Aberdeenshire Library and Information Service
www.aberdeenshire.gov.uk/libraries
Renewals Hotline 01224 661511

BRITAIN
FROM THE
RAILS

A Window Gazer's Guide

Benedict le Vay

Bradt

First published in 2009
Bradt Travel Guides Ltd
23 High Street, Chalfont St Peter, Bucks SL9 9QE, England
www.bradtguides.com
Published in the USA by The Globe Pequot Press Inc, 246 Goose Lane,
PO Box 480, Guilford, Connecticut 06437-0480

Text copyright © 2009 Benedict le Vay
Maps copyright © 2009 Bradt Travel Guides Ltd
Illustrations copyright © 2009 Bradt Travel Guides
Photos copyright © 2009 Individual photographers (see below)
For Bradt: Editorial Project Manager Anna Moores

British Library Cataloguing in Publication Data
A catalogue record for this book is available from the British Library

ISBN-13: 978 1 84162 277 4

Photographs
In-text photos From the Mary Evans Picture Library (ME): Mark Furness Collection (ME/MFC), Illustrated London
News Ltd (ME/ILN), Illustrated London News Pictures (ME/ILNP), Roger Mayne Collection (ME/RMC).
With thanks to Flickr: 3dCandy, Adulau, Athena's pics, Jez Atkinson, Atomicjeep, Cristophe Becker, BK59, Boliston,
Bonnet, Glen Bowman, Matt Buck 4950, Buildark, Phillip C, Roger C, Steve Cadman, Cayetano, cmdr gravy,
Conner 395, Crab chick, Damo1977, david.nikonvscanon, dearbarbie, DigitalLyte, Rachel Dorman, Einalem,
Elsie esq, Fimb, Foxypar4, Gary Photography, Ghat, Mike Gogulski, Gutobikes, hha124l, Jordon S Hatcher,
Andy Hawkins, Andy Haywood, histman, Hyougushi, I am Bruce, Ikkoskinnen, Ingy the Wingy, Jackspellingbacon,
K4dordy, kaet44, Kevinzim, Mike Laurence, Alex Layzell, le petit poulailler, Graham Lewis, Lhoon, manuel a 69,
Mairi McCann, Marilyn Jane, Martin, Mike 138, Steve Montgomery, mousyboywithglasses, Murky 1, Peter Pearson,
Dick Penn, Pfala, Piglicker, RBRWR, recursion, Redvers, Gareth JM Saunders, Scooby girl, Rob Shenk, Amanda B
H Slater, Jonathan Smith, David Spender, Andrew Starwarz, Gavin Andrew Stewart, Symmetry Mind, Neil T,
The Ancient Brit, thetim, Treehouse 1977, Vertigogen, Marcin Wichary, Wyberton. From Wikipedia Commons:
Chowells, Owen Dunn, Simon Ledingham, Russ London, James Kilfiger, Brian Robert Marshall, Akke Monasso,
Chris O. Other: Shighigdog Higgins, Ben le Vay, Vixen Moores.

Colour photos Arup (A), From Britain on View (BV): Val Corbett (BV/VC), Rod Edwards (BV/RE), Doug McKinlay
(BV/DM), Dave Porter (BV/DP), David Sellman (BV/DS), Star Attractions/Daniel Bosworth (BV/DB),
Colin Weston (BV/CW); Dreamstime (D): Andyb1126 (D/A), Dehew (D/D), Djaphoto (D/Dj), Paul Edward
(D/PE), David Gear (D/DG), Peter Guess (D/PG), Alex Hare (D/AH), Bridget Jones (D/BJ), David Marty
(D/DM), Mojonaz1 (D/M), Nicalf (D/N), Frank Spark (D/FS), D Turner (D/DT); Mary Evans Picture Library
(ME): Ad Lib Studios (ME/AD), Illustrated London News (ME/ILN); Flickr (F): Elsie Esq (F/E), B J Morley
(F/BM), Amanda Slater (F/AS); Richard Jones (RJ); Pictures Colour Library (PCL): AA World Travel Library
(PCL/AA), Charles Bowman (PCL/CB), Claver Carroll (PCL/CC), Alan Dawson (PCL/AD), Mark Dyball
(PCL/MD), Rod Edwards (PCL/RE), Brian Lawrence (PCL/BL), Graham Lawrence (PCL/GL), Tom Mackie
Images (PCL/TM), John Miller (PPCL/JM), David Noble (PCL/DN), Colin Paterson (PCL/CP), Clive Sawyer
(PCL/CS), Chris Warren (PCL/CW); Bill Smith (BS); SXC (SXC); Benedict le Vay (BLV)

Front cover design by James Nunn
Design, illustrations and maps by Artinfusion Ltd
Printed and bound in India by Nutech Photolithographer

Acknowledgements

John Gelson, Bill Smith, Robin Popham, John A U Woods, Lally Cowell, Hampshire libraries' railway collection at Winchester, and the train companies who have provided tickets and answered annoying questions. To the brilliant designers at Artinfusion, Chris and Lee, and the team at Bradt who have worked so hard to get this complicated book right. Any mistakes, however, are all my own. I know how picky railway fans are about history (and also how very sincerely they tell you something that clearly was never true). There will, I am sure, be points to put straight (no pun intended), suggestions and elaborations. Please write and let me know for future editions. Meanwhile, happy window gazing…

Dedication
To the great railwaymen and women of Britain

Not just the famed greats like the Stephensons, Isambard Kingdom Brunel, Nigel Gresley and Alan Pegler. The forgotten hundreds who died building Box Tunnel, the Forth Bridge and other massive monuments to engineers' visions, whose lives were cheap, and names usually unrecorded. The navvies whose sweat and cusses and blisters built the deep cuttings and huge embankments by hand, creating a new wonder of the world. The ordinary men and women who kept it all running through World Wars, under the Blitz's bombs and blackout. Who dug the trains out of snowdrifts for weeks in 1947 and 1963, often only to have the branch lines ripped up the next year. Whose backbreaking labour shovelling tons of coal into fireboxes got heavy trains over the summits. Whose professional dedication through long hours in lonely signal boxes got millions of us safely home billions of times. Who hacked out old sleepers and replaced rusted rails through the night at Christmas, while the rest of us feasted – or moaned about the railways. Who kept going through heartbreaking closures, cutbacks and botched reorganisations when interfering governments, stupid trade unions and the cynical travelling public seemed to be giving up. They carried on, waiting for the day when people would return to the rails, as they now have in droves, in numbers never seen before in peacetime, bigger even than when the network was a third larger.

Thanks. It really was all worth it.

Contents

RAIL BRITANNIA!

> They are our gates to the glorious and the unknown. Through them we pass out into adventure and sunshine... In Paddington all Cornwall is latent and the remoter west; down the inclines of Liverpool Street lie fenlands and the illimitable Broads; Scotland is through the pylons of Euston; Wessex behind the poised chaos of Waterloo.
>
> **E M Forster on railway termini, Howards End**

There's a magical romance about trains that no other form of transport can ever capture. Gathering speed through city, town and country, swooping across viaducts, rattling across junctions and whistling through tunnels. At long last you are in a small Sussex beachside halt, or a Welsh valley country station, beside a quiet Norfolk waterway, or winding through a remote forest high above a Scottish loch, and you dreamily think: do those same twin ribbons of steel *really* lead all the way back to the greatest city in Europe? Can this *really* be the very same seat?

Coming the other way, waiting on the planks of an isolated halt beside a Scottish beach, gazing for miles across rough sea and rocky islets, the huge skies bringing grey squalls across to the miles of majestic mountain faces across the water. The only other mammal you can see in this huge space is a seal basking on the shoreline. Lonely beauty.

Looking down the long single track into the gathering dusk, a welcoming hoot sounds from under a distant bridge and the headlights of a train heave into sight, reflected on the shiny rails... the train that leads back from this moody isolation to bustling coffee bars, theatres, department stores, bookshops, fine dining and great pubs. A magic carpet.

Or waking up in your crisp linen sleeper berth as the train rolls across the gigantic Forth Bridge, soaring way above the rooftops and high above the white horses of wind-whipped waves. Or rolling across the bogs of bleak, high Rannoch Moor while wild red deer stand in the wilderness and stare back at this long metal interloper into their wilderness.

As you look ahead from your dining-car seat, your excursion train takes a sweeping left curve south through Banbury. The platform ahead is crowded with commuters who shrink nervously back as the now-unfamiliar steam loco shrieks a warning whistle and roars through the station at 82mph; an unstoppable elemental force, followed by 700 tons of metal going *badang*

badang, badang badang, badang badang, badang rapidly over the joints. And then silence as the stunned, deafened bystanders are left open-mouthed and shrouded in a cloud of nostalgic steam and smoke. They had a glimpse of a sooty-faced driver in blue overalls peering intently ahead, the fierce yellow-orange glow of the firebox, glinting silverware on fine white tablecloths, and helpful uniformed attendants; so different from the humdrum train they were expecting. You take another piece of Yorkshire pudding from your roast dinner, a slurp of excellent merlot, and happily keep a look-out down this heavenly valley for Oxford, where pudding is promised.

None of the being treated like cattle in huge, ugly airport terminals with endless queues, prodded by security goons. No having to be there stupid hours in advance and answer endless intrusive questions. None of that divorce from reality as a plane plonks you down somewhere with no concept of the changes in the landscape on the way. Or the despair felt as your car rounds a motorway corner to see the brake-light trail of a jam, having just passed the only turnoff for 20 miles.

Just a gentle ride interrupted only by a pleasant visit to the dining car and perhaps a contented snooze, and then a comfortable ringside seat for the greatest scenery this wonderful kingdom has to offer.

A note on photography

No pictures were taken for this book by trespassing on railway land without permission, a habit of some enthusiasts which is dangerous and illegal. Pictures which appear to be taken by leaning a head out of windows were not and this practice is lethal from time to time. On the other hand, you are perfectly entitled to and should take above-ground pictures of our wonderful railway heritage and scenery, so long as you do not use flash, which can blind drivers to important signals. And don't let any busybody prodnose tell you otherwise...

▲ ME/AD

ROUTE OF THE FLYING SCOTSMAN

▲ F/BM

'There's a magical
romance about trains
that no other form
of transport can ever capture.
Gathering speed through city,
town and country, swooping across viaducts,
rattling across junctions and whistling
through tunnels... happy window gazing!'

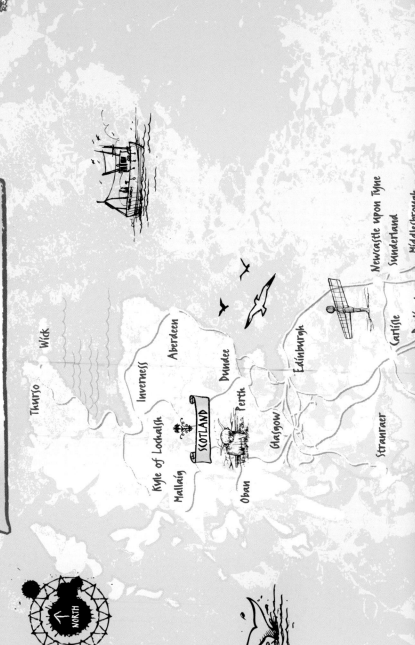

BRITAIN FROM THE RAILS

NORTH

SCOTLAND

Thurso
Wick
Inverness
Aberdeen
Dundee
Kyle of Lochalsh
Mallaig
Perth
Oban
Glasgow
Edinburgh
Stranraer
Carlisle
Newcastle upon Tyne
Sunderland
Middlesbrough

A WINDOW GAZER'S GUIDE

East Coast Main Line to Scotland

The Mallard: still the world steam record holder for speed

▼ PCL/CW

◄ BV/DM

4468

YORK MINSTER

DURHAM Castle and Cathedral

▲ SXC

▼ PCL/AA

NEWCASTLE The Sage building and bridges

EDINBURGH

ALNWICK CASTLE

Forth Rail Bridge

FLYING SCOTSMAN

The world's most famous steam engine

Scotland: Rails to Romance and Beauty

▼ PCL/CP

▼ PCL/TM

Bass Rock

▼ PCL/TM

Isle of Skye

Blackrock cottage on RANNOCH MOOR

Bridge of Orchy

'moo'

▼ SXC

THE JACOBITE
Britain's most successful
main-line steam service
goes from one beautiful
place to another through
sensational landscape...

MALLAIG   Fishing boats
in the scenic harbour

The bonnie banks of... LOCH LOMOND

AND NOW FOR SOMETHING DIFFERENT...

A proposed scheme to save money building new tracks. Needless to say it never caught on...

The Daddy Long Legs train between Brighton and Rottingdean – the only train with lifebelts, 1896

The platform for Harry Potter fans at King's Cross

PLATFORM 9¾

An alternative pub sign at Alton's Railway Arms

BLACKFRIARS BRIDGE
Britain's new invisible railway

Who is this book for? A lot of people...

- Visitors to Britain including those who have bought BritRail passes and want to know how to get the very best out of their tour.

- Green travellers who believe that flying or driving long distances to see beautiful places is also helping to destroy them. The carbon footprint of an electric train powered by hydro, wind or nuclear power, or even the other train braking on its way down the same hill, is zero. While that's the ideal, any train is ten-times better than any plane in pollution terms. Some trains are now powered by bio-diesel.

- Home-grown holidaymakers and British day trippers who want good-fare deals on the most rewarding routes but don't know where to start. I was approached by just such a lady at an Earl's Court travel show and she suggested this book. Thanks, Ma'am.

- People who already travel by train, including commuters, who want to know some fascinating stories about their lines. Heroism, murder, mayhem, blood, beauty, brilliance, humour – it's all between the lines. Local history fans too. Making the tracks you thought you knew a lot more fun.

- 'Romantics', who want to travel in style and really experience the country rather than being jammed in an Economy-Class aircraft and set down in a strange place, with no sense of getting there.

- Rail fans who want to hear more fascinating titbits about their favourite routes, the history, the weird accidents and the odd characters, and are open to suggestions for new routes.

- People who don't, won't or can't, drive or fly.

- People who love Britain, with its unrivalled countryside and landscapes, its heritage of castles, pubs, country towns, quirky customs and cathedrals (not forgetting viaducts, stations and tunnels) and want to know what to look out for.

The only people this book isn't aimed at are those who want to list all the locomotive classes by numbers and map every single station on the system and their long-gone timetables. I don't have the room, and I want this to be more interesting than any mere list, fascinating though that may be to that very eccentric British breed, the trainspotter. All I can say to anyone of that persuasion is that you too will find stories in here to intrigue, amuse and fascinate, and you don't need me to explain the difference between 4472 and 4468 anyway!

How To Use This Book

This isn't a mile-by-mile description of every single route. That would require something like a pair of the thickest phone books you ever saw, not too great for travelling with. And, frankly, some routes are just not that exciting, only useful for getting from A to B and passing through relatively dull places (actually that isn't entirely true – researching this and other books I found that everywhere, however unattractive, has *something* interesting).

While the system is outlined in this book, the maze of suburban lines is not detailed. Rather, what you have here are just the best: terrific treasures and genuine gems, with the detailed information you need to fully enjoy these lines from one end to the other, plus background features that will enhance the ride. You may have favourite lines you feel I have overlooked; drop me a line about your line, and I'll do the research for future editions (**E** info@bradtguides.com; **W** britainfromtherails.bradtguides.com).

What the symbols mean

Asterisks have been used throughout the book to rate certain lines in terms of their scenery. They will also be used in the text to alert you to bits you should put down your newspaper for:

*	well worth a look
**	really interesting and beautiful
***	terrific
****	a rare treat
*****	a simply staggering life-changing cosmic experience. That happens only once.

(r) Denotes a request stop. Standing on the platform waving will probably get you a hoot from the driver, who will stop. But you have to tell the guard well in advance if you're stopping off at one of these – it's no good saying so as you sail through, and in the Highlands it can be a long walk back.

In the route descriptions, each station is listed **like this**, as we pass it. A branch line or connecting route is written LIKE THIS when you can take it. Major railway features such as viaducts and junctions are written **like this**. Journey times quoted are for the fastest normal trains.

Useful information

You will find contact details for relevant steam railways and tourist information centres in *Appendix 2* page 307. Visit our web page at W britainfromtherails.bradtguides.com to find extra route suggestions, ideas for great railway walks, the latest news on fare bargains *plus* reader feedback.

Maps: don't always believe them

Some very useful maps are published in this book, and on featured routes, will be all you need. But a complete map/gazetteer of British railways is a large book in itself. Be aware when looking at route maps published by train companies that we have gone back to the silly pre-nationalisation state where other companies' lines are not always shown in an attempt to push you to use what is often a less direct route. For example, Cross Country was run by Virgin until 2007 and their route map showed the only way out of Brighton was up to Reading and the Midlands – clearly untrue. Equally, Northern had a map showing no way north from York (to Durham and Newcastle) except by crossing the country to Carlisle and back again. Madness! Often a light line and an arrow shows onward possibilities, but don't take one company's route map as gospel.

Equally, maps are often schematic for clarity (as with the London Tube) and show what order stations go in, without any accurate representation of the distances between them or real geography.

The regional sketch maps in this book show the routes covered as train track with other routes in grey. Where stations come thick and fast on a described route, not all are shown. For exploring on foot, bike, etc., we recommend the Ordnance Survey Landranger series.

Planning your trips

Britain's railways are too fast. That might seem like an odd complaint, and if you are merely travelling from London to Glasgow for, say, business and not in the least bit interested in your surroundings, fast is good.

But in a more leisurely age, people enjoyed the journeys for what they were. There were huge windows which actually opened so you could smell

the countryside and hear the birds (or the sound and smoke of the loco!).
Now you can whiz through places at 125mph and have no idea of where it
was because you can't possibly read the signs, nor take in much of the
countryside or architecture flashing past.

Of course, nature has kindly arranged that the most picturesque places,
on the whole, are the least populated and the most difficult for railway
building, so in the Scottish Highlands, Welsh cliffs, or Cornish bays we
always find we are at a speed where such beauties can be appreciated (and
with plenty of curves to get different angles on the scenery) whereas
relatively boring flat countryside on the way to all those places is traversed
at twice the speed. With exceptions, of course – there are some very slow,
sleepy branch lines (eg: Marlow, Bucks) in countryside that offers no great
obstacles, and if traffic demands it, just about any geographical challenge
can be ironed out by railways to the point where passengers hardly see the
place – the Channel Tunnel, for instance!

So, for time-pressed tourists is getting to the picturesque parts as quickly
as possible and then slowing down the best plan? Well, possibly yes, but I
wouldn't entirely agree. For that reason my advice is:

Don't always be in a hurry to take the fastest trains

A train that
stops at Durham, for example, will give you a much better look at that
superb view than one that whizzes full tilt over the viaduct. On the
secondary and branch lines, this advice will not apply because speeds won't
be that high and stops will be more frequent.

Don't always go via London if there is a cross-country route

London-centric people can't
imagine that you can go directly from Portsmouth
to Cardiff without going through London, or from Norwich to Liverpool, or
Manchester to Milford Haven, or Weymouth to Bristol. You can.

Not only in many cases will these routes be as quick as the high-speed
trains from London, because they are more direct, but they may go through
fabulous landscape, may be a lot less crowded and will travel at a speed
where you enjoy what you're going through, instead of being stuck in a
high-speed thing more like an airliner. And they can be a lot cheaper:
Portsmouth to Bristol cross country, for example, as I write is £44 *cheaper*
for an adult single than going via London Paddington and about *two hours
quicker*, yet many non-rail users assume via London is the only way. The
cross-country route is a gem, going through Warminster, Salisbury and
absolutely lovely valleys near Bath.

Those examples of cross-country routes are just direct trains. If you're
prepared to change once or twice, you can get to almost any station across
the country. So if your route *could* go cross-country rather than through
London, ask: can you get there a different way, how long does it take and
what does it cost? You might be pleasantly surprised.

Don't always take the most direct route For example, as I explain in the East Anglia section, you'd be mad to go direct from London to Norwich, if you've got plenty of time, when you can have a far more interesting route up via Cambridge and Ely, and back via Lowestoft and Ipswich. Equally, instead of going Swindon–South Wales both ways (how much of the River Severn do you see in the Severn Tunnel? Not much, I hope!), consider coming back via Gloucester, enjoying the Forest of Dean and glorious views of the Severn on one side and the beautiful Cotswolds on the other.

You can apply this to many routes: yes, the Preston–Carlisle part of the West Coast Main Line is quite interesting, but not a patch on the magnificent Settle & Carlisle Line along the Pennines, or the Cumbrian Coast Line which winds its way round the Lake District.

A word of caution: check tickets and fares are available via different companies' routes. If you have a BritRail pass or a regional Rover ticket (see *Chapter 9*) you should have nothing to worry about, but this advice may cost more due to the fact that lines are now run by rival companies less willing to share. Check exactly where Rover-style tickets end and don't overrun the edges or you could get fined. They may be for that company only.

If travelling at weekends, check with enquiries about engineering work For example, I recently wanted to go from London Paddington to Penzance at a weekend. A quick check showed that I'd have to get off at Tiverton Parkway and catch a bus to Plymouth where I'd join another train. What would have been a wonderfully relaxing journey would have become an endurance hassle and I'd miss the great sea views around Dawlish. Result, I did that superb trip another weekend. But suppose I'd paid and turned up to be told *then* what was going to happen?

Such engineering work is concentrated on weekends, nights and periods such as Christmas. We should be grateful to those who work in bitter cold and dark with dangerous, heavy equipment in hours when most people would rather be in bed, but it's hard to see it like that when you're turfed off your train to wait for a slow bus in the rain. Always check before booking – they announce engineering schedules weeks in advance.

Man is born free, yet everywhere he is in trains.

As Voltaire, or someone, nearly said.

Ben's Top Ten Rail Journeys

George Stephenson's *Locomotion*, Darlington

S.&.D.R. Nº I. 1825.

1 **West Highland Line** Come in by sleeper from London, and finish off with steam. This sensational route will change your life with indelible memories. Beautiful ones. See page 30.

2 **East Coast Main Line** Speed, style and scenery in abundance, plus the double drama of the Forth and Tay bridges. Two great capitals, with stunning views north of Newcastle. *The Flying Scotsman* route – rightly railway royalty. See page 1.

3 **The Wherry Lines** Charm on wheels. The layout of the lines is eccentric, like the waterways they follow, and defies explanation; their survival inexplicable too. Much overlooked gems. See page 203.

4 **The Skye Railway** This is what they mean by remote possibilities. Sea to shining sea, and a chance to avalanche on the way! A classic that tells almost incredible tales. See page 59.

5 **The Settle & Carlisle** A mad, moody, magnificent and mountainous main line – England's highest. Unmissable. See page 76.

6 **The Looe branch** – or maybe the St Ives, it's so hard to choose – in Cornwall. These Enid Blytonish short-but-sweet numbers will charm the socks off you, guaranteed. Do both in a day, go on! See page 146.

7 **The Cambrian Coast Line** Wales has a total treasure trove of railways, but this is the best. Made into a North Wales circuit with the help of the Ffestiniog line – it's simply superlative See page 169.

8 **The Great Western** It might be well known, but it offers constant joys: from 'Brunel's billiard table' in the Thames Valley to the viaducts over Cornish rivers, curving around bays and coves. See page 104.

9 **The Wessex Main Line** Very little known outside its region, it brings before you a glorious variety of scenery and, with its long arm to Weymouth, returns you to Hardy's Wessex. See page 155.

10 **West of England Main Line** The forgotten way west. As you near Salisbury it starts getting lovely and then just gets better and better. See page 243.

The Jacobite crossing Glenfinnan Viaduct

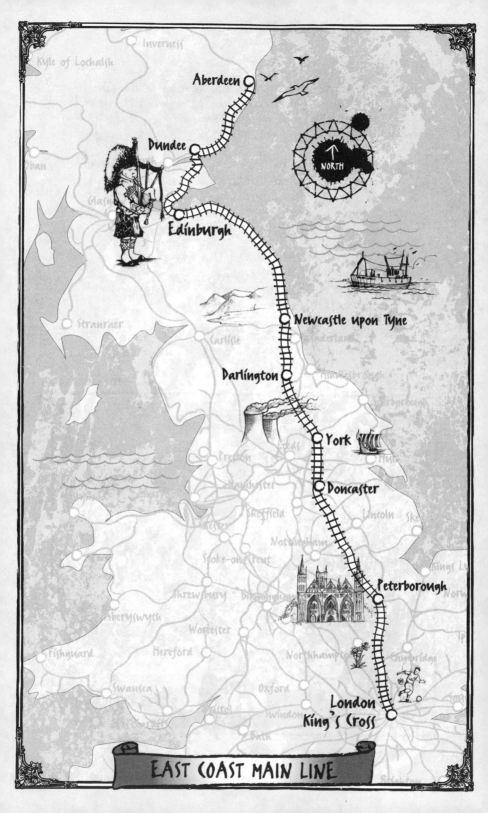

Inverness
Kyle of Lochalsh
Aberdeen
Dundee
Oban
Glasgow
Edinburgh
NORTH
Stranraer
Carlisle
Newcastle upon Tyne
Sunderland
Darlington
Middlesbrough
Scarborough
Preston
Leeds
York
Hull
Manchester
Doncaster
Sheffield
Lincoln
Chester
Nottingham
Stoke-on-Trent
Shrewsbury
Birmingham
Peterborough
Aberystwyth
Worcester
Northampton
Cambridge
Hereford
Fishguard
Oxford
Swansea
Swindon
London
King's Cross
Bristol
Bath

EAST COAST MAIN LINE

ONE

THE GLORIOUS
EAST COAST MAIN LINE
TO SCOTLAND

(4¹/₂hrs to Edinburgh, 393 miles)

Lots of main lines reckon they are important, but the East Coast Main Line really is the business. It has speed, style and scenery in abundance, and shoots north from London like an arrow across flatlands to reach the Scottish capital with no diversions. It has always had romance, records, racecourse speeds, relative reliability and real respect as a senior railway compared with the tiddler tramways – as fans of this line would see it – down south. It doesn't look down its nose at lesser railways, however, in the way that the Great Western always has. It doesn't need to. It's the no-nonsense chieftain of British railways, starting in the business-like terminus at King's Cross, arriving in the heart of Edinburgh and reaching right up to Aberdeen and yet, oddly, going through only one really big city – Newcastle – *en route*. The ECML, as it is known, features iconic landmarks, fascinating history and stunning scenery that are rare in such a modern high-speed main line. All aboard!

Newcastle, Edinburgh

Scarborough

York

Midlands

Leeds

Hull

Doncaster

Sheffield

Lincoln

NORTH

Newark Northgate

Nottingham

Grantham

Skegness

Lincoln

Leicester

Peterborough

Ely, Norwich

Huntingdon

Hitchin

Cambridge, Ely, Norwich

Stevenage

Hertford

Welwyn Garden City

Hatfield

Potters Bar

Hertford

Alexandra Palace

Luton Airport East Midlands (St Pancras)

Finsbury Park

West Midlands Scotland via WCML (Euston)

London King's Cross

Eurostar Paris, Brussels (St Pancras)

KING'S CROSS TO YORK:
record breakers* (2hrs, 188 miles)
(The first part of this route, until indicated, also forms the first leg of the East Anglia 'circular tour', see Chapter 6)

If you're a Harry Potter fan – and half the world is – then first pop across to the suburban platforms to *not* see Platform 9³/4 near Platform 8, or at least see its sign. The platform itself is invisible. If you're not a fan, you'll think I'm bonkers, so don't bother. If you have the choice, sit on the right-hand side of your train, facing forward.

The start of what is otherwise a remarkably level route to Edinburgh could not be more up and down. The converging tracks from the various platforms – known as the throat – dive into **Gasworks Tunnel** under the Regent's Canal, which having been built around 1820, got there first. Being wet, it wasn't easily made into a humpback bridge, so the railway had to dive under (or, at the St Pancras terminus next door, over). A lot of bother for something hardly used. Climbing again after the dip – which used to give long steam-hauled trains such a jerk that they could be in danger of breaking their couplings – we pass under a new large grey-tube bridge which carries the Eurostars from Paris and Brussels heading for adjacent St Pancras at 186mph. Well, not at that point, clearly, as it would be *zut alors* and *oh la la*! as they pranged into the buffers, but they do that speed between here and the Chunnel. Oddly, at this point, trains heading for Paris are heading roughly towards Oslo.

Even higher still is a bridge carrying the North London Line east–west, and deep beneath us somewhere nearby are various Underground lines, including a disused narrow-gauge Post Office one, and forgotten tunnels linking surface lines to Tube lines, making this the spaghetti junction of railways and canals. And King's Cross is just one of five huge termini almost in a row between here and Paddington.

Climbing up again into the daylight, the massive Emirates Stadium of Arsenal Football Club is soon on the right, with the remains of its Art-Deco predecessor visible further away as we speed through **Finsbury Park**.

After whizzing through **Hornsey** and **Harringay**, the massive site on a hill on the left is Alexandra Palace, or 'Ally Pally' as Londoners fondly know it. It's the twin of Crystal Palace on the similar hill on the opposite, south rim of the Thames Basin: they both had huge halls of popular entertainment (the Crystal Palace being burnt down in the 1930s), both had TV transmitter towers, and both had their own branch lines, both now gone.

* Reminder: stars = scenic rating

king's cross to york

After **Alexandra Palace** station a line takes off on our left and up and over to the right. This is the start of the HERTFORD LOOP which rejoins our East Coast Main Line around 20 miles later, a pattern of connections which recurs many times down this route. It is a useful diversionary route if anything blocks the narrow section at Welwyn ahead, and indeed if you're taking it while the main line is closed for repairs, a pleasant if not over-fast ramble through leafy northern suburbs into Hertfordshire, and only a mile or so longer.

Here on the main line, however, the route tunnels repeatedly through the low hills. As we pass **Potters Bar**, the gin-'n'-Jag belt of wealthy golf-playing commuters surrounds us. **Hatfield**, after some curves, is the site of the erstwhile De Havilland aircraft factory, home of the 'wooden wonder' Mosquito of World War II, the Comet and the 146 whisper-jet. Oddly, many battle scenes for the film *Saving Private Ryan* were filmed here.

Welwyn Garden City, next, was set up by idealist Ebenezer Howard who thought workers could live in leafy suburbs instead of slums, away from factories, which should be confined in industrial areas. Actually it was his second attempt, the first being near Hitchin further up this line, at Letchworth Garden City. Because the rest of the world copied them, they are rather boring nowadays (a bit like Aldous Huxley going on about zip fasteners as a fantastic futuristic thing in his book *Brave New World*). But garden cities changed the world: every neat suburb is descended from them.

Watch out just north of here, just after the tracks narrow (from four to two), for the superb Digswell Viaduct*, built with 13 million bricks, on which we soar above the leafy garden city in style. The train then rockets through **Welwyn North** and two tunnels, and regains four tracks beyond the bottleneck (which may be widened during the lifetime of this book) caused by these landmarks. **Knebworth**, of rock festival fame, follows.

Just before **Stevenage**, the HERTFORD LOOP rejoins from our right in a burrowing junction (that is, not a flying junction, as when it left us at Ally Pally, see above). Stevenage is recognisable at speed from the brick towers on the platforms, and within a few miles we are into **Hitchin**, 32 miles from King's Cross, where a flat junction lets the CAMBRIDGE LINE curve off to our right, next stop Letchworth Garden City. That's all three types of junction in one paragraph and one short journey, although Hitchin is supposed to get a flyover for the Cambridge trains soon. If taking the East Anglia circular tour, switch to page 195 now for the next leg.

The river at the small market town of Hitchin is the Hiz (in droughts, should it be the Hizn't?) and we have now left the Thames Basin. Whereas the rivers further south – such as the charmingly named Mimram which flows under the Digswell Viaduct – flow into the Thames, from here on they come out in The Wash (as your granny may have said most things do), which is that huge inlet of the North Sea above East Anglia.

As we speed through Ickleford village – where the ancient Icknield Way fords the river and crosses the line as a footbridge – and into Bedfordshire, the countryside becomes more open, wet, fertile, flat and ideal for high-speed railways. The first village, **Arlesey**, once had a huge mental hospital called Arlesey Asylum – unfortunately the source of more than a few suicides on the line. It was renamed Three Counties Hospital and then Fairfield in that odd way of renaming things to make them seem more pleasant.

Now, relax. There's nothing much to see except productive farmland and glimpses of the almost-parallel A1 road to Edinburgh – sometimes still known by its old name, The Great North Road – as we speed through small towns and see more and more waterways in this increasingly flat fenland. The drainage channels are always wet here, even after much dry weather. Larger towns like **Huntingdon** have stops, but many small villages such as the eccentrically named Offord D'Arcy and Offord Cluny, just before Huntingdon, pass in a flash with no stations or signs.

Approaching **Peterborough**, the ELY LINE from Cambridge and Norwich joins from the right, passing under us just before the river. When you consider that line needed Whitlesey Mere (the largest lake in southern England) to be drained in 1851 to be built, you can see how wet this area was until recently. The ending '–ey' in Whittlesey meant 'island', as once true at Chelsea, Bermondsey and Battersea in London.

Peterborough appears with its squat cathedral tower on the right, and further down a mosque. It's a meeting of cultures in other ways too – broad Norfolk voices will be joining the train saying stuff such as 'They didn't say change at Ely, what are they loike?' contrasting with the sing-song Geordie of the Newcastle train crew and the beautifully clear Edinburgh diction of those heading that far north.

A line south of the station and going west, by the way, links to a rather good steam line, the NENE VALLEY RAILWAY, although there are not regular through trains at the time of writing. To get to Peterborough (Nene Valley) station you'd need a bus, car or taxi, although it is walkable for most people. Its main claim to fame is that European-sized trains (bigger in cross section, but same tracks) can fit here, so it's great for making movies supposedly set in Europe. Usually I'm impatient with steam lines that fail to link up with the system, but with the amazingly busy ECML I see it would be difficult here.

Leaving Peterborough, there are New England freight yards on the right, with heavy locos standing waiting for their turn.

As we head north, the line that runs parallel on the left for a few miles and then diverges is the **LEICESTER LINE** that goes to Melton Mowbray – and if that makes you think of wagons of pork pies, it's worth noting we have just passed the village of Stilton, as in the cheese. A gourmet express possibly, but then this very route saw Britain's first railway dining car, which left Leeds for London King's Cross on 1 November 1879. The Pullman Car *Princess of Wales* carried only ten First-Class passengers and the carriage included a gentlemen's smoking room and a ladies' dressing room. Your dining car today, its direct descendant, is available without paying the two shillings and sixpence (12½p) surcharge. As far as I can see this pretty and useful cross-country connector has no official name or nickname – please put me right if there is one – so we can dub it the Pork Pie line.

Yet another route, the **LINCOLN LINE**, diverges right (east) for Spalding and that fine cathedral city (54 miles). As you might have gathered, Peterborough is quite a rail hub.

Further up here we start climbing Stoke Bank. It is a long, gentle and straight slope, ideal for racing downhill towards London, and as such became the site of a historic moment on 3 July 1938. In conditions of severe secrecy – in case the rival West Coast company LMS tried to steal a march by grabbing the place in the record books – driver Joseph Duddington, a man known to take calculated risks, crested Stoke Summit at the north of the bank at a creditable 75mph, coming towards London. He was driving the streamlined *Mallard*, a name engraved on the hearts of railwaymen around the world.

The A4-class loco was pulling a carriage with special measuring equipment – a dynamometer car – and although the track was officially passed for only 90mph, he was encouraged to give the Gresley-designed loco her head down the gentle slope. The speed crept up and up and eventually reached 126mph, a world steam record which has never been broken and probably never will be.

Now 4468 *Mallard* is exhibited in pride of place at the National Railway Museum, further along this route at York, with plaques on either side proudly stating her world record-holder status.

She and other restored examples of this brilliant design still pull trains around the country. But here's a thought: this amazing speed – which severely overheated the mechanical parts so it had to be towed for repair and had the press celebrating the driver as a hero – is matched every day on routes from London by regular trains such as the one you are sitting on.

At the top of Stoke Bank, after passing the 100 miles from London mark, we go through a tunnel and then whistle through **Grantham**. Not whistling madly, one hopes, as the *Scotch Express* was as it hurtled through Grantham against red signals in 1906. It was supposed to stop, but didn't, hitting points set for the severely curved Nottingham route and was wrecked against a bridge parapet. Recent re-examination of the mysterious crash shows that the carriage brakes must have been fixed off by railwaymen zealous not to cause delay at an earlier stop, and not restored, so the driver had only the engine's brake to stop on a slippery rail that night. Thankfully, such an error is now impossible.

Grantham's most famous export was 1980s' prime minister Margaret Thatcher. Like the *Mallard* above, she was heading south, tough, novel, unstoppable, and a record-holder – the first woman prime minister, and three-times elected too. But unlike the *Mallard*, Thatcher had little use for Britain's coal miners.

Talking of coal miners, we are approaching the Trent Valley, where Old King Coal played – and still plays – a massive part in our Industrial Revolution. More on that in a minute though.

A line diverges at Grantham for Nottingham, and after another short tunnel we cross over the route it connects with, the **POACHER LINE** which runs west–east from the city famous for its dastardly Sheriff to Skegness on the North Sea. Skegness was famously promoted with the slogan 'Skegness is so bracing' and the Jolly Fisherman (see page 101).

The odd thing about the East Coast Main Line is that it misses all the major cities only 20 or so miles to our left (west), such as Leicester, Nottingham, Sheffield, Derby and many more (served by their own Midland Main Line from St Pancras). It thus avoids their associated hills and rivers, racing instead across much flatter country for the prize of York, and later Edinburgh. At **Newark Northgate** we cross the **NOTTINGHAM–LINCOLN LINE** on an unusual and juddering flat crossing. Not unusual for a tram in some eastern European back street, but teeth-rattlingly odd for a main line aiming for 125mph speeds. Maybe it'll be replaced with a flyover by the time you get there, but meanwhile let's hope the signalmen keep this rather unnerving junction clear of crossing trains (don't worry, they always do and the safeguards are foolproof). It is often quoted as the only one in Britain. It isn't (see page 178).

Next we whiz over a recently replaced bridge over a canal – a waterway that still carries much freight, by the way, unlike that annoyingly empty one back at King's Cross – and then over the River Trent. The A1 road to Edinburgh, which has been shadowing us all the way, reappears on our right. We see power station cooling towers – those massive cylinders taller than cathedral spires, with concave sides – all the way up the Trent Valley, and at one time you can see three sets at once. They are here because the power demand is here, the coal is here (or was), and the river provided transport and cooling water. In fact the railway provided much of the transport, and still does, with lines frequently curving off to either power stations or collieries past and present. Of course, no-one had thought of global warming when these things were set up. Ideally, this train would be powered by some windmill or waterfalls up in the hills. In fact it'll probably be one of these power stations doing the hard work for a few years yet. Odd, when you think about it, that our sleek electric train is still powered by coal and steam, just as *Mallard* was.

We pass an old freight connection at **Dukeries Junction** (the area being so called because of the enormously powerful landowners including a whole bunch of dukes who lived here and got wealthy on the coal in the 19th century) and then speed through **Retford**, with the low-level station on a line crossing ours visible on the right.

There is more and more evidence of the industrial past as we approach **Doncaster**, Donny to some, a major junction and famous railway works. Lines come in from Lincoln and Derby and, beyond the station, diverge right (east) for Hull on the North Sea and left for Leeds and other Yorkshire towns. We head on towards York, freight lines all over the place, power stations on both sides and loops for coal trains alongside the main line.

One of the places on this route is called Heck, ironically as it turned out. A sleepy driver of a Land Rover pulling a trailer on a road crossing over the railway managed to drive down the embankment and onto the southbound track in 2001. A GNER (the then operating firm, and a good one) InterCity 225 train heading for King's Cross hit it and propelled the wreckage down the track at around 90mph. The leading vehicle, a driving trailer, stayed upright until it struck some points and was diverted by dreadful luck into the path of a freight train heading north. The collision was at an estimated 142mph closing speed, and ten people were killed.

The car driver was jailed for five years, and the young driver of the Freightliner freight train heading north, Steve Dunn, was commemorated with a new locomotive named after him.

In a little-known and bizarre twist, the loco at the back of the GNER train, which was propelling it southwards, had also been involved in a fatal crash at Hatfield a few months earlier (which was due to poor rail maintenance, now totally fixed). GNER renumbered the loco, which was undamaged in both crashes, in case people thought it was jinxed. And no, I won't give you the new number. It was just a coincidence.

Perhaps you don't want to read about crashes while you're on a train, but the reason they are interesting is because they are so very rare. Some years go by with no passengers killed on British railways, yet every year sees at least 3,000 road users killed. You could hardly be safer.

They are also interesting in the way the railway industry works: they rarely happen again, because it corrects itself. Road overbridges have been massively strengthened since the Heck crash and longer, stronger crash barriers put up; hundreds of miles of track have been replaced since the Hatfield crash because of a particular problem, and the whole system scrutinised on a far more frequent basis. Whereas on roads, exactly the same stupid crashes happen week after week.

Cheer up, we're approaching **York**✠✠ which, when the railway was built was the first town of any real importance on its route north, at around 188 miles out of King's Cross. It is still the most attractive city so far. Things to look out for (and visit if you are stopping): York Minster, the cathedral, on the right; on the left the National Railway

Museum, a branch of the Science Museum worth a whole day out, even if you think trains have steering wheels (in fact *particularly* if you think that). A 'visitor attraction' called Jorvik, the city's original name, makes much of the Viking origins of York. It promises streets as they would have been in AD975. So you come out with the plague and an arrow in your leg (that's a joke, but should New York really be New Jorvik?).

But York station itself is an absolute gem, with its huge, elegantly curved trainshed dwarfing the trains inside. Look for the happy details, such as the company coat of arms in the spandrels in the roof supports (spandrels, some might not know, are the flat bits between a pillar and an arch next to it). Less happy is the plaque beside one of the platforms marking the moment in the early hours of 29 April 1942, when a sister locomotive to the record-breaking *Mallard* mentioned above, the 4469 *Sir Ralph Wedgwood*, was destroyed by a German bomb in the so-called Baedeker Raids (Baedeker was a well-known brand of German guidebooks apparently used by the Germans during the war to help them make sneak attacks on picturesque ancient towns at night and bomb them without mercy).

MUCH RECOMMENDED SIDE TRIPS FROM YORK
On great lines: Scarborough, on the east coast (42 miles) and inland: interesting Knaresborough (16 miles) and pretty Harrogate (20 miles).

YORK TO EDINBURGH: to the world's first railway *** (2hrs 40mins, 205 miles)

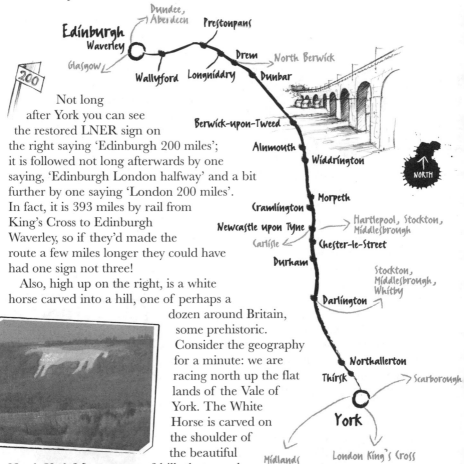

Not long after York you can see the restored LNER sign on the right saying 'Edinburgh 200 miles'; it is followed not long afterwards by one saying, 'Edinburgh London halfway' and a bit further by one saying 'London 200 miles'. In fact, it is 393 miles by rail from King's Cross to Edinburgh Waverley, so if they'd made the route a few miles longer they could have had one sign not three!

Also, high up on the right, is a white horse carved into a hill, one of perhaps a dozen around Britain, some prehistoric. Consider the geography for a minute: we are racing north up the flat lands of the Vale of York. The White Horse is carved on the shoulder of the beautiful North York Moors, a set of hills that march east for not many miles to the North Sea at Whitby. Looking left you can see the Pennine Hills, the backbone of England, with distant escarpments visible from the train. So we are racing up a gap only about 20 miles wide to reach the Scottish border. The West Coast Main Line races north on the other side of the Pennines, almost touching the Irish Sea at Lancaster, but then hits the Cumbrian Hills at the Lake District and has a hefty climb to Shap. We, on the ECML, are on much the best route. Only a madman would go up the middle along the Pennines – which is precisely what the Midland Railway did, beaten to the easier east and west coast routes, with its insanely ambitious Settle & Carlisle route in the hills to our left (details on page 76).

9

There are about ten former wartime airfields along this stretch, some still visible, mostly RAF Bomber Command, whose motto 'Strike hard, strike sure' came to have horrendous reality for Germany after those Baedeker Raids mentioned above.

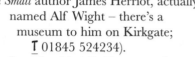

We speed through the little town of **Thirsk** (home to *All Creatures Great and Small* author James Herriot, actually named Alf Wight – there's a museum to him on Kirkgate; T 01845 524234).

Just after **Northallerton**, where freight lines diverge, there is a pretty, isolated chapel on the left. We are near a village with the charming name Danby Wiske.

Soon we are under the roof at **Darlington** – again the spandrels of the roof supports are worth a look. Home of the world's very first powered public railway, the Stockton & Darlington of 1825, on its opening day, George Stephenson's 'moveable engine' *Locomotion* did the nine-mile route in two hours. However, nearing the end of the trip he dramatically increased speed to 15mph. One passenger was so alarmed at this that he threw himself from the wagon and was badly injured.

In a Darlington park you can see evidence of the original track and its strange stone block sleepers. Fittingly, the first brand-new express steam locomotive made in Britain for many years, built by enthusiasts, was completed there in 2008: it is called *Tornado*. It's a beautiful machine and the boiler was made in Germany, where – the sad history of not many paragraphs before notwithstanding – the steam fans now have found many firm friends.

Tornado

From Darlington you can also take a particularly pretty route, the ESK VALLEY LINE, down to the sea at Whitby (see page 74). You may have to change at Middlesbrough.

Just after the station is a curious church on the right with three arches in its squat tower, known as the Railwayman's Church, not just because railwaymen worship there but because the railway architect designed it.

Be alert about 12 miles later for one of this route's great treasures. After we see the 'London 250 miles' sign on the right, and we curve sharpish left and right into a bit of a cutting, we shoot through **Durham**✝✝✝ station (or much better, stop).

The view on the right after the station is peerless: Durham Castle and cathedral sitting on their near-island in a loop in the River Wear. William the Conqueror realised he could create a near impregnable seat of power

YORK TO EDINBURGH: to the world's first railway ONE

here, and the view from the ten-arch railway
viaduct is just superb.

As we pass through the little station of
Chester-le-Street the striking
and enormous sculpture
The Angel of the North
becomes visible on the right.
Known locally as 'Rusty Rita'
and resembling a human figure with aircraft wings,
she stands beside the A1, which is yet again near our
tracks. Modern art isn't always good news, however.
In a bizarre and tragic accident here
at Chester-le-Street in 2006 two
women were killed when a giant
inflatable sculpture they were exploring was picked up by a gust of wind and
blown across a park.

Newcastle upon Tyne**, coming up, is fascinating and dramatic, so
watch out. The River Tyne flows through a deep cut heading east, and the
railways run at high level either side of this with junctions allowing us to
leap across the river on a high bridge. The Tyne was immortalised for its
five bridges in various songs, though of course there are now more, the
oddest being the low-level, winking-eye millennium footbridge, which
rotates to allow ships through (not while people are crossing it, one hopes).

There are castles and churches and weird modern buildings, some right
next to the tracks and some across the river, and views down to quaysides.
The thing like a huge mirrored pupa of an insect across the river (once
we've crossed it) is the Sage Building, a Norman Foster design (the man who
brought you the Gherkin in London). The weirdest thing I ever saw in
Newcastle was a black cat painted with white stripes to match the Newcastle
football strip: such cats are called 'Toon Cats' and given cats' desire
to keep clean, it is a cruel practice.
Recommended side route: to Carlisle
(61 miles) through the Tyne Valley.

Coming up is a real treat: one of
the world's best train rides, but the
first few miles after Newcastle are
unexceptional, with a Traincare depot
on the right. 'Traincare' evidently
dates from the recent past when it was
regarded as trendy to run English
words together as if we were speaking
German. In that language, I found

lokomotivfuhrer an excellent word for train driver, or Norwegian *lokstall* is
rather nice for engine shed, but I feel this habit is Orwellian in English,
trying to disguise a fact with vagueness and a forced emotion. Thus the

Railway Children's Home at Woking became 'Railcare'. Does that make it really more caring, or more meaningless? Actually it was originally called The London & South Western Railway Servants' Orphanage, which was at least accurate, informative and honest.

There are various colliery branches along this route, past and present. The coal workings around here extended for more than a mile under the North Sea, which we glimpse after passing a high viaduct at **Morpeth** and just before **Widdrington** station. Also on the right are two pill boxes, which remind us that even this far north the British feared invasion in 1940.

The fact that we have only just now glimpsed the sea after some 300 miles from London shows what a misnomer 'East Coast Main Line' has been so far. But we are about to make up for that, big time – unlike the poor souls on the even more misnamed 'West Coast Main Line', who glimpse the sea briefly near Lancaster and Carlisle then never again!

Here there are more rivers, and viaducts to cross them. One of the prettiest is soon reached at **Alnmouth✷✷**; the town is to the right by the river mouth. To our left after the station are the remains of the short branch to Alnwick town, visible a few miles away. Here Alnwick Castle is home to the Dukes of Northumberland – the ancient Percy family, immortalised by Shakespeare with the 'Hotspur' character in *Henry IV*. The Percys make the current Windsors in Buckingham Palace seem like Johnnie-come-latelies; the castle and gardens are well worth a visit. Here – a link with King's Cross – 14 flying Ford Anglias were crashed during the making of *Harry Potter and The Chamber of Secrets*, for the castle becomes Hogwarts in the movie. Or so I was told locally, perhaps by leg-pullers – weren't they computer generated?

Now concentrate on the views to the right. Here you can see the fabulous 'Holy Island' of Lindisfarne, cradle of Christianity and linked to the mainland by a tidal causeway, obviously visible more clearly at low tide with its refuge tower. At the south end (right, looking across) there is a village, a castle on its low, grassy mound, and several homes made from upturned, tarred-black boats with chimneys and windows cut in their hulls (like those described in Charles Dickens's *David Copperfield*). The rather sinister-

looking pair of obelisks on the right are leading marks, directing boats for the best channel to approach from the sea. Further to the right (south of Lindisfarne) is the stunningly located Bamburgh Castle. The railway viewpoint just couldn't be better.

The Lindisfarne causeway is cut off for around four hours around each high tide. It causes no end of fun with stuck camper vans, strange effects on the tide coming down from the north, and supposedly strange effects on the opening hours in the island's pubs. Well, legend has it anyway, about past publicans at least – how was the local cop going to get across once the tide was up?

The extraordinary saga of Flying Scotsman and The Flying Scotsman

At 10.00 every day since 1862, *The Flying Scotsman* train has left King's Cross for Edinburgh. True, the train at the start was officially called the Special Scotch Express and took 10½ hours, but at some point the nickname *The Flying Scotsman* took hold. The 'Race to the North' railway rivalry of 1888 ended with this service speeded up to 8½ hours.

By the 1920s, with private cars and airlines eating into the railways' dominance, the new London & North Eastern Railway (LNER), which had taken over this line, decided on a daring move. It introduced a new class of locomotive, led by one confusingly called *Flying Scotsman*. These brainchildren of genius Nigel Gresley could run non-stop the whole nearly 400 miles between the capital cities. This was possible because of the superb efficiency of the powerful design, and a special tiny corridor under the coal tender by which the crew could be replaced mid-journey, plus the scooping up of water from long troughs between the rails.

In the 1930s, the time on the route fell to seven hours and 20 minutes while the levels of luxury rose, with an onboard hairdressing salon, restaurants, cocktail bars and secretaries for businessmen. The war brought huge demand which sometimes saw *The Flying Scotsman* running as two trains of up to 20 carriages each, the corridors jammed with standing passengers, with delays for air raids and diversions round bomb-cratered tracks. Afterwards, the service sped up yet again to seven hours under the now nationalised British Railways.

1962 saw the introduction of the enormously powerful Deltic diesels and the time came down to six hours, then with better track to five hours and 20 minutes. In 1978, the 125mph High Speed Train arrived and did King's Cross to Edinburgh in just four hours and 35 minutes. In 1991, the route was electrified – in British Railways' last big effort before privatisation – and today *The Flying Scotsman* still leaves London at 10.00, now taking 4½ hours, less than half the original journey time. The first new operator at privatisation, GNER, was quick to paint 'the route of *The Flying Scotsman*' on all its carriages. After all, it was the world's most famous train. Now National Express run the route, keeping the name for the 10.00 train, of course.

Meanwhile, what happened to the steam locomotive by the same name? Scrapped long ago like her forlorn sisters?

Well, no, and it was all down to a small boy who climbed up on the footplate of *Flying Scotsman* at the British Empire Exhibition in 1924. The lad in short trousers and grey socks was one Alan Pegler. He was overawed by the beauty of the gleaming, almost brand-new machine with her flawless apple-green paintwork (she had been towed there under a bizarre immense padded duvet to ensure she was absolutely spotless!). She was massive, and the public and press loved her looks from the start.

As Alan Pegler grew up he heard of her record exploits – first non-stop run in 1928, first authenticated 100mph by a steam loco in 1934. Then came the war years and she was stripped of her glamour, and, by now dirty black, used to pull any old train including slow freights.

By 1963 with diesels taking over, she was heading for the

cutting torch in the scrapyard, as all 76 of her sister locos sadly had.

In stepped a now wealthy businessman, the very same Alan Pegler. He paid £3,000 for the loco and somehow won running rights on the network – by 1968 she ended up being the only steam loco allowed to run on the main lines.

Having re-enacted her famous non-stop run to Edinburgh, Pegler took *Flying Scotsman* for a tour of the USA. But governments changed, the Vietnam War was raging and with the Troubles flaring into warfare in Northern Ireland, some Irish Americans seemed to threaten the British locomotive's tour of the States, or at any rate boycott it. The tour was going to be a failure. But Pegler had promised to deliver some historic carriages to a museum, and decided to honour the deal at his own expense. He did it and went bust. Again she seemed doomed. American creditors wanted her, and Pegler hid *Flying Scotsman* in an old US air base.

Yet again, a miracle happened to save No 4472. Sir William McAlpine – yes, a relative of 'Concrete Bob' McAlpine who built the Mallaig line (see page 40) – bought her, shipped her back through the Panama Canal and repaired her, with the help of Pete Waterman, the pop producer and rail fan. She started her touring career again, taking in a trip to Australia where in 1988 she broke another record. *Flying Scotsman* established a new record for the world's longest non-stop steam run.

Another entrepreneur tried to save her, then she was threatened in another financial crisis. In 2004, at long last *Flying Scotsman* was bought for the nation, with the help of another knight, Sir Richard Branson. She has now been restored yet again to tip-top running order, this time at the National Railway Museum, and no-one was more pleased than one grey-whiskered old man in a wheelchair, Alan Pegler (who also helped save the Ffestiniog Railway in the Welsh mountains). He was honoured with an OBE in 2006 (a knighthood would have been better).

At some point in this tangled saga of the most-travelled loco in the world, amateurs were allowed to drive *Flying Scotsman* in the Midlands as a fund-raiser. I leapt at the chance.

Climbing up onto that hallowed footplate, I gingerly pulled the regulator handle down just about the width of a two-pence coin. 135 tons of steel, coal, water and steam – and not an ounce of electronics or computers – leapt forward like a Mini Cooper. The power available was immense, I realised as I blew that famous whistle for a crossing. For just a moment, it was like being allowed to play on Wimbledon Centre Court and win, or be the first man to walk on the Moon. Wow!

Years later I heard some expert say: 'And did you know in the 1980s some fool let amateurs drive *Flying Scotsman* up and down a track in the Midlands? What *were* they thinking of? Like using Concorde as a dodgem car. Bloody idiots!'

'Absolutely, tutt tutt. Bloody idiots,' I murmured.

Bet he never drove *Flying Scotsman*.

Flying Scotsman and admirers, 1963

◄ ME

Soon another real treat comes up, with **Berwick-upon-Tweed*****. Look out for the Tweedmouth Lighthouse. Passing that small town, which is across the river from Berwick, look ahead for a fine view of the Royal Border Bridge.

In fact three bridges cross this handsome river, which traverses much of the Scottish Borders (and indeed is the border for most of its course). There's the magnificent railway bridge we are purring across (the **Royal Border Bridge**, 28 arches, built by Robert Stephenson, son of George, above), the modern road bridge and a more ancient bridge below. Before that was built, there were ferries.

Berwick has famously changed hands a few times. It once came to be at war with Russia for more than a century by accident, with the Soviet Union sending an ambassador to sue for peace between Berwick and Moscow.

It's decidedly English now, and after the station you get a glimpse of the massive fortifications necessary to stop the kilted chaps grabbing it back. Just after that, you cross the border.

No route into Scotland can compare with that of The Flying Scotsman: the astonishing beauty of Berwick revealed suddenly as the train comes over the cliffs... the three great bridges, each a masterpiece of its day – and as the train slows and enters upon the loftiest of the three, Robert Stephenson's Royal Border Bridge, the passenger on The Flying Scotsman surveying this fair scene and watching his motoring friends below... has as JJ Bell once expressed it 'the advantage of the eagle over the sparrow'.

The late great railway writer O S Nock

We now climb the cliffs towards Eyemouth (where fishermen have a Herring Queen every year) and get superb sea views. Then it's inland through some hills, still dogged by the A1 heading for the same prize, and you can see the Scottish mileposts are now counting down towards Edinburgh.

Just after milepost 43, you see another one of those huge LNER signs, this one saying 'London 350 miles'. We get our first glimpse of the Fife coast to the north, looking way across the Firth of Forth.

Just after milepost 29 we whiz through **Dunbar****; look out for a superb view of the island of Bass Rock, and flat Fidra beyond. On the right, what looks like a mine slag heap in its conical shape is Berwick Law, a volcanic 'crag and tail' left scraped clean by glaciers after the last ice age. You can spot others in the landscape, particularly the one Edinburgh Castle sits on, coming up soon.

Behind Berwick Law – *law* is Scottish for 'hill' – lies North Berwick, as pretty a little seaside resort as you could hope for, reached from Edinburgh in about half an hour by the **NORTH BERWICK LINE** which joins us at **Drem** (see page 50 for the North Berwick excursion from Edinburgh). On a clear day you can see two hills in Fife, across the sea to the right. (Some call these two the 'Paps O' Fife', though as 'paps' go, these are more Gwyneth Paltrow than, say, the 'Paps O' Jura' – a pair of twin peaks on the other side of Scotland, which are more Pamela Anderson.) All of this gazing northwards might stop us seeing a fine pillar of a monument to the south (our left) about a mile away on a hill. It is one of two similar Hopetoun monuments (see Springfield in Fife, below).

Shortly afterwards, just before **Longniddry**, is a sandstone castle ruin on the right.

Now we can see the hills of Fife across the Forth more clearly, and exciting occasional glimpses of Edinburgh Castle and Arthur's Seat (Edinburgh's highest hill) ahead, as well as glimpses of the Forth Bridge beyond. As we whistle through **Prestonpans**, **Wallyford** and **Musselburgh** we can soon see Calton Hill, through which our train will tunnel. It is covered with fascinating monuments and absolutely worth the climb from the station for the best view of Edinburgh.

I can't here detail everything that's great about Edinburgh, but as you reach **Edinburgh Waverley✱✱✱** station, the Old Town and castle are high on the left, and Princes Street, the New Town and the Scott Monument are high on the right. Indeed, Scott's *Waverley* novels gave the station its name. If you are a first-timer, you have a treat in store! If you are a repeat visitor, you'll already love the place.

EDINBURGH TO ABERDEEN:
Firth to last**** (2¹/₂hrs, 129 miles)

This ride is scenically, geographically and, in engineering terms, one of the best – you will not be bored for a second. The monstrous, magnificent and breathtaking Forth Bridge being only one of many treats.

Starting off, we pass through an echoing canyon between Edinburgh Castle, high up to our left, and Princes Street to our right, through a tunnel to **Haymarket** station in the city's west end – a short distance that you could easily walk. Even odder, then, to recall that there once were two more stations in between (called Princes Street and Exhibition) plus *another* on a rival route nearby – all part of the expensive duplication of stations and routes by rival companies before grouping in 1923 and nationalisation in 1948. The huge stadium on the right just after Haymarket is Murrayfield, home to Scottish rugby.

Soon after the line to Glasgow diverges left, we go through **South Gyle** station, then past Edinburgh Airport where a new station is, it is hoped, to be built. Now you can see the mileposts counting up from zero again – at the 8¹/₂ milepost, there is an exciting glimpse looking ahead and a little to the right, of the looming **Forth Bridge***** (on the starboard bow, as a sailor on the train would put it). As we near the bridge, a line from Linlithgow joins from the left (just after we go under a main road) and then we reach **Dalmeny***** station. If you'd like to look at the fantastic Forth Bridges from ground level, and have a poke around the fascinating town of South

Queensferry, way down below on the shoreline, then Dalmeny would be the port of call by a local train. For the story of the Forth Bridge – one of the seven wonders of the world in engineering – see the box overleaf, but for the moment sit back and enjoy the astonishing views as you soar like an aircraft high over the roofs to South Queensferry and out above the waters of the Forth.

On the left is the much newer Forth Road Bridge, a far lighter suspension design compared with the staggeringly massive, cantilevered monster we are crossing. Both are built to be able to clear full-sized ships heading up to the busy docks at the head of the Forth (west, to your left) and any warships heading for Rosyth Dockyards (on the far shore). On the right are islands, some fortified from various wars (such as Inch Garvie, just below on the right), some with holy relics.

The last time I crossed this wonderful bridge, an autumnal sun was setting to the west, turning the Forth into a blazing cauldron of red and yellow, merging in the sky into apricots, blues and purples. Looking east into the inky blackness of the North Sea, a near full moon was rising, leaving a shimmering silver trail across the still, dark waters. Magic!

We hit **North Queensferry** – the name reminds us what was here before the bridges, and in fact lasted on another century after the rail bridge arrived – and get a view of Rosyth Dockyards to our left. **Inverkeithing** station is followed by a junction where we veer right and the FIFE CIRCLE LINE goes left. Look out after **Aberdour** station for the ruins of a castle on the right. There are excellent views across to Edinburgh here and sharply backwards, towards the Forth Bridge. You have to be this far away to appreciate its size.

Burntisland station is near oil-rig support yards: here I once spotted a fat seal close to the shore, swimming on his back and looking curiously up at the train. After **Kirkcaldy** (pronounced 'Kirkcoddy', and site of the last duel fought in Scotland when merchant David Landale shot dead the bank manager George Morgan in 1826), the line swings north, across old coalfields and into the fertile farmland of the 'Kingdom of Fife', a land cut off on three sides by sea and still very much its own place. (By the way, if foreigners find Firth of Forth a mouthful, they should try giving a football result such as East Fife five, Forfar four.) A supposed Edinburgh saying is: 'It tak's a lang spune to sup with a Fifer'. This may say something about Fifers' character, or just be a practical reality if you're trying to sup with them from Edinburgh!

THE RIVETING YARN OF THE FORTH BRIDGE

We are now in full view of the Forth Bridge – that stupendous undertaking which is, by universal consent, held to be the greatest engineering triumph of the kind that has ever been consummated.

From a 1904 traveller's guide

Constructing the Forth Bridge

The Forth Bridge, the railway bridge that opened in 1890, is an internationally recognised outline like that of the Taj Mahal or Statue of Liberty. Crossing it, you fly like a plane high over the rooftops of South Queensferry on the Edinburgh side, and the train – running 150ft above high water to allow shipping through – is completely dwarfed by the mighty structure.

It is far more massive than it needed to be because, not long before it was built, a trainload of passengers had disappeared under the waves when the Tay Bridge, on the next great inlet up the coast, had collapsed (see box on page 22). The same designer was about to build the Forth Bridge, so that project was swiftly shelved and thousands of tons of perhaps unnecessary steel were used to make it as strong as possible. It was also one of the first large bridges made of steel – as opposed to iron – so it was experimental in its tube and lattice construction.

It is $1^1/2$ miles long, the towers are 360ft tall and 55,000 tons of steel and eight million rivets were used to build it.

'Painting the Forth Bridge' (all 145 acres of steelwork on the $1^1/2$ mile-long structure) became an international phrase for something you could never finish, because when you got to the end

you had to start again to stop it rusting. When the cocked-up reprivatisation of the railways took place in 1996, they stopped painting it, and guess what – it started rusting, and had to be rescued at great expense. All is well again now, however.

Anyway, back to the spooky stuff – when the Forth Bridge was being built in 1890, the enormous cantilevered arms were reaching out to meet each other, but they were so huge that they couldn't exactly meet.

Although perfectly made and aligned, they were so big that the effect of the sun on the eastern side in the morning, and the west in the afternoon, could bend the structure enough to prevent perfect alignment. The solution was to send men inside the massive tubes, each itself large enough to take a London tube train, to light bonfires and 'trick' the bridge, as it were, into thinking that it was sunny on both sides. The ends aligned perfectly, the bolts were dropped in and the last plates riveted up. But did all the men get out of the smoke-filled tubes? Is that knocking and groaning you can hear just the bridge expanding or the ghosts of something else?

That much may be pure myth. What is true though is the staggering toll of workers who died building the thing, in accidents or blown off while walking the high girders: 71 deaths by the best count (see the memorial at South Queensferry).

Even more recently I have heard a local widow talk of how a man died when he tripped on the highest part, probably because he would keep his hands in his pockets against the cold and therefore couldn't save himself. It makes you realise when the Health and Safety mob festoon places like this with fussy walkways and handrails, they may have a point.

The bridge features in Hitchcock's great film, *The 39 Steps*, in an Iain Banks novel *The Bridge*, on some pound coins in your pocket and in the computer game *Grand Theft Auto: San Andreas*. It's very well worth a walk round South Queensferry at the south end of the two bridges, getting off at Dalmeny station. Spectacular.

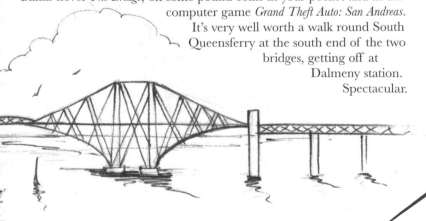

After a junction where the FIFE CIRCLE route rejoins, we whistle through **Markinch**, **Ladybank** (where the TAY COAST LINE to Perth takes off left), **Springfield** (the tall monument on top of a hill to the left is to Sir John Hope, Earl of Hopetoun, who by turning the fortunes of the Pensinular War in 1808 indeed gave Britain hope. He also has a similar monument further down this line past Edinburgh at Haddington in East Lothian – both are inscribed 'by his affectionate and grateful tenantry' – and a statue in St Andrew Square, Edinburgh), **Cupar** and then **Leuchars**. This is the station for St Andrews (on the North Sea coast a couple of miles east), the ancient university town, spiritual home of world golf, and place of pilgrimage for the sport's followers. It used to have its own branch line connecting here. If you don't see some wealthy golfers getting off the train with all their kit, being helped into plush minibuses to go to their swanky hotels… sell your shares; there must be a global recession.

It's also the station for RAF Leuchars air base, which spent much of the Cold War batting probing Russians back across the North Sea, and for Scotland's oldest university which famously produced Prince William as a graduate in 2005.

By the way, we are (at the time of writing) back in the land of semaphore

▼ ME/ILN

The Tay Bridge Disaster, the 'Diver' and Bird Poo

The Tay Bridge may not look as dramatic as the Forth Bridge, but it attracts different kinds of superlatives: the worst disaster, when the first bridge fell down on 28 December 1879; the longest rail bridge in Britain, at $2^{1}/_{4}$ miles; and the worst poem about a disaster ever written (by William Topaz McGonagall, who had just written two poems praising the strength of the bridge), which starts:

> Beautiful railway bridge of the silv'ry Tay
> Alas! I am very sorry to say
> That ninety lives have been taken away

It was the high girder section of the single-track bridge that blew down, taking a train and all 75 people on board to their doom. The fact that part of the bridge was gone was only ascertained by a worried railwayman crawling along the structure in the gale and darkness when he reached the gap.

signals (those waggling arms and manual signal boxes. South of Waverley, we had a 21st-century electrified railway with electronic computerised control; here we are in the 19th century, the lines little different from when they carried steam trains. Does anyone mind? No. Is it less safe? Certainly not. Is it less reliable? Nope.

On the very wiggly short run between here and the **Tay Bridge**✱✱✱, you glimpse distant views, sharply ahead on the right, then left as the train swings, of the city of Dundee, across the Firth of Tay.

Again, this firth offers great views. On the peaceful shore you may see a heron patiently stalking fish. To the west you can see the beautiful wide firth stretching up towards Perth; to the east the narrower entrance from the North Sea, and ahead, the city of Dundee. To the immediate right, down below are the stubs of the piers of the ill-fated first Tay Bridge (see box below). If you can't see them from up on the train, look back as we curve off the bridge down into Dundee.

At just over two miles, the Tay Bridge is Britain's longest railway bridge, so you've plenty of time to contemplate the view. The hill behind Dundee city centre is Dundee Law and a now-closed branch line round behind there had a station by the prosaic name Back of Law.

Designer Thomas Bouch had not allowed enough strength for the wind pressure of gales, or indeed any allowance for wind. The cast iron pillars and connecting work were badly made, patched up to look passable when they should have been rejected. The bridge was then poorly maintained; signs of deterioration were ignored. And as if that weren't a recipe for disaster, speed limits were also exceeded (even today, it's a long trundle).

Sir Thomas Bouch – he had just been knighted for his design! – lost a son-in-law in the disaster. Work had just started on his design for a Forth Bridge; this was rapidly scrapped and redesigned. The Tay Bridge was rebuilt to a far better design, but you can see the piers of the old one sticking above the water alongside. Bouch died in disgrace soon afterwards.

Surprisingly, after the central high girders were lifted from the river bed and the train found within, the repaired locomotive was run until 1919. And perhaps unsurprisingly, many railwaymen refused to drive the engine, nicknamed the *Diver*, over the new Tay Bridge which opened in 1887.

In 2003, when the current bridge was thoroughly refurbished and strengthened, 1,000 tonnes of bird droppings were scraped off! Grotty job, but good for someone's garden, perhaps. Now it's tip-top.

As we descend off the bridge and curve on to the
shore, we join the TAY COAST LINE running along the river's
north bank from Perth, and soon we arrive at **Dundee**
station, somewhat sunk into the city. Known for jute, jam and
journalism, Dundee has never been the prettiest Scottish city
but in recent years has cleaned up its act and made much of
its university (once part of St Andrews) and its links with great explorers.

The hinterland of Angus, behind the city, is as fertile and attractive as
Fife. My favourite products of Dundee are *The Beano* (a comic) and William
McGonagall, the world's worst poet.

After tunnelling under the town, we emerge by the docks
and run through the increasingly attractive seaside
settlements of **Broughty Ferry**, **Balmossie**, **Monifieth**,
Barry Links, **Golf Street Halt**, **Carnoustie** and
Arbroath✳✳. The last is home of the famous Arbroath
Smokie, a fish wonderful if done well (and there's little more
dramatic than the mobile smoking barrels some smokie
sellers have). By the way, as we run up from Dundee, there
are good views back to the bridge and Fife, exactly as there
were on the south of Fife, but across a different firth.

If you were told this section was laid in Indian-gauge with rails 5ft 6in
apart, you would be incredulous, as clearly normal British trains (which run
on 4ft 8½in track) would fall off. But this was true, because early railways
were isolated stretches which no-one dreamed would form a network.
Eventually the Dundee–Arbroath line had to be relaid.

Soon we are approaching Montrose. Before there, on the right, there's a
picturesque sandy bay with ruins. In fact, there is a series of bays. They
look inviting for a dip – but the water this far north is always achingly cold.

Montrose✳✳✳ is approached by an annoying (from a signalman's point
of view) single-track section, over a rumbling bridge that crosses the mouth
of Montrose Basin, an extraordinary stretch of water running two miles or
more inland (to a place called The Lurgies, as it happens). 'Basin' is exactly
the right word for this place, for after I looked across the broad expanse of
water on the way to Aberdeen and wondered if it was deep enough for
boating, I got my answer on the return train. The water had vanished,
leaving a muddy waste riven by streams and gullies. If the tide is running as
you cross the bridge, look at the piers of the parallel road bridge, and the
water that eddies and swirls dangerously against them. I can think of places
I'd rather be in a boat. So 'basin' is right – it's as if someone has pulled the
plug out twice a day!

The station is perched beside the water, with the town crammed into the
rest of the peninsula that almost encloses the basin. On leaving Montrose,
look to your left across a field to see the embankment of a converging
trackbed of a line that used to come round the north side of the basin, also
heading for Aberdeen, just as we curve right. Of course there must have

been 100 old trackbeds joining the line since we left King's Cross, but this is an important one, **Kinnaber Junction**, marked by the railway even today with a special signboard, and scene of the dramatic tussle between railway companies known as 'The Race to the North', a fierce 19th-century rivalry between the competing companies and routes.

Now, just as happened in Fife, the railway gets bored with hugging the coast and lunges across country and easier farmland to race north, crossing one river on a high viaduct. There are mostly closed stations in this rural section, although we pass the recently reopened **Laurencekirk**✳ (most useless information in this chapter: famous for the Laurencekirk hinge, an airtight snuffbox closure).

We reach the coast again at **Stonehaven**✳✳✳. Stonehaven itself is set down by the sea, a haven indeed. The short run along the cliffs to Aberdeen is a scenic highlight, similar to the coast near Berwick. As we leave, the view back to Stonehaven is highly recommended, across an old church and graveyard on this side of the town, and a castle on the other side.

We hurry along the cliff tops, impatient to finish the journey. There are spectacular views over the sea and down into dangerous foaming gullies and mysterious caves where the waves enter. We run through **Portlethen** station – we are in semaphore signal country again – and down over a river into **Aberdeen**.

This tough city of oil-rig workers, sailors and fishermen and no-nonsense, no-frills bars has various attractions I can't list here (and an onwards journey to Inverness and the Highlands by train). The tourist people would rather talk of 'The Granite City', 'The Flower of Scotland', or 'The Silver City by the Golden Sands'.

I'd just point out two things: one of the platforms (probably the one opposite where you came in) has an ancient milepost under its lip, midway along, down by the rails. It says Carlisle 241, though there's no direct route to that border city and the distance is wrong by train nowadays. But there was such a route, and it was the main line, further evidence of the Race to the North (see above).

The other oddity is down by the harbour, at Shore Lane. There's a business called the Shore Porters' Society, established 1498. *1498?* No, they're not joking. This was set up just six years after Columbus 'discovered' America (well, Cuba) and the Old World hadn't yet decided whether to do anything about the New (or just cover it up and pretend it wasn't there). This firm was set up *centuries* before Australia and New Zealand were even thought of, and yet is still going as a removals firm. Remarkable, though not the oldest business in Britain, but that's another story... For Aberdeen–Inverness, see *Chapter 2*, page 53.

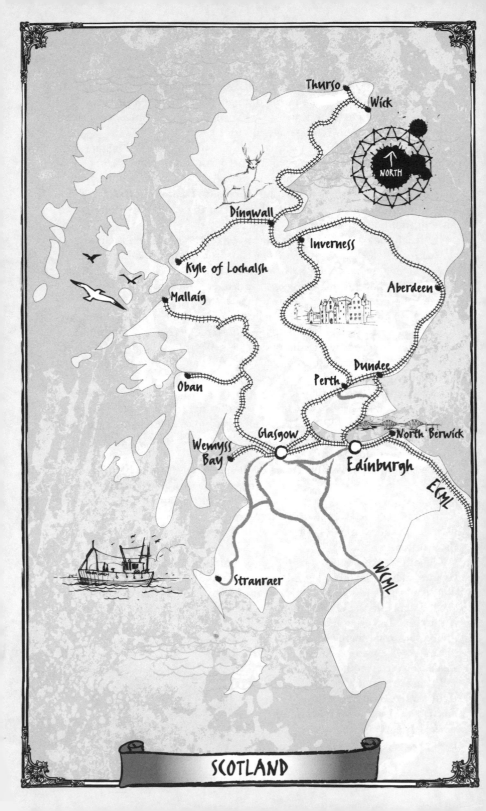

SCOTLAND

TWO

Scotland:
Rails to Romance and Beauty

The basic layout

No railway in Scotland is dull. They are truly one of the best things about this special country, and rail is the best way to enjoy the Highlands, by a long chalk. The 'iron road to the isles' does romance and beauty by the trainload.

But you need to know the layout and plan ahead up there. The basic layout of Scottish railways is like a letter 'H' with the Highland routes being on long unconnected upward arms and the two main lines to England and London being the lower ones, again unconnected (north of the border). The cross bar is the central Lowlands belt between Glasgow on the left (west) and Edinburgh on the right (east).

Of course it's not quite that simple. Both Highland arms have two long branches off them. And once you get near the Lowlands, things get complex with most cities such as Perth and Dundee enjoying separate routes to Glasgow and Edinburgh. These cross at places where you change trains to the other major city. In fact there are four Edinburgh–Glasgow routes.

In the southwest there are also two long secondary routes: one from Glasgow to Ayr and Stranraer (for ferries to Northern Ireland), the other through Dumfries to rejoin the West Coast Main Line at Carlisle. And Inverness is not only reached by the East Coast Main Line but also a wonderful line right up the middle. However, the fact remains that you can't get from one arm of the H to another without going through the central belt. The **EAST COAST MAIN LINE** into Scotland is covered in the previous chapter.

Glasgow and Edinburgh termini

Glasgow Queen Street (for the lines to the Highlands and eastwards to Edinburgh) to **Glasgow Central** (for lines to the southwest and England) is very walkable, even with a medium wheeled suitcase, so I wouldn't bother with the *Clockwork Orange* underground (subway) which goes only vaguely near each end. There's also a free bus for those holding onward rail tickets, but unless you've got three babies, an infirm granny, huge suitcases, hailstorm overhead or a gammy leg (or all five, in which case my sympathies), why bother?

Central was originally run by the Caledonian Railway and is the terminus of the route from London Euston and others south of the Clyde. Queen Street was the North British outfit and serves routes to the east and north, plus the north bank of the Clyde.

Queen Street is not as lovely as Central (which I enthuse about on page 49). Its layout has always been hampered by the fact that it immediately concentrates all the tracks into a dank, steep tunnel upwards. Originally, this was worked by a cable system because early steam locos couldn't manage it. After that way of operating finished, a steam train was once puffing and snorting so hard in the fume-filled tunnel that the driver failed to notice that it was slipping backwards, until it re-emerged humiliatingly in the station he'd just left! Of course back then the tunnel was wreathed in Stygian gloom. Today's diesels have less trouble and a lot less smoke. Vestygian gloom, possibly.

Given that danger of trains running down the hill – now completely under control with severe speed limits, I must add for nervous types – it's odd that the buffer stops are a lot less substantial than those at Central. There probably wasn't room here, as the longest trains just squeeze in sometimes. Safely.

There are also initially unseen low-level lines and platforms at the termini, but these mainly run in suburban networks.

Edinburgh Waverley is the only open British station to be named after a novel (now that Westward Ho! station in the West Country has closed). Author Walter Scott's totally over-the-top statue stands nearby. Waverley, in fact a through station not a terminus, is sensationally located in the deep trough between the Old Town and castle on one side and Princes Street and the New Town on the other. Once this was a defensive lake, the Norloch, but the draining of that left a deep cleft in which a massive railway and its station – around 20 platforms, more being built as I write – could be located without damaging the wonderful heritage and superb cityscape all around. It's a gem, and Edinburgh has **Haymarket** as another major station in the West End. Add in that fact the Scotland believes in railways, with Edinburgh getting two new (or reopened) routes and Glasgow having expansion too, and the picture is pretty positive north of the border. My favourite terminus is **Inverness**, and an odd detail is pictured left.

Planning ahead in Scotland

Plan ahead and check timetables in Scotland. It could save you time, as in the Highlands the trains are few and the lines are long. For instance, I sauntered down to Inverness station for the 09.35 train and sought a connection to Oban via Glasgow Queen Street. Result: a 12-hour journey (which didn't matter as I had much to do in Glasgow). Had I caught the 07.55 train however, it would have taken just seven hours 48 minutes. By the way, this illustrates what I was saying above about how you can't get from one arm of the H shape of Scotland's railways to another without going to the central belt.

Highland travel is in proper mountains, and even modern trains are not immune from the temperature changes. Carry a jumper and raincoat even in summer; in winter it is just possible snow will stop the train, so don't turn up in Jimmy Choo heels and a flimsy dress (and that applies to women, too).

First Class is very good and comfortable on the modern Turbostars, but don't assume this is available on all the Highland lines: most are Standard Class only. Check when booking. All the long-distance services have trolley catering, and some a counter service. Even relatively short lines such as the Oban branch have catering. Not Lowland commuter and city branches, naturally.

If the fewer trains on the remoter lines require planning ahead (rather than just turning up at the station), journeys involving ferries and islands need even more careful planning. But they are wonderful and absolutely worth it.

Useful Numbers

Rapsons Buses (Skye, Fort William, Inverness):
T 0871 200 2233

Royal Highland Hotel, Inverness (next to station, recommended)
T 01463 231926

Glenfinnan Monument T 0844 493 2221

Culloden Moor Monument T 0844 493 2159, Bus No 7 from Inverness (six miles)

Caledonian MacBrayne (ferries to the islands) T 08705 650000, W www.calmac.co.uk.

The West Highland Line: Glasgow–Crianlarich–Fort William–Mallaig and the Oban branch: the iron road to the isles✶✶✶✶✶ (5hrs, 164 miles)

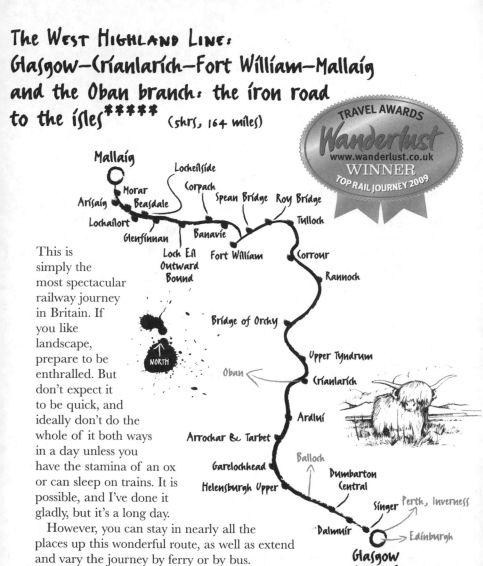

TRAVEL AWARDS
Wanderlust
www.wanderlust.co.uk
WINNER
TOP RAIL JOURNEY 2009

This is simply the most spectacular railway journey in Britain. If you like landscape, prepare to be enthralled. But don't expect it to be quick, and ideally don't do the whole of it both ways in a day unless you have the stamina of an ox or can sleep on trains. It is possible, and I've done it gladly, but it's a long day.

However, you can stay in nearly all the places up this wonderful route, as well as extend and vary the journey by ferry or by bus.

And this isn't just a great line for scenery and railway buffs; active types can bring (or hire) bikes, tents, canoes and boats; the hiking is superlative; and outdoor activities are all over the place. Pack midge repellent in late summer/autumn if you're doing the outdoor stuff.

Oh, and it's also starred in many films. *And* offers a superb steam-train ride. What are you waiting for?!

Glasgow Queen Street to Crianlarich: from Lowland bustle to empty Highlands in a few miles

(1hr 50mins, 58¾ miles)

The transformation that this route makes is simply staggering. You can't believe it's on the same trip. In London terms, it's as if there were a totally empty wilderness round about Croydon or Harrow. From bustling, industrial city with ugly tower blocks to real Highland bleakness and scenes of bewitching lochside beauty, it really is a special experience.

I'd sit on the left until Loch Lomond – and then change if possible to the right. No matter if you can't.

We soon leave the suburbs and pass through a station called **Singer** (where the sewing machines were made, employing 5,000 in the world's largest factory) stop at **Dalmuir** and get a great view of the Clyde Road Bridge, in a kind of suspension design. We then come down to the shoreline and parallel the Wemyss Bay branch on the far bank.

A call at **Dumbarton Central** and we cross the wide and fast-flowing River Leven (which drains Loch Lomond, not so far away to the north) before, about 23 miles out, at **Craigendoran Junction** we swerve suddenly right off the electrified line to Helensburgh and start climbing on single track, the start of the West Highland Line and the start of real adventure.

Helensburgh Upper means there's a lower station on the other line, which happens again later in very odd circumstances; but we have the Upper hand there too.

Soon we get splendid views of Gareloch on the left, a peaceful place – until you notice the nuclear missile submarine base on our side of the loch and a sinister black shape slipping out to sea. The theory is that these things won't start a nuclear war, they'll prevent one. Let's hope they're right.

Yet how can we think of such things: we are in lovely deciduous woods strewn with bluebells in early summer. There's a long view down Gareloch across the Clyde to Greenock.

At **Garelochhead** we meet the first of many passing loops, and take the right one, perhaps in deference to the ships in the loch below who like to pass port to port. The station's doubtless higher up the hill than the villagers would like, but then the West Highland is fighting for height.

We cross a high viaduct and then power through a rock cutting, emerging on a hillside with views of Loch Long – and no human habitation. Don't you suddenly feel you're reaching the Highlands? Rhododendrons thrive here, being Himalayan immigrants.

We climb higher and higher above the water, and then turn up Glen Douglas away from the loch. Now things are bleak and we *are* definitely in the pukka Highlands, still only haggis-chucking distance from Glasgow.

We reach a passing loop and some strange Ministry of Defence sidings, then emerge once more high above Loch Long – not a place to derail (which has never happened, I hasten to add!). There's a village and caravans viewed on the far shore as if from a plane.

Arrochar & Tarbet station often has timber being loaded. Suddenly we get a glimpse of a loch on the right, and fresh water this time. It's not *any* loch either, but the beautiful, legendary Loch Lomond, whose bonnie, bonnie banks we follow for miles. It's worth changing sides to the right if you can. You'll never get such a good view from the road, twisting even more than the railway below us, plus if you're driving you'll be watching those bends not the peerless scenery. No, this is definitely the way to do it. You can even read guidebooks!

There's a hydropower station, but it's discreet, not spoiling the indisputably bonnie banks of Loch Lomond. The largest expanse of fresh water in Britain, the other end goes almost back south to Dumbarton where we crossed the outlet a while back.

At **Ardlui**, we're told it's *officially* beautiful: we're in the Loch Lomond and Trossachs National Park. The latter are the hills. We veer into Glen Falloch, climbing and climbing, a great viaduct in a fantastic bit of railway building 143ft high above the river, and there are great views down to the river with a waterfall and strange-shaped boulders. Soon we

reach **Crianlarich** (tea rooms, loos), with mountains all round, the biggest being Ben More, 3,843ft, to the east. Sometimes here there will be a train carrying massive aluminium slabs from the Fort William smelter waiting for the single line southwards. All the way up this route, you'll see no traditional signals, by the way, but blue lights that flash when it's OK to proceed – a radio-controlled electronic version of the tokens seen on the Aberdeen line. It's as safe as houses, I'm told; if a train drives over the grids on the track without possessing the token (displayed in the cab) for that single-line section, the brakes will come on.

Result: dozens of closed signal boxes along this line, and a massive saving in costs. It seems a shame in employment and heritage terms, but it may have saved this route. The lovely **OBAN BRANCH** peels off left here and our train may divide for part to go each way. For the absurd story of its connection, and the route today, see page 42.

Crianlarich to Fort William: a lucky horseshoe, the last great wilderness and a gorgeous gorge
(1hr 50mins, 64½ miles)

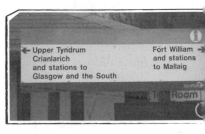

We take off, after the Oban line leaves us to the left, across a viaduct and up Strathfillan (meaning 'valley of the Fillan').

We pass a holy pool in which they used to test lunatics by binding them hand and foot and tossing them in to see if they would come up with a pebble from the bottom (yes, it was crazy) and soon reach **Upper Tyndrum** (see remarks on the Lower in the Oban section). Note how the original station buildings are still there, insanely large for the one or two walkers who join the train, and useless because it's all locked up. Let's hope they find a use before the vandals get there.

Talking of walkers, this is on the West Highland Way long-distance path which, like us, heads from Glasgow to Fort William. It's a terrific route if you're a Pennine Way type of person, and there's a fairly easy-looking section on the left as we head north. But of course suitable clothing, footwear, precautions, maps, torches, first aid (and helicopter, mobile Jacuzzi and self-heating madras curry), and telling people where you're going beforehand (and at some length afterwards), are all necessary before you start yomping all over the Highlands. I'm told some runners have done the West Highland Way in one go – 95 miles!

Tyndrum, by the way, was the centre of Scotland's not large gold industry, and the Crown Jewels (correctly the Honours of Scotland) were made from Tyndrum gold.

Pure visual gold is the totally perfect horseshoe curve coming up. Look ahead when you curve right at around milepost 44 (they are the yellow things on the left). You can see a piece of track heading north about half a mile away, but we will take two miles to get there, because we swerve right (east) into a perfect glacial valley, turn north around the end of it on two natty viaducts and then charge west up the other side to resume the course we were on. It's beautiful, framed by massive mountains, though you wouldn't have needed much more viaduct to carry straight on! The builders had run out of money and had to economise (hence so few tunnels between Glasgow and Fort William – one, I think). They simply went round obstacles in great curves. It's our gain – one of the best horseshoe bends you can see. Most countries' railways have at least one, but few as clear as this or as dramatically framed.

Bridge of Orchy comes next, with the station being used as a bunkhouse for trekkers. We leave the road which diverges left and start climbing fast for the most amazing bit of railway: Rannoch Moor, a true wilderness, a bottomless bog into which the railway nearly sank without trace.

This massive high-level treeless, roadless bog was almost as unknown as the surface of the moon when the railway was built, one of last great empty wildernesses of Europe. True, a few men had ventured in there but some of them had drowned in the mire or, lost, frozen to death. We leave the road to pick a different route through the mountains and are all alone on a single-track line to doom (well, Mallaig, but it *feels* lonely). Talking about lonesome, **Gorton loop** which is next in the roadless middle of nowhere would once have had a signalman living in a hut or two, with no way in or out but by train. Even water came daily by train, and once a year Father Christmas arrived on a special with a brake van full of toys for the railwaymen's children in isolated spots like this.

There are remains of old snow fences from here on; early trains were stuck for days but perhaps global warming, or more powerful snowploughs, have fixed that problem.

An early 1894 guide to the line says of this 20 square mile, 1,000ft-high moor: 'Monotonous it certainly is to the pedestrian… but from the window of a railway carriage it is the reverse of wearisome. There is an infinite solitude in its vast and open expanse that renders it a spectacle never to be erased from the memory…' Exactly, old chum.

Rannoch station (tea room, accommodation) was also cut off by impenetrable bog, but now has a road that the railway built. There's a carving at the north end of the face of Renton, the man who saved the line by donating money in the last months of construction, and who drove the last spike joining up the two ends. The cheering navvies were so pleased they grabbed a boulder and with their tools set about carving his likeness, which is still here.

FOR PEAT'S SAKE: RANNOCH'S GREED

Getting up to Rannoch Moor at either end was a miracle of engineering. Building a railway across the 20 miles of bleak, treeless, roadless, impassable bog of Rannoch needed more than a miracle. Men and horses would drown in the quagmire. There were no paths, and travellers would get lost. Skeletons of lost navvies were found later on. The great road builder Thomas Telford had been up here to consider what seemed to him, too, a logical route. He looked at the place and gave up.

The railwaymen tipped stone from cuttings blasted elsewhere into the mire. They tipped and tipped thousands of tons, and no bottom was secured – the stuff kept disappearing, swallowed up by the malevolent moor. They sent to Glasgow for trainloads of ash. That all disappeared into the bog too. They couldn't give up because so much money had been spent bringing the line up to this place on either side, and money was running out.

Then someone seems to have remembered what George Stephenson did with the world's first intercity railway, the Liverpool and Manchester line, 60 years earlier. He had exactly the same problem at the bottomless Chat Moss, and solved it by laying a raft of bundles of logs and brushwood, plus layers of turf, and then building the line on top of that. The raft sank, but it floated down there and held up the stone roadbed for the line. For all I know, the bundles of logs and twigs are still there – the peat preserves everything well. You can feel the train sway and, if you are on foot, the ground move.

The only alternative was to dig great pits down to something solid, keeping out the mire with boarding, and make a stone viaduct pier, which is what they did in a depression north of Rannoch station for 684ft. It must have been right mucky work.

As we leave there's a good view east (right) down over Loch Rannoch. It's a strange thought that not far beyond the end of that loch the lonely road snakes over a hill to the Highland Main Line round about Blair Atholl. It's about five hours and umpteen miles by rail, via Glasgow, Stirling and Perth.

There are wild deer frequently now, big enough to dent the front of the train. What seems to be a tunnel is in fact a snow shelter. It had a removable middle section which in the summer would let light in and smoke out. In Norway they still have heaps of these on their railways. We climb now in snaking movements to lessen the gradient. I would swear we're still floating on that raft of logs from the tipsy roll of the train.

At **Corrour** (walkers' hostel) is the 1,347ft summit of the West Highland (in fact it's just north of the station and well marked with signs). Read David Thomas's wonderful book on this line to hear how the early morning 'ghost' freight from Glasgow once slowed at the summit to pick up the tablet (for more details, see page 55) and took off rather too briskly down

THE JACOBITE: GET ALL STEAMED UP

(Fort William–Mallaig, 41 miles, usually done as a round-trip day out with time at Glenfinnan and Mallaig, from around 10.20 to 16.00)

This is Britain's most successful main-line steam service, and no wonder. It goes from one beautiful place to another through sensational landscape, the line itself being part of the spectacle, as well as the train. There are proper steam whistles, the roar of safety valves making waiting children jump, the chuff – chuff – chuff – chuffchuffchuff as the wheels slip on wet days. The clickety-clack of traditional Mark 1 unpowered coaches with that gentle shwooshing of the brakes downhill, huge windows actually lined up with the seats, windows that actually open (a miracle nowadays) to God's good air, more likely God's good steam and smoke, and slam-doors with drop-windows for photographing through. Brilliant.

It's not too long for a family outing, it's affordable, and it's reliable. It's also in a holiday area where people want this sort of day out. The West Coast Railway Company, based in Carnforth in Lancashire, have been running it every summer and if they can keep steam alive where so many others have failed, good for them.

the other side. The result was that the guard's van, which had not reached the summit at the rear of the train, snapped off – with the guard snoozing beside the stove. It rolled backwards with signalmen at Rannoch, Gorton and Bridge of Orchy not daring to derail it for fear of hurting the sleeping guard, who dozed on despite swaying alarmingly over viaducts and screeching round curves. Eventually a worried stationmaster tracked it down, stopped by a rising gradient, and woke the guard and told him where he was. 'Impossible!' he exclaimed, 'we were there two hours ago!' He had rolled back 20 miles.

Corrour station gets a role in the hit film *Trainspotting* (which I'm afraid is more about mainlining drugs and tunnelling into toilets than trains, so don't look for *Flying Scotsman*. They wanted somewhere bleak. Here it is!). The engines get a well-earned breather (as did the fireman stoking in steam days), and now the brakes need to guide us somehow down to sea level again – and what a totally superb ride it will be!

The engines aren't the tiny tank engines seen on some preserved lines, and they don't do those pathetic speeds either, but carry on doing a proper job over a decent distance, complete with sweaty blackened fireman and driver, much like they used to. Yes, it's nostalgia for more innocent times when dirty smut meant something in your eye. Mind you, it had its comic moments when a loudspeaker announced 'this is a non-smoking train'. At that very moment the engine was laying a huge duvet of grey and black smoke in the sky about 500 yards long.

A word of warning to those not used to this era of trains. Don't lean on the doors (they open outwards). Don't let your kids get their hands trapped in them (they are not called slam-door trains for nothing). And don't lean out of the windows to get that perfect shot on the camera/video. You will not see the lump of rock or tree branch on this limited clearance line. The picture will be posthumously viewed by your relatives, and the Health and Safety brigade will probably have the windows sealed up.

I even got to go on the footplate (they don't let everyone). When I stepped down, my carbon footprint was left on the platform. Marvellous. For contact details, see page 311.

We take swooping downhill curves, looking to lose height and soon encounter the tree line again. We emerge high above Loch Treig, whose beauty was totally unknown to the public before the railway came here. We turn right along its shore, but hundreds of feet above the water, and follow a remarkable route on a rock shelf, sloping a full five miles down to the water level far below. I've been told the hillside route has 160 bridges and culverts to carry the streams – every one of which must be cleared lest a washout takes the line away – but I'm afraid I haven't counted them for you. You can check the mileposts, however, as we go down – it's $73\frac{3}{4}$ at the top and $78\frac{3}{4}$ at the bottom, so it really is a five-mile slope. Meanwhile you have plenty of time to admire the can-do Victorians – contemplate the hostile opposite shore, for example – who looked at a bit of wilderness and just said: 'We can build a railway here.'

After a short tunnel comes **Tulloch**. Then keep your eyes peeled left for another scenic treat, the Monessie Gorge. You look down into fantastically carved stone cliffs, eroded by the swirling peat-brown water that's just begging to be made into whisky. It's signed helpfully from both directions. Gorgeous.

Roy Bridge station building was for many years used as a chapel, there being no other provision for the few inhabitants. There are fantastic views on the left in the next stretch, with Ben Nevis the bulky mountain behind Fort William. Britain's highest at 4,406ft, like Everest it is not dramatically pointed from any direction. We cross another river, with the water pouring over massive rock strata pointing upwards. It's only a couple of hundred years since men looked at these and pondered: if the world was created as it now is, why jumble it up like this? The forces involved in twisting it round like this must have been gigantic.

Spean Bridge is followed by an unaccustomed fair lick of speed into

Fort William. Notice on the right the MALLAIG LINE trailing in to meet us behind the signal box. As we reverse to gain that line at Fort William, you may wish to switch to the opposite side, facing the other way to continue.

Fort William to Mallaig: outrageous beauty and concrete evidence (1hr 20mins, 41 miles)

This is a truly, truly terrific journey, and for how to do it by steam, see box on page 36. We leave the town on the shores of Loch Linnhe and head along the waterside. A rare case of old-style signalling exists here and splitting semaphores (that is two) tell us which route we're taking – the road to the isles or Glasgow. This time we pass on the other side of the signal box then across the wide River Lochy. On the hills to the right are the massive pipes of a hydro-electric scheme, used by Alcan to make huge aluminium slabs, each capable of making thousands of rolls of kitchen foil. You may have seen some being hauled in the daily train south, and it's another thing that helps keep this line open, along with timber traffic and some oil.

Next is **Banavie**, which was the end of a short branch line before the Mallaig Extension was built. I said there weren't any more signal boxes beyond here. I lied – there is this one, not only the control centre for all radio signalling, but also guarding the swing bridge over the Caledonian Canal. Presumably because boats can't be detected by track circuits. That and the fact that you don't want a train ending up in the water, which happened surprisingly often in America, but not here. There's a truly massive bolt beside the track down on our left, worked by the signalman, which keeps the bridge in place. Nevertheless, there's quite a 'bong, bong' when you go over the gaps.

Do look right (landward) on the bridge to see Neptune's Staircase (designed by Thomas Telford in 1822), a great flight of locks which could just as well let Nessie escape as the sea god enter.

If you've ever looked at a map of Scotland, you'll have seen a gigantic slash running from here northeast to Inverness and the Moray Firth, as if God had sliced the Caledonian ciabatta with a galactic knife. Given that, it was an obvious way for boats to avoid the long and dangerous trip round the top of Scotland, and with Loch Ness, was already half-filled with water. It would also have been an easy way to get a railway to Inverness, and indeed a half-hearted attempt was made from Spean Bridge

A Man, a Horse and a Horseshoe: Concrete Evidence?

The fantastic, beautifully located Glenfinnan Viaduct, on a picture-perfect horseshoe curve, is allegedly haunted. It contains a macabre secret, or so local lore has it. The viaduct was a radical experiment by 'Concrete Bob' McAlpine but during construction in 1900, the story goes, a horse and cart fell through planks into one of the hollow piers. So there you are rounding the curve at the foot of impossibly beautiful mountains, with a dead horse sealed beneath you. Bizarre, if it's true, but no-one has ever found it (and some say it is in the next viaduct).

which reached halfway and then closed. It's a shame, because it's a mind-boggling, but very rewarding way round by rail through Glasgow. However, there were almost as few passengers as monsters.

Corpach follows with a bunkhouse in the station. The place name means, those staying there may not wish to know, 'field of the dead' – nobility were kept there *en route* to burial on Iona. The canal basin is on the left, and there are good views back to Fort William and Ben Nevis when the clouds clear. We follow the shore of Loch Eil, and indeed **Loch Eil Outward Bound** with hearty youths building rafts, etc, confirms the area's outdoor theme. The deciduous woodland near **Locheilside** (r) in late spring has carpets of bluebells (albeit a full month later than the south of Britain, but all the lovelier for that). We leave the A830 road to Mallaig (we rejoin later) and start climbing furiously. Next comes a highlight of highlights, with a stunning view that many judge as the best railway vista in the British Isles: the iconic Glenfinnan Viaduct (see box, above).

Glenfinnan station has a museum about the line, and a dining car (the steam trips stop here for about 20 minutes on their outward journey). Then there are overbridges, still standing in Concrete Bob's original material, and a dramatic rock cutting ends in a tunnel, followed by fantastic views to the right when we come out high above Loch Eil. The road has taken the further shore, so we are alone for several miles of great beauty, with waterfalls all around. Bonnie Prince Charlie hid in a cave here after his 1746 defeat.

The wooded islands are just lovely, and would look good in a Japanese painting. Who needs the Lake District or, indeed, Switzerland? Forests of these trees once covered this land in the great Caledonian Forest – until timber extraction and sheep farming got rid of them.

The viaduct has been used in a few films, recently in *Harry Potter and the Chamber of Secrets* where an old Ford Anglia swoops around the train. The *Hogwarts Express* in that story, you may recall, starts at an invisible Platform 9¾ at King's Cross. Ridiculous fantasy – it would be Euston, of course, to get to the West Highland.

'Concrete Bob' McAlpine went mad with his new material in the same way the Forth Bridge went mad with new steel, a few decades earlier. There's concrete everything up this line – a line which saved his life as he was rushed to hospital when badly injured. There's a museum of him and this place at Glenfinnan station after the curve. And note the pillar in the flat glacial valley we are curving around – it's a memorial to Bonnie Prince Charlie, who made this place famous by raising his standard here on 19 August, 1745. Romantic hero or yet another dithering Stuart loser, you decide. The views down the valley to Loch Shiel are, however, undeniably superb, and the great concrete viaduct is in sight long before and after on the curve.

The sharp curves often have check rails (an extra rail to prevent derailment turning into a disaster) you'll be glad to know. We cross the river draining the loch and there's a request stop at **Lochailort**, where during the line's construction there was a shanty town of 2,000 navvies, complete with hospital and shop.

More tunnels, a sea loch, Loch nan-uamh, to the left, curving and climbing very steeply, isolated Polnish Chapel on the left (it was featured in the movie *Local Hero*), more viaducts (concrete of course) and tunnels, then **Beasdale**, a request stop (because a local bigwig paid for it to be added as an extra station). A tunnel and viaduct lead us to **Arisaig** (Britain's most

westerly railway station) with a fine old signal box, a station building in concrete, milepost: concrete, platforms: concrete. Concrete Bob's legacy! Did the staff get paid in concrete, eat concrete sandwiches, and use concrete loos?

There's a lovely view of a sea loch and over to the islands on the left (Rum, Eigg and Muck, which sounds like a recipe for a hangover cure. Eigg is the long flat one with

the towering Sgurr peak at one end). Soon we are seeing white-sand beaches with Skye beyond. Another viaduct, descending to cross a peat moor, and **Morar** has not only a 900ft deep loch to the right, but also a beautiful view to a bay on the left. The films *Local Hero* and *Highlander* were partly shot on the beaches here. And then we're there: seagull-squawking **Mallaig**, as far as rails could possibly reach on the rugged West Coast, you may think. Until you discover the Dingwall–Kyle line…

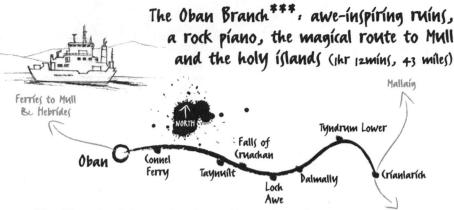

The Oban Branch***: awe-inspiring ruins, a rock piano, the magical route to Mull and the holy islands (1hr 12mins, 43 miles)

The Oban line is just enchanting, and were it not for the exalted company it keeps – the West Highland and the Skye lines – it would be the best, most remote, and it could put in a good claim for the loveliest. I'd sit on the left.

Finished in 1880 as the Callander and Oban Railway, it was an entirely separate route by a different company striving to get to the West Coast. It crossed the West Highland at a right angle just after **Crianlarich**, where our train divides from that bound for Mallaig. You can see the arch for the old line in the bridge of the Mallaig line to your right. A spur from the one line to the other was put in for freight, but as the quarrelsome rivals fell out again a piece of line was removed to make it unusable, and not restored for three years. It was 35 years before Oban line passengers' pleas for a direct service to Glasgow were heeded. Until then they had to scramble from one station to the other and train times seemed designed to prevent any useful connection.

Meanwhile the old route was earmarked for closure in the 1960s, but nature did it first with a landslide in Glen Ogle.

So this history explains why there are two stations at the next stop, **Tyndrum**, ours being Lower, the other Upper. It's given many a holidaymaker fun trying to race between the two to catch the train on the other line (which can usually be gained at a more relaxed pace by staying on to the junction at Crianlarich).

You can walk from one to the other easily in ten minutes, and you can cut out some of the road by taking a path marked by an old rail (on the way up) or turning left by the white bungalow (on the way down). You could even go by train from one side of the village to the other, if you're bonkers. I did this and it took an hour and nine minutes and 11 miles, via Crianlarich. By the way, if Waterloo Station was Britain's busiest station with 84 million passengers in the most recent year, Tyndrum Lower was the least busy with just 17 (and one was me)! However, it's probably bad statistic-keeping, for a local tells me he's seen about a dozen passengers in one day.

Soon comes **Dalmally**, and a mile or two further keep an eye out for on your left for the most romantic view of a ruined castle on a promontory

▼ ME

sticking out into Loch Awe. Look how it guards the loch entrance with the opposite promontory; we cross the entrance river on a viaduct. **Loch Awe✠✠✠** station is soon right on the water's edge. There's an old coach parked there which has been a tea room recently. The road keeps us company along the shore for miles now and the charming wooded islands are just too *Swallows and Amazons*-ish to be true. Loch Awe is awesome, but we can't see the full extent of the loch because we're following one short arm. The main run southwest is more than 20 miles.

Next is **Falls of Cruachan✠✠✠**, a summer-only request stop, handy for a tour of the underground power station. This is a line without traditional signalling and signal boxes, so the two-faced semaphores high on the left are a surprise. The strange signals all the way along here are controlled not by the signalman but by rock. They are connected to a set of wires running all along the hillside, nicknamed 'Anderson's Piano'. Any rockfall triggers a pair of signals to fall to 'Danger' showing each way. The apparatus is on the right, like a weird wired fence. It would probably be done with lasers nowadays, but there's no electricity in this fantastic contraption. Mind you, it must be a devil to reset if a demented deer crashes into it.

We leave the loch behind, following the river which drains it, and cross a superb high viaduct over the River Awe, descending west as we are, and after **Taynuilt** loop and sidings we soon reach the sea water again (on the right) where fish farms can be seen in Loch Etive.

The dramatic bridge at **Connel Ferry** can be glimpsed ahead on the right – we stick to this side of the water. It was an odd hybrid road–rail bridge where road traffic had to stop to allow trains across on a now-closed branch line. It was shut so long ago that you can now only just make out the joining embankment after the station.

▼ ME

Come to think of it, why couldn't they do this at Dornoch – just inset the rails into the bridge?

Down and down through woods and rock cuttings to **Oban✠✠✠**, an achingly beautiful harbour, where the friendly red-funnelled MacBrayne boats await to take you to Mull, thence perhaps to the holy island of Iona, cradle of Christianity in the British Isles. Or trips to Rum, Eigg, Muck or even Fingal's Cave. It's a beautiful scene – not always so in winter though; islanders take refuge in Oban hotels during great storms.

Recommended is the Oban Caledonian, the old railway hotel in front of you as you leave the station. It's not in the least bit fuddy-duddy, being modern, spacious and luxurious. Get a room with a harbour view, if you can. Perfect. If you can smell kippers in the breakfast room, I apologise. It'll probably be me.

The Highland Main Line: Inverness to Glasgow (and Edinburgh) ***

(3½hrs to Edinburgh or Glasgow,
118 miles Inverness
to Perth then about
another 60 miles
depending on route)

Inverness

Far North & Kyle

Aberdeen

Carrbridge

Aviemore · Strathspey

Newtonmore · Kingussie

Dalwhinnie

Blair Atholl
Pitlochry

Dunkeld & Birnam

Dundee

Perth

Fife,
Edinburgh

Gleneagles

Dunblane

Bridge of Allan

Stirling

Alloa

Lenzie

Larbert

Bishopbriggs · Croy

Mallaig
(West Highland Line)

Glasgow
Queen St

Edinburgh

Summit special in railway building: Britain's highest

This route is spectacular, speedy by Highland standards, useful and never, ever boring.

Leaving Inverness's curious triangular railway station behind, we take the left set of lines at **Milburn Junction**, compared with the Aberdeen route. This seems wrong but is soon rectified as we soar over that route.

Immediately we start climbing and climbing. There are fabulous views across the Moray Firth though soon we are ascending through woodland. We reach the great **Culloden Viaduct** with a slight curve to the west, then the A9 road, which we will be seeing a lot of today, crosses us.

This spectacular 1898 viaduct has 28x50ft stone arches, and one leaping 109ft across the River Nairn. Its brilliant engineer, Murdoch Paterson, was born at a farm a few miles from here and he died here too, while supervising its completion. It is said that his last request was to be pushed across the nearly completed viaduct on a trolley. Shades of Brunel and the Tamar Bridge!

Culloden Moor was, of course, the site of the battle that finished Bonnie Prince Charlie's 1745–46 rebellion. Whether it was a good or a bad thing for Scotland in the long run that he lost must be debated elsewhere, but don't let tour guides mislead you with talk of 'the English side' and 'the Scottish side'. There were more Scots on the government side than the rebel one. What is indisputable is that this moor was soaked with much blood, sweat and tears that terrible day. It's worth noting if you are rail touring Scotland, that the other end of Charlie's dream was at Glenfinnan on the Mallaig line.

You may miss it – I confess I did while making notes – but we soon cross a somewhat smaller but very rare timber-trestle viaduct of five spans. It is probably the last remaining one in Britain – the others having been replaced after rotting away. This is, amazingly, Paterson's 1897 **Aultnaslanach Viaduct**: I wish he'd made my back door frame, rotten after just 40 years! But all is not what it seems – a concrete inner viaduct was added in 2002 to take the weight off the ancient timbers.

Soon there is another more spectacular viaduct, the **Findhorn Viaduct** south of Tomatin. Built in 1894, steel trusses were used here instead of stone arches. This time the road has its own viaduct to our left (east) but the best view is right (west) down the broad valley.

After some deep rock cuttings, comes **Slochd Summit** (the sign is on our right, and you don't pronounce the 'D') – altitude just over 1,300ft or 370m, which is high – but we will go considerably higher soon. At this point we are within yards of the remains of one of the consequences of that Jacobite rebellion: General Wade's military road. Like the A9 and the railway, Wade had to aim for the same narrow pass.

Downhill to **Carrbridge** (milepost 90) which is signed as part of the Cairngorms National Park, and what seem to be grey clouds in the distance are actually magnificent mountains. Talking of clouds, a quite extraordinary cloudburst here in 1914 swept away several bridges in the ensuing torrents, and the line was closed for seven weeks.

Aviemore comes next and is the junction for the steam **STRATHSPEY RAILWAY**. You will see Aviemore Speyside platform on the left, but that dates from the bad old days before the steam trains were allowed back into the main station. There's also a fine signal box and a turntable.

Aviemore station proper is, looking at the buildings on the left, a fine old station with traditional canopy and lighting. The semaphore signals fit in with all this.

Kingussie, pronounced 'Kinoosie', has a large lake to the left, and a boat club for sailors with altitude.

Newtonmore has one platform rather devoid of population and another crowded – but only with gorse bushes. Next there is a girder viaduct running over a broad river, still the Spey, but we are shortly to turn up Glen Truim, for the Truim joins the Spey a little way further up (on our right).

That we are getting high is evidenced by the old snow fences on the left. Another way of getting high is provided by the Dalwhinnie Distillery, just before the **Dalwhinnie** station. On

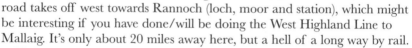

the right (west) just after it there is a dam and behind it the lengthy Loch Ericht, a hydro-electric project with a much bigger dam at the other end.

More snow fences and a classic glacier-carved valley can be seen to the left.

Look out now on the right for the sign announcing **Drumochter Summit** at 1,480ft (452m). This pass is the highest point on the entire British railway system (barring weird mountain funiculars). We are in the Andes of Britain.

Now the brakes go on as we descend, which is more difficult to control than climbing. At Calvine a road takes off west towards Rannoch (loch, moor and station), which might be interesting if you have done/will be doing the West Highland Line to Mallaig. It's only about 20 miles away here, but a hell of a long way by rail.

Blair Atholl station has proper semaphore signals and a signal box, and befitting for this aristocratic kind of place, the following bridge over the river has castellated ends. Whether this is pompous or not is not for me to say, but the Duke of Atholl who lives in the castle is the only individual in Great Britain allowed to keep a private army. It is a ragtag outfit of kilted gardeners, etc, and has not recently fought many battles.

Talking of battles, keep a look-out for when the train slows to 30mph for the Pass of Killiecrankie, where road, rail and river must squeeze through a gap in the hills.

There are precipitous views on the right down into the river's swirling salmon pools, and a short tunnel as we screech round dramatic curves. The 1689 Battle of Killiecrankie was a forerunner of Culloden in that it was the Jacobites (supporting James II or VII of Scotland) versus the Protestants (pro-William III). The side usually called 'the English' were in fact largely Lowland Scots. On this occasion they lost, but soon won elsewhere.

Famously, a Highlander almost impossibly leapt the river here to escape the claymores of the enemy.

Pitlochry, known for its Festival Theatre, has suitably arty sculptures on the platform. It is followed by miles of the shallow wide river on one side and the A9 road on the

Pitlochry Festival Theatre

other, then a long girder bridge to the other bank. After a viaduct and tunnel, we reach **Dunkeld and Birnam**. If you've read *Macbeth*, you'll remember the witches' curses about Birnam Wood coming to Dunsinane comes true when the attacking army carry tree boughs to disguise their numbers, an early case of camouflage (books on that subject are naturally very hard to find). It looks like the cast-iron spandrels supporting the station canopy have been decorated by the three witches too.

The 330yd **Kingswood Tunnel** is followed by signs of the old main line to Aberdeen trailing in from the left (this features in the 'Race to the North', mentioned on page 25, where we saw the other end of this old route).

We're now crossing fertile farmland, and if the potatoes seem behind those in the south of Britain, they are also a lot more disease-free which is why southerners are keen to get Scottish-certified spuds.

Perth is a substantial station as befits the capital of Western Australia. Or Perthshire. It's slightly shabby mock baronial in style, and note the wonderful old station clock high up on the right (and an even better one on the northbound Platform 7, in which case it's also on your right). An equally ancient wrought-iron bridge leads across to the opposite platform where the little-used line is held in with wooden wedges in cast metal chairs (our own track is much more modern). No need to go to a museum, then! A museum, by the way would explain that the wedges were driven in the direction of travel to counter a strange phenomenon called 'rail creep' where the rails would slowly move that way, perhaps encouraged by train brakes. Modern track doesn't.

All in all a splendid station with far more space than Glasgow Queen Street and with, perhaps, a tenth as many passengers!

In late May/June it's lupin city round here, unless someone's gone mad with the weed-killing train since.

The line that joined us from the left in this station was the **TAY COAST LINE** from Dundee along the north banks of the Tay. It leaves us again after the short **Moncrieffe Tunnel** at **Hilton Junction**, with signal box, and heads across Fife to Edinburgh via the Forth Bridge.

We cross over the Tay somewhat more easily than the line directly south from Dundee does, and speed to **Gleneagles**, a world-class hotel with its own station, and signs of an old branch platform on the right. Not long

ago, the G8 world leaders including Tony Blair and George W Bush gathered here, Bush famously falling off his mountain bike after colliding with one of the cops sent to protect him.

There's a lovely view south (left) of a glacial valley and semaphore-signalled loops. Approaching **Dunblane**, we cross two rivers. Our route onwards to Glasgow is correctly called the CROY LINE.

A tunnel is followed by **Bridge of Allan**, and views to the left of the striking Wallace Monument tower on a hill. This is roughly the hero of the film *Braveheart* (well, it's Mel Gibson) and looks like a stone space rocket. It has the most elaborate Scottish crown, festooned flamboyantly with more pinnacles than Zsa Zsa Gabor had husbands. Anyway if flamboyant means flame-like, then that's exactly what it's like. (In which case, the reader demands, how can it be a rocket with flames pointed upwards? Blast!)

We cross a river with newly laid tracks to the north crossing alongside us on their own bridge, and this is the 2008-reopened ALLOA BRANCH (well done, Scotland, for investing in railways!).

At the time of my last visit, **Stirling** was semaphore heaven (those waggling old signals). Once all railways were signalled like this, and soon none will be. I mean, how many signalmen have been on duty from Inverness to see our train through when computers could do most of it? But see this 19th-century technology now before it's in the aforementioned museum: wouldn't you rather see a clipper ship under sail than gutted, stuffed and done up like a turkey? And if it gives employment to people up in the Highlands keeping us safe, I'm not complaining.

After **Larbert**, a triangular junction with signal boxes at each corner epitomises this traditional way of doing things (but electric signals will probably be in place by the time you get there), as we join a major east–west route (the east corner going to Edinburgh). Now it's high speed through **Croy** as we make up for all that slow screeching round mountain curves back up the line. We pass **Lenzie**, **Bishopbriggs** and Eastfield depot on the left and then the new Cowlairs depot in a rail triangle. After some less than romantic housing schemes, we plunge down a tunnel to **Glasgow Queen Street**, our terminus (for comments see page 28). You have just completed the highest main-line trip in Britain. Quite a ride!

The striking Wallace Monument

SEASIDE EXCURSIONS: two great days out from Scotland's two big cities

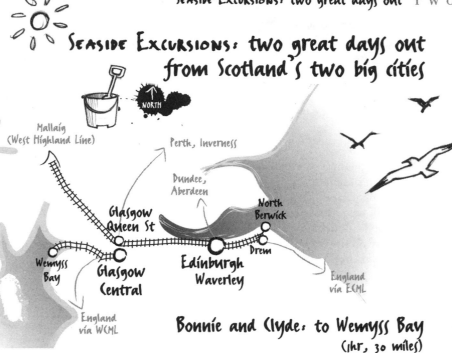

Mallaig
(West Highland Line)

Perth, Inverness

Dundee, Aberdeen

Glasgow Queen St

North Berwick

Wemyss Bay

Glasgow Central

Edinburgh Waverley

Drem

England via ECML

England via WCML

Bonnie and Clyde: to Wemyss Bay
(1hr, 30 miles)

Glasgow has a great network of suburban lines, some pretty and some, frankly, not. Paisley Canal, one of the termini, is not exactly Paisley-patterned. One that I loved is the hour-long trip to **Wemyss Bay** (pronounced 'Weems Bay') from **Glasgow Central**.

Central Station is by far the better of the city's termini, and the interior is spacious with many fascinating details, such the splendid covered carriageway on the street, the elliptical wooden buildings inside the concourse and, on your left looking towards the trains, the 'CR' initials carved above a passageway – standing for Caledonian Railway.

The station is always busy, with trains to many parts of England as well as south-of-the-Clyde Scotland. Clearly the Caledonian expected the Sassenach trains to arrive in a great hurry, judging by the massive buffer stops.

I said south-of-the-Clyde, but we're not. We leap quickly across the Clyde and rapidly diverge right. There are all sorts of junctions for the suburban lines you can see on the route map in the carriages, and we whiz through some uninspiring suburbs. Never fear, it gets a lot better. After a stop at **Paisley Gilmour Street** (near the airport on our right, which is shortly getting its own branch) we swing right, back towards the Clyde. After Port Glasgow there are bonnie views of the Clyde

Estuary, with its massive shipping-lane markers making clear its importance, past and present.

Soon we are diverging left on our own ten-mile-long branch (the mileposts are on the right if you like that sort of thing). Strangely named stations such as **IBM** (because of the factory) and **Inverkip** follow and then we reach **Wemyss Bay**, the most perfectly preserved Edwardian station in Scotland. Take a while to walk around the concourse near the booking office and appreciate the glazing that floods this cheerful place with light, unlike so many gloomy stations of that era.

A ramp leads down to the waiting Caledonian MacBrayne steamer to **Rothesay** on the beautiful island of Bute. I'd take a boat there and back myself, as there isn't a lot to do in Wemyss Bay. But if not doing a lot is what suits you, you can take a walk along the beach to look at the views, perhaps paddling across the stream (to the left looking seawards), or crossing it on the bridge, in which case you have crossed into Ayrshire (and you can give yourself Ayrs) and entered the village of Skelmorlie. Or lazily sit in the Sea View Café across the road and enjoy their great salads and cakes. Here you can watch the splendid clock tower of the 1903 station, and marvel how the ferry manages to come in just before your return train departs. On returning to the station, notice what's carved above one of the windows: *CR*.

North Berwick: for Quality Street... and Black Magic (30mins, 22 miles)

A day out to North Berwick from Edinburgh is fun and quick, being less than 40 miles along the coast to the east. It is connected by a fast, clean, reliable, direct train (33 minutes) which takes a four-mile branch off the East Coast Main Line on its way to the other better-known Berwick. It goes from Haymarket or Waverley stations. Here's a brief guide:

Someone once ludicrously titled North Berwick 'the Biarritz of the North'. One wonders if they had seen either of them. But it's guaranteed to be worthwhile on any half-decent day because of the superb location – wide clean sandy beaches, rock pooling or scrambling around rocks, plentiful seabirds – and the best view you can imagine.

The less-than-grand railway station is on the edge of town, the engineers having understandably decided not to try to reach the much lower level of the town but stay up on the coastal plain. The branch line opened in 1850 and transformed North Berwick's economy, but the feebleness of early steam engines meant that the service to here from Drem on the main line was for a while one horse-drawn carriage.

Go left out of the station and then right (noticing St Baldred's squat church opposite, and there's a Blackadder Church elsewhere in the town) down Station Hill. Carry on down Beach Road to the beach. We go left down Victoria Road down the far side of the little harbour which includes pretty fishermen's cottages and a lifeboat station.

At the end, notice the touching memorial to Glaswegian student Kate Watson, who aged 19 gave her life here to save a drowning child in East Bay in 1889. The boy was saved and though she died, here she is immortalised rather beautifully.

▼ ME

Just beyond are the ruins and remains of St Andrew's Kirk, a scene of the most gruesome witchcraft four centuries ago – if the stories extracted under torture are to be believed. It was the reality behind Shakespeare's *Macbeth*. It is an extraordinary tale, and you'll not find better evidence of witches anywhere.

On a somewhat sunnier subject, here is a great view of Berwick Law, the conical hill right behind the town (and note the thin arch on the top) and Bass Rock, another volcanic plug a mile or two out at sea.

The Berwick witches, St Andrew's Kirk

Now Bass Rock – despite its having been once a prison, let's not call it the Alcatraz of the East – is home to thousands of screaming gannets. You can go out on a boat for a look at this and the dramatic coast nearby in summer months (book on T 01620 892838). It also has a strange natural tunnel going right through it, visible at low tide.

But you can get a close-up by other means. Down by the shore is an ornithologist's dream, the Scottish Seabird Centre, which by means of live TV cameras gives you close-ups of gannets doing whatever they do, as well as puffins, which look like silly toy birds made up for paperback book covers but which turn out to be something like sea-going rabbits in their behaviour – burrowing holes to live in, etc. Wonder if they're any good in a pie?

This promontory was once linked to the town by a bridge at high tide, and the chapel was important for medieval pilgrims making their way across from here to St Andrews in Fife. Going back up Victoria Street away from the sea, you will find in Quality Street (straight ahead) plenty of places to eat plaices and other food, as well as tourist information and toilets up the far end.

Why Quality Street? Are the people toffee-nosed (for North American readers, it is a brand of British sweets – candies – once much loved by Saddam Hussein of all people, but if we are on a box-of-chocolates theme North Berwick is much more like Black Magic with its witchy history)?

Actually toffee-nosed is exactly it. The people who once lived here thought themselves above the average, hence the name.

Go right at the top of Quality Street and pass the subsequent St Andrew's Church (also ruined) and then left up Law Road towards Law School at the very top.

We are heading for the 613ft hill itself which is so dramatically and apparently artificially emerging from the plain that it looks as if it could be a spoil heap for a mine. But this is no slag, it's a crag – crag and tail, or a volcanic plug left when the landscape was scoured out by glaciers, as is Edinburgh Castle rock and many more round here.

The path towards the Law is a rough road to the left, through a stile and around the hill's right flank. Soon the path to the top goes off left. I'd advise sticking to the paths as much as you can because otherwise you may find yourself clambering over dangerously steep wet rocks and damaging fragile hillside too. I wouldn't take tearaway toddlers and wheelchairs are quite out of the question. It's all at your own risk.

But it is absolutely worth it for one of the greatest views in Britain on a fine day, and I don't exaggerate. At the top you can look back south inland over Traprain Law six miles away, another crag and tail formation where the Romans encountered a tribal settlement. Beyond are the lovely Lammermuir Hills, combed towards the southwest by great glaciers. Slightly to the right are the Pentland Hills and Arthur's Seat in Edinburgh.

Back towards the sea we have a bird's-eye view of the town and Bass Rock seems close enough to touch. On the coast facing it is the romantic ruin of tantalising Tantallon Castle, easily visited if you are carborne.

Further out there are flat islands such as Fidra, formed by the liquid rock of magma intruding in horizontal shelves into whatever landscape there then was. Beyond them is the Kingdom of Fife and beyond that, if it is very clear, I'm told you can see the Grampian Mountains of the real Highlands. And to the east (if you are reading this in an armchair rather than on the hilltop), the North Sea stretches to the wide horizon.

The thin arch which we saw from the town turns out to be made out of a whale's jawbone. Whaling was once a vital industry locally, and the first whale jawbone was landed in North Berwick in 1709, although it has been replaced over the years.

Not surprisingly this excellent vantage point, easily seen from Edinburgh's Calton Hill, has been used in conflicts over the centuries, from a medieval flaming beacon to a tower to warn of Napoleonic invasion (the unlikelihood of his coming by this route didn't seem to have stopped the Scots joining in the national anti-French hysteria) and a World War II bunker which probably did have something to look at as Nazi bombers lined up for their run west. The remains of both eras are obvious here at the top.

If you are returning to the station, you can save your weary feet a hill descent and climb by going left at the crossroads at the beginning of the hill down to town and following Clifford Road round on the level to the station.

The Great North of Scotland Railway: Inverness to Aberdeen **

Whisky and canals: a funny thing about its history...

A vainglorious title, possibly, particularly if you realise that 'Great North of Scotland Railway' only reached halfway, from Aberdeen to Keith. But then the English could do a more ridiculous title than this, by a long chalk (see page 117).

The Scots are both inordinately proud, and sometimes savagely scornful, of their railways and regiments – I mention both together because at both Inverness and Aberdeen there are wonderful war memorials worth seeing (outside and inside the stations, respectively) and also great proud memorials to the railways themselves. As related elsewhere, the railways round here were often self-financed, there not being the industry and population to draw in outside money. So they should have been, and should still be, proud of their achievements.

But you have to laugh when you read E L Ahrons on this line in 1922:

> Why it was ever allowed to be called a railway at all passed comprehension. As a matter of fact, part of it between Aberdeen and Inverness was not originally a railway but a canal, and the company thoughtfully scooped in the canal, baled it out, and made their line on the remains. After which some people in the district bethought themselves, when it was too late, that the canal would have been infinitely preferable. The stopping trains... set the pace of a glacier, only a glacier would probably have got there first.

Satirical exaggeration, but in 1880 $4^1/4$ hours got you only as far as Elgin from Aberdeen (now it's less than $1^1/2$ hours).

And the truth about that canal jibe is even funnier. O S Nock, the railway historian who quoted the above extract, goes on to tell how the original route from Kittybrewster (on the northwest side of Aberdeen) to Huntly was indeed to be built on a canal. But because the contractor couldn't be bothered to wait for the legal paperwork, he simply cut a hole through the canal bank and let the whole contents pour into the River Don. This left all the barges still in transit loaded with their cargoes and sitting on the muddy canal bottom! The outrage was such that it had to be repaired, refilled and then drained when the boats had all gone!

Another odd thing. When the GNoSR reached Aberdeen in 1855 it was to a separate Waterloo Station, not the one you reach from the south. So you could have booked a very, very roundabout route from London

Waterloo to Aberdeen Waterloo for a few years. The two Aberdeen stations weren't merged, cutting out a lot of bother for footsore travellers, until 1867.

One more funny thing: because the GNoSR was built from Aberdeen, and the joining-up railway from Inverness, the result is that the mileposts count up from both ends, so milepost 10 is at two places, miles apart, for instance.

The route described: from Inverness to Aberdeen
(2hrs 20mins, 108³/4 miles)

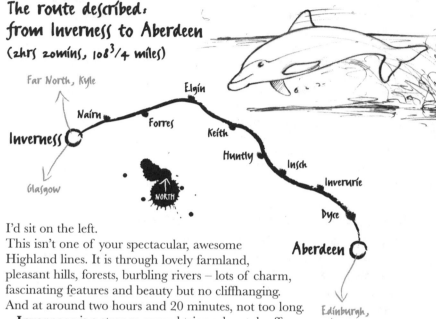

I'd sit on the left.
This isn't one of your spectacular, awesome Highland lines. It is through lovely farmland, pleasant hills, forests, burbling rivers – lots of charm, fascinating features and beauty but no cliffhanging. And at around two hours and 20 minutes, not too long.

Inverness is a strange curved triangular stub off a line running east–west, just long enough to put the station at the bottom apex in the town centre, and a depot in the middle. The line west (left) goes to Kyle, or Wick and Thurso, and the line right goes to Aberdeen, or Perth over the mountains. So the Highland capital is also the rail hub.

Some platforms in Inverness lead left (west and north), and some right (east and south), and one short one is connected both ways. In the old days, expresses that were continuing would go past Inverness station on the Rose Street curve, and then back in so the loco was ready to take off again. How quaint, I thought – until my train from Kyle to Inverness did exactly that the other day, because it was continuing to Aberdeen.

We turn right and probably spot a snowplough on the left. This is no anachronism. They have been needed on our route today; they are often needed on the lines to the west and north. Even at the beginning of June you can look across the waters of the Moray Firth and see snow on mountain tops. The two lines to the left of us are the **HIGHLAND MAIN LINE** south to Perth and being the wrong side, soon cross over us (right after the tunnel under the A9 road).

We get glorious views of the sea, and the Moray Firth usually manages to look cold. You may see seals on the foreshore. And is it just me, or does that house on a headland ahead left look like a stranded ocean liner from this angle?

Castle Stuart, about half a mile on our left, has a Scotch Crown spire, and probably flies the Saltire. Inverness Airport is close by on the right. Good farming country.

Next stop, **Nairn**, which had a pleasantly Ruritanian signalling system until a few years ago. There are two signal boxes, now boarded up, at each end of the extremely long platform. Because the one signalman used to hurry from one box to the other, they were issued with a bicycle to do so more rapidly, much to the bemusement of the passengers on the train. Now they have colour light signals here and such picturesque goings-on are history.

But along this line you will see much of the old ways in railways. Entering single-track sections, or leaving them, the driver slows or stops to hand over to the signalman the Tyer tablet. This is a 19th-century bit of cast iron that fits in a machine at either end, a bit like putting chocolate back in a vending machine. But only the right one fits the machine. Drivers are only allowed to continue with the tablet marked for the right section – so they are legally obliged to take it out and look at it.

And this is the clever bit – the signals can't be changed without the right tablet being in the machine. Usually the train would go into a siding or trap points if it passed the red signal, but not into a head-on crash. It's a Victorian-era system. Yet it's safer than some modern systems, it's cheap and it works.

I said red signal, but much of this route is, or was on my last visit, manually signalled with semaphore arms. So when they stretch out straight, it means 'danger'. When they are at a slope, either up or down, they are 'off' – the equivalent of 'green'. What with jointed rails giving the old-style clickety-clack and the telephone poles still standing alongside the track, Hitchcock could still film *The 39 Steps* here.

There are still beautiful views across to the mountains up the coast (possibly 20 miles away as the crow flies, more like 60 by rail!). We cross the River Findhorn on the high-sided iron viaduct.

Forres, which uses semaphore signals, was once a totally triangular station, which explains the odd curve of the platform.

At $12^1/2$ miles, we reach **Elgin**, which produces not marbles but equally well-carved Walkers Shortbread by the tonne. Next there is a girder bridge over the wide Spey, and we enter a twisting hilly section with deep cuttings, constantly changing views and forests. This is the only section where we part company with the A96 road between the two cities for very long.

ODDEST ACCIDENT 1

One of the oddest railway accidents in Scotland didn't involve trains, didn't involve a railway line, nor rail staff nor passengers nor rolling stock, and there was no fatality and no person even injured. A local man drove up to a level crossing at Dunragit near Stranraer when the automatic arms came down and he stopped sharply. A following car banged into the back of him. Both drivers got out, and a pedestrian walking his dog came over to act as a witness. As they were concentrating on the car damage, none of them noticed that the train had come and gone and the crossing arm, to which the pedestrian had tied his Scottie dog's lead, had gone up… leaving the poor creature dangling and gasping out of reach. It wasn't until the next train came that the dog came down, apparently little the worse for its experience. It sounds urban myth, but examination of the original report shows names and addresses of the local people involved.

Soon we come to **Keith** and the warehouses defended by barbed wire and set carefully apart, with stringent fire precautions, just like munitions stores for the army. They are in fact bonded whisky stores. This is a spirit which is far stronger and more explosive than the stuff you can buy, so the precautions are necessary – also because tax has not yet been added to the stuff. There are sometimes thousands of barrels stored on the left here too.

We get plenty of time to look at all this because for some reason the passing loop where we have to wait is outside the station.

Huntly has the by now usual splitting semaphores – that is, one for each track at a loop, so you know which way you're going at the points – and therefore a signal box too.

There's a particularly beautiful old (closed) station on the left, on a long left curve across a valley at Kennethmont. If you like a wee dram, you'll probably be looking the other way at the Ardmore Distillery, home of Teacher's Whisky (and don't teachers need that stuff from time to time?).

Insch has basic wooden shelters and old signals, and **Inverurie**, next, has some splendid examples too. In between there are endless old stations to spot, some overgrown, crumbling platforms, and some with residual buildings and charm, such as Pitcaple (Pitcaple Castle is on the left). You can dream about buying an old station and living amidst castles and distilleries, like 1,000 others, no doubt! Dreams, unlike drams, are free.

After Inverurie there is a strange, conical mound in the graveyard on the left. It's next to the infant River Don which we follow for most of the rest of the route. Soon, for about ten miles, there are great sweeping meanders on our left in a particularly handsome valley.

Dyce, the next stop, is bustlingly busy, yet the nitwits in charge had it closed for some years. Now it's reopened, and adjacent to the airport and industry which are booming still thanks to North Sea oil (hence helicopters to land on oil rigs). Note the splendid signal box high up on the left.

Talking about closed stations, there are now no stops between here and Aberdeen. Yet there were once seven in this populous stretch – and they wonder why road traffic is so bad in Aberdeen! Some may soon be replaced.

Anyway, there's a point down here called Kittybrewster – a name lovelier, perhaps, than the place. The railway that went on to the docks to the left (still there) was that original line to Waterloo, and we are on the later connector to Aberdeen Joint (as it was called). Just before we reach Aberdeen through a gloomy set of bridges and build-overs, there's a rather cute turntable pit scooped out of the rock to the right. I say cute, because their engines must have been small in those days.

And here we are at **Aberdeen**, another granite city, set between the rivers Dee and Don. An excuse to tell you a story about a lady fishing mid stream in waders up the River Dee, near Balmoral. She saw another woman walking down the bank and realised it was the Queen Mother, and curtseyed correctly as she was greeted. Her waders part filled with water and the fisherwoman floated off downstream, still smiling at her puzzled Majesty... More about Aberdeen at the end of the East Coast Main Line chapter, page 25.

ODDEST ACCIDENT 2

Most of us have taken a naughty swim when we weren't supposed to. A whole train did so in 1939. The story that starts with a breakdown in the Haymarket Tunnel near Edinburgh Waverley. The firemen and then the driver got down to find the fault with the brakes, and eventually found a loose connecting pipe between two wagons. They put it on, only to realise the engine was still set to go, with the brakes set to pump 'off'. They hurried back to the engine as the wagons began to roll past them, but the fireman tripped over his lamp and the driver came a cropper on top of him. By the time they'd got up again the train was running away too fast to catch, with no driver up front.

They rushed to a signal telephone and called the signalman, who calculated that he couldn't let the train crash into passenger trains along the line, and couldn't let it crash into a dead-end brick wall, but could have a chance of saving it by sending it down the Granton Dock branch, luckily empty. At the back of the train was a guard's van occupied by Angus Panton, a happy man unaware of the danger. He might have been able to slow the train with his brake, and save himself too.

At the station, the signalman had organised a gaggle of people to warn Angus, and posted them halfway down the platform. They started running as the train passed and yelled: 'Ye're on the road to Granton, there's no-one on the fuitplate!' Unfortunately, they all yelled over each other, and old Angus, whose birthday it was, thought they were saying 'Hurrah for Angus Panton, Many happy returns mate!' He puffed on his pipe, smiled and waved fondly as his brake van disappeared from view. How nice of them to arrange a surprise. Which indeed it was.

Only when the engine, 37 wagons and brake van went through the buffers and off the end of the dock into the water to the horror of startled dockworkers did Angus take the plunge, and save himself.

THE SKYE RAILWAY: the very strange story of 'the most beautiful line in Europe'****

The romantic iron road to Skye

The line from Inverness to Kyle of Lochalsh, the iron road to Skye, rightly attracts superlatives. Some call it most beautiful railway in Europe. I can understand that, although I haven't seen them all (yet). But I have spent much of my life travelling every line in Britain, however, and can swear this is among the most scenically dramatic of them all.

True, you have to want awesome mountains, rocks and rivers, jaw-droppingly beautiful lochs, red deer and eagles and a journey from sea to shining sea – rather than the chocolate-box villages of thatch and cream teas of the south, so it depends what you're after. If it's wilderness and majesty and nature, this is one of Britain's best, rivalled only by the other two lines in the Highlands, plus the Settle & Carlisle.

It also has the benefit of being not too long, less than $2^1/2$ hours from Inverness to Kyle, and having a definite start and finish – the chilly North Sea to the rolling Atlantic right across Scotland. With Inverness accessible both by overnight sleeper train from London and by plane, it's not as remote as it once was, and for whole touring trains or individuals, it's hard to beat.

Having said all that, it does have a remarkable sense of connecting somewhere to nowhere through a lot of, er, nowhere. But it has survived many perils against the odds and those locals who once resisted it being constructed now fight just as doggedly to save it. It should be up there with Stonehenge and the pyramids as an international asset to value for all time. Before describing the route (and all the towns it doesn't go through!) here's a look at its fascinating history.

Kyle of Lochalsh

History: from feudalism to internet-age — democracy in just 150 years

▼ ME

Crofters meet to discuss the Clearances

In 1864, when locals in Inverness mooted the building of this line, the Highlands were still almost feudal. Great lairds held power over vast tracts of countryside, while their tenants and crofters lived in poverty and hardship (which is one reason why Australia, New Zealand, the US, Canada and Hong Kong are full of people of Scottish descent. Neither were the emigrations always voluntary, with the disgraceful Clearances telling a sad tale of croft-burning and poor people being herded off the land like cattle by rapacious landlords).

The Highlands held no great reserves of the coal or iron ore that were powering Britain's industrial revolution, and there were no great towns or cities to connect. The geographical obstacles were huge, the snowdrifts often deep. But men could dream, and sometimes dreamers make things happen.

This backward land could be brought directly from the 14th century to the 19th, it was argued, by building a railway through the only glens that linked directly and relatively easily across the Highlands at this level. By providing a pier at which a steamship from Skye and the Hebrides could connect with the railway, Inverness would be reachable in a few hours instead of days of struggling over rough mountain roads or dangerously round the rugged storm-tossed north coast. The locals in the west otherwise had to take long and sometimes perilous steamer trips to Glasgow to shop for supplies from the outside world.

The teeming fish of the west-coast lochs could find a market in England if trains reached here. Sheep would no longer lose a quarter of their weight walking to Falkirk if they could ride by train in a day. The few horses and cattle would no longer break their legs boarding steamers.

As with the other railways around Inverness, it was very much a self-build project. There was no help from outside, so this part of Scotland hauled itself up by its boot straps and joined the modern world. And outsider investors were absent, it must be said, because they could see through all is optimism that there was a virtual desert along the route, virtually no pulation and not a few bloody-minded landowners and no cities at the er end. All there was was lots of scenery, and would that buy tickets? But it would eventually *sell* them.

A BATTLE, A WAR AND A HIJACK!
THE SKYE LINE'S UNBELIEVABLE SEA OF TROUBLES

The Dingwall and Skye Railway got it wrong about sea transport, which was the one thing supposed to make sense of its route through nowhere to nowhere, and then got it wronger. Its first suggested terminus which was supposed to bring in steamer-loads of passengers and goods from the Hebrides was at Attadale, but wasn't built because it was too far up shallow waters. The next terminus and pier at Strome Ferry was still so far up Loch Carron that shipping companies that took trade up and down the west-coast islands point blank refused to make the 28-mile extra journey up to Strome.

At the last minute, the railway decided it had to become a maritime power and bought two vessels to run to the islands. One was soon wrecked and the other frequently broke down. Tight-fisted local bigwigs on Skye and Lewis charged such huge rates for landing the ferries that they could never make money. A smaller paddle steamer was acquired to reduce the per-ton charge for landing on Skye. The fees were doubled, so no saving was made.

A faster, more reliable boat was eventually acquired, the *Ferret*, and the service settled into something of a pattern, with the Highland Railway taking over shipping (and eventually the loss-making railway). Then the unbelievable happened. The *Ferret* ended up being hijacked to Australia.

It would be too far-fetched for Freddie Forsyth fiction, but it happened. To steal the Highland Railway's *Ferret*, 347 tons, 171ft long, was bizarre. She was chartered dishonestly in 1880 and 'wrecked' off Gibraltar, the railway claiming insurance on the sinking. In fact, although lifeboats and debris had been planted in the sea, she had actually been renamed and repainted.

She was put up for sale in Melbourne, Australia, but someone who knew the Highland Railway's ships (how unlikely was that!) became suspicious and the authorities alerted. In the ship's log, they found a sheet of Highland Railway notepaper and the game was up.

She was indeed sold in 1881, to reimburse the insurers, and traded legally until 1920 when she really was wrecked at Cape Spencer, South Australia. A fair way from Strome Ferry.

Meanwhile in another unbelievable episode, the Battle of Strome Pier, local west-coast fishermen who were strict Sabbath-day observers – the 'Wee Frees' – were angry at the east-coast men scooping up all the herring in the area and sending them off in the early hours of Sunday to make London's Monday fish markets. Working on Sunday caused them great offence.

On Sunday 3 June 1883, their small boats converged on Strome Pier and took it by force, wrecking the crane. The one policeman covering the whole area was absent, and even six more sent by train from Dingwall were helpless against the mob. The protesters sang a hymn of victory and slipped away, vowing to stop trade again the next Sunday.

But the authorities were this time having none of it. A strong police detachment arrived, and 74 troops were sent from Edinburgh Castle in a special military train, held near Inverness (but the fact that it was there, and they were armed, was carefully leaked along the line). A sullen demonstration took place, but the trains were loaded with fish. The ringleaders were arrested, the police being pelted with stones by their womenfolk. They were released, feted as heroes, and life returned to normal.

Meanwhile the rival lines to Oban (see page 42) and later Mallaig (see page 30) were eating holes in the valuable fishing traffic. The era was known as 'the fish wars'. All three companies which had built through the Highlands with such monumental effort sent agents to the fish market at Stornoway. Sometimes they got a third of the traffic each, which went on three steamers to their respective piers, then three trains to London, but before they reached England were joined into one fish train! It was insane, or at least very illogical.

In 1897, after the government had considered various ways to assist this poverty-stricken corner of Great Britain, the subsidised extension of the railway from Strome Ferry to Kyle of Lochalsh was finally opened. It really was the iron road to Skye (nearly).

official policy that everything should end at Inverness. The Kyle line went through the closure process in 1971 and escaped by the skin of its teeth thanks to oil exploration, which looked as if it needed freight trains to the west coast. In this sense it was saved by its biggest rival, the motor car. Now these wonderful lines are recognised worldwide for their tourist potential, bringing in special touring trains, and locally as invaluable community assets, it is unlikely they will ever be closed. But as the Skye Railway's utterly amazing history shows, anyone who even suggests such a thing will have one hell of a fight on their hands.

That all three of the once-rival lines to the west coast have survived is astonishing. It was seriously proposed in the 1960s that there should be no railways north of Glasgow and Edinburgh, and then it was

The route from Inverness and Dingwall to Kyle, and its story

(2¹/₂hrs, 82 miles) For the first few miles, setting out from Inverness to Dingwall, read from page 68 (and it will return you here at the right spot).

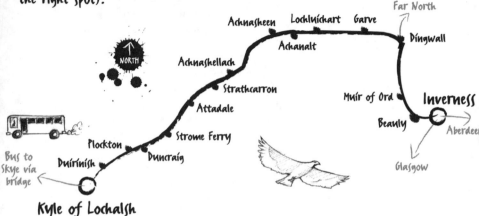

The building of the Dingwall–Kyle route met obstacles from the near-feudal lairds some of whom had, after all, cleared people from the land to enjoy expensive solitude and weren't willing to change. Many of them just wanted the route altered to look better from their grand houses, and private platforms for their convenience, which they were granted.

Worse, one of them insisted that the railway at the start from **Dingwall** (on the existing line to the north) could not take the obvious route through Strathpeffer (the valley of the River Peffery), which denied it access to the only town (of the same name) on the route. This condemned it to climbing up to a summit at Raven Rock for ever more, causing no end of trouble with snow in the winter. It was not a good start, although scenically, it is our gain.

That it was a last-minute change is shown by the way we suddenly swerve right after 2¹/₂ miles (the mileposts zeroed again at Dingwall) across the main road. We do not rejoin it for half a dozen miles by which time we've missed Strathpeffer, which oddly we can see clearly down in the valley on the left at 3³/₄ miles. Useless fact: when Strathpeffer did eventually get its branch line, now gone although the station is preserved, it was sometimes run by railway engines built for Uruguay.

The engines work hard up the steep gradient towards Raven Rock (a not-too-obvious prominence amid the forests) and a 458ft-high summit, and then the line enters a small rock cutting and emerges into a very different, more Highland landscape from the valley we left below.

We pass amid great long views of Loch Garve on our right with mountains all round. A halt comes at **Garve**, beside the loch, and here the main road which has rejoined us takes off right (northwest) to the fishing port of Ullapool (which would have been the western terminus of this line had the final approach been less steeply down). Garve station was laid out with double lines for trains to pass, and the tracks are curiously far apart. The reason was because of a plan to ship not just fish but entire fishing boats from one coast to the other when the seasons required it (thus obviating a tedious and dangerous trip around the north coast, or up the tediously diagonal Caledonian Canal). Special cranes and trucks were ordered, but like so many of the Skye line's dreams, it came to naught. It's a shame, because it deprived us of the curious sight of a fleet of fishing smacks cruising over mountains at several hundred feet above sea level, skipper sitting on deck puffing on his pipe.

Beautiful and vast Loch Luichart soon comes on our left, and there's a **Lochluichart** (r) halt after a hydropower station on the right (look, no pollution!). We follow the river to find two more picturesque lochs, A Chuilinn, the long wide one on our right, and then we cross to the north side of the water in this valley, Strath Bran, and Loch Achanalt is on our right, followed by **Achanalt** (r) station. We follow the River Bran on our left, the line dead straight for a while, with the A832 road on the right keeping rail and river company, to **Achnasheen**, meaning 'field of rain' which it often is. Strath Bran has a lonely bleak beauty of emptiness. Loch Gowan, the double one on the right, is the last connected to the North Sea. There are awesome mountain views to the left and ahead.

We climb hard through bleak near desert above the tree line to **Luib Summit**, 646ft, not marked that I could see, amidst beautiful scenery of little lochs and mountains. Railwaymen were warned by locals about one of these close by on the right, Loch Sgamhain, which apparently harbours a kelpie which devours swimmers whole, leaving only their lungs to float to the surface. Nice.

By the way, if you find the landscape bleak, consider that the lengthsmen – who patrolled the line checking the joints, etc – were not provided with any accommodation or shelter for the first few years, and had to sleep under their coats, in caves and culverts, snowdrifts or not. Later there was a more paternalistic attitude evident, with the record showing a train making a weekly stop at lengthsmen's cottages so their wives could do the week's shopping in Dingwall. Wouldn't do for Paris Hilton, but better than sleeping in a cave.

Now the River Carron is often keeping us company, heading west like us, for we are in the beginnings of Glen Carron. There are impressive views of brooding 3,000ft mountains to the left.

Where we cross the infant River Carron, there was once Glencarron halt, built as a private station for the nearby Glen Carron Lodge 'for the setting down or picking up of the proprietor… or his servants'. Later, it was open to the public, who had to operate a pair of lower-quadrant semaphore signals to stop trains (which must have been fun). Mind you, the eccentric chatelaine of the house, Lady Cobbold, was a great traveller and the first western woman to enter Mecca (or the first to get out and tell the tale). She is buried standing up in the gardens here, facing towards Mecca. So semaphore signals must have been a doddle for her.

Achnashellach (r) is still open, in an increasingly pretty wooded valley with a large freshwater loch on the left, and first views dead ahead of brutal-looking Fuar Tholl, 2,975ft, and the surrounding mountains.

In October 1892, the railway suffered an embarrassing runaway here. One of its questionable mixed trains – where goods trucks were marshalled next to engines with passenger carriages at the back – was being shunted at night. Having taken out some trucks, it was necessary to nudge up to the remaining part of the train to get the coupling hook on. The trucks and carriages (holding nine passengers) began to roll back over the small

summit, with engine and guard stumbling along trying to get the heavy shackle over the hook. It was hopeless.

The crew then made a bad mistake and set off into the pitch black to catch the train. Of course it had rolled up a further slope, stopped, and was now heading back toward them. The first truck was smashed to pieces, and it was a miracle that no-one was killed.

We reach wide Loch Carron soon after **Strathcarron** station, and the clear views to the right of Fuar Tholl are more and more majestic along the next few miles.

Attadale (r) was the original planned site for the western terminus, complete with a pier and hotel, being the first bit of salt water on Loch Carron that the cash-strapped railway reached. But it was too far up and shallow for steamers. After a rethink, Strome Ferry was decided on, and the station, pier and grand hotel to be built there instead. Except that the hotel could not be afforded, and the station was a rudimentary platform.

Attadale had a simple wooden shack in the 1950s, and a red flag was provided for 'intending passengers' to wave to stop trains. Eventually the shack blew away in a storm, taking the flag with it.

There's a good view, left, up Attadale Glen with its river, and right across the loch to the village of Lochcarron. The line now curves sharply, and has been troubled here by rock and snow falls from the early days. It even passes into an avalanche shelter. Indeed, in late 2008 a train was derailed

Plockton

by a landslide here, with no injuries. The frequent curves from here to the end of the line give the benefit of sweeping your window views across the magnificent outlook, and anyone who reads a book – excluding this one! – for all of this stretch should be chucked off the pier at Kyle. You can see Strome Ferry narrows ahead, for example, and through them the peaks of the Cuillins, 30 miles away on the Isle of Skye.

Strome Ferry was the original terminus, and as the name suggests, Loch Carron narrows to a few hundred yards here. The line was eventually extended to Kyle, reaching there in 1897.

There is a superb view back to the Strome narrows on the next stretch (back right, and a rather small ruined castle on the far shore), showing the dramatic way the water or rather ice cut through the mountains, and then after **Duncraig** (r) (odd octagonal waiting room) comes **Plockton** (restaurant, loos, bunkhouse, original buildings). There's another fine view ahead right over Plockton bay, with boats moored in it and the village beyond framed by far distant mountains. The village is so pretty, it starred in a TV series, *Hamish Macbeth*.

After **Duirinish** (r), the long views across the sea are just fabulous. On a fine day you can see mountains up to 30 miles away, such as the Quirang, 30 miles northwest. Closer to hand the Crowlin Islands stand in the sound, about five miles away. This whole section was hewn from solid rock to make a shelf above the sea. Soon we are rattling into Kyle itself, and the trip ends at the pier and the still-substantial **Kyle of Lochalsh** station (loos, gift shop and rather good little museum). There's no need to go over the sea to Skye any more, as now there's the road bridge and a connecting bus.

Congratulations! You have finished one of the great railway journeys of the world. There's another funny thing about the Dingwall–Skye line. It's built with commendable Highland economy, with not one tunnel or great viaduct that I can recall. That's why it fits in so perfectly.

THE FAR NORTH LINE: from Inverness to Wick and Thurso ***

(3¾hrs, 154 miles to Thurso, 175 to Wick, because you do the Thurso bit twice)

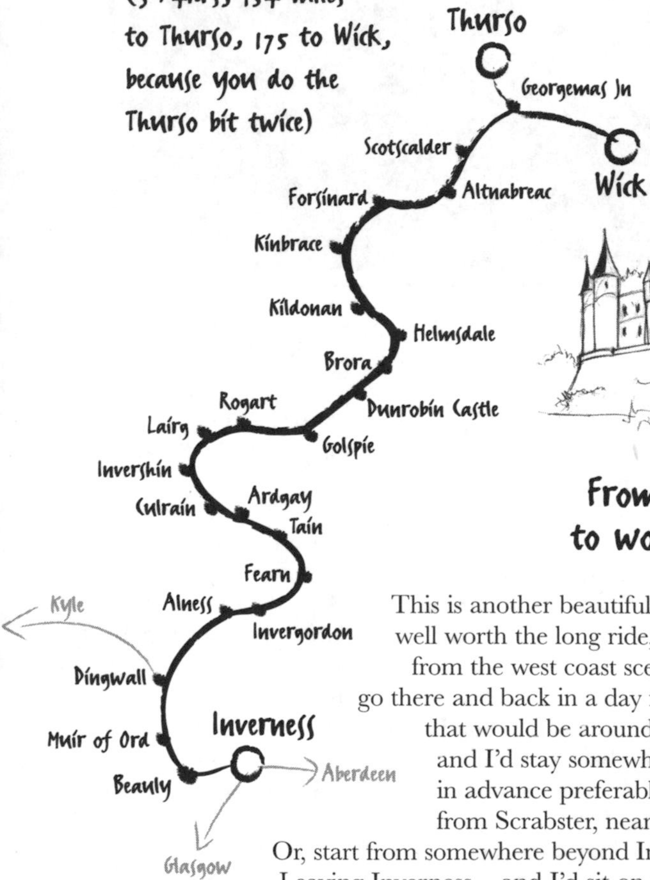

Thurso

Georgemas Jn

Scotscalder

Forsinard   Altnabreac   Wick

Kinbrace

Kildonan

Helmsdale

Brora

Rogart   Dunrobin Castle

Lairg

Invershin   Golspie

Culrain   Ardgay
Tain

Fearn

Kyle   Alness

Invergordon

Dingwall

Muir of Ord   Inverness

Beauly   → Aberdeen

Glasgow

From the slightly Ord to wonderfully remote possibilities

This is another beautiful route well worth the long ride, and very different from the west coast scenically. It is possible to go there and back in a day from Inverness, but that would be around seven hours on trains and I'd stay somewhere at the top, fixing it in advance preferably. Or go on by ferry from Scrabster, near Thurso, to Orkney. Or, start from somewhere beyond Inverness.

Leaving Inverness – and I'd sit on the right – on the west side of its railway triangle station, we cross the fast-flowing River Ness (which drains the legendary monster's lair). This bridge was swept away by floods in recent years, so the trains on the two lines north of here had to carry on in splendid isolation, with buses doing the last bit.

Next we come to the **Caledonian Canal swing bridge**, protected by proper signals a decent sliding distance from the water's edge – and thus very safe – and needing a 10mph speed limit for trains (if not boats). You still get that 'bong, bong' of the wheels going over the crack. You may have seen the Atlantic end on your rail touring of the Mallaig line near Fort William (see page 39).

Caledonian Canal
swing bridge

The wide inlet of the North Sea on the right is the Beauly Firth, an extension of the Moray Firth. The view of the spectacular road bridge to the Black Isle (back right) is great, although that place – one of a series of massive peninsulas divided by vast sea inlets – is neither black nor an isle.

We speed on past flowering broom-lined track and gentle farmland inhabited by happy-looking cattle. No hint of Highlands yet; it could almost be Devon or Cornwall.

We cross one big river into the new station of **Beauly**. Ahead looms the distant mass of Ben Wyvis, 3,433ft, from which summit you can see the North Sea and the Atlantic (I'm told). What was that about 'like Devon and Cornwall?'

And another big river bridge into **Muir of Ord** station is followed by the spacious and original **Dingwall**, next to the Cromarty Firth. It's a Viking name: before them it was Inverpeffer. This is the junction for the SKYE LINE to Kyle of Lochalsh and thence Skye on the west coast (if following that, switch to page 64).

To start with, once the lines diverge after Dingwall, the Far North Line runs through some pretty verdant and lovely countryside completely unlike the rugged Atlantic end of that line. Foulis Castle on the left, then two distilleries. We pass through good Easter Ross farmland, gently undulating.

There is none of the wave-lashed bare rock and railway blasted out by dynamite. Perhaps this trip will be all amidst this gentle almost West Country-style scenery, you wonder. **Alness** and then **Invergordon** follow, and here the latter's strategic naval position is evident from the gap into the North Sea across the water. Nigg Bay on the right is where many North Sea oil platforms were launched (if that's the right word).

The railway is in no hurry; when we turn west again after **Fearn** and **Tain** (followed by two more distilleries and Skibo Castle on the right), up the Dornoch Firth, we loop inland into Sutherland and re-emerge after 40 rail miles only ten miles up the coast. This isn't because there are obstacles to navigate around: the railway builders deliberately took long inland loops a few times on this route to open up inland areas to rail traffic. Look how the A9 road sensibly cuts across Dornoch Firth to our right (due north).

Skibo Castle

We instead follow the convoluted Dornoch Firth through **Ardgay** to **Culrain**, then the bridge to **Invershin** and next up a steep gradient across more highland country to **Lairg**, which is well inland. The railway swung this far inland to tap into the rural hinterland, as the village stands at the head of the inland Loch Shin and thus is the junction of a whole set of highland roads to remote places.

The railway was used for taking out great trains of sheep, fish, stone, timber and whisky and bringing in oil, coal, newspapers, tools and tourists with dozens of specials laid on for seasonal demand. O S Nock's book tells of five special sheep trains leaving Lairg in less than 24 hours; today there are none.

Then fleets of buses met the locals and tourists. Today, if you're lucky, a handful of people get off the admittedly faster and more frequent trains, and no staff meet them; one wonders if the 30-mile diversion from a more direct route is still worth it. There have been rumblings about building a rail bridge at Dornoch to cut out this inland stretch and speed up the long journey north.

I take the view that one has come to see the scenery, not to hurry, and this route gives such great variety. The special trains today are touring trains. The timetable is more intense in the summer and trains lengthened. Anyway, it's not all gloom on the freight side. Timber and stone trains have been seen again on this route, some of it marble bound for Italy via the Channel Tunnel, which makes it a coals-to-Newcastle story if there ever was one, and a pretty long train ride. It is amazing that this line was built, and amazing that it has survived. Looking out of the window at sea, valleys and mountains (or should that be straths and bens?), it still is amazing. And startling that once or twice one is briefly heading slightly south when going north!

Indeed, after climbing steeply to **Lairg Summit**, we descend southeast along a suitable valley. We pass through **Rogart**, heading (oddly) slightly south and a lot east. Rogart was piled high with smelly wreckage one winter's night about 100 years ago when 22 wagons broke away from a fish train and ran back (continuous brakes on wagons not then being compulsory). The quick-thinking signalman at Rogart heard them coming and threw the points to divert them into a siding instead of smashing into the following passenger train waiting at the station. No-one was killed, but a lot of herring were damaged in the mountain of wreckage.

Soon we see on the right an embankment called The Mound which the great highway engineer Thomas Telford threw across here in 1815 (like The Mound in Edinburgh) and brings the A9 road back beside us. In fact a branch line from here south to Dornoch once used the same embankment. Now we see the North Sea proper. Through **Golspie**, and then **Dunrobin Castle** – the fairytale historic castle is glimpsed to the right overlooking the North Sea as we pass through what was the Duke of Sutherland's private station of the same name. In fact the line building had stopped short at Golspie because money ran out, until the duke saved the project.

After **Brora** (followed by a distillery, and the spot where the last wolf in Scotland was killed in 1700) we and the A9 follow the coast until **Helmsdale**, where we turn sharply inland again even though Wick is only 30 miles up the coast. We follow the River Helmsdale on our right for miles, and Strath Ullie. We climb through increasingly bleak countryside, through **Kildonan** (scene of a short gold rush in 1868) and **Kinbrace**. We pass close to Loch An Ruathair on the left, and the remote halt of **Forsinard** (the village is nearly a mile further up the road north). This is seriously bleak country now, and we climb over empty Caithness moorland to 708ft. There have often been snow fences built up here, and not without cause – passengers have sometimes been marooned on trains for days with only a humorous guard to keep them sane until rescued, in at least one case on one of these Highland lines, by an Arctic Snow Cat, a tracked vehicle more usually seen in polar regions, which could climb over the snowdrifts.

There are odd halts such as **Altnabreac** and **Scotscalder**, but one wonders if the railways swerved inland to serve more population, where are they all? There is little visible except miles of peat bog, great for birdlife, not for nightlife. On the right, the River Thurso rushes through the landscape and, eventually, under the train.

Eventually we descend into flat country and a settlement is reached at **Georgemas Junction**. The train can go straight on for 14 miles to **Wick**, a pleasant run past Loch Watten, or reverse left seven miles, still with the A9 road, to **Thurso**. It chooses reverse first. It's slightly bonkers that people going to Wick see Georgemas Junction twice in 20 minutes, but locals have got used to it. The reason is that this Wick/Thurso line got here first, and it's not worth having a train stationed at the junction to shuttle the last few miles. Neither town is particularly dramatic, nor is the landscape, but the sense of place is magical. The real aim for most people is the last village in the British mainland, John o'Groats, easily reached by bus or taxi if you are staying here. There you may look toward Orkney across the Pentland Firth, where the whirlpools and overfalls of water reveal how the swirling cold waters of the North Sea and the Atlantic struggle and collide.

You have crossed unique landscape to reach a rail extreme point. There's nowhere remotely like it.

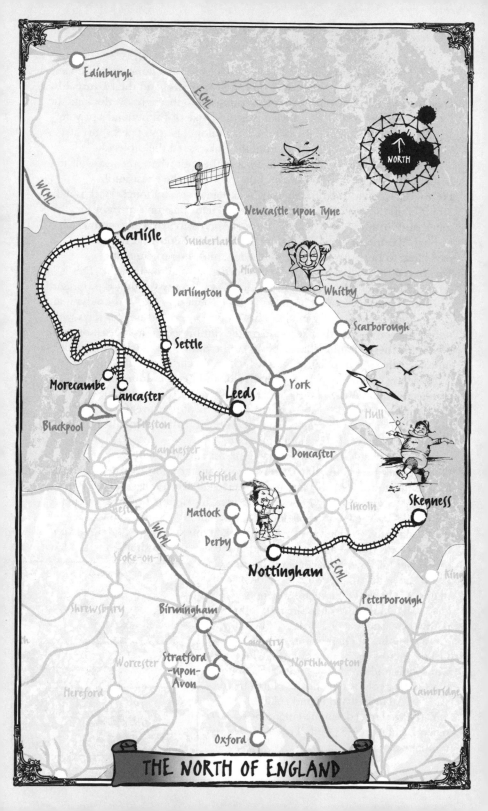

THE NORTH OF ENGLAND

THE NORTH OF ENGLAND:
(CHUFFING 'ECK THAT'S GRAND!

Controversially, perhaps, I'm not to going to detail routes

Midlands mentions (briefly, before heading north)

in the Midlands as a region – to some extent because they come elsewhere in this book (though don't get confused with the Midland Railway, which created the Settle & Carlisle line in the north and St Pancras in London).

THE EAST COAST MAIN LINE gets the full treatment (see pages 1–25) and passes through the East Midlands. In its quest for speed, however, it avoids all the big East Midlands cities. Also, the Midlands to Welsh borders and their wonderful railways come into *Chapter 5*.

Oxford–Worcester–Hereford comes into *Chapter 4*. The very fast and modern WEST COAST MAIN LINE passes through Birmingham and many West Midlands cities (having loops along its length) but doesn't warrant a mile-by-mile description. Equally, the web of lines around Birmingham are too dense and too ordinary, on the whole, to need full details.

The East Midlands cities of Leicester, Nottingham, Derby and Loughborough, (and indeed Sheffield as the line reaches the North) all of which have something to offer, are well served from beautiful London St Pancras (with useful Eurostar connections there) on the MIDLAND MAIN LINE*. But scenically the main line, and the cities, are not in the top ten. There are a few gems, however:

Midlands treasures to highlight

DERBY TO MATLOCK*, a short route also known as the DERWENT VALLEY LINE which gets up into the Pennines and reaches fab places such as **Cromford*** and **Matlock Bath***. Note the extravagant architecture of the stations, eg: French chateau, alpine chalet. These towns are historically fascinating. The fact that the line used to go on to Manchester is now, sadly, academic. PEAK RAIL, a steam operation, continues from Matlock Riverside to Rowsley South (see page 309).

OXFORD TO BIRMINGHAM* is a fine old Great Western route, running fast up the pretty Cherwell Valley to **Warwick**, in company with the Oxford Canal. In wet seasons the railway becomes a causeway across flooded meadows, to the delight of swans. At Aynho (near **Banbury**) the CHILTERN LINE from London Marylebone, a pretty route through the Chilterns, trails in from the east, also heading for Birmingham.

STRATFORD-UPON-AVON, a great tourist destination, is perhaps oddly the terminus of a stub of railway heading south from Birmingham (useful but not gorgeous), from which it is easily reached. But there is a useful linking single-track line across from the nearby Oxford–Birmingham route (above), so some trains from the south and Marylebone go directly there.

NOTTINGHAM TO SKEGNESS*: It's SO bracing; a top seaside day out – see page 101.

The North of England: overview and recommended lines

There's nowt like the North. Very much its own part of England, the region offers spectacular and charming railways, beautiful and sometimes scary scenery ranging from rugged fells to delightful dales, great days out, fascinating, exciting or historic places and delightfully do-able circular routes. There are three routes to the Scottish border, four if you include the Cumbrian coast route, plus myriad local lines in the North which cannot be described in detail but form a web around Manchester and the Yorkshire cities. Excellent places to base yourself for several days exploring are Carlisle (six great routes north and south of the border), Lancaster, Leeds, and York. For details of relevant tourist information centres, see page 311.

Some recommended lines in the North

Some lines are described elsewhere in more detail, and the East Coast Main Line gets its own chapter (pages 1–25), but recommended in brief are:

THE ESK VALLEY LINE* Darlington from Middlesbrough to Whitby. Just lovely, connecting with the North Yorkshire Moors Railway (steam from Grosmont to Pickering, sometimes runs down to Whitby details on page 309), and reaching the sensational harbour town down a pretty valley, with many long views *en route*. A batty reversal *en route* at Battersby, under the scarp of the North York Moors.

What you can say about Whitby is that Captain Cook left, monks and Dracula (in fiction) arrived and steam stayed. The fantastic Coast-to-Coast walk mentioned at St Bees (see page 98) ends near here, at Robin Hood's Bay. Oddly, there were at least three Esk Valley lines around Britain, two still being open.

THE WEST COAST MAIN LINE* Of the admittedly very fast and useful WCML, which goes all the way from London Euston to Glasgow, the only really   great bit scenically is Lancaster to Carlisle. Here we zoom up the Lune Gorge alongside the M6 motorway, with views of the Pennines to the east, and the Lake District mountains to the west; the summit comes at Shap, 916ft. Look out for a terrific, redundant viaduct joining from your right before this. This can be combined with other routes to make great days out. You don't really see much west coast on the WCML. Euston, we have a problem!

THE TYNE VALLEY LINE (NEWCASTLE–CARLISLE) ** This is a beautiful line across   the narrow neck of Britain, usefully connecting the ECML and WCML. Hexham is well worth a visit *en route* (Hadrian's Wall, museums, scenic beauty), plus – what a name for a station! – Haltwhistle. To use a Scottish word for a hill, it's all law and border. The Tyne Valley Day Ranger ticket extends the run to Whitehaven in the west and Sunderland in the east. Great value.

MANCHESTER–SHEFFIELD* Via the lovely Edale and Hope Valley, this offers great Peak District landscape, country walks and Victorian architecture. Includes the three-mile 950yd Totley Tunnel near Sheffield and, at New Mills, note how many transport systems can be squeezed into one narrow valley.

YORK–LEEDS* Go via Harrogate to enjoy a line of great beauty, the castellated Bramhope Tunnel and terrific viaducts. Reaches the East Coast Main Line at York (site of the superb National Railway Museum) where it links with:

THE SCARBOROUGH LINE* A lovely route from York, and not too long. Often used for steam excursions at timetabled, affordable prices. Seaside resort Scarborough station has two bonkers features: the world's longest platform seat (which can accommodate more than 100 people), and a clock tower of crass and clashing proportions (so say the experts, you decide). It still receives long excursion and steam-hauled specials so its extra-long platforms are needed.

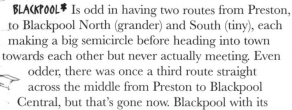

BLACKPOOL* Is odd in having two routes from Preston, to Blackpool North (grander) and South (tiny), each making a big semicircle before heading into town towards each other but never actually meeting. Even odder, there was once a third route straight across the middle from Preston to Blackpool Central, but that's gone now. Blackpool with its tower, pier, beach and roller coasters is the ultimate cheap-and-cheerful kiss-me-quick, mill-girls-on-the-pull, stag-night resort. Genteel it ain't. Great fun, bags of accommodation. Also has a tram system that never closed, providing runs up to Fleetwood.

THE WONDERFUL SETTLE & CARLISLE RAILWAY: don't Settle for anything less! ***

Mmmmm...

The Settle & Carlisle is a mad, mountainous, miraculous, marvellous, mysterious, mean, moody, magnificent, massive and masterful main-line Midland railway.

Mad and mountainous because only a fool would choose this route to Scotland. There's the East Coast Main Line, there's the West Coast Main Line, picking the obvious routes, and in between there's a north–south row of seemingly impossible and virtually uninhabited mountains, the Pennines. The S&C charges along these bleak mountainscapes at a level where only the hardiest of sheep survive, in fact too high for most of them. It was insane – by far the hardest way to reach Scotland, and passing the fewest potential passengers, apart from those sheep, on the way.

Miraculous because it was very nearly never built, and it came within a whisker of being closed within my lifetime, but something special saved it time and time again.

Marvellous because it has the best views in England plus the finest set of lovingly restored stations anywhere.

Mysterious because of the spooky atmosphere that saw the healthy young Australian surveying the route cursed by an early death, and passengers doomed on the line one appalling Christmas Eve. More later.

Mean and Moody because the weather that swept down from the fells sometimes threatened to blow carriages off the rails. The very turntables needed stockades round them to let the engines be turned against the wind and not whirl round, and snow fences had to be built to try to stop the line being blocked – in two 20th-century winters, massive snow-plough trains battered in vain at the deep drifts. The ploughs still wait at Carlisle for the next time.

Magnificent because the sunlight on the glorious peaks can produce magnificent views unequalled in England, bee-buzzing blue skies above the heathery hills in June and July giving a seemingly benign outlook, the weather changing in hours back to the bleak, bare cruelty of the ascetic, treeless fells, icy streams, tumbling scree and deep snow in winter. Yet going down to the Eden Valley it seems one has indeed reached paradise on earth: has any line in Britain such contrasting beauty?

Main line and *Midland* both ought to surprise. A mountain railway is usually a slow thing clinging to the contours and winding tightly through ravines and gullies to gain or lose height. As with the Welsh and Scottish highland lines, the wheel flanges should screech on sharp bends that have to be taken at only 20mph, gradients reducing engines to walking pace. Yet the S&C has none of that. It is built to main-line standards, with sweeping curves that can carry 80mph trains, high massive viaducts across apparently bottomless swamps, huge tunnels blasted through hills that lesser lines would have curved around. It even avoided most of the few towns and villages that there are up here to take the best and fastest route. The surveyors were clearly in a fix-bayonets, take-no-prisoners frame of mind as they charged through here.

Its engineering is *Massive* and *Masterful* indeed.

But why *Midland* when it isn't in the *Midlands* but in the North? Aye, there's the rub that explains it all.

Sleepless in Settle ... and carless in Carlisle: a brief history of the 'S&C'

When the Midland Railway formed in 1844, it was just that. No pretensions to national reach, and totally centred around Derby. Most railways just carried minerals a few dozen miles from mine to dock or factory. Railways were local things (except to dreamers like Brunel).

As the railways boomed in the middle of that century, long-distance express services became the name of the game. The Midland realised too late that it had to reach London and the South, and Scotland too, to get a share of this and lucrative long-distance freights; but other companies had got there first.

Its battles for the South were long and legendary. Using the rival London & North Western Railway's (LNWR) route from Rugby south to Euston caused all sorts of problems, so a route was pushed south through Bedford to Hitchin and thence onto the Great Northern's tracks to King's Cross in 1857. But attempts to play off one rival against the other backfired, with obstructions (such as slow goods trains being sent out in front of Midland expresses deliberately to delay them) and a disastrous accident at Welwyn.

Building St Pancras Station

Eventually the Midland was forced, at vast expense, to make its own route to London St Pancras, through St Albans.

In the West, its tentacles reached Bath, much to the fury of the Great Western, and even Bournemouth after misadventures and bankruptcies. You begin to see why such duplication of routes led to stations serving only tiny villages (and then not very near them) and nationalisation brought rationalisation.

But the way north to Carlisle and Scotland concerns us here. Carlisle had been reached from Lancaster by the 'enemy' LNWR, and yet in Scotland that company's enemies waited to ally themselves to the Midland if they could only somehow connect.

The great rivals in the English northwest were building short branches to outsmart and block each other. The Midland used these to gain access to Liverpool and Barrow-in-Furness, and set up ferries to the Isle of Man and Ireland, which the LNWR had thought its private prerogative. But the Midland found itself obstructed getting trains to Scotland. Passengers who left its trains at apparently connecting stations found the spiteful LNWR just left them standing with no onward connections. Endless negotiations about running rights over that route were started, encouraged, dashed and disappointed over and over again. Typically, in 1866–68, the enemy company offered a last-minute peace deal to try to get the Settle & Carlisle project stopped before it was started. The Midland agreed, but parliament, which had passed the act to build the S&C, was having none of it. The astounding project to build up and over the fells and moors was on.

The engineer-in-chief was John Crossley and the surveyor on the ground was Charles Sharland, a young Tasmanian. Sharland, a genius, was not to survive to see their line open and Crossley would little outlive its first train.

Sharland was only in his early 20s, but well respected and seemed to be destined for greatness. He walked the entire length of the route surveying it for the line, making record time despite being snowed in at a bleak moorland inn for three days. He designed a masterful, no-expense-spared route but the effort exhausted him and he died not long afterwards, aged only 26. The obstacle these engineers met with and how they were overcome will be described with the route below.

The through passenger service started on 1 May 1876. Any train heading for Scotland tended to be known as the *Scotch Express*, and the average speed of 41mph was identical to the rival LNWR over Shap, but by the 20th century expresses were making 80mph runs from the summit down to Carlisle.

THE BATTLE OF SETTLE & CARLISLE: HOW ORDINARY PEOPLE DREW A LINE

As various tyrants have found over history, you can only push the British so far, then they dig their heels in. For instance, steam railways were officially finished with in 1967. Result: 20 years later there were still 100 of them around, run by 100,000 volunteers! So it was with the Settle & Carlisle line. British Railways decided in 1981 that the line wasn't needed and blamed the impending closure on ruinously expensive repairs to the Ribblehead Viaduct. The fact that they had run the track to tatters and closed all the local stations, plus run an inconvenient timetable, suggested we were facing a conspiracy to wreck this magnificent masterpiece of railway building.

The vandals in charge had got away with this dishonest process elsewhere, but this was pushing people too far. So how did the British respond? From a base of 93,000 passengers in 1983, numbers soared to 500,000 by 1988. Thousands of people from around the world joined the Friends of the Settle-Carlisle Line. Locally, town councils, villages, MPs, schools, churches, women's institutes and pensioners got behind the battle. Over 100 excursion trains were run by enthusiasts from all parts of the country. Eventually the government caved in, the local stations were not just mostly reopened but wonderfully restored and that troublesome viaduct repaired at – guess what? – a fraction of the estimated cost. Now the pattern of freight has changed and this line has been busier than ever, so much so that the track has had to receive much overdue renewal to cope with the traffic and signalling has been doubled up. Volunteers from the Friends of the Settle–Carlisle Line run shops at Settle and Appleby and organise a fabulous set of guided walks pretty well twice weekly from stations on the line. For information, E walksinfo@settle-carlisle.co.uk or send a stamped addressed envelope to FoSCL Walks, Settle Station. For steam excursions, see page 311.

The route described: heaven and hell in 72 miles (2hrs 45mins, 72 miles)

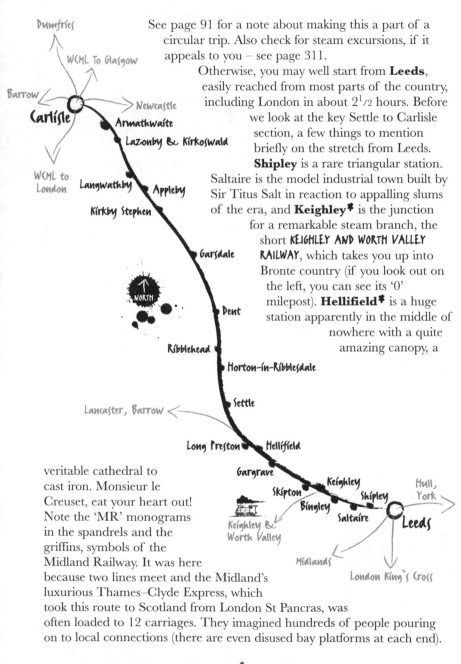

See page 91 for a note about making this a part of a circular trip. Also check for steam excursions, if it appeals to you – see page 311.

Otherwise, you may well start from **Leeds**, easily reached from most parts of the country, including London in about 2¹/₂ hours. Before we look at the key Settle to Carlisle section, a few things to mention briefly on the stretch from Leeds.

Shipley is a rare triangular station. Saltaire is the model industrial town built by Sir Titus Salt in reaction to appalling slums of the era, and **Keighley*** is the junction for a remarkable steam branch, the short KEIGHLEY AND WORTH VALLEY RAILWAY, which takes you up into Bronte country (if you look out on the left, you can see its '0' milepost). **Hellifield*** is a huge station apparently in the middle of nowhere with a quite amazing canopy, a

veritable cathedral to cast iron. Monsieur le Creuset, eat your heart out! Note the 'MR' monograms in the spandrels and the griffins, symbols of the Midland Railway. It was here because two lines meet and the Midland's luxurious Thames–Clyde Express, which took this route to Scotland from London St Pancras, was often loaded to 12 carriages. They imagined hundreds of people pouring on to local connections (there are even disused bay platforms at each end).

Last time when I was there, two people did, and only the east end of the massive platforms is used by ordinary trains. Still, the community has found a use for all those buildings and elsewhere the cast iron would have been smashed down and a ghastly bus shelter put up. Well done, Hellifield. Just keep it properly painted, please…

Not much further west, the S&C route from **Settle Junction** northwards took the obvious route – following the top end of the River Ribble's course, providing a do-able slope over 13 miles, with the usual road, gully and river crossings but nothing extraordinary… to start with anyway!

True, 'the long drag' was the enginemen's nickname for this route from Settle Junction to **Blea Moor Tunnel** near the top, so unrelenting was the climb, but the magnificent engineering kept the gradient within the capability of an express train. The fireman had to work hard to keep the fire filled with coal and the steam pressure up, but if nothing went wrong it was possible to make good time to the summit.

Indeed, you can see from the diverging Lancaster line, on our left and below us, that we're climbing from the very junction.

Settle⚹, altitude 510ft, is a station like most on this line – superbly restored and lovingly tended. It's followed by two short viaducts and then the short **Stainforth Tunnel**. A difficult section of the valley a mile further on sees two more short viaducts – **Sherriff Brow** and then **Little** – where the Ribble had to be diverted to allow construction. A mile further on and we cross the river on yet another viaduct before reaching **Horton-in-Ribblesdale⚹⚹** station, altitude already 850ft. A couple of miles east, away to our right, is the dramatic peak of Pen-y-Ghent, 2,272ft and one of Yorkshire's famous three peaks. We'll see the other two, Ingleborough and Whernside, soon.

Next station after some bleak, empty country, is **Ribblehead⚹⚹** and, as the name suggests, we can no longer rely on the south-flowing river to form a route: it peters out in, or rather starts from, a great bog. The Ribble is a dribble in high summer. Even worse, beyond that is a massive watershed fell of 1,753ft which there was no way round for fast express trains to take. It was necessary to cross the sinking mire with a huge, still-climbing viaduct and then plunge straight into the hillside with a deep and long tunnel. The boldness seems massive, even after it was done.

Ribblehead Viaduct, rightly famed for its sensational setting and magnificently clean design, has 24 arches and is on a curve and an incline. The piers are up to 105ft high but go way down into the bog below. The thing seems to be constructed entirely out of local limestone but in fact a walk below reveals the arches are brick for strength. Even so, every sixth pier is a 'king pier', massively built, so that in a catastrophe the whole lot wouldn't go down like dominoes. You will be relieved to know they were never needed and hopefully never will be.

Look left (west) from the viaduct to see Ingleborough, 2,373ft.

A shanty town of 3,000 people plus hundreds of horses sprang up hereabouts, as did roads across the empty moorland. Now there's little trace. Not because of any 19th-century concern for the environment – the concept and attitude didn't exist – but because at this altitude the weather soon wipes away anything temporary. After the viaduct we soon enter a cutting to line up for the coming tunnel. An aqueduct carries a stream, and footpath, over our heads a few hundred yards from the tunnel mouth.

On Blea Moor Tunnel on the Settle & Carlisle

What is a mile and a half of Styx in seventy miles of delectable mountains?

(Hamilton Ellis

Blea Moor Tunnel, 2,629yds, is an incredible achievement, given the candlelit picks, shovels and hand-drill techniques of the day. To be ready in time, 14 working faces were needed, so seven shafts had to be first dug down from the moor up to 500ft above and winding engines installed at their heads – no easy task in isolated rugged landscape 1,500 ft above sea level. They worked day and night, seven days a week. It was the last main line that navvies built by hand before machines started doing the hard work, although the men in the tunnel had one advantage – dynamite had replaced the much more dangerous gunpowder.

Three of these shafts were kept for ventilating the tunnel, and even today when steam trains visit the route, a distant roar, rumble and perhaps a whistle from the depths of an apparently peaceful mountain are followed by clouds of smoke ascending incongruously from the chimney-like shafts. Thankfully the gradient in the tunnel flattens off and even goes down slightly, giving winded boilers – and firemen – a chance to build up pressure again for the last climb in steam days. Our modern diesels just take it all in their stride.

Keep an eye left after leaving the tunnel for truly wonderful views down Dentdale, looking down on the farms as if from an aircraft.

We cross **Dent Head** (ten arches – I won't make a habit of it throughout this book but because of the astonishing numbers and beauty of the viaducts up here, I'll mention how long each one is in arches), and then **Arten Gill** (11 arches) viaducts. When I first travelled this line, here stood snow fences which sought vainly to defend the line against drifts – their skeletal remains are on the right. In the terrible winters of 1947 and 1963, hundreds of men and steam-powered snow-ploughs battered against snow-blocked cuttings for months. Some trains became stuck for weeks.

On Dent station...

Visitor: Why did they build Dent station so far from the village?
Native: 'Appen they wanted it near t' railway lines.

Quoted in Andrew Dow's excellent Dow's Dictionary of Railway Quotations (Johns Hopkins University Press, 2006)

Dent** is the highest main-line station in England at 1,150ft. It is the epitome of bleakness, but therein lies its beauty, you may think. The station has extra slate lining and double glazing when that was unheard of elsewhere, so cold was it up here.

The railway had some brass neck calling this isolated station Dent, as the village of that name is about four miles west (left) and 550ft lower in beautiful Dentdale. But it's staggeringly moving country.

Dent Station

Perhaps the station should have been called Dent Road. (Dent's Dents, however, would be a fine name for a car-repair workshop hereabouts.)

Rise Hill Tunnel, 1,213yds, follows and soon we are in **Garsdale****, once a junction for a lonely single-line branch to Hawes (closed in the 1950s). Like the River Ure that starts here and goes east, that branch headed down Wensleydale towards the east coast and reached the North Sea. You can see the lonely trackbed peeling off right after the station. Imagine puffing up here on a bleak winter's dusk – in the middle of nothing. Only sheep commute up the track now.

Here at Garsdale there was a turntable for the banking or pilot engines, which would have helped us (pushing or pulling respectively) up from either direction, to be turned and sent back down to do it all over again. This famously had a stockade of sleepers round it because the engines couldn't be turned against the wind. According to one commonly told version, one engine here whirled round uncontrollably like one of those advertising signs that work on the wind – until the fireman thought of shovelling coal onto the circular track those things turn on.

One more push to the top – we climb over Dandry Mire Viaduct (12 arches) through tiny Moorcock Tunnel, over Lunds Viaduct (five arches) through little Shotlock Tunnel and we are at Ais Gill Summit, 1,169ft and marked as such on either side of the line. The highest English main line. You might catch a glimpse of Hell Force on the right, a waterfall that is one source of the River Eden which, now we are over the watershed, heads north for Carlisle, like us. For the hellish double disasters that happened here, see page 88.

Ais Gill Viaduct (four arches) is small and we are now visibly descending with the at-first tiny River Eden down to our right. The summit beyond it is Mallerstang Edge, at a height of 2,328ft; the slopes of imperious Wild Boar Fell on our left reach a similar height.

Many stations on this route have been closed and then reopened, but on this stretch there have never been any – because there is no-one here. There was a long time ago, mind – Pendragon Castle's ruins are down on our right guarding the valley.

A couple of miles after Birkett Tunnel, 424yds, we reach Kirkby Stephen*. Actually the town is 1 1/2 miles east and 320ft lower, but the Midland insisted on the line gradient being maintained which meant not going through the town.

Kirkby Stephen did get a station in the town thanks to a now-gone NER line from Barnard Castle to Tebay on the WCML – we soon cross over that closed route in the first arch of the dramatic 12-arch Smardale Gill Viaduct, the line's highest at 130ft high, although not so dramatic as Ribblehead. Not that you can see the old route for the trees down there. It is rapidly followed by Crosby Garrett Tunnel and Viaduct over the village of that name, and a cutting which used to house their station.

By the way, the local term for a stream is a beck, and just now we crossed the intriguingly named Scandal Beck. Good name for a barmaid.

On over Griseburn Viaduct (seven arches) and Helm Beck and through Helm Tunnel, the former station and Ormside Viaduct (ten arches) over the Eden, then past various railway relics on the left into Appleby* station (see box opposite).

THIS OTHER EDEN: COMPLETE WITH TEMPTING APPLEBY

Appleby has a typically pretty restored Midland Railway station with ornamental bargeboards and old lamps. It is a charming town, said to have the finest main street in Britain – although an 1890 guide pronounces surprisingly 'Appleby is a notable example of decadence'. It's a trap of the language changing: not moral decay, but decaying in population to a quarter of its previous size (although the population swells massively in early June for the annual Horse Fair, where hundreds of gipsies meet to trade horses, wash them in the river and race them. Some of the Romanies make the trip by horse-drawn caravan even today).

On our left at Appleby station is a memorial plaque to the great railway fan Bishop Eric Treacy who died here on 13 May 1978. His plaque is marked: 'Railway photographer, Lover of Life and Railways and Pastor to Railwaymen' which just about says it all. He was a 'reverse engine spotter' – when he was out photographing trains, he would wear a white armband for crews to spot *him*. They knew if they wrote to him confirming details of the train and the date, time and place, they would get free copies of the picture (and he would get train information for his captions). When this hugely liked man died – doing what he loved, photographing a steam engine called appropriately *Evening Star* – his many friends organised a tribute steam special from London, pulled over England's most magnificent railway – the Settle and Carlisle – by the world's most famous steam engine, *Flying Scotsman*. She put up a cracking show.

Bishop Eric was not unusual in combining railways with the Church – think of Reverend Awdry, creator of *Thomas the Tank Engine*, to name one of dozens. The bishop saw God's work in this landscape and in the railwaymen who worked through it. It's not for me to say whether his departure from a place called Eden – the Eden Valley runs from here to Carlisle – was fitting, but it seems a short step from a place like this to paradise.

Down we go, with long views of the Lake District mountains to the left, over Trout Beck and **Long Marton Viaduct** (five arches), past busy gypsum sidings at Kirkby Thore on the left, and with views of Cross Fell, 2,939ft on the right.

More old stations, **Crowdundle Viaduct** (four arches), **Culgaith level crossing** and two tunnels follow. The Eden now becoming sizeable thanks to the confluence, which you can clearly see on the left, of the Eamont which flows from Ullswater to the west. All that Lake District water has to get out somehow.

Langwathby follows, then another old station and viaduct then on our left the derelict **Long Meg signal box**. Worth a mention because there is a quite peculiar stone circle, Long Meg and her Daughters, on our right but sadly out of sight from the train. There are 66 stones with Long Meg being the

tallest and not part of the circle. Legend has it that Meg was a witch and the others her petrified coven, but she also lines up perfectly with the midwinter sunset. An early Mystic Meg.

Eden Lacy Viaduct (seven arches), brings us over the Eden again and through a short tunnel to **Lazonby and Kirkoswald‡‡**

station (they are actually two villages, this being charming Lazonby. Just look on the right at the churchyard and old station house). The increasingly stately river is meandering around majestically to our right.

Now we are in the pretty wooded part of the Eden Valley, a part which the great O S Nock called 'the most beautiful of all on the Midland Railway'. Two short **Barron Wood 1 and 2 tunnels** and then a mile further on the third is called **Armathwaite**, as is the viaduct (nine arches) and station.

We are now more than 100 miles from Leeds and about 800ft lower than Ais Gill. **Dry Beck Viaduct** (seven arches), a level crossing, and **High Stand Viaduct** (four arches) follow, and the Settle & Carlisle line ends where it joins the **TYNE VALLEY LINE** from Newcastle (joining from our right) at **Petteril Bridge Junction**. At **London Road Junction**, tracks leave us to curve south on to the **WEST COAST MAIN LINE** from Lancaster and Shap, and also the **CUMBRIAN COAST LINE**. We finally join these two to arrive at **Carlisle**, tired but pleased like the mountain hikers we are, 113 miles from Leeds and almost back to sea level. What a ride!

CARLISLE STATION: LONG MEMORIES

Carlisle Citadel station, built in Tudor Gothic style, had no fewer than seven railway companies operating over eight routes at one time – the most of any British station – and even today it has several companies operating six routes radiating either side of the border. So it has three long platforms for through trains and three short bays facing north and south, all used. Busy? A recent Wednesday saw 169 passenger and 84 freight trains pass through.

There are plenty of odd details to look out for. Some are obvious – the gargoyles on the tower, the strange circles in the main inside roof trusses, the coats of arms on the front, or the Tudor arches (and no, that's not another gargoyle, it's that irate guard from the Dumfries train leaning out of a window). There's something odd in the square outside the station. No, not the actual cannon used to repel Bonnie Prince Charlie's army, proudly displayed at the top of English Street.

Tucked away by the archway on the right of the square is a curious blue enamel sign, saying: 'London Midland & Scottish Railway: Private Road and/or footpath.'

I hope some thieving magpie hasn't whipped it by the time you get there. The company ceased to exist in 1948. Mind you, railwaymen tend to have even older memories. They still refer to the various routes from here in nicknames that recall the companies before even LMS was formed in 1923. 'The Caley', 'the Lanky', 'the M&C', 'the Cumbrian' or 'the Southwestern'. Or so I was told…

As if to confirm this, as I left on a train south the lettering on a long building on the right announced *Maryport and Carlisle Railway Goods Depot*, one of those early companies that ceased to exist in 1923. Now that *is* old…

HELL AND HORROR IN THE HIGH HILLS

Two notable disasters happened on the same high-level stretch of the S&C in the early 20th century, both caused by tragic human error and both impossible today because of safety procedures – imposed partly as a result of these crashes.

Christmas Eve, 1910

▲ ME/ILN

The first was all the sadder because it was on Christmas Eve, 1910, and some of the victims would have been expected for happy family reunions. Although it was the small hours of the morning, the line was busy. Seven expresses came up to Ais Gill from Settle and their pilot engines (assisting at the front) had to be detached, run back to Hawes Junction (now Garsdale), moved onto the siding, turned on the turntable, and run back downhill, sometimes in pairs. Two southbound expresses also had to have their pilots detached and sent back to Carlisle.

The Midland had a small engine policy, using assistance when required, which made all this necessary. And bosses insisting that the pilot engines weren't detached conveniently at Hawes, as had happened before, but continued the three miles further to the summit at Ais Gill made things more complex.

In charge of all these movements, whipping engines in and out of sidings and across main lines, without delaying expresses, was just one signalman at Ais Gill and one at Hawes, doing 12-hour shifts and communicating by bell codes. Everyone had to remember where the engines were and it was pitch black and stormy; beating rain poured down.

The two engines to be returned to Carlisle from Hawes were eventually put on the Down main line to wait at a signal while other movements were undertaken. Time passed, and the waiting engines were forgotten about. According to the rule book, the drivers of the engines should have blown their whistles after a while and then sent their firemen to the signal box on foot to remind the signalman they were blocking the main line. On this dark, vile night, they didn't.

Eventually the midnight St Pancras to Glasgow train came rushing up from Settle, and the signalman sent it onwards to Ais Gill. But in clearing the signals he let the two forgotten light engines start their leisurely journey on the same line as well. The last

THE WONDERFUL SETTLE & CARLISLE RAILWAY

thing that could have saved the express as it hurtled past Hawes was the tail lamp on the light engines in front, but as fate would have it, Moorcock Tunnel prevented it from being seen.

The collision between the express doing 65mph and the two engines doing only 30mph happened just beyond the tunnel. The carriages, wooden and gaslit, 'telescoped' (fitted inside each other, with drastic results for those on board) terribly and caught fire at once. Some of the 12 who died were still alive when the flames reached them. A Canadian lumberjack, a surviving passenger, was heard crying out for an axe to get through to the trapped passengers in front of him.

No tools were at hand.

Back at Hawes, the signalman who made the mistake was asked by another worried engine driver what had happened to the light engines. He said he thought they'd been sent to Carlisle – but a quick check with Ais Gill signal box found they had never been offered the route officially. Had the Glasgow express gone through safely? No, it hadn't arrived. It was clear that something had gone wrong.

It was now 06.00, and the day signalman arrived. It was still dark but an ominous orange light was reflected in the clouds to the north. The night man said grimly: 'Go to the stationmaster and tell him I have wrecked the *Scotch Express…*'

Why it couldn't happen today As a result of this accident, the Midland invested in track circuits. A similar technology works today. A train standing in one section is detected by electrical currents passing from one rail to the other, and this locks the signals behind it to prevent another train following too closely. Wooden coaches are now long gone, and modern tubular carriages can withstand such an accident without 'telescoping' and indeed have survived very much faster ones. And dangerous gas, candle or oil lighting has also long gone.

The second disaster near here was again in the small hours of the night, just north of Ais Gill summit. Again it was human error, but again if the Midland had provided more powerful engines it would not have happened. A train from Glasgow on 2 September 1913 had too many carriages attached at Carlisle, so the driver asked for a pilot engine. He was told none was available, and to make matters worse the coal was very poor. The crew battled valiantly, doing only 20mph by Kirkby Stephen, but eventually pressure fell so low that the brakes leaked on – ironically a safety feature – and the train stalled tantalisingly only half a mile from the summit. They would have to wait while boiler pressure rose.

A second express, from Edinburgh, was storming up from Carlisle 14 minutes behind. It was doing better, although the driver complained about the coal: 'If she'll steam on this, she'll steam on anything.' As with the first train, the fireman and driver worked like furies to get the fire to burn properly. The driver had to go out on the outside of the locomotive, right round the front, with an oil can in one hand while clinging on to the bucking engine with the other, and like this went through Birkett Tunnel. He should have checked the Mallerstang distant signal, and said he 'thought it was clear', but when he got back in the cab there was another emergency with the boiler dangerously low of water and the injectors that would fill it up properly not working owing to falling steam pressure. This potential disaster (if not attended to, he would have had to stop and throw all the fire out on the tracks with a shovel to stop the boiler being damaged) was no excuse, but he missed the next two signals.

They failed to see the tail lamp of the previous train standing on the line, or the guard frantically waving a hand lamp, until it was too late. Again the wooden wreckage of crushed carriages burned. Sixteen people died, just two miles short of the very recent disaster on the line going the other way.

We have noted how there is aptly an Eden (Heaven) further down this route. The nearest natural feature to this lonely spot of double disaster was a force, or waterfall, appropriately called Hell.

Why it couldn't happen today Again modern carriages could withstand this speed on impact and no fire would result. Drivers don't have to perform the arduous and distracting duties described above. And modern track and signalling means a SPAD, 'a signal passed at danger', as happened here, brings on the brakes automatically. In fact as I was writing these words in 2007, a Virgin Pendolino express crashed at Grayrigg not far from here on the parallel West Coast Main Line. It was doing 90mph and the carriages tumbled down the embankment. An 84-year-old woman was killed, which was bad enough, but what a tribute to modern carriages' design that hundreds of people survived. And, it must be said, on the same day around 12 people would have died on Britain's roads and no-one would have taken a blind bit of notice.

LEEDS TO LANCASTER AND MORECAMBE**: a useful connector, brief encounters and a great comedian

This interesting cross-country route not only allows you to get onto the Settle & Carlisle line, changing at Hellifield, but also the WEST COAST MAIN LINE (WCML) at Lancaster, by which you could quickly reach Carlisle again, allowing one great circular route. A westward route carries on to Barrow (described in the next section) and the line up the west coast of Cumbria back to Carlisle, allowing two more spectacular circular routes – the S&C and Cumbria Coast, or the WCML and the Cumbria Coast. Either way you can start at either Carlisle or Lancaster or points between, but do your timetable work to make sure you can connect round in the direction you want. Not using the WCML makes the day longer, but a lot more interesting. And, of course, the Leeds to Morecambe route also does what it says on the tin – connects the Yorkshire metropolis usefully to the Lancashire seaside resort. It doesn't have to be part of some grand circuit to be enjoyable.

The route described
(2hrs–2hrs 40mins, 70 miles)

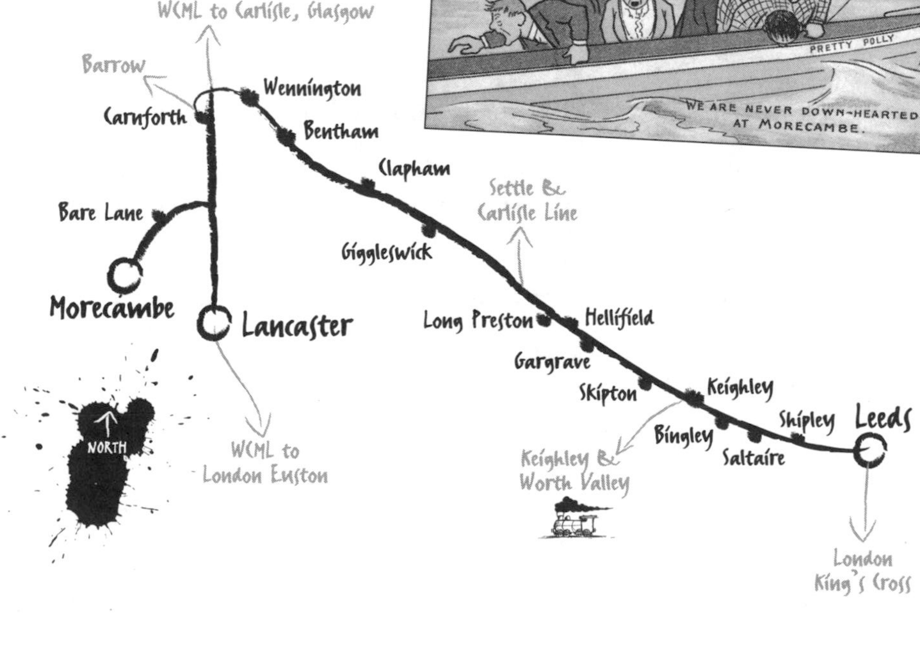

PRETTY POLLY

WE ARE NEVER DOWN-HEARTED AT MORECAMBE.

WCML to Carlisle, Glasgow

Barrow

Wennington

Carnforth

Bentham

Clapham

Settle &
Carlisle Line

Bare Lane

Giggleswick

Morecambe

Lancaster

Long Preston

Hellifield

Gargrave

NORTH

Skipton

Keighley

WCML to
London Euston

Bingley

Shipley

Leeds

Keighley &
Worth Valley

Saltaire

London
King's Cross

The highlights of the route from Leeds to **Hellifield** are described above with the Settle & Carlisle line (see page 80). After **Long Preston**, we rattle over Settle Junction and head in a more westerly direction as the S&C climbs away from us to the north (right). The next stop, **Giggleswick**, is in easy walking distance of Settle on that line. The dome on the right (north) is the chapel at Giggleswick School.

The rocky fell behind is Giggleswick Scar. We rattle over a high viaduct to **Clapham** – which once connected directly to the West Coast Main Line, so the hills up here had the original Clapham Junction. Not many people know that...

We have crossed the watershed and are now in the valley of the Wenning, heading for the Irish Sea. The next

Giggleswick School

station, **Bentham**, makes you realise how lovely the restored stations on the S&C really are!

We cross into Lancashire, and at **Wennington*** , the view of cottages and rivers on the right is much prettier. After Melling Tunnel, 1,230yds, we race across a river plain of the Lune Valley, needing two viaducts totalling 13 arches. This major river is responsible for the Lune Gorge which cuts the hills northwards from here and is used by the WCML and the M6 to get up to Shap on their way to Carlisle; in the other direction is 'Lune Castle', which gives Lancaster, and the whole county, its name. The area is thick with remains of Norman castles, having been very heavily fortified in that period.

Having crossed two rivers, and passed under the M6 motorway, we cross the WCML on a flyover to reach famous **Carnforth***. Note the Steam Town loco sheds and train depots on our right as we curve round – there's always something interesting going on there, and this is where excursion trains are based. Note also the locomotive coaling tower. They were once a common sight on railways but are now nearly all gone, not being a lot of use for diesels.

Carnforth station, as we swing round to join the main line and the Barrow line, was immortalised in the film *Brief Encounter*, about duty overriding forbidden passion (so not a modern one, then!). It featured the refreshment rooms, which have now been reopened. There's also a visitor centre, and don't miss the splendid clock by Joyce of Whitchurch on the left.

On the other hand, Carnforth clearly isn't as important as it once was, because the platforms on the adjacent WCML have been demolished to let expresses hurtle past safely. The task of junction has been delegated to Lancaster (to which we are heading) so in that respect Carnforth is a shadow of its former self. For a while it was very run down, but has been lovingly restored to its present state.

We run on to the WCML and get good views of Morecambe Bay to the right (west). If you're in one of the little four-wheel nodding donkey railcars, and I hope they've been scrapped by the time you get there, you will feel a little exposed as Virgin Splendifocos whoosh past at 125mph. A bit like a milk float on a grand prix course. This short diversion gives much better connections for the main line and access to the city of **Lancaster⚑**, great for shops, pubs, museums, and more.

We leap dramatically over the River Lune to reach the splendid Lancaster station, battlemented with arrow slits – perhaps they expected the Scots to arrive in a bad mood. Or maybe it was to fit in with the nearby castle.

That this was once the start of the Lancaster & Carlisle Railway can be seen by the 0 milepost on the London-bound platform (which must come as a surprise to some of those Scots – 'what, Angus, London already, laddie?'), and also L&C marked on the grand chimneys.

If you're heading to Barrow or the Cumbrian coast, you will probably have to change here and cross to the bay platforms on the far side (see overleaf).

If continuing to the seaside resort of Morecambe, you usually stay on the train and it reverses and heads back the way we have come a little to take the curve seawards, through **Bare Lane** to **Morecambe⚑**. Here, don't miss the LMS Railway's fabulous Art-Deco Midland Hotel. The town's most famous son was the late great comic Eric Morecambe, born Eric Bartholomew there in 1926, later taking the town's name as his own.

He's remembered with a statue on the seafront, still – optimistically you may think – seeming to sing his theme song *Bring me Sunshine*! Lucky he wasn't born in Scunthorpe or Ramsbottom, he might have joked. On the other hand, Giggleswick up the line might have suited rather well…

Some trains reverse and go south, to continue to **Heysham** in connection with Irish ferries from there; the odd layout is because this is a remnant of a Midland Railway incursion into 'enemy territory'. And occasionally Manchester Airport to Barrow trains turn down the Morecambe branch, heading back up to their east–west route at Carnforth. In which case the lucky passengers get to stop at Bare Lane twice. Barely enough, I should imagine. But for a day out, Morecambe is wise.

THE CUMBRIAN COAST LINE: right round the Lake District**

(1hr plus 2¹/₂ hrs in two stages, 120 miles)

First step, from Lancaster to Barrow: splendid views, a lovely coast, vanishing engines and furnaces in Furness (1hr, 24³/4 miles)

After leaving **Lancaster*** on the WEST COAST MAIN LINE we turn off at the famous station of **Carnforth** (both described above) and turn left (west) while the Leeds line turns the other way, and crosses over the WCML.

There are splendid views from the left of the train over the salt marshes back to Morecambe and ahead of the Furness Peninsula, where we are heading. The Morecambe sands between these two offered an apparent short-cut from Lancaster to the Furness coast, but are treacherous in the extreme, with sinking sands and very rapid tides, so expert guides were

needed to get the earlier horse-drawn stagecoaches through. Because the coast we are heading along is riddled with long inlets and rivers, travel overland was tedious, but the dangers of picking the wrong route over the shifting sands, when the tides seemed to offer a chance of a short-cut, were immense. You may recall that 22 Chinese cockle pickers drowned here just a few years ago.

We pass the pretty stations of **Silverdale** and **Arnside** (in my case, after the driver has shooed a cow off the track; Carnforth had the movie *Brief Encounter*, here we had Beef Encounter!). Viaducts link the sea to massive inlets, the water swirling dangerously through. The first is the **Kent Viaduct**. We cut through what was clearly once a rocky island and reach **Grange-over-Sands**✝✝, which gives us a fantastic outlook towards the sea as we run right along the promenade. **Kents Bank** is a request stop and we then run through **Cark** across more salt marshes, a causeway and approach the long **Leven Viaduct**.

This viaduct over the tidal river estuary is clearly at a windy spot; local lore says that a train was once blown on its side on this bridge, although thankfully not into the sea. Records of any such accident are strangely missing, but 1915 Furness Railway records state that: 'A wind pressure gauge is fixed at the west end of Leven Viaduct and when the wind is of such a pressure as to make it dangerous to cross, alarm bells will ring in the signal boxes...', so something must have happened.

In 2006, a tedious 20mph speed limit was scrapped and the decaying 1857 bridge decks were replaced in a mammoth operation which should make the bridge good for another 150 years. Another bit of local legend – that the bridge once had a lifting section to allow shipping through – was confirmed by examination of span 37, longer than all the others. No way of operating it could be discovered, though, apart from one written record saying it could be worked 'by a man and boy'.

Note the insanely big monument above the next town. It's been nicknamed 'The Lighthouse without a Light', 'The Guardian Angel of Ulverston', 'The Pepper Pot' and more often 'The Hoad Monument' after the hill it stands on. It is a monument to local boy made naval administrator and traveller, Sir John Barrow (died 1848). I can't quite see why they loved him so much, as he didn't return to Ulverston after 1796, yet on the day of the foundation stone laying the whole town was bedecked with flags and virtually the entire population marched up the hill behind a military band.

The extraordinary edifice was modelled on Eddystone Lighthouse. It has never had a light at the top, although in recent years the outside has been floodlit.

Ulverston✱ has a grand station with a tower which has somehow survived the barbaric ripping out of similar features elsewhere. The cast-iron spandrels contain the letters 'FR' which doubtless stand for Furness Railway (well if they stand for Ffestiniog Railway, that's one heck of a tunnel, boyo!).

One of the world's oddest railway accidents happened at Lindal Bank between Ulverston and Dalton-in-Furness on 22 September 1892. A six-wheel steam loco and its tender sank into a mining subsidence hole that appeared beneath the track. The crew jumped clear and for a while it seemed as if the engine could be saved, but it kept sinking Lethe-wards and only the tender could be pulled out by a crane. The railway poured hundreds of tons of material into the hole and laid steel plates and 36ft-long timbers over the pit.

It's been suggested from time to time that steam buffs should dig the loco out, as at least we know it was in working order when buried. However, it is probably too far down and they find it easier to locate, repair and repatriate derelict locos in Java, Greece or Turkey than to delve down under Cumbria. And as the mine that swallowed up the loco was an iron working, the earth was in effect reclaiming its own. (There's also said to be a similarly lost loco under Wembley Stadium, which sank into a mud pool when the original stadium was being constructed.)

We pass through a tunnel to **Dalton**, then after another tunnel comes **Dalton Junction** for Barrow trains to go left (south), and any heading straight round the Cumbrian coast to go right.

We pass the ruins of Furness Abbey, a small tunnel and **Roose**✱ station, and reach the dock and curve sharply west. The huge building in the town contains a shipyard that makes the world's most advanced submarines, those powered by nuclear reactors and/or carrying ballistic missiles. They can go

▼ ME

three years without refuelling, unlike ourselves who may be looking out for the Barrow tea room.

Barrow once featured fast ferry services to Fleetwood (near Blackpool) and the Isle of Man, and the Furness Railway's two handsome paddle steamers, which were low with raked-back funnels. They were doubly war heroes because they 'volunteered' not only for cross-Channel service in World War I, but answered the call to Dunkirk in World War II, where they were both sunk.

Fleetwood paddle steamer to the Isle of Man

Another was named *Phgilomel*, which locals of course nicknamed 'Full of Smell'. The FR's fleet even extended to steamers on two lakes – Coniston and Windermere – to which it had branch lines.

By the time we reach **Barrow** station, we are heading northwest again. You may well have to change if continuing up the coast to Carlisle. Check before you dive into the refreshment room; there's usually time.

Barrow to Carlisle: Cumbrian coast from lakes to nukes (2¹/₂hrs, 73¹/₂ miles)

Who wants to breathe a Millom air?

Going out of Barrow we curve north by some sand dunes and then contrive to curve due east briefly – as if we were heading back to Lancaster – before sharply turning north to rejoin the main coast line.
In truth, Barrow has been a huge loop which has brought us back to the main line less than a mile from where we left it.

After **Askam**, we race along the flats with truly magnificent views of the mountains across the great horseshoe-shaped bay to our left. Note a church spire across the Duddon Estuary, perhaps two miles away.

> Dad: Should I take the kids down the line for an outing?
> Mum: Ask 'em. Dad: No, Barrow.

The views, on both sides, of the Lake District mountains are splendid and inspiring, so you might miss the little request stop of **Kirkby-in-Furness⚜⚜**. We soon reach pretty **Foxfield⚜⚜**, which once had a lovely branch to Coniston, and we cross a bridge over the River Duddon. **Green Road⚜** is a well-loved station and great for walks. Next we reach **Millom⚜**, which offers a folk museum and made its fortune out of huge iron-ore deposits from the 1860s. Note the spire, which was two miles away when we last saw it. It's taken us 14 minutes and more than ten miles to get here round the bay, but with views like this, who's complaining?

(As a matter of fact it was three times proposed to build a line straight across the mouth of this bay, the first time when the 'Father of Railways' George Stephenson was asked to survey a West Coast Main Line that would have gone round the coast to reach Scotland, unlike the route over Shap that was eventually built. He included in his plan a huge tunnel from Ulverston straight under the hills and then a great viaduct to leap across to Millom. This would have been seven miles instead of 25¹/₄, but if you're a tourist, not a commuter, today's route is a far more fun.)

More FR spandrels in the vintage station, and we start seeing more and more wind generators on the hills. Look out right for a superb view up a mountain valley, before we reach **Silecroft** and **Bootle**. In the sand dunes at Eskmeals, a little further up the line, thousands of rabbits lived in huge warrens, many presumably deaf. This is because Vickers shipyards at Barrow used to test battleship guns here, and the hot cross bunnies didn't get ear protectors. It's still a military range.

There's another long bridge over the River Esk Estuary, and we soon reach **Ravenglass⚜⚜**, a pretty name for a pretty place, a confluence of rivers and the connecting station for the 'La'al Ratty' line – properly the **RAVENGLASS & ESKDALE RAILWAY**, a 15in-gauge miniature line which gives a seven-mile run through the loveliest scenery to Dalegarth, where suitably prepared walkers can access England's highest peaks. The loveliness of this route belies the fact that this was originally a 3ft-gauge iron-ore line.

After so much gentle beauty, what comes next might be a shock. We pass through **Drigg** and the level of security on the left suggests something's up; meanwhile odd towers are looming in the distance. On through **Seascale** and there's a huge industrial complex on the right (inland) – one of the world's biggest nuclear sites, **Sellafield** (rebranded from Windscale after a serious 1950s' accident).

Whatever you think of nuclear power – and you can't help but wonder if this coast got this, plus all those windfarms because the people were poor, so not very listened to, and desperate for work, or simply because it was remote from cities – there was consequently no question of this railway ever closing. That's because of the trains (you can see them on the right, with their own Direct Rail Services blue locos) bringing nuclear flasks to and from this site. This place, and the Barrow shipyards, also kept a commuter traffic going after the mining industry vanished.

From hereon the coast gets more rugged and the industrial history more evident, not that it doesn't have a kind of beauty. At Sellafield there's a fine old water tower for steam locos on the right, and we picked up a single-line token for the narrow bit to St Bees ahead (possession of the token means only one train can be on that line, avoiding head-on crashes). In the meantime we pass **Braystones**, and see increasingly stern sea defences, including lines of concrete railway sleepers armouring the embankment against winter storms. Note the ramshackle shacks along the shore. Once pleasantly cheap dwellings full of cast-off furniture and old pots and pans, these have become very expensive.

Birdlife is fantastic along here. Cormorants (the black ones drying their wings because they don't have the oily feathers of other sea birds), puffins (which look like toys and live in cliffs) and shags (yes, no puerile jokes *please*, I know they sound like the American dance).

Nethertown follows, then **St Bees**✱✱ which is the prettiest place for miles, a perfect station with signal box and passing place. The beach and cliffs here are lovely (although whilst having a paddle with the children, I did suddenly remember Sellafield's waste pipes discharging into the sea round the corner). It's also the start of the great fell-walking guru Alfred Wainwright's *Coast-to-Coast* walk. Having done it, I can thoroughly recommend it as one of the world's best walks (it takes two weeks, get his

little book). But just to be
infuriating, he takes you in the
wrong direction, down to the beach
and along the cliffs (to see the
puffins and views) before crossing
this track heading inland about
two miles north (wave at the
hikers, they will soon be facing
three ranges of mountains). He does the same trick at the North Sea end,
when you're desperate to get there. Cat and mouse, he calls it.

More single line through **Corkickle** and a tunnel to **Whitehaven** (one
of Britain's first planned towns, with 18th-century terraces, churches and
quays) with platforms for services terminating from Carlisle on the left.

Now there are staggering amounts of industrial archaeology around: old
mineral workings, ruined engine houses, former rail tracks snaking up into
the hills, for this coast was at the heart of the Industrial Revolution,
supplying coal and iron to the burgeoning furnaces of the 'workshop of the
world' (particularly the West Midlands).

After **Parton** – if you look for the twin peaks that made Dolly name
herself after here you probably won't spot them, because I've just made
that up – there's a fantastically rugged bit of coast which we creep round
on a ledge at 15mph. The hillside is meshed and bolted to stop it pushing
us into the sea, and the shore is heavily armoured with rock defences. Even
so, a railwayman told me, the line gets eroded from time to time. 'It's a
nuisance for travellers, but I get a few days off while they fix it.' The hills
far ahead left are Scottish, in Dumfries & Galloway across the Solway Firth.

There's the sweetest little harbour at **Harrington**, then note the sea-
damaged old railway to the left – it seems we have been moved inland here.
Workington had a huge steelworks on the left; as I passed it they were
loading long rails onto trains for installing round the system. It was closed
in 2006, because the railway wanted even longer rails and this would have
meant extending quite a long way out into the Irish Sea. They will be
made elsewhere.

A pity for local employment, and also because there was a time when
every part of the British Empire was bound together with steel bands made
here. I remember puffing up into the Himalayas on the Darjeeling steam
train to stop at Ghum Monastery. Buddhist prayer flags, rancid yak milk tea,
Tibetan refugees – and a turntable with rails proudly stamped 'Workington'.
Another time, in the 1990 Gulf War, we saw 'smart bombs' on TV, taking
out railway bridges in Iraq. The twisted wreckage was stamped 'Workington',
puzzled TV crews found. My grandfather put them there in another war.

We pass a little harbour, a wide river and what looks like a top-security
prison on the right (it's a shopping mall). **Flimby** follows, then **Maryport**
(which has only one platform so trains have to cut across to it, as with the
original Brunel stations.

This rather pretty town and port on the mouth of the River Ellen has a maritime museum, although to be frank, local lads have not always been too happy at sea. Fletcher Christian led the mutiny on the *Bounty*, and Thomas Ismay's firm owned the *Titanic*.

Aspatria (what a lovely name, it sounds Latin but just means 'St Patrick's ash tree'). Plus a fine footbridge, adjacent cheeseworks and a mattress factory; followed by speeding across miles of pleasant but unremarkable farmland. **Wigton**, **Dalston**, then a freight line takes off left to reach the routes east and south of Carlisle while we swing round to join the main line from London, which would have got us here from Lancaster in around two hours less! But you would have missed a wonderful, wonderful ride. And we roll triumphantly into **Carlisle**.

THE LAKE DISTRICT BY TRAIN? What are those words worth?!

The Lake District interior is not directly accessible by trains, which run all round it but not into it, mainly because steep mountains and very deep wet bits got in the way, and three good routes which did reach into it were cut off by the total morons who were in charge in the mid-20th century.

However, don't despair! Two routes still head in from the sides to penetrate the wonderful landscape. On the west, the RAVENGLASS AND ESKDALE** (see page 98) miniature line from Ravenglass on the Cumbrian Coast Line, and on the east the WINDERMERE BRANCH* from **Oxenholme** on the WCML.

The ten-mile Windermere branch has at least survived, and from Oxenholme reaches **Kendal**, mintcake capital of the world, then picturesque **Burneside**, **Staveley** and **Windermere**. It's a pleasant rural ride, although one waggish postcard from around 1910 shows a cartoon train with the caption: 'Our local express: to Windermere and back in a day.' The train is preceded by a man on a donkey and a woman holding a flag saying: 'Not too fast'. In the foreground some of the train crew are playing golf, while on the coal tender another man uses a punting pole to push the train along.

It doesn't reach the lake, however, with a bit of a walk needed (around 15 minutes), or a bus. One railway which does reach the lake is the LAKESIDE

AND HAVERTHWAITE RAILWAY, which reaches Lakeside at the south end of Windermere, and gives the pleasure of a steam ride through lakeland. How a railway that is cut off from the former main-line connection at Ulverston can provide any useful alternative to road transport – surely it must generate more – I really can't see. A pleasant enough ride for tourists though.

No missing Lincs in Lincolnshire:
Nottingham to Skegness
(2hrs 15mins, about 78 miles)

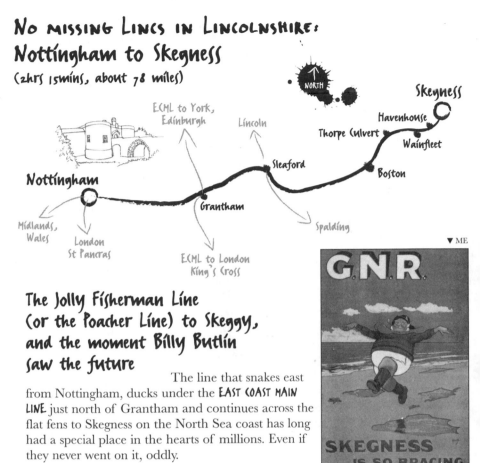

ECML to York, Edinburgh

Lincoln

Skegness

Havenhouse

Thorpe Culvert

Wainfleet

Sleaford

Boston

Nottingham

Grantham

Midlands, Wales

London St Pancras

Spalding

ECML to London King's Cross

▼ ME

The Jolly Fisherman Line (or the Poacher Line) to Skeggy, and the moment Billy Butlin saw the future

The line that snakes east from Nottingham, ducks under the **EAST COAST MAIN LINE** just north of Grantham and continues across the flat fens to Skegness on the North Sea coast has long had a special place in the hearts of millions. Even if they never went on it, oddly.

For those that did, it was the line that took millions of Midlands factory girls and mineworkers to their first seaside holidays, and the first Butlin's holiday camp. And for those that didn't, the line became known for another reason – the comic *Jolly Fisherman* artwork invented by the Great Northern Railway, taken over by the LNER in 1923, used by British Railways in their half century in charge, and now used by train operators to the extent that the whole route is called the **JOLLY FISHERMAN LINE**.

It was a brilliant bit of marketing of what was an isolated, tiny, cold place with few facilities, and very little in the way of geographical interest, being at the edge of flat fen country.

You may recall the rotund Michelin-man-style fisherman, beaming smile, sou'wester on his head, pipe jammed in his mouth, skipping over a puddle on the beach, his arms outstretched as if he were trying to be a seagull. The slogan said: 'Skegness is SO bracing.' Which was, oddly, selling a place on the fact that the North Sea is always flipping freezing. Perhaps it was wry irony, even then, but the effect was comic.

The line which had earlier reached Boston and then Wainfleet was opened to sleepy Skegness in 1873, and straight away the railways began running cheap excursion fares for day trippers from inland towns, sometimes for the races at Skeggy, as it was affectionately known. Even as early as 1874, newspapers were reporting the resort 'overcrowded beyond all precedent'.

By the end of the 19th century, huge numbers were arriving at Skegness and attractions such as a pier and switchback railway were built. In 1908, the railway first used John Hassall's *Jolly Fisherman* oil painting as its poster in London, and trippers flocked to the rapidly expanding town, reaching their destination in three hours from King's Cross.

After World War I, factory workers started to get a paid week's holiday, and for East Midlands cities, Skegness was the nearest resort to visit.

THE SWIMMING POOL, BUTLINS HOLIDAY CAMP SKEGNESS.

In 1927, a certain Canadian-raised businessman called Billy Butlin stepped off the train from London and looked quizzically at the resort. He had been persuaded by friends to make the trip to Skegness to see if it afforded any holiday business opportunities. He had been discouraged by the fens on the last part of the journey, he recalled later. 'We rattled on through flat featureless fields stretching to the distance on either side...Was Skegness at the back of beyond? I began to have doubts about the whole idea.' When he arrived and saw two streets, on a wintry day, there seemed little to encourage him.

But then came the realisation of what could be there, and what a pent-up demand there was for entertainment and recreation from the industrial Midlands cities. He imported the first bumper cars from America the next year, and set up an amusement park in the town. But as he watched the tough landladies of the cheap boarding houses, he noticed how they turfed the holidaymakers out of the door between meals, whatever the weather. He determined to provide something better.

He soon bought 30 acres and started work on his first holiday camp, just in time for legislation forcing employers to give workers paid holidays.

Butlin's slogan was 'a week's holiday for a week's pay' and he realised working-class people would love the concept of a camp where, once you were in, all the food, rides and entertainment were free. Butlin's – with the interruption of World War II where it became a navy camp – never looked back, with a chain of such camps around the coasts. He made a point of giving the infirm and elderly free holidays from the early days. Sir Billy Butlin died in 1980, and what is carved on his tomb on his retirement island of Jersey? A picture of that original Skegness holiday camp, and, I'm told, the *Jolly Fisherman*.

It was in Skegness in 1937 that the 'prostitutes' padre', the disgraced Harold Davidson, Rector of Stiffkey, was mauled by a lion in a cage and later died.

Lincolnshire, being flat and next to the North Sea, was thick with air bases in World War II to carry the war to Germany while Britain stood alone and Europe enslaved. This made the county a target for retaliation, and 'K Fields' were built, dummy airfields with wooden planes, lights and fake runway markings. They were bombed frequently and repaired in time for the next night's attacks. Meanwhile the railways round here were busy with construction material for real bomber airfields, supplying them with everything including bombs.

The route described (well, the last bit anyway!)

The strange shape of the last part of the railway to Skegness can be explained only by the missing routes. You take off dead straight northeast from **Boston** across the flat fens but then in the middle of nowhere the train slows for a sharp screeching curve to the right so tight that you are now heading south. If the train's long enough – and some of those old excursion trains were – you see the back of your train across the fields still going north!

This is because the original line went on to Firsby, just a mile or so up the line, then to Louth in north Linconshire, or another coastal route. These have all gone, in 1970, and we're left with a ludicrous layout here.

The train heads south to the prosaically named **Thorpe Culvert** (which like other stations on the line was once busy with fertile produce – corn, potatoes, carrots, etc – of the rich dark soil round here). An old gentleman who lived here in the mid 20th century bought a season ticket to Skegness and spent his retirement years happily travelling to the seaside town three times a day, going in the morning and back for lunch, taking an afternoon trip and back for tea, and then just for a change, an evening excursion. Sometimes he would ride in the steam engine's cab, and if the weather was cold or wet, wouldn't even get out of the train at the seaside. He wasn't at all keen on heading towards Peterborough and London, however. Nasty foreign places.

The line then swings east again to **Wainfleet**. This was once the end of the line, and is a quiet and pleasant market town, with a Roman predecessor called Vannona, then a Danish settlement in the Viking era. Later, William Waynflete not only founded Oxford's Magdalen College, but also provided a remarkable school with two octagonal towers here, near the River Steeping.

Then it's on to **Havenhouse** and at last **Skegness**. Brace yourselves!

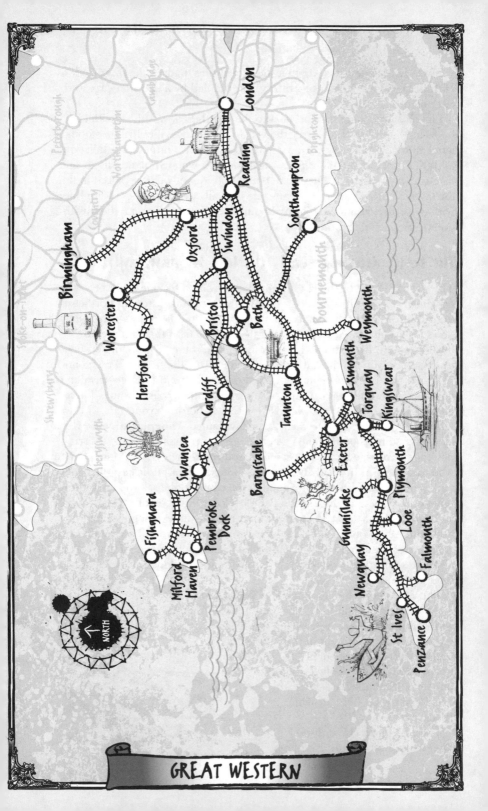

GREAT WESTERN

FOUR

GREAT WESTERN:
GOD'S WONDERFUL RAILWAY

The GWR: trunk, branches and twigs

The shape of the Great Western routes is like that of a tree, with its main trunk at Paddington, dividing at: Reading with the Berks & Hants route splitting off (though it later rejoins); then again at Didcot with a limb for Oxford; at Swindon with another medium limb for Cheltenham; and then a huge part heads for south Wales while the rest goes on – and on – for Penzance. Meanwhile there are little branches, many mere twigs, from the very start at Ealing to the very end at St Erth.

Those branches, some wonderful lines, have been trimmed back to perhaps a half of what they once were, but despite that – or because of it – their layout is often completely mad. Several – such as those at Marlow, Gunnislake and Looe – set off in one direction then reverse and head in another. One literally loopy one (loopy Looe again) sets off in totally the wrong direction, loops around under the main line, heads the wrong way again then reverses towards the seaside. Yet another one crosses under the main line twice before making up its mind where it's going. You couldn't make it up.

The reason for such madness is the history of many different companies striving to reach the same places, or to invade each other's territory. At nationalisation in 1948, many routes were found to be expensive duplicates, and then again in the infamous Beeching cuts of the 1960s, some branches and secondary routes just weren't considered viable (although they would be kept open today).

So those reversals in the middle of nowhere are because another lost route carried on from the junction.

But one thing is assured – the Great Western still has by far the prettiest and most fascinating set of branch lines in the kingdom. And it is, 60 years after the Great Western Railway (GWR) formally ceased to exist, still very much its own railway with its own way of doing things.

Keeping great company: the GWR's great history

It is hard to overestimate the loyalty to, and affection for, the Great Western Railway (the routes west out of London Paddington), or 'God's Wonderful Railway' as some called it. It has always stubbornly gone its own way, and in the government-forced grouping of Britain's railways recovering from World War I in 1923, only the GWR retained its name and its identity. At nationalisation in 1948 – guess what? – the Western region again retained much the same shape and livery, and in privatisation guess whose name lives on: Great Western.

Even today, it is possible to travel from London to Vladivostok on the Pacific by modern electric railway all the way. But not in 2010 from London to Swindon or Oxford, thanks to GWR 'we know best' attitudes that once had its trains running on a completely different track gauge from the rest of the country, and later used completely incompatible diesels.

Author Michael Bonavia put the attitude of superiority like this: 'Paddington speaks only to Swindon, and Swindon speaks only to God.'

Two funny stories about the GWR that give an insight into its intensely conservative nature:

One is that a GWR horse water drinking trough at Reading was marked to be used by GWR horses only, as if such horses deserved superior water, or other ones could read.

The second, also at Reading, has a London-bound train wait for a Newbury branch train to unload its passengers. An impatient top-hatted gent leant out of his First-Class compartment and urged the guard to blow his whistle to hurry the passengers along. The guard declared sniffily: 'Sir, one does *not* blow whistles at people from *Newbury*.'

Two stories, did I say? One more amusing GWR vignette. At Acton a cockney station hand would call out to arriving passengers: 'Hacton, Hacton!' as cockneys are wont to do. A despairing Sir Daniel Gooch, chairman of the GWR who was on the train, ordered: 'Dear me! Let that fellow be transferred to Hanwell. He can't give us too much H there!' Soon the porter was up the line yelling: ''Anwell, 'Anwell!'

Decades after nationalisation (in 1948) there were country stations in Wales, Devon and Cornwall where on special occasions the cap with the gold braid proudly announcing GWR would mysteriously reappear despite attempts by British Railways to ban the things.

Mind you, not everyone was pro-GWR. Some of the other companies' staff trying to work with them after nationalisation called them 'Broad

Gauge Bastards' – and when you consider what they did to rivals' lines they had gained control of after nationalisation, that wasn't without reason.

God's Wonderful Railway? Before the Severn Tunnel was built giving direct access from London to south Wales, so a journey through Gloucester was necessary, the initials were taken to stand for Great Way Round. And the most hurtful of all lampoons was a reference to Gresley, the great designer of the world-record *Mallard*, run by the rival LNER (London & North Eastern Railway), that finally eclipsed Swindon's locos for all time for speed and fame, if not elegance. That railway's staff claimed GWR stood for 'Gresley Was Right'. Ouch!!

The unknown Isambard Kingdom Brunel: suspenders to suspension

If you like travelling by train, you'll surely have heard of Isambard Kingdom Brunel (1806–59), creator of the Great Western Railway and pioneer of the technologies that totally transformed the world by rail, bridge, tunnel and shipping. So let's look at a few *less* well-known but fascinating facts about him.

The fabulous name, to start with. 'Isambard', which he shared with his engineer father Marc Isambard Brunel (1759–1849), means 'Man of Iron' in a Germanic language, hugely appropriately. 'Kingdom' came from his mother, Sophia Kingdom from Portsmouth, who was staying in France as a young girl and met royalist Marc in the turmoil of the French Revolution. Eventually they fled, and not for the first or last time Britain benefited from continental intolerance.

Marc, besides inventing mass production (of pulley blocks for the Royal Navy during the Napoleonic Wars against his former homeland) a century before Henry Ford thought he did, and building the first tunnel under the Thames, also had a job at Chatham Dockyard. There he, interestingly, installed a dock railway with a broad gauge of 7ft. Whether this impressed his then young son I K Brunel, sitting on one rail looking across at the other, as to what an ideal railway should be, who knows, but it seems likely when he came to design the GWR.

Father and son made dozens of brilliant innovations, but were not always in top form in either health or financially. For example, Marc set up mass production of army boots, just in time for the Battle of Waterloo and the outbreak of peace to make his products near worthless. If there were huge triumphs in their lives, it was only after huge disasters such as the flooding of the Thames Tunnel, or the Clifton Suspension Bridge going bust before it was built, or Box Tunnel workers being killed, or the *Great Eastern* ship exploding. Ill health and debts pursued them to the end, and their successes were hard-won.

Neither were they shining advertisements for Victorian virtues. I K Brunel was sent to the seaside after one of his many close shaves with death but his family unwisely chose Brighton, then as now synonymous with the 'dirty weekend'. Instead of convalescing Isambard exhausted himself in 'exertions with actresses', his biographers note. He was sent off to relatives

DID BRUNEL'S 'ATMOSPHERIC RAILWAY' SUCK? WAS IKB AN IRRITATING KID BUNGLER?

What exactly was Brunel's ill-fated Atmospheric Railway from Exeter to Teignmouth? OK, it wasn't a train flying *through* the atmosphere, but surely, some locals thought, he was crackers even to think heavy trains could be driven by the atmosphere!

Well, no. Think of a drinking straw. When you suck on it, you think you draw the drink up the tube. You don't. It is driven up by the atmospheric pressure – 14lb per square inch – on the surface of the rest of the drink. When your sucking makes a partial vacuum, the drink must go up the tube. It would go 33ft up the tube if you could create a total vacuum and your straw was strong enough.

Make the tube 15 inches wide, pump the air out at one end, and you've got a considerable force on a piston (potentially about 28,000lb). The piston shoots along the pipe, pushed by the atmosphere (or sucked as we would see it).

If this 15in tube is a pipe laid between railway lines to power trains, there is one huge snag: how to attach a train, *outside the tube*, to the piston *inside the tube* without letting the air in. Any normal engineer would give up here. It was madness. But Brunel wasn't a normal engineer. He joined the piston to the train by a flange or blade which travelled along a slot in the top of the pipe. To stop air rushing into this slot, it was closed by a flap which had small wheels on the flange opened and resealed behind itself.

It shouldn't have worked – but it did, pretty well for a while.

Starcross pumping station

in a quiet part of the West Country, and then genteel Clifton in Bristol. So without those actresses' exertions, the wonderful Clifton bridge would never have been designed. From suspenders to suspension, possibly.

Brunel's triumphs and disasters are explained later in this book at the places where they occur on the GWR: at Bath, Bristol, Plymouth and south Devon, for example. But several patterns emerge. That Brunel created with a brilliance and daring when faced with any obstacle. That he added elegance to engineering, but economy too – such as west of Plymouth.

Carriages reached the unheard of speed of 70mph pulled by the wagon attached to the piston.

True, you needed pumping stations quite often – one still stands at Starcross – to draw the trains along, but then at this early point in the rail age many railways were worked by cables wound by stationary engines. By these methods the still feeble and unreliable steam locos didn't have to carry their own weight up hills and down dales, so steep inclines, such as those faced in Devon, could be tackled. And two small-scale atmospheric railways had been shown to work before – although not along the seafront, as in Devon, or over such distances.

Brunel's Atmospheric Railway, which started operating in 1847 and soon reached Newton Abbot, immediately ran into difficulties. The leather flap needed constant greasing to keep it airtight, and the gangs who did this were in danger of being run down by near-silent trains.

The flaps became more brittle, were affected by rats chewing them, and by sun, sea spray and frost, causing tremendous leaks. The whole thing became a disastrous error and normal locos, which had rapidly become powerful enough to cope, took over only a year later. The huge slotted air pipes between the tracks were sold for scrap, and all lost – or so it seemed. One piece, used for a beach drain for many years, was discovered in the 20th century and installed on a bit of replica broad-gauge track at the steam centre at Didcot, so we can see what the track looked like. Very strange!

Didcot Steam Centre – 'Atmospheric Railway'

The Mirror

That the Brunels' designs were so far ahead of their time meant they sometimes found a use only later.

For example, the first Thames Tunnel, which was used only by pedestrians as the approach roads could not be financed, was later sold to the Underground railway and is still used daily today for a purpose Marc didn't consider. The *Great Eastern*, an enormous ship which could sail round the world without refuelling, was built for a market that didn't yet exist. It found a use (after that engine explosion, caused by bad handling, not design) laying the first intercontinental telegraph cables, building the first world-wide web.

▶ ME

Ironically, when ships of such size were really needed, and one of them, *Titanic*, struck an iceberg, had she been built with Brunel's double skin she would have survived.

And I K Brunel would always go his own way, usually but not always with good results. His broad-gauge rail track of 7ft $^1/4$in (the extra quarter he thought would contribute to smooth running) was expensively abandoned later in the century and all the tracks converted to narrow-gauge 4ft $8^1/2$in (thereafter called standard-gauge). But it wasn't because 4ft $8^1/2$in was better – after all, it was based on a Roman horse's bum, not any engineering need.

No, it was similar to the battle between VHS video tape and two other systems. VHS won not because it was better – it was the worst – but because it was more common, and it was too expensive to go back.

So it was with the GWR's broad gauge. In fact many railways were other odd gauges because initially no-one imagined they would all connect up. Some believe that Brunel *was* thinking ahead, but thinking defensively, to keep other companies' trains out of his empire. After all, later in the 19th century totally pointless lines were built to block off rival companies from accessing certain towns.

But I imagine Brunel just started with a blank sheet of paper and thought what would be best in engineering terms, in speed and comfort, in spaciousness, in boldness and grandeur. Perhaps a distant memory of his father's spacious dock railway at Chatham figured in that first doodle…

Brunel's Atmospheric Railway (see box on previous page) was one of his epic failures and, it must be said, not the only one. He insisted at the beginning of the Great Western Railway that track should be laid on longways sleepers, resting on piles at each end. This gave a disastrous switchback motion to the ride and resulted in broken rails. We now know that rails have to float a little in their stone beds, or on rubber mountings, to give a satisfactory ride – watch the rails under a passing train.

Brunel's odd choice of a broad gauge for the GWR was another hugely expensive mistake. Everything had to be transhipped where the GWR joined standard-gauge railways. Every single passenger, parcel, lump of coal or potato had to be moved across from one train to the other. And while Brunel's railway was fast and comfortable, the broader the gauge, the wider the curve must be (which is why mountain railways always are often narrow-gauge, and why the boundary walls on the GWR often sweep much wider than the present track curves). And as the French and Japanese have shown, standard gauge can reach huge speeds safely.

The GWR was adapted in many places with a third rail to take both sorts of train: the cost and complexity of pointwork at junctions was horrendous.

In the end the whole GWR was converted, amazingly, in just one weekend in 1892. Of course all the broad-gauge engines, trucks and carriages had to be got off the system before the rails could be levered closer by armies of navvies. And it was not quite as simple as that, when you consider that on curves the outer rail would end up too long, or the inner one too short.

It was an amazing achievement in one weekend; particularly when you think that the railway at Hatfield which suffered one broken rail and an accident in 2000 took *five weeks* to reopen.

Brunel's broad gauge was his being bloody-minded and individual as usual. He should have compromised but didn't.

So he had his failures. But his mistakes were rapidly ridden over by changes and adapting them: that's how progress goes. The successes endured – the Great Western Railway, and its stations, bridges, tunnels, docks, steamships and hotels, a staggering achievement. Every country in the world and every railway, civil or marine engineer is in Brunel's debt.

Meanwhile the thought might have occurred to you that a pneumatic railway might have worked if the tube was big enough to take the whole train – a piston-shaped train fitting tightly in an underground tube railway.

Well it was tried in the USA. It worked, as a train. But the passengers got off in agony, their eardrums burst.

Clifton Suspension Bridge

LONDON TO PENZANCE: the best of the West
(5hrs, 304 miles)

Paddington to Reading: Brunel's billiard table*
(25mins, 35 miles)

Marlow

↑ NORTH

Henley

Taplow   Slough

Maidenhead   Burnham   Langley

GWR Continues...

Twyford

Windsor

Reading

Guildford, London Waterloo, Gatwick

Berks & Hants to west

Basingstoke

You can't separate the Great Western Railway, as the route from London Paddington to Bristol will always be known, whoever runs it, from its famous creator, Isambard Kingdom Brunel (see previous pages).

It is known as 'Brunel's billard table' because it is so flat – there are no tunnels as he followed the Thames westwards, even making a huge bend north to Didcot (unlike the railways going north and south of London which repeatedly tunnel through hills with much steeper gradients). The other reason for spaciousness in many Great Western stations, bridges, etc, is that Brunel famously and quixotically chose a broad track gauge of 7ft ¹/₄in, which was later abandoned.

The directors of the GWR has asked for the cheapest quote for the route. Brunel point-blank refused to make economy but vowed instead to build 'the finest work in England'. They agreed. He did.

Paddington station is largely original Brunel, with its famous three-faced clock and roof details much as he left it. True, as we set off west we can see for a moment electrified Tube trains run to our right to Royal Oak station, then cross under us left and after Westbourne Park, disappear off south.

There are also overhead wires on the main line, but this is so far just for **THE HEATHROW EXPRESS**, and soon **CROSSRAIL** trains from Essex, under London and following us as far as Maidenhead. Not for the main line.

On the right here is a monstrous, even Stalinist in its severity, but to some minds beautiful tower block called Trellick Tower and designed by take-no-prisoners architect Erno Goldfinger, who gave his name to the James Bond villain. The land beside it is charmingly called Meanwhile Gardens because development, which never happened, was delayed and they were to be gardens 'meanwhile'.

We pass a complex set of junctions near **Old Oak Common**. The West Coast Main Line to Glasgow is at this point not many yards to our right, and two routes from the south cross ours overhead to get to it. We are here also close to Kensal Green Cemetery, where Isambard Kingdom Brunel and his father lie fittingly within bone-rattling distance of these great main lines. Old Oak Common is a large train depot on the right – a place of pilgrimage for Great Western fans past and present who descend on its open days in their thousands – and nearby is another called confusingly, as a destination, **North Pole** (after a pub). Another depot services the Heathrow Express and we pass through **Acton Main Line** – one of seven Acton stations.

Soon another two Tubes join us, on the right, to reach **Ealing Broadway**. This was a small country village when the railway opened in 1838; now Ealing has four stations. A junction for the GREENFORD BRANCH takes off right after **West Ealing**. The long footbridge across many tracks here is known locally as Jacob's Ladder.

Watch out after picturesque **Hanwell** ✻ (restored GWR notices, brickwork and gas lamps) for the second viaduct, the superb **Wharncliffe Viaduct**. Named after a bigwig of the day who backed the route and whose coat of arms still adorns the 891-ft long brick structure, it has eight typical GWR elegantly flat arches, best seen from the park below, where the River Brent crosses our route.

Next is **Southall**, a great centre for Indian food and temples, though the landmarks are (on the right) the strangely castellated water tower and the huge gasholder. The latter is marked on top with an arrow saying effectively 'this way, stupid' after a dozy jumbo pilot landed at Northolt RAF base, out of sight on our right. The runway was so short that all the passengers, luggage and even the seats had to be taken out for the subsequent one-minute hop across the main line to Heathrow. The huge gasholders around the country, by the way, are always next to railways because until the 1970s the gas was made from coal brought in by train. A neat double benefit for the railway in this case was that a by-product of the gasworks was used next door in a plant to creosote wooden sleepers.

After **Hayes & Harlington** is **Heathrow Junction** where the four-mile tunnel to the airport starts, with a flyover so Up trains don't have to cross the main line. Between **West Drayton** and **Iver** we reach Buckinghamshire and also pass under the M25 London orbital motorway.

After **Langley** comes the bigger town of **Slough** which didn't have a station to start with, perhaps because the Act of Parliament for the GWR specifically forbade any station within three miles of Eton College (whether to stop the scholars going up to London or riff-raff coming down is not clear). In fact the whole line was kept three miles clear.

Despite that, nowadays the WINDSOR AND ETON BRANCH✱ takes off left (south) here, the trains rattling over Brunel's original wrought-iron bowstring bridge.

Slough was the first stop out of Paddington where 'slip coaches' were used, a strange practice whereby a guard would pull a pin between some coaches, allowing the rear portion to fall back and stop under a handbrake after the express had run through. Strange because the safety bods would have a screaming hissy fit at the very idea nowadays – although I can't recall an accident from the practice, which continued for 102 years until 1960. It clearly didn't work going back, when all the carriages had to be collected with much shunting.

Industrial Slough was famously ugly – although it perhaps makes up for it by producing Mars Bars and Horlicks – and was attacked in poetry in the 1930s by John Betjeman who wrote: 'Come friendly bombs and fall on Slough/It isn't fit for humans now.' A certain Mr Hitler arranged just that activity two years later (much to Betjeman's mortification).

Very soon afterwards, after whizzing through **Burnham** and **Taplow**, we cross the Thames on a rightly famous Brunel bridge. Brunel had faced two conflicting demands – the river authorities wanted clear passage for the barge traffic (which the GWR would in the end pretty well kill off) and yet he refused to spoil his smooth gradient from London to Didcot by raising the railway to a hump. Typically, Brunel didn't compromise but pushed the technology to new achievements. Maidenhead Bridge has staggering low and beautiful brick arches, 128ft wide with a rise of only 24ft (the widest and lowest in the world then). So much so that the authorities in 1838 were convinced Brunel was being too daring and a train would end up in the water.

He was ordered to leave the timber supports used to create the arches just in case but – and this tells you a lot about the man – he let them down a little with an inch or two to spare, so they weren't supporting his bridge at all but seemed to be. They eventually rotted away and here we are nearly two centuries later, with trains far heavier and faster than then envisaged, and the bridge is fine.

It also became famous because of its strange acoustics – if you walk underneath, the Sounding Arch gives a strange echo – and because Turner used it for his painting about the arrival of the industrial age, *Rain, Steam and Speed – The Great Western Railway* (1844, see it at The National Gallery).

Maidenhead Bridge

At **Maidenhead** you can take a MARLOW BRANCH** train right (north) to the pretty town of Marlow (which oddly reverses *en route*) and then another, right again at **Twyford** for the HENLEY BRANCH**, both these towns being on the near-parallel Thames. For details of the Thames Valley branches, see the next three pages.

Soon comes the exceptionally deep Sonning Cutting, with its bridges high up above – it is two miles long, more than 60ft deep and Brunel wanted to build a tunnel. The GWR directors felt people were not ready for travelling so long in the dark, so 1,200 navvies and 20 horses dug this all out by hand. Ironic, given that it was dug out to steady people's nerves, that the Sonning Cutting Disaster on Christmas Eve 1844 saw eight people die as the wooden carriages were crushed between their engine that had hit a landslip and the heavy goods wagons behind them.

Then, after a Thames-side marina on your right, comes **Reading** with its five thriving rail routes and trains to many parts of Britain. Whatever the weather, you can always spot a trainspotter at the end of the platforms here.

Trains from Paddington to Bristol, Bath, Oxford, The Cotswolds and south Wales, plus some West Country ones, take the Didcot and Swindon route (four tracks, train depot on your *left*, first station Tilehurst). If, however, you take the alternative BERKS & HANTS ROUTE (two tracks, depot on your *right*, first station Reading West) flick over to page 140.

Did you know?

- Reading was the birthplace of Oscar-winning Kate Winslet, on 5 October 1975.

- Reading was nicknamed 'Biscuit Town' and the football team the 'Biscuit Men' because Huntley and Palmer (the 'most famous biscuit company in the world') were based here.

- The town hall holds a biscuit museum plus a full sized copy of the Bayeux Tapestry.

- In St Lawrence's churchyard there's a memorial to a man killed by a whirlwind at Reading station in 1840.

- The football team now play in the magnificent modern Madejski Stadium because a lowly sales chap, John Madejski, who worked for the Reading Evening Post once had an idea: what if car-for-sale ads had pictures with them? Result: multi-millionaire.

- T E Lawrence 'of Arabia' left his first draft of The Seven Pillars of Wisdom in Reading station waiting room in 1919 – not that much wisdom, clearly – and had to spend three months writing all 250,000 words again.

Royalty and Thames branches: does one come here orphan?

There are three open, plus one preserved, branches off the Great Western in the Thames Valley between Slough and Didcot and they are all recommended. All were opened between 1849 and 1873, all are short, and all make for the pretty riverside towns that the main line misses – although that probably tells you more about Brunel's obsession with making the GWR straight and flat than people's need to go boating. However, they all give access to fabulous riverside walks, charming towns and even better villages.

The SLOUGH TO WINDSOR* branch includes a Brunel bowstring bridge over the Thames, a fine brick viaduct across the meadows and the option of taking the rival Waterloo line's route back to London from Windsor and Eton Riverside station. It is just $2^1/_2$ miles long and next to where it curves south from the main line at **Slough** was once the British Orphan Asylum, a case of calling a spade a spade which certainly wouldn't happen nowadays. Odd, too, that the most privileged boys in Britain were at Eton on the same branch line.

Windsor, of course, is a hugely historic town with the royal castle: the oldest such continually inhabited one in the world. The terminus station is **Windsor and Eton Central***, suitably grand with an imposing entrance and with an exhibition about royalty and railways. Both rival railways managed to get their termini surprisingly close to the castle walls.

The MAIDENHEAD TO MARLOW* branch – known to railwaymen since the early days as the 'Marlow Donkey' – is the most charming of the lot to ride and curiously involves a reversal *en route*. The line swings away north from the west end of **Maidenhead** station, and the next stop **Furze Platt** is one of those places that sounds more interesting than it is, a sprawl of housing. **Cookham** is the next village, or group of three (Cookham Rise, Cookham Dean which is where the station is and Cookham on the river, about half a mile northeast which is prettier). There's a museum/gallery devoted to local painter Stanley Spencer (and the village would make a good address for dodgy accountants – The Books, Cookham).

We then rattle over the Thames on a
viaduct with good views each way and
roll into Buckinghamshire and **Bourne
End**✢. This station is worth a look –
clearly it was laid out with
double track (as
was the whole
branch so far,
but most of the second track has
been lifted) and from the sweep of
the platforms

Marlow
Bourne End
Cookham
Furze Platt
Maidenhead Slough

Windsor
& Eton
Riverside

London
Paddington

Windsor &
Eton Central   London Waterloo

it was an express route heading north. Instead it abruptly ends in
buffer stops. It was in fact the first railway to High Wycombe, opened
by the GWR, and we are about halfway on that former route which
became unimportant after Wycombe gained its own direct line to London.

The route – once much used by trains carrying locally made blotting
paper, hardly in demand by the trainload today – shut when the ink had
dried on the closure order in 1970. Stationery trains became stationary
trains, as it were.

But sharply curving west from the south end of Bourne End station is the
single-line Marlow branch, now a branch off a branch. It fact this tiny
route was initially called the Great Marlow Railway, the most ridiculous use
of the word 'Great' one can imagine, before the GWR took it over in 1897.

Our train creeps over a series of open crossings (gates being too much of
an investment) which gives us a good view from the low **Marlow Viaduct** of
the creek we are crossing. **Marlow** itself once had a pretty station like that
at Bourne End but today the route has been cut back to some sort of
ghastly bus sheltery thing. The Mayor of Marlow should be ritually thrown
in the Thames each year and pelted with soggy blotting paper until they
rebuild the old station. But the town is lovely and well worth exploring;
walk onwards as it were.

The **TWYFORD TO HENLEY**✢ branch takes off in a way that results in an oddly
curved Up slow platform. 'Mind the Gap' wouldn't be sufficient for a train
coming from Reading if it stopped short – the chasm could be several yards.

Next stop is **Wargrave** which has a village well to the east. It has a pretty
high street but no river frontage. The boating club was once alleged by

tabloid newspapers to be the setting for rather fruity goings-on: leading to jokes about rowlocks, oars and cox, no doubt. It turned out that the claim had been a website spoof and the behaviour of the boating types totally above board.

The village's other claim to fame was that suffragettes once burnt down the church, but they torched the wrong one. The vicar at the next place down the line had preached against women's emancipation. The protesters thought they were at the right place.

I wouldn't make any comments about women and map reading if you don't want to be burnt down yourself.

That next stop, **Shiplake**✝, is reached after a short trip through lovely meadows and a bridge across the Thames into Oxfordshire, plus another short viaduct over a brook.

Again it is slightly to one side of its village, this time to the west. Finally we reach **Henley-on-Thames**✝. The town has excellent pubs, lovely riverside walks, a rowing museum and upmarket shops. Crowded in Regatta Week (early July), and a tendency to elect big-haired MPs (recently Boris Johnson and Michael Heseltine) who might or might not have had fun at boating clubs.

The one preserved branch is from **CHOLSEY TO WALLINGFORD**, nicknamed locally as 'The Bunk' and which closed in 1959. It is operated by enthusiasts on a limited scale: for details call ☏ 01491 835067.

The GWR, and then British Railways and today's modern operators, are to be congratulated on saving these three little branch lines. Other routes in Britain would have high-handedly chopped off the branches – I can think of perhaps 100 examples – and expected people to drive to the former junction. They don't, they stay in their cars. Here the railway has even retained the facility for running rush-hour trains off the branches up to London instead of totally isolating the lines, and have helpful guards on trains (where others would have only drivers), thus stopping vandalism and fare-dodging. Well done, Brunel's heirs!

Reading to Swindon* : river run
(30mins, 42 miles)

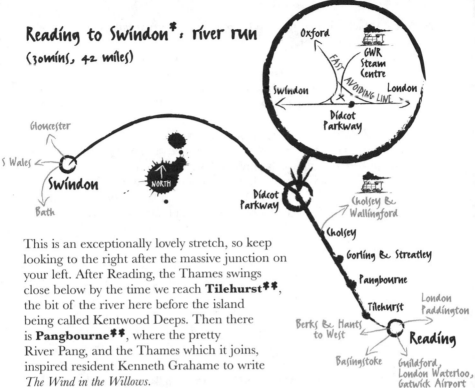

This is an exceptionally lovely stretch, so keep looking to the right after the massive junction on your left. After Reading, the Thames swings close below by the time we reach **Tilehurst****, the bit of the river here before the island being called Kentwood Deeps. Then there is **Pangbourne****, where the pretty River Pang, and the Thames which it joins, inspired resident Kenneth Grahame to write *The Wind in the Willows*.

We and the Thames are now heading up a most beautiful stretch of the wide river valley for the Goring Gap in the Chiltern Hills which both squeeze through. Didn't H G Wells, who cycled all around here, write a short story about the Gap being closed by an earthquake and in consequence being able to row a boat over a huge lake looking down on Oxford's dreaming spires?

After **Goring and Streatley****, yet another short branch takes off right at **Cholsey**, this time a short preserved railway to Wallingford. Oddly, you may think, as we are to come shortly to a huge collection of GWR steam locos and trains at Didcot which most of the time have nowhere to go.

Didcot Parkway* – the place was called Dudcote until the railway arrived – is the triangular junction for Oxford and Birmingham to the north (right). As we approach, a high-speed ladder of points lets fast trains access the rightmost tracks without slowing down much, and a fast avoiding line (the East Curve) sweeps away towards Oxford round behind the steam centre. But as you can see after the station, there's also a line allowing trains that called there still to go to Oxford (this oddly being called **Chester Line**

Junction, on the basis that the GWR could take you that far). So a smaller triangle within the big one.

There's always something to look at here – a train of light-armoured vehicles, or a set of freight locos waiting their turn, or activity in the steam centre beyond (which has replica broad-gauge tracks, working steam trains and even a piece of Brunel's bizarre Atmospheric Railway, detailed on page 120).

Beyond the station, another line curving from the direction we are going towards heads to Oxford, making a huge triangle on our right. There's also a massive power station, which draws in long and frequent coal trains – from the Midlands down through Oxford from Wales, and imports through Bristol on our route, and even the way we have come from Southampton docks via Reading.

Now there's a fast, empty run to Swindon, with all the charming GWR branch lines and stations on this stretch sadly long closed. The main thing to look out for is the White Horse carved on a hill on the left. Unlike most of the others in Britain, this is truly ancient (about 3,000 years old). The broad valley of the River Ock we are joining is therefore known as the Vale of the White Horse, which sounds better than Ockdale. All the way along we skirt between the Berkshire Downs to the left and the hills to the north.

Swindon was the main base of the GWR and the railway made the village into a thriving town, taking the population from 2,500 in 1841 to 33,000 50 years later. The massive railway works were the key to this: hundreds of locomotives, and thousands of wagons and coaches were built and maintained here. Some 14,000 people were employed at what was for more than a century the most famous railway works in the world.

One of the great railway engineers here at the start of the 20th century was George Jackson Churchward, born in 1857, who designed and built at

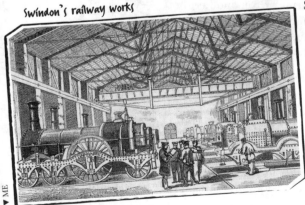

Swindon's railway works

Swindon many of the GWR's greatest locomotives including the record-breaking *City of Truro*. He was killed by one too, crossing the line on foot in fog in his retirement in 1933. This former Mayor of Swindon was buried in nearby Christ Church where a black marble memorial tells the story.

▲ ME

It turns out the 76-year-old was checking a defective rail joint he'd spotted as he crossed, which was promptly fixed: even in death he served the GWR.

Churchward's greatest triumph was the Star class, the first being *North Star* in 1906. One of the first locos on the GWR had been *Morning Star*, built by Robert Stephenson in 1838 to get Brunel out of a hole (he was no good at locos), so this carried on that theme. The very last steam locomotive built for British Railways was built

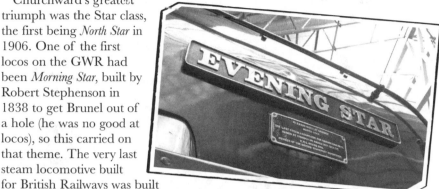

here too, appropriately *Evening Star*, named in 1960 and still running in preservation today. (Incidentally, when Chittaranjan works produced India's last steam loco in 1972, it was called *The Last Star*, surely an affectionate nod to the GWR.)

Swindon works finally closed in 1986. Much of it was demolished, though part was made into a shopping centre and another bit into a railway museum called Steam – encapsulating a national trend from heavy industry to retail and heritage. Meanwhile Swindon has thrived as a new technology, retail and overspill housing centre although not, frankly, as a tourist destination.

In the 19th century, Swindon was much hated by railway passengers because an unwise deal had been made with caterers that all trains had to stop there for ten minutes (food on the trains had not yet been thought of). And the food was just awful. As Charles Dickens said: 'The tea is indistinguishable from the soup, the soup is indistinguishable from the tea, and the sandwiches seem to be filled with sawdust.' The place was nicknamed 'Swindlem'. In the end the railway company had to buy the caterers out.

And the 'Swindon disease' referred to rampant asbestosis caused to workers and their families when this material – not then known to be deadly – blew around the loco works like snow. The apprentices made snowballs out of it, and not only did they die from it but children who sat on their knees when they came home from work died too.

Some things have improved a lot.

Swindon to Bristol*: a plunge into Bath

(45mins, 41 miles)

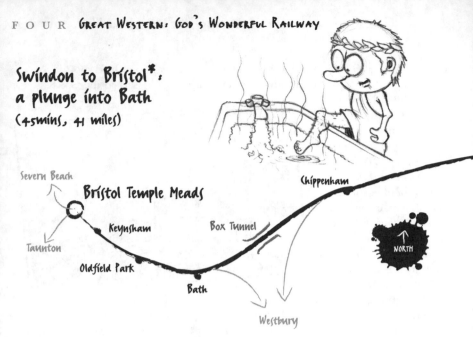

After Swindon, the Great Western divides like the trunk of a tree. Just after the station, the **GOLDEN VALLEY LINE** takes off right (northwest) through the Cotswolds for Stroud, Gloucester and Cheltenham (recommended, more on page 144). A few miles further the greatest split takes place where the **SOUTH WALES LINE** takes off to our right at a place called Wootton Bassett. It races west for the Severn Tunnel (that route isn't described in detail) while we head southwest in increasingly pretty and rewarding surroundings.

The infant River Avon starts winding under the train's route – for we have crossed a watershed from the Thames catchment to one heading west for Bristol, as we are. If you have ever wondered why there's another Avon at Stratford, it might be because the Welsh for river is still *Afon*. I wonder; if

the immigrant English pushing out the Ancient Britons heard them calling their river 'avon', did they accidentally end up saying River River?

Be that as it may, having crested a gentle summit after Swindon, we're now going downhill fast. We speed through closed stations such as Christian Malford and then the open one of **Chippenham**. A line to Trowbridge takes off left before we arrive at one of Brunel's masterpieces, **Box Tunnel** (and yes, the signal box at the now-vanished station here was known as Box Box).

This was one of his daring strokes in his scheme to link London and Bristol (his aim was New York, as it turned out). His river-

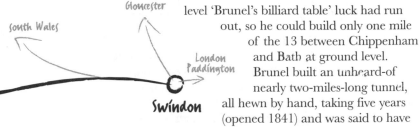

Gloucester

South Wales

London
Paddington

Swindon

level 'Brunel's billiard table' luck had run out, so he could build only one mile of the 13 between Chippenham and Bath at ground level. Brunel built an unheard-of nearly two-miles-long tunnel, all hewn by hand, taking five years (opened 1841) and was said to have cost the lives of 100 men, with many more maimed. The west portal is particularly grand, and as magnificent as when Brunel completed it.

The tunnel descends at a 1 in 100 gradient, (whereas before Swindon the gradients were remarkably gentle, often 1 in 1,320). MPs debating its construction warned that trains would emerge out of control at an undreamt-of 120mph (which would surely suffocate everyone aboard) and that no-one would dare enter it. Trains on this route routinely do that speed today.

The portal architecture is as grand as a route approaching Georgian Bath should be. It is spacious inside, partly because it was built for bigger broad-gauge trains. There are many legends associated with this tunnel. One is that the sun shines right through it only on Brunel's birthday: 9 April. Others insist it does so from 6 to 8 April.

Another persistent rumour is that a secret tunnel branches off in the middle of it and inside the hills there is a depot with Britain's 'strategic reserve' of steam locomotives, all wrapped and greased against rust, stockpiled during the Cold War.

This would seem steam-nut wishful thinking, and there is no junction halfway through the tunnel (although some steam nuts were once arrested trying to break through the wall halfway through). It is the steam equivalent of King Arthur slumbering under Camelot waiting for the nation's hour of need.

But there *is* an until-recently secret town under these hills, yes complete with its own hospital, telephone exchange, dormitories, etc. It was one of those Cold-War things, and it *did* have its own railway tunnel entrance, to the right of the main line one at the London end.

The short **Middle Tunnel** follows then, at Bathampton, just before Bath, the cross-country **WESSEX MAIN LINE** route from both Weymouth or Southampton/Salisbury (both recommended) trails in from the left.

Bath Spa★★ is incomparably pretty, its golden stone houses set out in Georgian elegant orderliness to catch the neatest aspect of the surrounding hills, and made famous by the Romans,

Beau Nash and Jane Austen (who despite using Bath as a setting, rather disliked the society there). Some of its beauty can be seen from the train, which having approached through suitably grand landscaping luckily emerges on a high level near the typically spacious GWR station.

A short run through **Oldfield Park** and **Keynsham** takes us to **Bristol Temple Meads✱**, which we reach after a long tunnel then a short one. In case you're wondering, the name means 'meadows in the Bristol parish of Temple' (as in Knights Templar,

Da Vinci Code fans will want to know). The reason why the great station is built on a curve is historical. There were two separate routes, both built by Brunel, which met at a right angle and with their own adjacent stations. In fact the Bristol and Exeter Railway, from the south, opened on 14 June 1841, and the first through trains from London arrived at the other station two weeks later.

Eventually, in the 1870s, the Great Western and Midland railways jointly built the station on the curve, leaving Brunel's original Tudor-styled station to become a goods depot, then a car park, then to house the Empire and Commonwealth Museum. It is a fine structure, rightly listed as Grade I to preserve it, said to be the oldest railway terminus building in the world.

The current station is beautiful, with many Tudor arches on its curving site, and there's a brilliant pub at Bonaparte's bar. Credit where credit's due.

For Brunel fans, Bristol also has his Clifton Suspension Bridge (more on page 131), a daring and spectacularly located bridge over the Avon Gorge (designed by IKB but not finished in his lifetime) and one of his great ships, the SS *Great Britain*, wonderfully rescued, restored and displayed within walking distance of the station.

The fact that this vessel, the first screw-driven passenger ship in the world, was finished in 1843 shows that Brunel was thinking of the Great Western as just part of a through route to New York.

You can go part of that distance on the **SEVERN BEACH LINE**, a 45-minute ten-stop suburban route to the north side of the Avon's exit into the Bristol Channel, with much industry at the end of it. Not particularly recommended.

Bristol to Exeter, Somerset Levels and record runs (1hr, 75 miles)

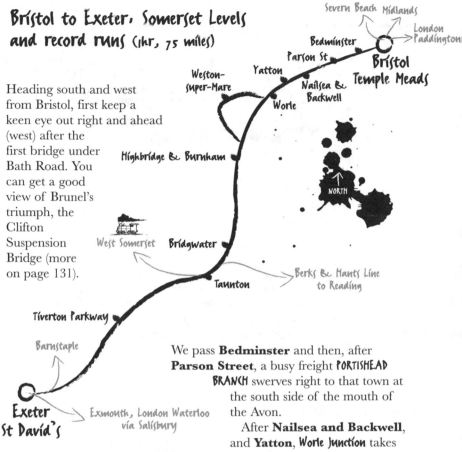

Heading south and west from Bristol, first keep a keen eye out right and ahead (west) after the first bridge under Bath Road. You can get a good view of Brunel's triumph, the Clifton Suspension Bridge (more on page 131).

We pass **Bedminster** and then, after **Parson Street**, a busy freight PORTISHEAD BRANCH swerves right to that town at the south side of the mouth of the Avon.

After **Nailsea and Backwell**, and **Yatton**, Worle Junction takes route for the seaside town of **Weston-super-Mare** right. This resort station is on a loop which rejoins the main line four miles later at Uphill Junction. We speed almost due south, on mostly level and straight track, to **Highbridge and Burnham** and **Bridgwater** (like Bristol, up a muddy creek from the Bristol Channel).

Coming up is Cogload Junction, a flyover where we, that is Down trains coming from Bristol do the flying, to allow the BERKS & HANTS LINE, which we had parted company with way back at Reading, to rejoin – or leave in the opposite direction – without conflict. Next to it (on the right) is part of the Taunton and Bridgwater Canal, which the GWR once owned. Note the pillboxes from World War II which sought to make the canal a defensive line, near where we cross under the M5 motorway. On our left the River Tone coming off the Somerset Levels meanders, and sometimes floods.

When we reach **Taunton** the canal, however, ends abruptly at Firepool Lock on the left before the station. It was brutally truncated by a railway goods depot and the Great Western Hotel being built on its route westwards.

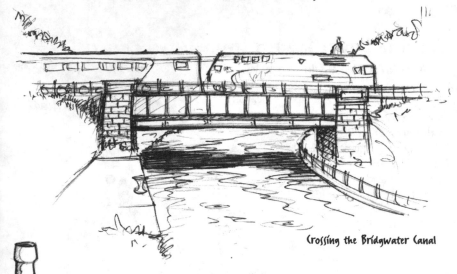

Crossing the Bridgwater Canal

Just outside Taunton going west is Norton Fitzwarren, famous for three things, two of them pleasant and one not.

First is cider, or *zoider* as *Zomerzet* toypes might call it. Second is the junction for the **WEST SOMERSET RAILWAY**, Britain's longest preserved steam line, which runs 23 miles northwest along the base of the Quantock Hills and reaches the seaside at Watchet, continuing to Minehead. Sadly, for some ridiculous reason, the trains don't often run into Taunton (except for main-line excursions) but start from Bishops Lydeard, which is connected by bus. Stations of the WSR include Stogumber and Blue Anchor, which hints at some of its real charm.

Third was a very strange accident here in 1940. Four tracks extended west from Taunton to here, and then the outer slow or relief tracks merged with the middle two fast lines. A night sleeper train running in the difficult conditions of wartime blackout set off west from Taunton, the driver of *King George VI* – named after the reigning monarch – clearly thinking he was on the main line. He must have misread the signal at the platform end showing which way the points at Taunton were set. Having made this one mistake, he consequently read the green oil lamps and tilted signal arms set for that parallel line. In fact he was on the slow line, which would run out at Norton Fitzwarren.

As a safety precaution, when such a route is signalled to a stop by yellow and then red lights, as it indeed was, a set of trap points directs the train away from the main line into a short siding to prevent a two-train pile-up.

While this may have been useful for overrunning slow-speed goods trains, or runaway wagons, for a full-tilt express it turned out to be utterly disastrous. The driver of the sleeper was virtually at the end of the track when to his horror he saw a mail train overhauling him on the main line. He knew in an instant that his train was doomed.

It overturned and 27 people were killed. The guard of the overtaking train heard strange sounds – which turned out to be ballast, the large stones under the tracks, thrown up by the derailing sleeper alongside, hitting his compartment. Under the 'stop-and-examine' rule, he applied the brake and the train halted perhaps half a mile further on. Having found nothing wrong, he allowed his train to proceed completely unaware of the ghastly disaster unfolding just out of earshot.

Oddly – given that very few accidents have ever happened to sleeper trains in this country – another fatal accident occurred with a sleeper near here in 1978 when 12 people died as a result of a fire, the good news is that both kinds of accidents are now pretty well impossible. Sleepers are much more fireproof and have smoke alarms throughout, with more attendants. And the exit doors are not locked.

The remains of that truncated canal – the Grand Western – are on our left, and together with the M5 motorway we often run close together on the way south; three eras of transport, as it were, sharing one route. The Grand Western, overtaken by history, never got south of Tiverton; luckily the Great Western did.

Soon the superbly sited Wellington Monument, an obelisk you can climb up inside, can be seen on the hills to our left. We pass through the town of Wellington, which has lost its station, and though we have been following the valley of the River Tone since Cogload Junction, we now climb steeply out of it up **Whiteball Bank** with 1 in 80 and 1 in 90 gradients ('Brunel's billiard table' now forgotten). It was here that railway history of a better sort was made on 9 May 1904 when the then-new loco *City of Truro* headed downhill with a London-bound train at a staggering 102mph.

Although verified by only one timekeeper, not the officially required two, it is widely accepted that this was the first train in the world to reach 100mph. The famous engine was on display in museums for much of the 20th century but was thrice restored to running order to delight rail fans, which she is doing as I write, more than a century after her moment of glory. In fact she ran down this very bank on the centenary of her record run, although at a more sedate speed. Not bad for a 100-year-old lady.

In steam days, trains struggling to the top of Whiteball Bank slowed to a measly 30–40mph; goods trains required 'bankers' shoving from behind on the long slope. Today we barely notice it.

Whiteball Summit, 392ft, and **tunnel** (1,092yds, note the house perched right above) takes us into Devon. After **Tiverton Parkway**, we then join the valley of the River Culm, near Cullompton, before this river joins the southbound River Exe for the last few miles into Exeter (you can see the rivers' junction to our left as we cross a girder bridge). In fact the truculent Exe, meandering around this wide valley, sometimes gets a little too close, being prone to flooding and damaging the tracks. I once travelled down to Penzance where torrential rain fell all weekend. On the return, the train was running across a causeway on a vast, swirling lake. I was lucky: the next day the track was submerged and trains halted. The reason is the high ground of Exmoor, first of the three great West Country moors, which lies to the north and catches Atlantic rain clouds in sometimes massive quantities.

Joining us trailing in from the right over the river at Cowley Bridge Junction is the long TARKA LINE branch from Barnstaple on the north Devon coast (see page 146). Nice and noisy for the Tudor-styled Cowley Bridge pub, famously very close to the tracks on the left at the junction. You can see those both better on your return.

We reach **Exeter St David's** – note a broad-gauge goods shed on the right – which boasts being the home of the Met Office. Hence all that rain, I suppose. Here another line, misnamed the WEST OF ENGLAND MAIN LINE, diverges to our left which would, eventually, lead us back to London Waterloo by a completely different route (see page 246).

In the privately owned railways before the 1948 nationalisation, many cities had a choice of routes and stations, an expensive duplication which was ruthlessly pruned away. When privatisation returned in the late 20th century, choice would usually be one of operator on the same route – such as two companies' trains operating from Bristol to here as well as First Great Western. Except at Exeter, which kept its two separate routes to London and stations, ours being Exeter St David's, Waterloo's being Exeter Central.

The Waterloo route, run by the rival London & South Western, however, lost its onward westward line to Plymouth, which turned off west at that Cowley Bridge Junction we recently passed (so rival Plymouth-bound trains could pass each other on that short stretch). This was a mistake, strategically, for that left our onward route in the hands of Brunel's occasionally very dodgy Dawlish seaside run, as we shall soon see. An inland route would have been useful for diversions in times of storm and landslide. But then their mistake was our scenic gain. It's the Exe factor!

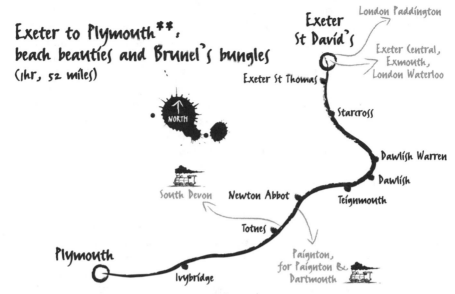

Exeter to Plymouth**,
beach beauties and Brunel's bungles
(1hr, 52 miles)

London Paddington

Exeter
St David's

Exeter Central,
Exmouth,
London Waterloo

Exeter St Thomas

NORTH

Starcross

Dawlish Warren

Dawlish

South Devon   Newton Abbot

Teignmouth

Totnes

Plymouth

Ivybridge

Paignton,
for Paignton &
Dartmouth

This section is highly scenic – one of the best stretches in the country – and
it is recommended to sit on the left. Our train gathers speed through
Exeter St Thomas* and a view to the left gives us a glimpse of the simply
superb Gothic masterpiece that is Exeter Cathedral (the square towers, not
the tall spire). Then we're following the west side of the Exe Estuary. After
we run on an embankment between Cockwood Harbour and the Exe,
watch out at **Starcross*** for the tower on the right, the most visible sign of
Brunel's ill-fated Atmospheric Railway (see box on page 108).

Soon there are views across to the seaside town of Exmouth (and yes,
what with Ply*mouth*, Fal*mouth* and Sid*mouth* there's a river theme here. The
Celtic equivalent is *Aber*- or *Inver*-, which can also mean 'confluence of two
rivers.' And a geographical point: whilst southern Devon and Cornwall is
all great estuaries and harbours giving on to the English Channel, perfect
for messing about in boats but useless for surfing, the north of those
counties is rugged, surfable, exposed to the Atlantic and best
avoided by sailors except during southerly storms).

We are soon arriving at **Dawlish
Warren****, a sand-duney place and the
beginning of a great seaside stretch. Actually,
at Dawlish the railway *is* the seaside, which
on a pleasant day is, well, pleasant, giving
wonderful opportunities for seaside/train
pictures. Stormy weather, however, sometimes
causes problems for track and trains, with waves
breaking over the carriages. As remarked at
Exeter, closing the inland route to Plymouth
wasn't such a brilliant idea.

But it has to be admitted that Brunel miraculously achieved an almost level route between Exeter and Teignmouth, separated by hilly country, by using the two river estuaries and the foreshore, but the latter has proved a continual nuisance for the maintenance crews. You can't build a railway along the foot of storm-lashed cliffs without a constant battle to shore up the track. In fact in the 1930s, the GWR bought land and designed a line cutting inland, but the war put a stop to that.

To see how serious it can be, note that points (crossovers) are installed at Dawlish Warren and Teignmouth to let trains run on only the track furthest from the sea during storms. Normal train-detecting track circuits cannot be used here because the lines are, from time to time, deluged by waves breaking over them.

The engineer's loss, by Brunel's bungle (or creative cheating to save costs), is our gain. It is an exceptional, exquisite pleasure on a nice day to be running right along the beach. **Dawlish**✸✸ may have lost much of its beach to the railway, but then the bucket-and-spade brigade have been carried there by train. There would have been no resort without the railway.

We thread through the cliffs in short tunnels (the building of one of these uncovered a secret smugglers' tunnel) like a needle heading through gathered cloth, reaching another -*mouth* place, **Teignmouth**✸ (pronounced 'Tinmuth', note a World War II pillbox on the left as we leave the seaside), and follow the Teign Valley, then swing south to **Newton Abbot**. After that the **RIVIERA LINE**✸ to Torquay and Paignton (recommended, leads to the **PAIGNTON AND DARTMOUTH STEAM RAILWAY**✸✸, see page 150 for both) goes on south while we diverge right (west). This is the real Devon countryside: thatched cottages, charming millside streams, apples, cider and milk cows for cream teas, as we climb steeply to **Dainton Summit and Tunnel** and then down again the other side.

Totnes✸ brings us to the River Dart with yet another charming steam railway branch, the **SOUTH DEVON RAILWAY**✸✸, leading off on the right (north) to Buckfastleigh (its station is on the right just before ours, with a footbridge across the river linking them. Totnes is also reachable by boat from Dartmouth on the sea up this prettiest of valleys, when the tide permits, so there are excursions which would take in both Devonish steam railways if you wish. Totnes also has a castle, pretty shops and a vaguely hippie atmosphere (if you wear sandals with tie-dye skirts and use joss sticks and patchouli oil you are called 'TQ9ish' locally, which is Totnes's postcode). And a terrific cheese shop. In a very different era, Totnes station was bombed in October 1942, killing two people.

There's now a decent run to Plymouth, starting with a long climb up **Rattery Bank** with Dartmoor's hills visible on our right. **Marley Tunnel** (867yds) just before Brent station is one of several on the system that were totally unnecessary but were for visual reasons, insisted on by the local landowner. The summit comes about a mile after a viaduct at a place called **Wrangaton** and at 455ft is the highest point on the whole line – or to put it another way, about 100ft higher above the English Channel than the tunnel to France dives below it.

There are little towns such as **Ivybridge*̃**, which we pass high on a curving viaduct. On the next big viaduct, the curving one at Blatchford, (and certainly at other ones in Cornwall), you may notice old piers as if another viaduct stood alongside. They did – Brunel built in wood with stone bases, to save money in this frankly poor end of the country, but of course they didn't last for ever and stone replacements were built alongside.

Down to Plymouth and the Plym Estuary on our left, then we pass **Laira railway depot** in a triangle formed by a line down to the docks, before reaching **Plymouth** station after the short **Mutley Tunnel**. The city is a funny mixture of historical – Plymouth Hoe down by the sea, where Francis Drake finished his game of bowls while the Spanish Armada neared, being well worth exploring – and the frankly ugly or indifferent, the place having been bombed to hell in World War II (so you see that driver observing the blackout in the accident at Taunton was right to be worried about the Luftwaffe this far west).

I do recommend reading the box on the Royal Albert Bridge here (see below) because you will want to look at the views when crossing it, not at the book.

BRIDGED BY BRILLIANT BRUNEL: THE PUZZLES BEHIND CLIFTON AND TAMAR

The **Royal Albert Bridge**, which leaps so dramatically across the Tamar from Devon to Cornwall, has often been described as Brunel's masterpiece, and so it is – and more.

It was opened by Prince Albert – Queen Victoria's other half – and named after him, but this bridge is really Brunel's memorial, as 'I K Brunel Engineer 1859' proudly emblazoned in huge letters on the portals shows.

It was also Brunel's swansong. He was dying as it was

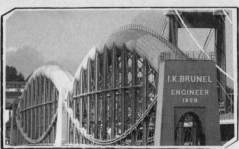

completed, and was drawn carefully over it lying on a flatbed truck.

It's a bridge of triumphs, daring, genius and puzzles, ugly to some eyes, beautiful to others, but in-your-face engineering that gets it noticed because it is so odd.

First, the very odd bowstring shape, and the description 'railway suspension bridge' (it is the only one in the world) which have often puzzled people, including me. After all, at first glance it doesn't look like a classic suspension bridge with the usual drooping cables between towers holding everything up, but more like an arch bridge, like Sydney Harbour Bridge.

But then it isn't that either, for the arches don't reach the ground at either side, but stop at the towers on each portal.

Consider a normal suspension bridge with the familiar two towers and saggy cables shape, looking like a very droopy letter 'M' from the sides, as with the more recent Tamar road bridge alongside, or the Golden Gate in California. The bridge deck in those cases hangs from the huge cables, and the weight is carried to the top of the towers and down the other side to massive anchors in the rock at either end. Cut those cables and the bridge falls down: the towers can't possibly hold all that sideways force.

Brunel knew full well how to build suspension bridges, as we saw with his elegant Clifton Suspension Bridge back at Bristol. There the cables are anchored in caves in the cliffs of the gorge.

Here at the Tamar the problems were very different and needed a new technology to be invented. The railway needed to curve south at either end, particularly in Cornwall, and yet the bridge had to be right here between those hills because the admiralty had insanely insisted on 100ft headroom for ships (sailing warships were becoming obsolete and the height was never really needed). As the approaches curved, there could be no in-line cables from the shore, holding back the forces of the suspension bridge, and nothing to anchor them to either.

A classic iron arch or arches bridge was not possible either, because the Admiralty wanted the space under the train deck to be clear.

Brunel's brilliant masterstroke was to build those massive elliptical tubes (made of wrought iron, steel not being easily available yet; if Brunel had steel, he would have surely done it in one jump, not two). Those massive bow-shaped tubes which arch across from tower to tower in two spans don't hold the bridge up, as the Sydney Harbour Bridge arch does. They hold the towers *apart*, so that the suspension girders and ties underneath can hold up the track. If you look closely you can see the classic line of suspension bridge chains beneath them.

Those chains (made of very long links, not a chain in the

usual sense) themselves are part of a triple puzzle. They are, largely, the chains made for the beautiful **Clifton Suspension Bridge** in Bristol that Brunel had earlier designed (and well worth a visit because of the road bridge's spectacular Avon Gorge location). Because of financial problems, that project had stalled and was not completed in his lifetime, so these chains, standing idle for 20 years, were used to speed things up on the Tamar. So what holds up the Clifton Suspension Bridge? Oddly, when it was finally restarted in 1860, yet another of Brunel's wonderful bridges – the **Hungerford Footbridge**

▶ ME

Hungerford Bridge, 1846

across the Thames in London – was being demolished to make way for the railway bridge to Charing Cross from the South Bank. So *both* Brunel's most famous bridges are held up by the wrong, secondhand chains. Bizarre.

By the way, the Clifton bridge was well known for

suicides and has had Samaritans' phones at each end. But in 1885 a woman called Sarah Ann Henley, 22, jumped off, not realising her hooped crinolene dress would act as a parachute, which it did. She was rescued by a man in a rowing boat and lived well into her 80s. There is perhaps an argument for making all depressives wear hooped crinolines. Even more macabre is the fact that Clifton suicides don't drown. They suffocate in the mud beneath.

Oddly, the Clifton bridge isn't completely flat because Brunel realised this would look wonky because of the landscape, so its deck slopes a few feet from one end to the other, so it *looks* flat.

But here, back at the Tamar, problems were dealt with more dramatically: how to erect thousands of tons of metal 100ft up in mid-air across a deep river they could not span in one go?

The two monstrous 1,060-ton spans were assembled ashore. Meanwhile the central pillar had been built on the river bed by sinking a massive vertical bottomless cylinder with pressurised air chambers in it down to the bottom. Men in the near-dark and the mud dug out the river bed down to solid rock under these infernal and dangerous conditions. Some gave their lives or health, as the 'bends' – the divers' disease then not understood – took hold. Massive iron rings were added to the underwater tower as it sank towards the bedrock, until the central pier stood strong above the waves.

The iron spans were floated out on pontoons to align with the bases of the stone piers, beneath their final positions, and then raised by huge hydraulic rams, the masonry being built foot by foot until the massive height was reached. I wouldn't have liked to have stood under the bridge while 1,060 tons of ironwork was jacked up, but Brunel knew what he was doing.

A series of high iron spans on the curved approaches – eight in Devon, nine in Cornwall – also needed high masonry piers. The total cost was only £225,000, Brunel having saved perhaps

£100,000 by making it single track. In fact, impoverished Cornwall thought it would have to settle for no bridge at all, and the Act of Parliament provided for a train ferry to cart the carriages and wagons back and forth across the Tamar. Brunel had other ideas, but he had to keep costs down.

There are certainly no frills. At a time when classical pillars, frilly lanterns and filigree finials were added to almost everything from bridges to public toilets, this has a magnificent, modern muscularity. It is pure function that cannot date.

While Clifton bridge is an elegant Keira Knightley of a bridge, the Tamar is a Schwarzenegger bridge. But it worked then, in 1859, and despite 150 years of increasingly heavy trains and seaside gales, it still works. Nothing like it had been done before, or since.

Brilliant, Brunel.

Plymouth to Penzance**: viaduct Viagra and mineral mileposts (2hrs, 79 miles)

Leaving Plymouth, we immediately cross a curving viaduct which was the newest part of a three-sided triangle – the original Plymouth Millbay terminal was down a line to our left, and trains to Cornwall would reverse there before the curve we are travelling on was

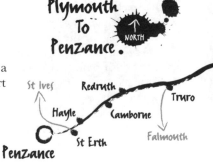

built. You can see the old piers in a park to our left with a completely
bonkers sculpture on top of them – well, you may like it. Or it could be
some ship part that never made it to the scrapyard.

Millbay services were abandoned abruptly after the city suffered terrible
World War II bombing. Among the victims of the carnage at Millbay in
April 1941 were 32 railway horses burnt to death in their stables.

By the way, as we started that curve on the viaduct, we crossed a road
called Pennycomequick Hill, the district at the top being known as
Pennycomequick. This charming name could be one of three things: a call
to a girl; a very profitable piece of land; or in the ancient British language
pen-y-com-cuick, meaning 'head of the valley of the creek'.

We climb through **Devonport** and, after a short tunnel, only about 30
seconds later **Dockyard** (which partly explains what the wartime bombers
were looking for – look left for warships, etc) followed by **Keyham** on what
is clearly an intensive city service (built to beat trams). There's a branch
sharply back into the HM Dockyards (guarded by machine-gun-toting
sailors). Then after a long girder bridge which once crossed a muddy creek,
since filled in, a branch line leaving to our right does a very odd thing. It
crosses underneath us twice within a mile, having first had a station to rival
our **St Budeaux Ferry Road** in the form of very nearby St Budeaux
Victoria Road. It is more evidence of once-rival companies – the branch
was a London and South Western route which once went separately but
alongside all the way back to Plymouth, the connection here being made as
a wartime emergency which became permanent.

But we will soon be far too entranced with the coming Tamar Estuary
and the spectacular **Royal Albert Bridge**✷✷ to notice this track, the
TAMAR VALLEY LINE✷✷, sneaking under this end of the bridge
and heading for 14 enchanting miles up to Gunnislake.
Keep that for another day
(see page 151).

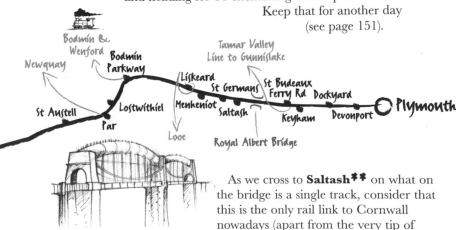

As we cross to **Saltash**✷✷ on what on
the bridge is a single track, consider that
this is the only rail link to Cornwall
nowadays (apart from the very tip of
that Gunnislake branch), so if anything happens to either of the lines we
are running on, them thar Cornish trains are going to stop in Cornwall!

The road bridge alongside was completed in 1961, but as at many estuaries, such as the Forth and Severn, for many decades previously car ferries continued while the trains could cross. You can still see the slipways here far below.

Along this next stretch is the remains of a station by the intriguing name of Defiance. It served a naval engineering base, *HMS Defiance.*

Just how hilly and riven with river valleys this next part is can be judged by the fact that there were originally 26 viaducts between Plymouth and St Austell, a number reduced only by two by a diversion to a more inland route at one point. Even so, Brunel seemed to be on viaduct Viagra the way these things sprouted all over the shop.

Indeed we rapidly cross the 28-arch **Nottar Viaduct**✢✢ and then the 17-arch **St Germans Viaduct**✢✢ before reaching **St Germans**✢. Now we have safely crossed the viaduct, I can tell you that two days after the Cornwall Railway opened, a train fell off the previous wooden trestle here and ended up upside down in the mud of the creek, killing three crew members. St German was a 5th-century bishop/warrior, but a Cornish saint and place names become increasingly strange – one village even revered St Disen for a century, before finding out it was supposed to be St Denis. You could get bed and breakfast in an old GWR carriage at the station here last time I looked.

Next station is **Menheniot**, after two short viaducts. Look out after milepost 263 for signs of Britain's most insane branch line. Another three viaducts lead us into **Liskeard**✢, with the **LOOE VALLEY LINE**✢✢ hidden way down below by the third one. This bonkers branch is supposed to go south to the sea but takes off northeast from the station, descending fast, does a horseshoe curve back under the viaduct we have just crossed and having wandered round a nice bit of countryside does a curve round to head *north again* under the next **Moorswater Viaduct**!

Here it has reached what was once a completely separate railway from Moorswater to Looe, at a level much lower than the main line, and *now* it can reverse and head off down to the seaside, a journey of just $8^3/4$ miles in total. You'll have to travel it to believe it.

We climb to a summit near the closed station of Doublebois, then across the long **St Pinnock Viaduct**✢ to **Bodmin Parkway**. This was originally called Bodmin Road, but both styles of name indicate that it was nowhere near the town it purported to serve – it's about three miles away. The county town languished with little development as a result, and although it eventually gained a branch line from here (now a steam railway, the **BODMIN & WENFORD**) it never really prospered and Truro took over as Cornwall's county town. Bodmin has meanwhile been famous for a large lunatic asylum and a *Hound of the Baskervilles*-style creature apparently often spotted on Bodmin Moor, the 'Beast of Bodmin'. This, the second of the three great West Country moors, lies north of the main line.

Much of the branch traffic was china clay, a massive local industry without which glossy magazines and shiny book covers, such as the one you're holding, wouldn't be possible. It is a form of broken-down granite, unlikely though that seems. The branch to Bodmin General in the town gave eventual access, after a reversal, to the picturesque branch from Wadebridge to Padstow on the north coast, still a terrific country walk. The steam railway should reopen all the way to that popular fishing port if they want tourists to flock there.

Next we descend to the beautiful wooded valley of the River Fowey (pronounced 'Foy') and the station of **Lostwithiel**✱✱. We cross the river after the station; the town is across the river on our right, the road on this side being called Brunel Quays.

Notice we are now in the 19th century technologically – with signal boxes linked by levers and long wires (not carrying electricity!) to semaphore signals (the ones with waving arms). I suppose it'll all get ripped out one day as it has been elsewhere, but meanwhile it works, it's safe, it gives people jobs and it's charming.

On our left after the station a branch goes off down the valley to the oh-so-pretty town at the start of the estuary which by West Country logic should be Foweymouth, but is just Fowey. Sadly, the station there closed in 1965 and the main rail traffic today is china clay.

Next is **Par**, the junction for the long branch to the surfer's nirvana on the north coast, Newquay, called the ATLANTIC COAST LINE (see page 153). There are docks here and you get a glimpse of that harbour to our left.

Then we reach **St Austell**✱, sometimes lazily pronounced 'Snozzle'. It has become better known in recent years thanks to the domes of the Eden Project nearby (T 01726 811911). If you see strange-shaped hills, however, they are probably remains of china clay workings.

Soon, climbing hard, we cross the 206yd St Austell Viaduct✱, and look sharp ahead left to see another – there are around seven more in the switchback route to Truro. On the way, after about five miles we cross the young River Fal heading for still-distant Falmouth (it is under the second of two nearby medium-length viaducts).

The cathedral city of **Truro**✱✱ features two massive viaducts on its approaches, giving us splendid views over rooftops and gardens. The station serves the MARITIME LINE✱ branch for Falmouth from the leftmost bay platforms, and such were the crowds of holidaymakers that once used this service that two footbridges were, unusually, provided between the platforms. The 300 miles from London post is on the opposite Up platform.

Soon afterwards, there is the short **Highertown Tunnel** and the line for Falmouth diverges left at **PENWITHERS JUNCTION** (or rather we swerve right and it doesn't): we head on over **Penwithers Viaduct**.

Although many people think of Cornwall as charmingly rural, the land around these last few miles of the GWR was once heavily mined for tin, copper, lead and arsenic. The evidence is all around in ravaged, lumpy landscape, lost branch lines, old engine houses and chimney stacks. One of these last is at Wheal Busy, close to the tracks on the left before **Redruth***, which station follows after a short tunnel. You may see the Cornish black-and-white flag flying from the Town Hall or Mining Exchange. Here, as in the mining areas of Wales, the nonconformist chapels were, and are, much in evidence, some of them huge.

We curve around on a viaduct and all the while we can see on a large hill called Carn Brea a spectacular monument to the Peninsular War (the Spanish, not Cornish Peninsula). The next stop, **Camborne**, was also once heavily industrial and the surroundings suitably grim. In the 1860s, these two towns were booming with 49 mines operating; in fact Camborne is still home to a School of Mines for pitmen from around the world.

Another great Cornish theme is the prehistoric stone circles and burial mounds. In this, as in 100 other things, it is like its French counterpart sticking out into the same sea, Brittany. (Both places have similar place names, Tre-something and Lizardieu, for example, because both used the same language, more or less. Both used to send trainloads of fresh vegetables such as new potatoes to their capital cities. Both adjoin a less rugged region – Devon and Normandy – that produces endless cream, cheese and cider. Both have rocky coves, black flags, lifeboat heroes and rugged seafarers – one could go on!)

We now descend from this mineral-rich plateau the four miles down to **Hayle****, where we cross the town on a viaduct with fine views of the harbour, rapidly reaching the junction station for the **ST IVES BRANCH, St Erth***. In fact it was hopefully called St Ives Road until the branch to that arty town opened in 1877 (see page 154).

We run down to the south coast in a few minutes, reaching the beach at Marazion****, whence we can see the spectacular island of St Michael's Mount, a Cornish version of Brittany's Mont St Michel. Marazion meant 'little market' but it sounds lovelier.

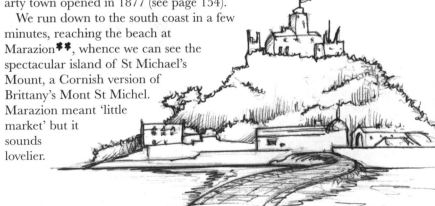

Now there's a short level run round the bay to the terminus at
Penzance✦, stopped by the most westerly signals in England.

In southerly storms and at high tide, waves here in Mounts Bay crash
right onto the trains. Here we must get off. Trains for the little St Ives
branch, for distant Midlands and Scottish cities, sleeper cars for London –
they all have to start from here, the end of the line. For us, it's been 325
miles 37 chains from Paddington (the mileposts showing slightly more
because of later deviations). Or 21 miles fewer if we came via the Berks &
Hants line (that is, through Westbury, not Bristol). Either way, after milepost
326 and a half, it's time to stretch our legs.

A walk up the pier to our left, as you explore the town, shows by the old
tracks you could once in fact have caught a train from a few hundred feet
further towards the sea. But only if you were a lobster, crab or pilchard…

THE NIGHT RIVIERA SLEEPER TO DEVON & CORNWALL

There are also sleeper trains between London
Paddington and Penzance, with stops at major stations west of
Exeter. These are great fun but I hesitate to recommend it because
Cornwall needs to be about 200 miles longer to make it truly
worthwhile. Since the day trains have speeded up to get it done in
half a day, and with it being such a beautiful line that you mustn't
sleep through anyway, there's less point. Having said that, if you
wanted a weekend or day in Cornwall and had limited time, great;
or one-way by day, one-way by night. If you just buy an Anytime
ticket, this costs £119.50 single. Off Peak costs £80 (you can go
today, but out of peak times). However, Advance brings it down to
£50.50 for the next day, or £15 for a month ahead. These are just
normal seated fares, not
sleeper berths, but cheap it ain't!

There's a certain adventure
in getting off your long
sleeper train, with cosy bed
and buffet car, at tiny
St Erth and seeing the
screeching seagulls while
waiting for the little St Ives
branch train in the magic
morning light.
Marvellous.

THE BERKS & HANTS ROUTE**: Kennet Valley and Vale of Pewsey
(1½hrs, 106 miles)

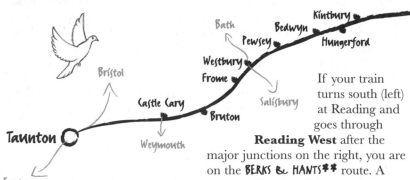

If your train turns south (left) at Reading and goes through **Reading West** after the major junctions on the right, you are on the BERKS & HANTS** route. A huge misnomer, as it never enters Hants and it's more Wiltshire and Somerset than Berks, but a scenic route nevertheless – and a quicker one to the far southwest than the Bristol main line. Mind you, I know even less about the railwaymen's nickname for this section: *The Toot and Bunny*, which I hope isn't something rude but just describes the wildlife.

It's an increasingly pretty, rural route through totally charming English countryside. Yet in its first 25 miles it bizarrely takes in four most unlikely links with unimaginably terrible death and destruction.

Just after Reading West, the BASINGSTOKE LINE diverges left as we turn right (west) at Southcote Junction. For the next 30 or so miles we follow the same valley as the River Kennet, a tributary of the Thames which joins it at Reading, and the Kennet and Avon Canal.

You see these two occasionally until after we cross under the M4 motorway, which thankfully takes a different route west. We speed through **Theale**, with its freight yard on our right, then **Aldermaston** (as unlikely a place for building nuclear bombs as you can imagine, but many thousands of people marched here from London in the 1960s' and '70s' protests: the bombs built here could end all civilisation, or arguably deter such).

Next comes **Midgham**, **Thatcham** and **Newbury** (which has the luxury of two stations, the first one just for its racecourse). In the Civil War, the first Battle of Newbury in 1643 saw 6,000 slain in the king's failed attempt to stop the parliamentary army returning to London; a year later the two sides again clashed here, again with no decisive victory.

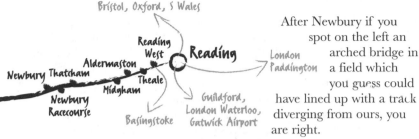

After Newbury if you spot on the left an arched bridge in a field which you guess could have lined up with a track diverging from ours, you are right.

It went south to Winchester, having started from Didcot to the north, and we next pass under the busy A34 which follows the same route.

Now we are into increasingly rural and charming surroundings, climbing up the upper Kennet Valley, passing **Kintbury*** and **Hungerford*** (after a freight passing loop on the right) with the river and canal keeping close attendance all the way. Note the World War II pillboxes tucked in close to the canal and railway all along here. These are in groups covering each other all along this canal, which the military obviously thought would form a 'stop line' for German tanks racing up from the south coast. Several of the canal bridges still have enormous 'tank trap' concrete blocks on or beside them. How effective all this would have been was, thankfully, never put to the test.

It's odd to remember this canal was derelict and not navigable only a few decades ago, the restoration right through to Bristol having been achieved by monumental efforts.

Charming Hungerford is known not only for its amazingly picturesque customs such as scrambling for pennies and driving horseshoe nails into the heels of newcomers at the town hall (the tower on your left after the station), until they buy everyone a drink, but sadly also for a massacre. A deranged gunman called Michael Ryan in 1987 killed 16 people, including himself. It led to a severe tightening of gun laws.

After Hungerford you see how much we climb by the locks on the canal, as well as the river flowing the opposite way. On the hills to our right is the ancient Savernake Forest. At the village of Little Bedwyn the railway and canal come within feet of each other and there's an achingly pretty spot with the church and footbridge over both routes – but no station and no main road.

Bedwyn* station is next at Great Bedwyn village, again astonishingly pretty and much recommended for a walk. Oddly the stopping trains from Paddington stop here and these small local trains make for the refuge siding on the right to allow expresses to roar through, then reverse back to make for London once more. There is a fine view of the church and footpath to the village on the right here, with the canal to our left.

A bit further up at Crofton, an ancient pump house stands beside the track on the right, marked by its tall chimney. It's a working museum with coal-fired beam engines. If you have time, there are some great walks beside the track and canal here. You'll need boots for the canal towpath after wet weather, but there's a parallel country lane on the other side of the railway.

We are now in Wiltshire, but not for long. After crossing the canal at milepost 70 we are at the summit of the Berks & Hants, at about 400ft. So after here the rivers will, like us, be heading west. In fact at the summit, where there used to be two rival stations called Savernake but now are none, the canal runs beneath the tracks in the 500-yard-long Bruce Tunnel. It re-emerges low down to our right in a cutting.

Onward to **Pewsey**✱ where we part company with the canal, now on our right, as it heads up the Vale of Pewsey towards Bristol (and reappears on page 162). Meanwhile we speed at possibly over 100mph, heading slightly further south in this great wide valley, a real rail racing ground.

After some cement works and sidings on the right we come to **Westbury** where we can either go into that junction or swoop left and take the high-speed avoiding line.

In the latter case we pass under the WESSEX MAIN LINE which came from Bath to our right through Westbury and is heading southeast to Salisbury and Southampton (see page 158 for the charming story of Dilton Marsh Halt, very close to here).

Just four miles later the same thing happens again at **Frome**✱ (pronounced 'Froom') which we can either call at via a single-track line to the right or avoid on the fast tracks to the left. Frome somehow retained its original GWR overall timber roof (making it the joint-oldest through station in the country). Next comes **Bruton**✱ (look for the picturesque ruined dovecote on the hill to the left and also the folly, Alfred's Tower, on the left – south – skyline further away). Bruton, home to the oddly named Sexey's School, is as pretty as a peach, as is the next small town along this valley of the River Brue, **Castle Cary**✱, (where the hugely recommended single-track HEART OF WESSEX LINE to Yeovil and then Weymouth on the south coast takes off left). The mileposts, by the way, are now wrong, showing about 14 miles too much, measuring the route from London by an old route via Swindon.

You know you're in the West Country, and in particular cider-soaked Somerset, simply because of the village names near the track here: Wyke Champflower, Hornblotton Green, Shepton Montague and Lydford-on-Fosse – the last marking a Roman road, the Fosse Way (now the A37, the dead-straight road we cross over diagonally about five miles after Castle Cary).

Onwards, past Charlton Mackrell, Huish Episcopi, Curry Rivel, Oath and Middlezoy (no, I zwear I'm not making this up!) and onto the wet flat river plains of the Somerset Levels. The odd mounds you see, sometimes topped by a church or an ancient hill fort, were once islands – as with the famed Glastonbury Tor, out of sight a few miles north of our route.

Here we rejoin the GWR main line at **Cogload Junction**, diving under the Down line coming from Bristol (see page 125).

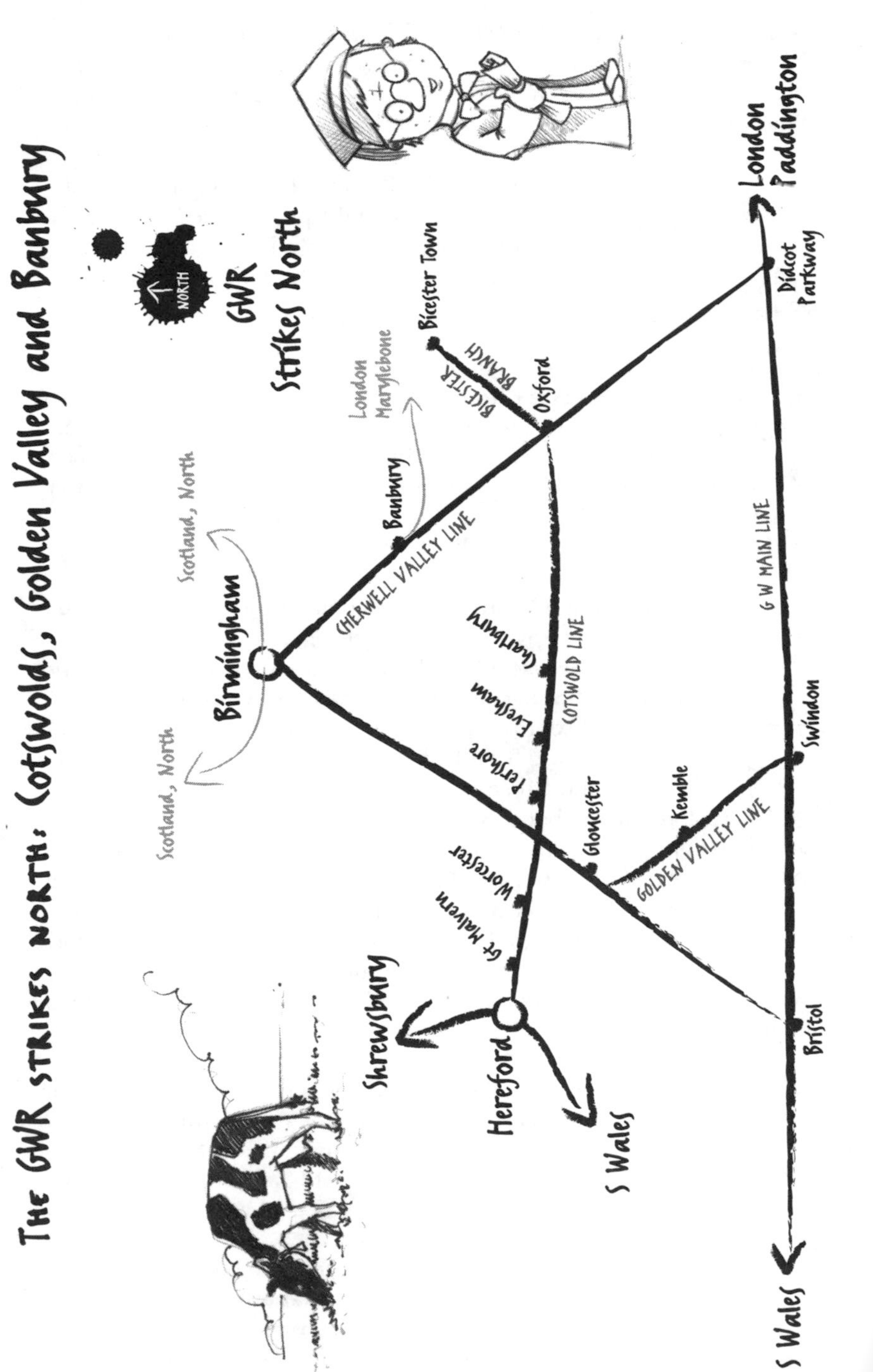

The GWR strikes north: Cotswolds, Golden Valley and Banbury

GWR
Strikes North

NORTH

London Marylebone

Bicester Town

BICESTER BRANCH

Oxford

Banbury

CHERWELL VALLEY LINE

Scotland, North

Birmingham

Scotland, North

Hartbury (Hartbury)

Evesham

Pershore

COTSWOLD LINE

Gloucester

Kemble

GOLDEN VALLEY LINE

Swindon

G W MAIN LINE

London Paddington

Didcot Parkway

Bristol

Worcester

Gt Malvern

Shrewsbury

Hereford

S Wales

S Wales

North of the Thames Valley/Severn Tunnel east–west main line, the Great Western launched north to create a great set of secondary routes offering much charm we can still use today. A bunch of these start from **Didcot Parkway** (steam museum) and north to **Oxford✳✳**.

The main **CHERWELL VALLEY LINE✳** continues north at main-line speeds up the picturesque Cherwell Valley to **Banbury** (16mins, 23 miles) and ultimately Birmingham; more in the Midlands section on page 73.

The very minor **BICESTER BRANCH** goes northeast from Oxford to **Bicester Town** (26mins, 12 miles) (which nevertheless gives great country walks from **Islip✳**). That this line once went all the way to Cambridge is now, er, academic. Or maybe not, as parts of this useful route are going to be reopened within the next five years, giving an Oxford–Bicester–London Marylebone service, and an Oxford–Milton Keynes–Bedford service too.

More significantly, Oxford is the junction for the great **COTSWOLD LINE✳✳** which runs a long way west through the lovely and fertile Vale of Evesham to **Worcester✳** (with links south to Gloucester and Bristol, and north to Birmingham) and ultimately to **Hereford✳** (3hrs 86mins from Oxford) in the Welsh Marches (with links north–south from there to Cardiff and Chester). There isn't room here to give a station-by-station, mile-by-mile guide to this 86-mile line (from Oxford, that is) but if you get the chance to ride it, take it. There are stations with great rural village names, such as **Ascott-under-Wychwood✳** and **Moreton-in-Marsh**, country towns well worth a visit, such as **Pershore✳** and **Evesham✳**, and stations that are absolute gems in themselves such as **Great Malvern✳✳** (you will not find prettier Victorian ironwork anywhere, nor a better station café). Two stations on this line get good poems written about them: Adlestrop (now closed) and Pershore (see booklist in *Appendix 2*).

The **GOLDEN VALLEY LINE✳** is very much shorter (44 miles in all) but cuts across a corner of the Cotswolds, north–west from the Great Western main line at **Swindon** to the Bristol–Birmingham line at Cheltenham. If you see London, Birmingham and Bristol as a great isosceles triangle, this neatly cuts off the bottom left corner.
Trains stop at **Kemble** (station for Cirencester and Tetbury which no longer have their own branches), **Stroud✳**, **Stonehouse** and **Gloucester**. Here trains going on to **Cheltenham** have to reverse as the main line skirts the station. Note at Gloucester the longest platform in Britain at 1,977ft 4in.

THE BREAK OF GAUGE AT GLOUCESTER.

▲ ME/ILNP

This was because the break-of-gauge between the GWR with Brunel's broad gauge and the Midland Railway with its standard gauge happened here, with every passenger, parcel, potato, pig, parnsip and parson having to be transferred between trains while the other lot were being transferred the other way. Much-lampooned chaos resulted. This platform is as much a monument to Brunel's bloody-mindedness as his great bridges and tunnels.

Talking of tunnels, on the way, the train passes through **Sapperton Tunnel** (1 mile 104yds then another bit at 353yds) which is useful to remind us of the pioneering work done by the canal builders. The Thames and Severn Canal's nearby Sapperton Canal Tunnel opened in 1789, was at the time the longest tunnel ever dug in the country at 3,817yds or just over two miles. Without the canal builders' pioneering tunnels, viaducts (well, aqueducts), deep cuttings and embankments, the navvies (which as you probably know, at the time meant 'navigators') could never have switched over to build the railway network a few years later. At the time of writing the canal and partially collapsed tunnel were being restored. You could take boat trips in the good end. Spooky.

WEST COUNTRY BRANCHES: Devon and Cornwall's cream

Instead of wittering on about how many pasty-powered branch lines in Devon and Cornwall have been lost, lovers of rural railways should be yelling from the rooftops how many truly great ones have been saved. Stunning seaside views, lovely wooded valleys, delightful burbling rivers and charming villages of thatched cottages and church spires with smoking pub chimneys, glimpsed in cosy valleys, dramatic seaside cliffs, even the strange lunar landscape of the Cornish china clay industry.

There are eight full-time pukkah ones run by and connecting with the main line. Each is delightfully different and filled with interest and, at times, breathtaking beauty. There's one part-time route, to Okehampton.

Then there are also three steam lines, all connecting well with the main line (and three that don't). It's a perfectly possibility-packed peninsula. Here are the full-time branches, where they go and what's good about them:

The Tarka Line*
(Exeter–Barnstaple, 1hr 10mins, 39 miles)

This line runs north to Barnstaple, a rare haven on the rugged north coast. (The first part from Cowley Bridge Junction to Coleford Junction was also mentioned on page 128 as part of the London and South Western Railway's battle to get to Plymouth across Dartmoor.)

Why Tarka? Well, you may be of an age where it's just an item on an Indian restaurant menu, but for 1950s' and 1960s' kids, it was *Tarka The Otter*, Henry Williamson's wonderful book about the adventures of that creature along these lovely river valleys we are about to explore. (And if you don't know your Indian food, tarka dhal is a vegetarian dish with no whiskers in it, and no it doesn't come from Otter Pradesh!)

Memories of the Waterloo line's control are still evident in the fact that trains start from 'their' station, **Exeter Central***, before plunging downhill,

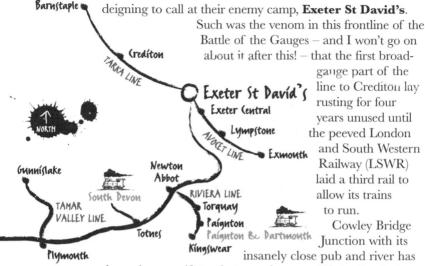

deigning to call at their enemy camp, **Exeter St David's**. Such was the venom in this frontline of the Battle of the Gauges – and I won't go on about it after this! – that the first broad-gauge part of the line to Crediton lay rusting for four years unused until the peeved London and South Western Railway (LSWR) laid a third rail to allow its trains to run.

Cowley Bridge Junction with its insanely close pub and river has always been a gift to photographers, and if the Exe isn't roaring too high, we cross the river to reach **Newton St Cyres*** , the station being in fact at Sweetham, with a particularly good pub.

We follow the Creedy up to **Crediton**, a decent-sized station originally the terminus of the 1851 branch. Note 'L&SWR' carved into the footbridge, stamping their ownership. The line appears to run double-track north. In fact the two branches are run as separate single lines, which is why the signalman has given us a token for ours. After sleepy **Yeoford**, the 15-mile **DARTMOOR RAILWAY** takes off west to Okehampton. A relic of the old inland Plymouth route, this sees massive stone trains from Meldon, and a summer Sunday service from Exeter, and the Dartmoor Railway's own trains from Okehampton to spectacular Meldon. Long term this may be restored as a through route.

Just before **Copplestone*** we reach a summit of 350ft, and the watershed between the Yeo flowing south to the English Channel and the separate Yeo heading north to the Bristol Channel. Bonkers? But then there are 11 Yeos in the West Country. Yeo, man, it's daft!

Next stop is **Morchard Road, Lapford***, with the River Taw on our left now in an increasingly beautiful wooded valley; **Eggesford*** (with a passing place, change of token, open crossing gates). Chulmleigh, the little village up the hill on our right as we cross the Little Dart, oddly never had a station, whereas the next stop, **Kings Nympton** is, frankly, in the middle of nowhere. This is the ultimate cheek in station misnaming. Not only is it three miles from its remote village, it was originally called South Molton Road in a hopeless attempt to trick people heading for that village, nine miles' walk away on a rival line!

Junction Pool on the right is a river junction, where the Taw and its tributary the Mole meet. **Portsmouth Arms** is named after a pub named after a local bigwig named after that city; three viaducts later sleepy **Umberleigh** still has its Southern Railway (1930s) concrete sign; **Chapelton*** is well maintained and we run over two more viaducts in the increasingly wide valley into **Barnstaple***. This coastal town was once the hub of five lines, two of which you can rediscover by hiring bikes and taking their wonderful routes either side of the estuary seawards. Another route, the LYNTON AND BARNSTAPLE, is as I write being restored as a narrow-gauge line over the hills up to rugged Exmoor. Part of it is open already. Otterly wonderful, the Tarka Line.

The Avocet Line*
(Exeter–Exmouth, 25mins, 11 miles)

South from Exeter to Exmouth along – how *did* you guess? – the Exe Estuary, this short and sweet route follows the east bank whereas the main line to Plymouth and Cornwall takes – again obviously – the opposite bank. As the name suggests, this line's great for spotting wading birds. In fact the avocet is so named because it was adjudged by the French to be dressed like a judge, so you can in winter look out for the black-and-white chaps with upward-curving beaks. The birds, not the French judges.

Some Exmouth trains start on the north coast at Barnstaple (see above) which takes you rather neatly from sea to shining sea. Most start from **Exeter St David's**, climb the hill to **Exeter Central**, may call at suburban **St James Park** (the third saint's station in the city), through Blackboy Tunnel before splitting from the Waterloo main line, which diverges left, at Exmouth Junction and heading south. At the junction the Southern Railway had a concrete works between the wars where all those concrete platforms, station signs, fences, footbridges, huts, signal boxes and so on still redolent of that Southern Railway era were made.

Polsloe Bridge, the next halt, has evidence of this concrete fad. **Digby and Sowton** follow and after crossing over the M5 we reach **Topsham**, where there is a fine old station and the only passing loop. So where's this estuary, then? After a deep cutting we at last get a view of the river and with a bit of luck its wildlife, crossing the River Clyst, a tributary, on a short viaduct. At simple (the place, not the people!) **Exton*** halt you can often see trains on the far side of the water; whatever you do, don't get off at the next stop **Lympstone Commando**, which serves the training camp alongside. There's a notice telling you not to get off without good reason, and a sentry with a loaded automatic weapon. Beyond the razor wire are hundreds of commandos trained in cutting your throat noiselessly and slipping a blade between your ribs, so stay on the train, noting the fearsome-looking assault course, and either get off at the next halt **Lympstone****, a pretty fishing harbour village which we enter at rooftop height (note the strange Peters Tower right on the waterside, modelled on St Mark's Venice), or run on down to the terminus, **Exmouth***, for a wander round the port, the impressive seafront and maybe fresh fish and chips.

The Maritime Line*
(Truro–Falmouth, 25mins, 11³/4 miles)

This short up-and-down route is packed with interest and things to visit, and is well used by local shoppers, commuters, students and schoolchildren. Starting at the cathedral city of **Truro***, usually in the bay platform on the left as you enter, we set off into short **Highertown Tunnel**, then part company with the Penzance line at **Penwithers Junction**. The fact that we simply go straight on suggests, correctly, that this was once the main line, and as it was built for broad-gauge trains the bridges, tunnels, etc have a feeling of spaciousness.

We climb over high embankments to a summit at a deep flower-filled cutting just before **Sparnick Tunnel** (491yds). Then we cross the high **Carnon Viaduct**, with good views. As often in the West Country, the piers of Brunel's original timber viaduct are down to the right. An old tin-mining railway trackbed underneath makes a good walking and cycling trail to Devoran and its sleepy harbour about a mile along the River Carnon.

First stop is **Perranwell*** (note the old sign) and then it's down to **Perran Viaduct** and **Perran Tunnel** (374yds) **Ponsanooth Viaduct** with that village on the right, then **Penryn*** (17th-century buildings, worth a walk round, and a new passing loop), whence the line falls sharply downhill and crosses **Collegewood Viaduct** with great views across this town and its river inlet. **Penmere**, or Penmere Platform as the old sign made out of disused rails still calls it, is well tended with GWR benches and flowerpots.

Next is **Falmouth Town*** and the end of the line; **Falmouth Docks**, which station has evidently seen busier days, with rusty dock railways running off to one side. Great things to see here are the dockyard, the branch National Maritime Museum (best from Falmouth Town) and Henry VIII's Pendennis Castle, clearly built to command the entrance to this important anchorage, on the point sticking out into the sea – all within walking distance. Falmouth was once the communications gateway for Britain, with the Post Office's fast packet ships sailing to 63 countries around the world until 1850 – which is why the local paper is, unusually, called the *Falmouth Packet*.

The Riviera Line** (Exeter and Newton Abbot–Paignton, 45 or 17mins, 28 or 8 miles, with a steam continuation to Dartmouth)

This bit of superb mainline and short branch leads through splendid scenery to what the railway has long promoted as 'the English Riviera' – the seaside towns of Torbay, and connects with a great steam line. The beautiful and dramatic run along the seawall through Dawlish to **Newton Abbot*** is described with the main line on pages 129–30. Although the divergence from the main line comes at Aller Junction, it isn't really one, as to simplify trackwork, we've been on the branch line since Newton Abbot. Passing through now-stationless Kingskerswell we reach the slight summit of the line, and down under the often-jammed-solid bypass to **Torre**, with Great Western-style running in boards (that means the larger signs as you come into the platform), and the last time I looked, period signal box and footbridge. The train descends (in altitude,

not social class, the snooty locals who for a while stopped the railway getting beyond Torre would point out) into **Torquay***, a hotel-festooned part of the 'Riviera', and then climbs slightly so you can see the sea.

We come into **Paignton*** amidst endless hotels and bed and breakfasts, the locals waiting for our train to clear the crossing. This is where the regular service trains end, and very nice too, but the line continues as the glorious PAIGNTON & DARTMOUTH STEAM RAILWAY***, a line of real charm and beauty. Even if you are not travelling on it, a dip in the sea at **Goodrington Sands** (walkable from Paignton) will be accompanied by the splendid sight, sound and smell of copper-chimneyed Castles, Halls or Granges pulling rakes of chocolate and cream carriages up the steep bank behind the beach to reach the summit at **Churston**.

If it's all redolent of Agatha Christie books, then it's because the author lived nearby at lovely Greenway on the Dart, preserved by the National Trust. Then the train descends past there, amidst great beauty, to the Dart Estuary. In fact the railway never reached Dartmouth but ends at **Kingswear** across the river, where a convenient and included-in-ticket ferry nips across that estuary. If you've come from Exeter, that's three superb estuaries in one trip, the Exe, Teign and Dart. Exe-cellent!

The Tamar Valley Line**
(Plymouth–Gunnislake, 45mins, 14 miles)

This eccentric and by no means fast little line offers startling beauty, engineering drama, constant interest and above all a quirkiness that is pure West Country. The first part from **Plymouth** to St Budeaux is described with the main line on page 134. It is only worth adding here, to make sense of the completely crazy layout of the Tamar Valley line, that once LSWR trains would be heading this way to reach London (albeit on their own vanished parallel tracks) and could pass GWR trains also heading for London but going in the opposite direction!

Nowadays the Tamar Valley line splits off from the Cornish main line just before **St Budeaux Victoria Road** – this was originally an emergency wartime connection between two separate systems – and thus the two lines still have two almost adjacent stations, the main line's being St Budeaux Ferry Road. Having picked up the branch-line token, which means no head-on crashes are possible, and perhaps noted a milepost which says 227 (measured from Waterloo via that long-gone route), we then cross under the main line twice, because while it is trying to gain height to reach the glorious Royal Albert Bridge, we want to run along the banks of the Tamar, not cross into Cornwall (well, not yet – we get some splendid bridges of our own later). Thus we get a great view of Brunel's masterpiece, and the road bridge, as we cross under them (see box on page 131 for the full story).

There's a huge naval depot and perhaps signs of the maritime activity that compelled Brunel to build such an insanely high bridge. The long bowstring **Tavy Viaduct** takes us across that river, with great views all round (when not in cuttings!) on this peninsula until we reach **Bere Ferrers***, where there is a rail-related museum and old signal box, then across a high embankment, into more cuttings and to **Bere Alston***. This pretty station was where the old line to London Waterloo continued across Dartmoor (yes, the same one whose severed remains come down through Okehampton to join the Tarka Line, and was indeed part of what is still called east of Exeter the West of England Main Line) but was ripped up in the 1960s' short-sighted retrenchment (but may be restored in parts shortly).

So after the guard unlocks and changes the points, we reverse and take what was a branch line to continue our journey. We screech around sharp bends and descend to emerge seemingly in mid-air, high on the elegant **Calstock Viaduct** which takes us across the Tamar into Cornwall. This bridge is the photographer's friend, for when the river is unruffled by wind, it gives a great mirror image of the high arches, built in the then novel material, concrete. The first Cornish station is **Calstock***, and the train then takes such a long steep horseshoe curve – usually including a stop for a gated crossing – that walkers who get off the train can reach the top first! Heading north, with many a hint of this area's long-gone industrial past, we soon reach **Gunnislake**✦, the terminus. Almost needless to say, the station isn't in Gunnislake but more than half a mile south at High Dimson. Or possibly Drakewalls. Or near Albaston. Being Cornish, it isn't entirely clear.

The Looe Valley Line✦✦
(Liskeard–Looe, 28mins, 9 miles)

This quaint line is just lovely, and again as West Country eccentric as if built by the biggest clot in clotted cream. Literally loopy. You'd do well to start off sitting backwards on the platform side. Why? Well, in the main-line section, I call it Britain's most insane branch line and add: 'This bonkers branch is supposed to go south to the sea but takes off northeast from the station, descending fast, does a horseshoe curve back under the viaduct we have just crossed and having wandered round a nice bit of countryside does a curve round to head north *again* under the next Moorswater Viaduct!'

Now, having reached what was once a completely separate railway from Moorswater to Looe, at a level much lower than the main line and at right angles to it, it can finally head off down the Looe Valley to the seaside. There is a station in this coombe, or deep valley, **Coombe Junction Halt**, but most trains don't call there and head on south, past the stumps of the old timber viaduct next to the current one above us. In fact there was no linking railway until 1901, so passengers had to struggle up the steep lane to Liskeard, possibly lugging suitcases and cussing the Great Western. This one was primarily a freight line, and still is, to a cement works up the valley. **St Keyne Wishing Well Halt**✦ is the first stop and maybe one for newlyweds: the nearby well bears the legend that the first of a couple to drink from it after their wedding will dominate the marriage. The 19th-century ballad *The Well Of St Keyne* by Robert Southey tells of a bride who outwitted her bossy groom by smuggling a bottle of the well water to church under her dress. Just as well she had a dress, because after she drank it, she definitely wore the trousers!

There's also a mechanical music museum here. The valley with railway and river becomes increasingly pretty, particularly in spring. There are remains of an 1828 canal visible here and there – it was converted into a railway by 1860. **Causeland**✦ seems rather remote from the modern world. Some Cornish place names are impenetrable, but **Sandplace**✦ was the place where sand was unloaded to improve the fields nearby. Now the river is on the right – so see, you did sit on the right seat back at Liskeard! – and the views superb, the train at one point on a causeway across the water. Amidst much hooting we crawl over an ungated level crossing and then rattle down the last mile to the waterside terminus of **Looe** to explore this strange seaside town, or pair of towns divided by the river.

The Atlantic Coast Line
(Par–Newquay, 45mins, 21 miles)

Why call this line by this name, you may wonder, as three of the West Country branches run from the English Channel to the Atlantic? Well it's because of the stunning success of Newquay in presenting itself as the surf capital of Britain. With miles of wide sandy beaches exposed to Atlantic rollers without Ireland or Wales getting in the way, this coast can be spectacular. And it's also been the post-exam destination of choice for many teenagers in recent years (so it's busy in June–July). But it's still a great route in its own right, and those wonderful beaches have a fascination year-round. There's room enough for everyone out there.

Par, where we leave the main line, is very Great Western, with working signal box, lower-quadrant signals (dipping arms, that is), and all that. We curve sharply around past the St Blazey freight depot, still busy with locos for china clay workings, to join the line (built for that traffic straight to Par docks) near St Blazey signal box. Here we pick up the single-line token. Soon we are in the Par Valley beside the river and canal, then climbing sharply through lovely woodland – once a hive of industry. We pass under a very early viaduct of the old Treffry tramway, which also carries within it milk-white water, stained by china clay, which once powered machinery. We cross viaducts ourselves, then through the short tunnel to **Luxulyan***, a village and setting of great beauty.

Soon we are passing a much less arcadian landscape, up on the edge of Bodmin Moor, seeing past and present china clay workings which have been likened to lunar landscape because of the treeless scars. At Goonbarrow Junction the token is exchanged with the signalman, the junction being for china clay trains. Next comes **Bugle**, still scarred by industry, and then **Roche**, after which we parallel the A30. We cross bleak Goss Moor, a boggy scrubland with the china workings still visible to the south, and wind farms sprout up here and there. **St Columb Road** is, as the name suggests, nowhere near the village: St Columb Major three miles away. A deep cutting and a short tunnel leads to **Quintrell Downs**. Trenance Viaduct leads us into **Newquay***, and although there is but one platform nowadays, it is long enough to still receive through trains in the summer from London and the Midlands. The route hasn't been all picturesque and hasn't offered much view of the sea. But it has offered the true Cornwall – deep rural beauty, fascinating history and industrial bleakness all in a few miles. Plus, finally, a coastline that's hard to beat.

The St Ives Bay Line**
(St Erth–St Ives, 12mins, 4¼ miles)

This little line has big views, big history, big artistic connections, and big rewards for the visitor, who would be crackers to try to get into St Ives by car in the summer (it's jammed, see Lelant Saltings below). In sheer prettiness you can't better it, with the arrival round the cliffs to the pretty fishing port something out of a novel, or at least Enid Blyton. **St Erth**, which is really nowhere, being not really at that village which is half a mile up the hill, and across the bay from the sizeable settlement of Hayle, the previous main-line stop, but sited simply for the junction, offers traditional station, signal box and single-line token (some trains run through from Penzance). This branch was the last broad-gauge line ever built in Britain and until it opened, St Erth was known as St Ives Road.

The next station at **Lelant Saltings**＊ – still seemingly within a pasty's throw of Hayle across the harbour – is a recent addition, to make a park-and-ride facility for people to get into St Ives, and has worked well to reduce traffic pressure and perhaps introduce a few car addicts to the pleasures of trains. (This is to be replaced with facilities at St Erth, but if you're coming by car, that'll be signposted.) Next follows **Lelant**, a much older station, and now the little train has to work hard to climb to the cliff tops, with sharp curves. The summit is just before **Carbis Bay**＊＊. Note how the footbridge over is made to allow broad-gauge trains through. Out at sea there may be fishing boats, yachts or, if the weather's bad, naval vessels anchoring in the shelter from the prevailing southwesterlies battering Penzance.

Carbis Bay

Up on these cliffs when this line was built, the pilchard spotters would watch for the coloured patches the shoals of fish made and signal to the fishermen in the bay with flags.

We follow the cliffs round slowly, on tight curves and, after Porthminster Point, St Ives Harbour comes into view and we run into **St Ives**＊＊ station, still well above the water level to which we can descend on foot through pretty lanes. The town was famously the home of great artists such as sculptor Barbara Hepworth, painters Whistler and Sickert, potter Bernard Leach, with Henry Moore and Virginia Woolf also turning up at some point. Today it's home to the fabulous Tate St Ives Museum, plus many private galleries. Wander round the narrow paths and seafront and you will soon see why artists were drawn to this unique and creative place… yes, the terrific pasties, obviously.

Wessex Lines: undiluted Old England at her best

Two wonderful yet little-known (to outsiders) routes linking the south coast of England to Bath, Bristol and Cardiff are the **WESSEX MAIN LINE** to Southampton and its long, more westerly branch, **THE HEART OF WESSEX LINE**, making a huge upside-down 'Y' shape, to Weymouth.

Wessex doesn't exist, of course, except historically as an ancient kingdom, in Hardy's novels, as a title for the Queen's youngest son and as a vague concept of a beautiful southwest Englishness, which is why it works well here rather than precise county names which couldn't fit these routes.

These are just lovely, lovely routes and traverse not only some of the most charming countryside in the world but also cross various completely contrasting types of scenery. The Wessex Main Line runs from the south coast through chalk downs and trout streams to the rolling openness of Salisbury Plain to deep-cut Bath stone valleys and the Severn Tunnel and South Wales – all in a couple of hours. On the Weymouth line, instead of Salisbury Plain you get the unspoilt Hardy-esque charm of little Dorset and Somerset farms, thatched cottages and villages that on a fine day seem an unspoiled heaven of undiluted Old England at her best.

Oddly, you cross three separate River Avons on the Southampton route and two River Fromes on the Weymouth one, which just goes to show how unoriginal the English can be.

Because the trains at the time of writing are unutterably small, I would urge you to book a seat (which costs nothing and usually doesn't restrict you to that particular train unless your ticket type is Advance) or turn up early and stand where the train is likely to stop (see two-car stop notices in black and white facing the driver and stand just before that). Advance booking saves money and see the Rover section (see *Chapter 9*) for a terrific deal on a holiday based on these and nearby lines.

In railway terms the two routes are full of interest because you cross the main east–west routes, like a country lane threading through hills between major highways. You start on the busy, electrified south-coast lines, cross the Waterloo to Exeter route at Salisbury (or at Yeovil on the Weymouth route), cross the Paddington to Plymouth route at Westbury, and the Paddington to Bristol route at Bath and then you can get on to the Paddington to Swansea line. Many of these you join for a short while, and each has its own types of traffic busily hurtling past while we, a tiny interloper, dash across between the high-speed intercity and booming freight traffic like a Citroën 2CV caught up in a motorway. Without the risk.

The route described from the south
(1hr 40mins, 66 miles from Southampton to Bristol)

If you are starting from Weymouth jump to the section headed *Weymouth connection* on page 60. And, if so; make sure you are not booked via Southampton or Taunton (which may be the next logical train) if you want to see the Heart of Wessex Line.

If you are starting from **Southampton** (see pages 226–8 for more on that station and city, and you could of course have commenced at **Portsmouth** or **Brighton**), we take the Waterloo–Weymouth coastal line for a while, so you can see the massive docks and all their rail traffic on the left, but after **Millbrook** and **Redbridge** whiz past we diverge right up the Test Valley.

Notice the old stone bridge on our left shortly after we've left the coastline, and the lovely meandering river up from here with its flood meadows. If you're a trout fisherman, you'll be almost drooling. It's world class.

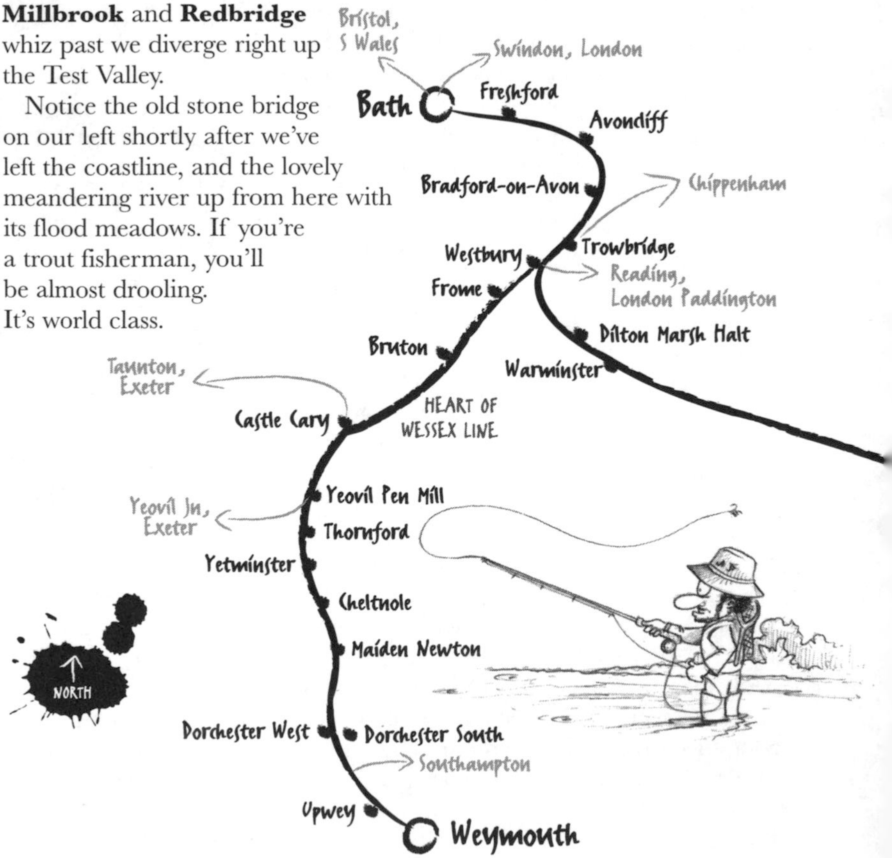

Bristol, S Wales
Swindon, London
Bath
Freshford
Avoncliff
Bradford-on-Avon
Chippenham
Westbury
Trowbridge
Reading, London Paddington
Frome
Dilton Marsh Halt
Bruton
Warminster
Taunton, Exeter
Castle Cary
HEART OF WESSEX LINE
Yeovil Pen Mill
Yeovil Jn, Exeter
Thornford
Yetminster
Cheltnole
Maiden Newton
↑ NORTH
Dorchester West
Dorchester South
Southampton
Upwey
Weymouth

Soon the line reaches **Romsey✦**, slowing for a curve which brings a direct line from Eastleigh on our right. (This kind of slowing down for a screeching curve for no geographical reason but because our route was joining a straight line that got there first happens a lot around Britain and often persists when the original route has gone – if you came from Portsmouth at Fareham and approaching Southampton too on this journey.)

Romsey is a small town which lies on that trout-stream nirvana, the River Test. It was birthplace of the Rev W Awdry, creator of *Thomas the Tank Engine*, and of titian temptress, gardening guru Charlie Dimmock. Lord Mountbatten, last Viceroy of India, lived here, until blown up by the IRA.

We speed through **Mottisfont and Dunbridge⚹**, and the tiny halt of **Dean⚹** right on the Hants/Wilts border. Look sharp left ahead for the tallest cathedral spire in Britain, Salisbury Cathedral, immortalised in Constable's painting. There is a triangular junction with the Waterloo line coming from our right, a short tunnel and a steam-era water tower.

After **Salisbury⚹** we follow the valley of the River Nadder and soon reach the junction where the WEST OF ENGLAND MAIN LINE to Exeter goes west (diverging left, described fully on page 243) and our line heads northwest. At this point, both railways had a station, Wilton North and Wilton South, so the tiny town absurdly had two stations. Even more absurdly, when you think it gave its name to Wiltshire and a type of carpet made here, it now has none.

Our line now follows the lovely and otherwise rather remote valley of the Wylye towards Warminster. The little rivers helpfully have cut down through the surrounding high chalk of Salisbury Plain to hard gravel beds, making perfect railway routes.

There's a kind of openness about Wiltshire whether you visit by rail or road that is unique and lovely. Note the curving inviting valleys to our left and the female shapes of hills to the right, some ringed with Iron-Age hill-fort ditches. It is quite unlike the counties around it.

All along here were sidings and branches (now vanished) for the army camps for which Salisbury Plain is famous. In fact at Heytesbury on this route, in World War I, a line took ambulance trains straight from the Southampton dockside to tented operating theatres in Sutton Veny Camp.

On the right the big sweeping hills are Scratchbury Hill and Cotley Hill, both more than 600ft above sea level. Indeed, war poet Siegfried Sassoon wrote a poem *On Scratchbury Camp* here.

Around appropriately named **Warminster**✤ the area is still much connected with the infantry, and military trucks line the tracks. After that summit it's downhill towards Westbury.

Oddly, when so many small halts have disappeared, **Dilton Marsh Halt**✤ on the slope down to Westbury is still open. Originally just a few planks, its 'ticket office' was quaintly bizarre. I have seen the official notice saying:

> *British Railways, Dilton Marsh Halt:*
> *Will passengers please obtain tickets from*
> *Mrs H Roberts 'Holmdale' 7th house up the hill.*

Perhaps it was not closed because the lover of railway travel, and poet laureate Sir John Betjeman wrote a poem about it. When it eventually got a proper platform in 1994, his daughter reopened it, read the poem and dedicated a plaque. I don't know if Mrs H Roberts attended, but I hope so.

DILTON MARSH HALT

Was it worth keeping the Halt open,
We thought as we looked at the sky
Red through the spread of the cedar-tree,
With the evening train gone by?
Yes, we said, for in summer the anglers use it,
Two and sometimes three
Will bring their catches of rods and poles and perches
To Westbury, home for tea.
There isn't a porter. The platform is made of sleepers.
The guard of the last train puts out the light
And high over lorries and cattle the Halt unwinking
Waits through the Wiltshire night.
O housewife safe in the comprehensive churning
Of the Warminster launderette!
O husband down at the depot with car in car-park!
The Halt is waiting yet.
And when all the horrible roads are finally done for,
And there's no more petrol left in the world to burn,
Here to the Halt from Salisbury and from Bristol
Steam trains will return.

                                   Sir John Betjeman

© John Betjeman, by kind permission of the Estate of John Betjeman.

Betjeman's poem perfectly expresses the wistful longing for an England that is nearly lost and the inner peace that such places offer.

In fact – and this is going hopelessly romantically too far I know – the theme of longing for the real England, of nostalgia, of a paradise lost that can be regained has been a theme for 1,000 years. Betjeman talks of 'the Halt unwinking/waits through the Wiltshire night' as others talk of King Arthur lying under these Wiltshire hills, in a lost Camelot of a perfect England, who will return one day. In Betjeman's case, King Arthur becomes steam engines.

Quick – back to reality. A GWR nut pointed out to me that the little gate at the end of the footpath to the lane – the only surviving feature (in fact the only feature!) on this station – was made at the railway workshops in Swindon. That's *detail* for you.

Before Westbury we pass over a 2¹/₂-mile-long loop, **The Westbury Avoiding Line**, not a personal slight on the town but a way to speed non-stop West of England expresses and freights using the **BERKS & HANTS LINE** that we cross at Westbury (see page 140, it links Paddington and Plymouth) while avoiding the speed limits and congestion at the station. It was built in 1933 using government funds intended to alleviate the Great Depression.

Weymouth connection: Hardy, a Maiden and Wessex girls
(3hrs, 80 miles)

If you are coming from **Weymouth*** (if not, skip to Westbury opposite), you start from a seaside town and Georgian resort that has tracks running through its streets to a Weymouth Quay station (now not used, sadly) and after **Upwey** you pass the site of the oddly named Upwey Wishing Well Halt just before the tunnel. The massive Iron-Age hill fort of Maiden Castle is up to our left.

At Dorchester the electrified Waterloo line turns off right, and even though it's been the main line for London for more than 50 years, it's still on a screeching curve as a result of being built second. We head on straight track to **Dorchester West**, whose station buildings are now used as a rather good Indian restaurant. You can easily walk to Dorchester South if making connections with that line (and you pass another historic earthwork between the two).

We enter another tunnel, which Brunel was persuaded by locals to build instead of making a deep cutting and destroying the Poundbury hill fort above. (Prince Charles's model village, also called Poundbury, is at the west end of Dorchester.) Across the valley of the Frome we go, and the A37 road which is heading, like us, for Yeovil. This Frome is heading south and then flows east alongside the Waterloo line into Poole Harbour.

At **Maiden Newton***, the rolling chalk hills are closing in a bit, and the track of the pretty (but closed) Bridport branch, which had its own platform and bridge, arch to our left. You can see the embankment curving left as we leave and tank traps which were supposed to stop invading German Panzers rolling up here. This is very much Hardy country – he lived near Dorchester, which he called Casterbridge in his novels. He named this village Chalk Newton, which is why the rather good pub in the village is called the Chalk and Cheese.

There are sleepy halts at **Chetnole*** (r), **Yetminster*** (r) and **Thornford*** (r) (to which Betjeman's comments and poem above could apply; they are all request stops, as described at Avoncliff below) before we cross under the South Western's Waterloo to Exeter WEST OF ENGLAND MAIL LINE at Yeovil. Again you can walk to Yeovil Junction on the other line. It's a legacy of the rivalry between companies before the 1948 nationalisation. It led to rationalisation with just one station per town where possible, but not here where we arrive at **Yeovil Pen Mill*** after crossing the River Yeo.

The countryside is just too perfect as we roll up to **Castle Cary✳✳** (which was in the territory of the same company, GWR, so we use the same station as the Paddington–Plymouth BERKS & HANTS LINE which we join for a few miles).

Bruton is yet another pretty Somerset town and at **Frome** (which, like the next station, Westbury, has expensive avoiding lines to the right for expresses and freights to avoid the station) we pass under the wooden roof, which is GWR original. This makes this the second-equal oldest through station in Britain. The other River Frome here runs north like us and joins the Avon at Freshford, where we will soon call at too. It turns out there are five River Fromes in England (which must at least make some places seem like home from Frome for local yokels).

Next stop is Westbury, so continue here with your Southampton co-explorers.

When you get into **Westbury**, which has Y-shaped junctions at both ends, note the white horse carved into the Downs to the south. It's a busy junction with great long trains carrying stone from the West Country, track-repair machines, expresses and local trains all falling over each other to get to their right tracks. You see why the avoiding line was a good idea. If you have to change trains, note the high-tech passenger information system on Platform 1. *Knock on window* it says. I try it and a cheerful head appears and instantly gives me the right information. Well, if it ain't broke…

Leaving Westbury, we take the left fork and note there is a triangular junction beyond. Next stop is **Trowbridge** (which claims to be Wiltshire's county town, despite Wilton's name and the more obvious Salisbury), and then a line branches right for Chippenham in what is a massive train triangle, with the London–Bath line being the far side.

Note after that the River Avon joins us for the rest of the way to Bath.

We pass through a tunnel into **Bradford-on-Avon✳✳**, a thoroughly charming station for a thoroughly charming town, and the start of an unmissably beautiful section to Bath. Now we really are into Great Western Railway country, the accents of locals have become more Zomerzetty.

As mentioned elsewhere, the loyalty to that company which after all disappeared in 1948 is oddly insistent, but very English. There are GWR ends to the benches of the platforms. I inspect them to see if they are original and some have been replaced – 60 years *after* that company was nationalised. There is a GWR plaque inside that station and details of a very dedicated railwayman. Further down this section some stations have new signs done in GWR brown style. The railway company operating this route at the time of writing incorporates Great Western in its title.

To be accurate, I note one seat at Bradford, as

locals call it, has 'BR (W)' on its end, which means it went up in the 1948–82 period when there were regions such as British Railways (Western). Even that has a historical feel now.

History and stone-built charm is what Bradford-on-Avon offers so well, like a small-scale Bath. It's also here that the Kennet and Avon canal joins the club of rail–river–canal to enter the winding Limpley Stoke Valley (not quite a gorge but very pretty) for a lovely dozen miles to Bath. Because of the excellent all-weather canal towpath and small stations along here, this is top walking or cycling territory.

Next stop is **Avoncliff**✻✻(r). My rural England charm-o-meter goes right off the scale. The canal, which was on the left of the valley beyond the River Avon, takes a sudden right-angle jink by an inviting riverside pub and leaps across river and railway on an impressive stone aqueduct, takes another right angle and resumes its parallel progress to our right.

Look at the station – GWR benches, reproduction gas lights, it's just lovely, the setting lyrical. Having walked here up the canal from Bradford-on-Avon, I am delighted to find that you are supposed to flag down approaching trains to stop by request (obviously not *any* trains, but the timetabled ones). There's a good straight bit of track under the aqueduct and the driver obligingly hoots to warn us as he curves round the wooded valley beyond. A boy puts his arm out and the train draws to halt. Jenny Agutter ripping up her red petticoat would have been nice (as in *The Railway Children*), but even so it's just too perfect.

Constantly pleasing vistas open up all around, the valley beyond gets even prettier, and we cross the river on a fine arched bridge before reaching **Freshford**✻ station (the village is up the hill to our left) and then another noble aqueduct brings the canal back across to this side of the valley. Eventually this journey of delights brings us to the main line and into **Bath Spa**✻✻, whose charm is much better known. Then it's a short run through **Keynsham** (where the Avon and canal have now merged, on our right), **Bristol** and under the Severn Tunnel to south Wales and **Cardiff** (see page opposite).

A note on mileposts On this route the mileages given mostly on the left side are completely and utterly insane; counting in big and small numbers, up and down, and then up again, etc. The reason is that it's a collection of small routes. Even in the middle of a straight, if an old route joins, that mileage (from eg: Paddington) pertains even if that route has gone. It's very British and totally bonkers. Pay no attention to them, unless you'd like to try to work out where on earth they're measuring from!

GWR Route Into South Wales: branch lines to Dai for

The **GREAT WESTERN MAIN LINE** runs simply east–west from the Severn Tunnel to all the South Wales major cites, including **Newport**, **Cardiff** and finally **Swansea**. Beyond that another great line continues to **Fishguard** for the Irish ferries. There is no need or rather room to describe all this in detail save for a few comments about Cardiff and just one favourite branch in detail below. And to remind you that the rest of Wales, with the principality's scenically best lines, is dealt with in detail in its own chapter, page 166.

Cardiff Central has Great Western Railway emblazoned across its frontage, 60 years after that railway supposedly vanished into nationalisation. With a fab Art-Deco interior, it's the busiest station in Wales and gives access to the **VALLEY LINES**, a complex bunch of routes running up to former coal-mining areas in the hills to the north. Don't forget that Cardiff usefully has direct trains to Nottingham, Portsmouth and North Wales, as well as the obvious expresses to London and Swansea.

On a north–south line, the **BUTETOWN BRANCH**, there's Queen Street station and a funny little terminus, Cardiff Bay (which was first called Cardiff Docks, then Bute Road), plus plenty of other suburban stations.

A sleepy Welsh branch line: Swansea to Pembroke Dock
(2½ hrs, 72 miles)

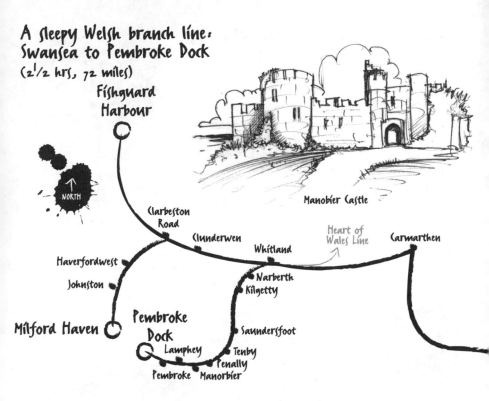

Manorbier Castle

The single line leaves the main **Swansea** to Milford Haven/Fishguard line at **Whitland**, past a set of semaphore signals. Mostly trains are small diesel units from Swansea, but summer Saturdays see through trains to/from London Paddington, often named the *Pembroke Coast Express*.

It passes through the Lampeter Valley – pretty but unspectacular countryside. And nowhere near the town of Lampeter. Over the hill on the right is the village of Llanddewi Velfrey, not to be mistaken for Llanddewi Brefi, so the only gay in the village will not come trolling over the hillside (as in the TV comedy *Little Britain*). Most stations are request (r) stops.

It climbs pretty steeply up to the town of **Narberth**, then begins a long descent towards the sea, marked by caravans and holiday parks, past **Kilgetty** and **Saundersfoot**✱ to the wonderful seaside resort of **Tenby**✱✱ (two platforms, unusually!). After leaving the town, on your left is a golf course and at the end of it, just before Penally, a glimpse can be seen of Caldey Island, which still has a thriving Cistercian monastery. The line has halts at **Penally**✱, **Manorbier**✱ (where there is a great castle and antique level crossing) and **Lamphey** (ruins of an ancient Welsh bishop's palace), and the train stops for several ungated level crossings. At the end of the trip, which takes just under an hour, you get a view down the Pembroke River to Pembroke Castle, birthplace of Henry Tudor (Henry VII and father of

Henry VIII). The train stops at **Pembroke** and finally the terminus at **Pembroke Dock**, a soulless boarded-up station last time I was there. There are ferries to Ireland from Pembroke Dock and used to be a ferry across to a lost GWR branch on the other side of the estuary, though now there is a road bridge. This was a big naval base from Napoleonic times to the 1920s, and during the war was a Sunderland flying-boat base; it's been a bit of a dump more recently. But the best use of this branch is to get to lovely Tenby. Fascinatingly useless fact: this line had its own police force until 1897 because of the munitions being transported to the naval base.

Swansea and Whitland on the **WEST WALES LINE** – they form a trident of branch lines – give access to the **MILFORD HAVEN BRANCH** which leads to that town and oil terminal on the other side of the estuary from Pembroke Dock but further down river (fascinating facts: it would have been part of a mad 'Manchester and Milford Haven Railway', never completed, the trains still ending up in Manchester by a different route. And the name is a tautology as the 'ford' part meant 'Haven' in Viking times, as in 'fiord'. So it's Mil Haven Haven). Finally there's the **FISHGUARD BRANCH**, or maybe that's the main line, ending up at that ferry port for Ireland.

Heart of Wales Line

Llanelli

Cardiff, London

Swansea

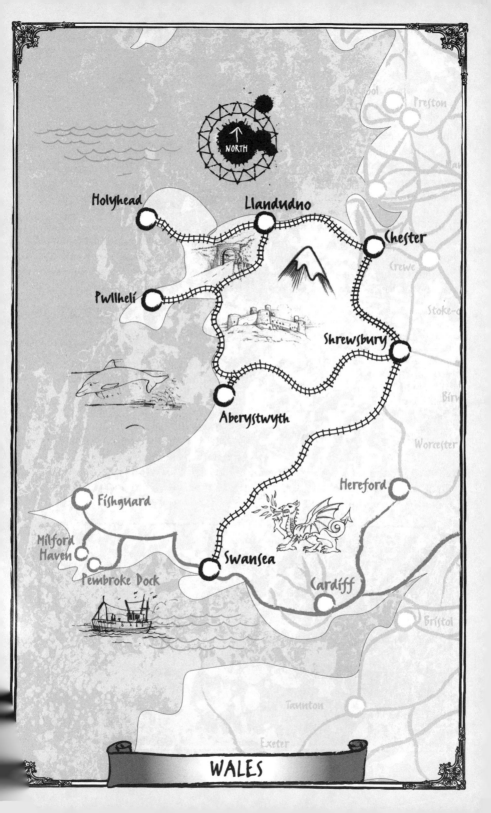

WALES

WALES RAILS

Fire-breathing dragons and going for a spin with the best connected

Wales is a fabulous principality, with plenty to be proud of and scenery so magnificent that it would be hard to leave out any main line or branch. It also has the world's best collection of narrow-gauge, steam and mountain railways, collectively known as the Great Little Trains of Wales. The enthusiasm is unbelievable. You could spend a fortnight on Wales rails and never repeat yourself and never get bored. They are still building new ones as I write. And what more apt way to charge up the hills of fire-breathing dragon country than to be pulled by steam engines?

The main-line railways are just magnificent – the Conwy Valley and Cambrian Coast lines are musts and world class.

But – did you sense a but coming? – the Land of our Fathers, of Men of Harlech, of great rugby, beer and Catherine Zeta-Jones suffers from one serious bit of spin in railway terms: the idea that it is one unit.

Now I'm not the sort of Englishman who feels threatened by Wales's welcome cultural, political and language resurgence – actually I have Welsh blood but no English. No axe to grind, Dai. But the geography of the place means, in railway terms at least, it is two regions. North Wales and South Wales are connected by rail (and best by road) only through England, because of the sparsely populated mountains between the two.

The South was always Great Western territory, ruled from London Paddington and the North was LNWR and then LMS, ruled from Euston. The two mega-powers fought it out at various junctures such as Blaenau Ffestiniog, while smaller Welsh companies mopped up in between.

Recently it has become politically essential to put 'Wales' in the train companies' titles, and run more trains round from Holyhead to Cardiff (through England) to try to bind Wales together. I hope this works, but forgive the rest of us for thinking Great Western along the bottom, and Euston along the top. And for putting Shrewsbury and Chester in this chapter.

Having said that, it's simply superb that two lines still cut across the waistband, as it were, of Wales, and that the **CAMBRIAN COAST LINE**✳✳ still screeches round the corners clinging to the cliffs of Cardigan Bay. These lines may not be fast, but they are beauties.

Meanwhile the politicians in the Welsh Assembly could do something useful, railway-wise, to further unite this lovely land: reopen the line from the south coast, from Carmarthen to Aberystwyth. Then you could travel from South Wales up the Cambrian Coast Line to Porthmadog, up the Ffestiniog to Blaenau Ffestiniog, up the Conwy Valley Line to Llandudno on the north coast. You'd have stayed in Wales all the way, you'd have taken for ever and a day when anyone sane would have gone round through England, and you'd have had a treat and a half. Bonkers, but put me down for a ticket (I've done most of it but for the missing few miles)! And on a more practical note, it would link the middle of Wales much better to the south in a useful way. Go on, chaps – if the steam nuts of the Welsh Highland Railway have just restored a magnificent 30 miles on a shoestring, why can't you do the same?

Welsh rare bits and best bits

In terms of picturesque, dramatic scenery and railway interest, north and central Wales has by far the best lines. This chapter will therefore describe only those in detail. Most are included in a possible circuit, but it is by no means essential to do all this in one go. If you do the lot in one long day (and it's great, with a bargain fare covering the whole route), plan ahead to make sure the timetable works in the direction you wish to go (or go the other way). If you are starting your day from further afield – such as the English Midlands, Bristol, North or London – definitely don't try to do the whole circuit in one day. It would be exhausting (I've done it from Hampshire; it's a bit much!). In other words, best be somewhere on the circuit first thing to do the whole of it in a day. Otherwise, just one part of it will be reward enough. For the GWR in Wales, see the previous chapter.

A note on place names

A lot of places in Wales have Anglicised (or plain English) names and also Welsh ones. I have stuck to the former where there is a choice (Swansea, not Abertawe) because readers of this book in, after all, English, will be more likely to recognise them. Where the Welsh is now the standard, I'll of course use that – Conwy instead of Conway, for example.

This is not to disrespect Welsh culture: it is thrilling to hear young people chattering away in Welsh on the trains even across the border at Shrewsbury, when you consider the whole culture very nearly went down the tubes half a century ago. As with the saving of so many steam railways, it was a miracle, surely worth it, and came entirely from the commitment of the people involved. To use entirely the wrong language, *vive la différence*!

NORTH WALES AND THE MARCHES: a fantastic circular route or splendid separate days out

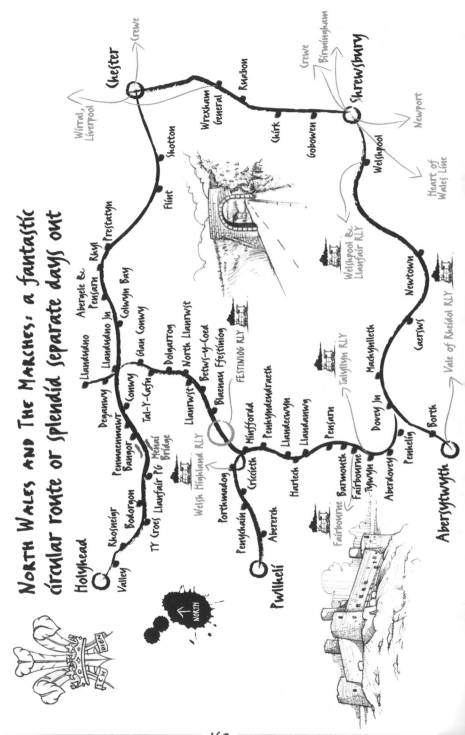

Crewe →

Chester

Shrewsbury

← Crewe

Birmingham

Crewe

Ruabon

Newport →

Wirral, Liverpool

Wrexham General

Shotton

Chirk

Gobowen

Welshpool

Flint

Prestatyn

Heart of Wales Line

Rhyl

Abergele & Pensarn

Llandudno Jn

Colwyn Bay

Welshpool & Llanfair RLY

Llandudno

Newtown

Deganwy

Glan Conwy

Caersws

Conwy

Tal-Y-Cafn

Dolgarrog

Llanrwst

Penmaenmawr

Bangor

North Llanrwst

Betws-y-Coed

Machynlleth

Menai Bridge

Llanfair PG

Blaenau Ffestiniog

FESTINIOG RLY

Dovey Jn

Vale of Rheidol RLY

Rhosneigr

Bodorgan

TY Croes

Welsh Highland RLY

Minffordd

Penrhyndeudraeth

Talyllyn RLY

Borth

Valley

Porthmadog

Criccieth

Llandecwyn

Llandanwg

Pensarn

Aberdovey

Penhelig

Holyhead

Penychain

Abererch

Harlech

Fairbourne

Barmouth

Tywyn

Abersytwyth

Pwllheli

Fairbourne RLY

NORTH

Chester to Holyhead**:
coast and castles (1hr 45mins, 85 miles)

The just-English station of **Chester**, easily reached
from London, the Midlands and the North via Crewe
is a rather ugly station from the inside, but of some
stature from the outside, even handsome some might
say. It was built by local boy made good, the great
railway contractor Thomas Brassey, in 1848. Brassey
built not only the route to Holyhead but also great
lines all over the world (his swashbuckling style is evident in the story of the
Portsmouth Direct line, page 236), and is rightly remembered with two
busts in Chester and two street names.

Ugly or not, Chester station gives access to great beauty: glorious lines to
North Wales and south to Shrewsbury. I will describe a circle of routes
going Chester/Llandudno/Blaenau Ffestiniog/Porthmadog/Machynlleth/
Shrewsbury/Chester. As said in the preamble, you could do all that in one
glorious day and one ticket, if you've got the stamina, but there's absolutely
no need to cram it in or do it in that order.

Chester to Holyhead trains diverge from the third-rail electric route to
the Wirral and Liverpool on the right as we swing past a train depot. After
a tunnel you might glimpse canal locks sharp left.

The Chester Racecourse on the left used to witness an odd sight:
expresses both heading for London passing each other in opposite
directions at full speed once a day. They were of different companies
heading for different termini.

We cross the River Dee and enter Wales. A junction on the left marks the
line from Shrewsbury (see page 185) by which you might return in many
hours if making a circular expedition. Then comes the Airbus factory,
marked by old Russian fighter jets standing near the line, where wings are
made for Airbuses. The ordinary ones are collected by an immense 'Guppy'
aircraft of considerable ugliness, big enough to swallow a huge wing, before
being assembled in France. But the new super jumbos are so huge that the
wings have to be taken by barge down the Dee and to France that way. A
500mph bit of aerospace wizardry being hauled along at the speed of that
200-year-old canal we just crossed!

Shotton station comes in an increasingly industrial area, with the
widening river to our right. There's also a Shotton high-level station on the
WREXHAM-BIDSTON LINE that crosses above us. **Flint**, which gives its name to a
county, follows. Miles out in the bay are the huge arms of a wind farm (or
they could be nuclear-powered propellers pushing the Wirral towards
Liverpool, as they seem to turn when there is no wind).

On this side there are a succession of traditional signal boxes with
semaphore signals, at Holywell Junction, Mostyn and Talacre. After the first is
the slightly surreal sight of a ship on our right, *The Duke of Lancaster*, which

appears to have arrived so fast it came completely
ashore. She was a former railway ferry across to
Ireland and was a 'fun ship' in the 1980s, but looked
rather neglected as I passed. If she's not there, she's
been scrapped, but locals and ship fans are battling
to save her for a new use.

Prestatyn gives you long views up the valley to
the left and is followed by **Rhyl**, also a seaside
resort. The No 1 box at this end is clearly busy, with
point rodding and signal wires all over the place,
but the huge box at the other end appears disused.
A through line allows overtaking here. We cross the
River Clwyd which comes out of the beautiful
broad valley to the south.

There are many so-called mobile homes here;
they are an eyesore. Ignore them.

Ahead there are long views of the Great Orme Peninsula as we reach
Abergele & Pensarn. After a tunnel **Colwyn Bay** has a bit of a pier; soon
the A55 trunk road and railway are jostling to fit in on the coast. We reach
Llandudno Junction which is the jumping-off point for the incomparable
CONWY VALLEY LINE✷✷ (skip to that below if needed) and the short LLANDUDNO
BRANCH. The junction is a handsome station in a not-so-handsome-town.

Ahead, the railway leaps across the broad Conwy River towards the town
and castle of that name on the far bank. The last part is on Stephenson's
famous box-tube bridge with its castellated far entrance to match the
adjacent castle. This bridge is a promise of greater things to come down
this line, but of course you can't see a whole lot from within the tube!

We run beside the castle and enter **Conwy**✷✷ station through a
mock-medieval arch made to match the town walls, see page 173. This
town is well worth a look round, being one of very few towns still enclosed
by its original walls. Next there are long views to the right, a tunnel and

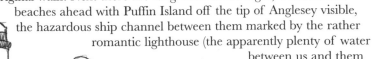

beaches ahead with Puffin Island off the tip of Anglesey visible,
the hazardous ship channel between them marked by the rather
romantic lighthouse (the apparently plenty of water
between us and them
being too
shallow).
Mountains to the
left have been
heavily scarred by quarrying – you may see a train loading stone on the left
– and after **Penmaenmawr** both road and railway have a hard time
squeezing past. The pretty Anglesey town of Beaumaris is visible on the far
side of the Menai Strait and after an interlude of farmland huddling under
the massif of Snowdonia to our left we come to the town of Bangor (same
name as the town across the water in Northern Ireland).

The castle on the hill to our right is a fake. Two short tunnels and we're in **Bangor** station, whose buildings (at least the eastbound side) feature crests with 'C&H' intertwined, the emblem of the original Chester & Holyhead Railway.

Then it's across the Menai Strait on (or rather in) Stephenson's famous bridge and the first station is Britain's longest place name: **Llanfairpwllgwyngyllgogerychwyrndrobwllllantysiliogogogoch** on the line to Holyhead. It may usually be seen with tourists being photographed alongside, and is often shortened to Llanfair PG.

But it has a real meaning: St Mary's church in the hollow of the white hazel near a rapid whirlpool, and the church of St Tysilio near the red cave. But Welsh readers would already know that.

The column on the right just before this, by the way, is one of four monuments to the Marquis of Anglesey and his missing leg. He lost it at Waterloo (the battle, not the station) and called out to Wellington after a cannonball took one leg right off. The Marquis, then Lord Uxbridge, said: 'By God, I've lost a leg!'. 'By God, Sir, so you have,' said Wellington, who then carried on observing the French through his telescope.

You can walk to the monument from Llanfair PG (turn right along the main road out of the station and you can see it ahead, on the left of the road after half a mile) and climb it, for great views over the Menai Strait, for a small fee.

We speed across the ancient and fascinating island, known to the Romans as Mona Insulis (which they conquered in a bloody invasion, using flat-bottomed assault boats and swimming the cavalry across the treacherous straits at slack water). According to one version, the Romans got such a spring tide that troops could wade across. In Welsh, however, it is called Ynys Mon, and steam excursions to Holyhead from London are often called the *Ynys Mon Express*.

We pass through **Bodorgan** (station but no such town), **Ty Croes**, **Rhosneigr**, **Valley** (watch for low flying jets from the nearby RAF station, and glimpses of great beaches to the left) and then run across a causeway onto Holy Island and the ferry port terminus for Ireland, **Holyhead**.

Conwy Valley Line**: a beautiful line to the roof of Wales

The marvellous, spectacular and picturesque CONWY VALLEY LINE, if you include the short stub to pretty Llandudno on the shore of north Wales, forms a cross with the east–west coastal main line. But it does far more than follow the river inland: it offers sublime and dramatic scenery and an amazing transformation from gentle farmland, wooded hills and curving rivers to wild, bleak moors and eventually an inhospitable mountain moonscape next to the highest mountain in England and Wales. All within 28 miles and an hour from the Junction.

The line's aim was the same as that of two other railway companies that pierced the mountain fastnesses of Snowdonia – to reach Blaenau Ffestiniog, then slate capital of the world. It is hard to overstate the importance of this industry. One way is to look at any British town: if you see rows of slate roofs you can date the buildings to the time between when the rails reached the quarries up here and the onset of cheap roof tiles in the 1930s. It's as easy as that.

At its 1890s' zenith, this industry employed 17,000 men in harsh and dangerous toil producing 500,000 tons of slate a year. Apart from a last boost to slate traffic given by Hitler's bombers damaging roofs in the 1940s, it was all downhill economically, as well as literally, for slate from the 1930s.

▼ME

But as the tonnage of slate fell, the numbers of tourists grew. From the very first the line's scenic splendour had been noted, and in the 20th century the railway laid on observation cars to highlight this (at a higher fare, of course). The first diesel units from the 1950s had huge windows and ones at the back and front, great on this route.

But as Brits fell in love with the Spanish costas and the car, tourist traffic by rail declined and the Blaenau route looked doomed. Two unlikely and rather beastly commodities saved the route – nuclear waste and explosives.

Not what you'd want rumbling past your door, perhaps, but the nuclear power station at Trawsfynydd, just beyond Blaenau on a short remaining bit of the GWR line, needed its armoured flasks to go in and out by rail. Closure of the power plant in the 1980s led to an increase in traffic heading for the nuclear site in Cumbria for a decade.

The explosives factory at Penrhyndeudraeth also produced traffic that couldn't go by road. You knew which wagons were carrying this cargo as there were several empty flat wagons between it and the loco or any other traffic – just in case. Either of these goods running away down this steep branch hardly bears thinking about, and both together… (in fact the flasks are very safe). Yet together these unlikely saviours, now finished with, preserved the route until a resurgence in tourism and political changes that meant this wonderful line was safe again. With the 1982 direct link with the fabulous Ffestiniog Railway narrow-gauge line at Blaenau, it also provides a useful link from North Wales to the Cambrian coastal railway (see page 178) to points south. But above all it's just darn beautiful.

If you have even the slightest love of beauty, of nature, of railways, of the great outdoors, or a hint of romance, a day out up here in half-decent weather can't go wrong.

The stunning route described: from sea to mountains (1hr, 28 miles)

Sit on the right, if going south. If you are picking up a train standing at Llandudno Junction, and are not sure which side that is,

it's towards Platform 4 and the cinema, not the large half-timbered pub.

Llandudno (a separate town down a short branch northwards, not essential to make the southwards journey to Blaenau but worth the ride) was once, and now is again, a fashionable seaside resort of quiet Edwardian elegance. Tucked under the hill called Great Orme, it boasts a great curve of pebbled beach. It's like Brighton without the cockney spivs, mods and rockers, gay bars and dirty weekends. Whether that is good or bad is up to you. A kind of seagoing Tunbridge Wells.

The station's remaining 1890s' signal box only hints at how busy it was in the 1930s, with one summer Saturday seeing more than 80 specials arriving and departing. There were just too many locos to coal and water here, so they were sent coupled in fours up to the Junction.

The station is huge but was run down at the time of writing. I hope it can be rescued with new uses for parts of it; meanwhile note the 'LM&SR' monograms on the gates, relics of a railway that disappeared in 1948.

Deganwy, the first stop coming inland, was the site of the quay which the railway hoped would seize all the slate traffic, which it never did, but ran from the 1880s until it petered out in the 1930s, just as the day trippers boomed. There are great views right (west) to the heavily quarried mainland, Anglesey and a lighthouse guarding the narrow channel between that island and little Puffin Island at the end. Ahead, Conwy Castle stands across the river, but the strange tubular rail bridge is somewhat messed up by having a road bridge in front of it.

Llandudno Junction is the crossing point for the Chester–Holyhead line (built 1848) as the branches go north and south. On the latter, we head towards Chester a little, then loop around to follow the east bank of the

Conwy. You will probably see a solitary heron stalking the shoreline, plus curlews and oystercatchers. In the early morning mist on the river, with the pink of dawn lighting the castle and the far shore obscured, the peacefulness of nature is powerful.

In fact the first part of the shoreline isn't really natural, having been formed from the spoil when the A55 coastal express road was taken in a tunnel under the river rather than ruin the crossing by Conwy Castle with a huge new bridge. It was a good decision, and wading birds have made this shore as natural looking as anywhere.

After **Glan Conwy**, the road, which has been accompanying us, takes a more direct hike over the hills while the railway takes the river's rambling route. The view improves

The impressive Conwy Castle

– the Carneddau Mountains to the right are the biggest high-level hunk south of Scotland – and after meeting the road again we pass through **Tal-Y-Cafn**, where a manual crossing forces us to halt. There was a Roman road crossing on the way to Segontium (Caernarfon), and later a coaching road, because the modern flat route along the north Wales coast was then of course barred by wide rivers and marshes. The legions marched over the skyline to the right through the pass where the pylons do today.

The near conical peak to our right is Pen-y-Gaer, on which Iron-Age people built a hill fort.

Dolgarrog halt (r) was closed briefly in the 1960s, as was Glan Conwy. Dolgarrog hit the headlines in 1925 when the dam supplying the aluminium works across the river with hydro-electric power burst, killing 12 people.

A long straight takes us through the village of Tan Lan. Rock reinforcement of the embankment shows where the track was undermined as the Conwy flooded in recent years.

The small town of Llanrwst was the terminus of the branch from 1863, and on the opening day, *Rule Britannia* was sung in Welsh (neatly showing both loyalties). There's a passing loop and a signalman exchanges the token for the section we have just finished for the one for the second half of the line (thus allowing two trains to be on the branch totally safely). The signal box is on the right and the original line went straight on.

So there have been three stations here: the original terminus which was to our right; the one built on the route when diverted round the town (still here, now called **North Llanrwst**), and the 1989 one a bit further along under the bridge, **Llanrwst**, which gives much better access to the town.

Back to the early days – in 1868, the line had extended via trestle-steel and stone-pier bridges across the river to **Betws-y-Coed**, a tourist magnet for

scenic Snowdonia and nearby waterfalls. The disused platform opposite our train is now occupied by the Conwy Valley Railway Museum, complete with miniature railways. From here, Sherpa buses take you on mountain routes.

Now the line leaves the troublesome Conwy to follow the Lledr Valley towards Blaenau Ffestiniog, climbing hard, with both road and rails on shelves clinging tight to the hillside. We are within the Snowdonia National Park and beauty is about to be replaced by majesty.

On this stretch is the massive Gethin's Bridge, named after the mason who built it. The steep climb levels out halfway along this, giving a brief breather to the firemen shovelling coal in steam days. Note the castellated refuges for track-workers to dodge out of the path of trains. The way the viaduct is jammed in the landscape means it is impossible to photograph. Now sinewy curves try to gain height (and avoid expense on track building).

A four-mile climb takes us through a short tunnel to **Pont-y-Pant**, popular with hikers and campers, then **Dolwyddelan** in increasingly wonderful scenery – note the romantic 12th-century Dolwyddelan Castle, birthplace of Prince Llywelyn the Great, guarding this route on the right and bleak Moel Siabod, 2,861ft, beyond. **Roman Bridge** halt (the name is complete baloney) is followed by remote countryside before a sheer wall of rock blocks our way ahead. The tunnel at the valley's head takes us under Crimea Pass. This tunnel contains, near the far end, the line's summit at 790ft (the road climbs to 1,263ft).

The two miles 206yd tunnel, Britain's longest single-track one, under part of Moel Dyrnogydd took five years and several lives to build. They had to use special drills as the rock was so hard, but the tunnel interior is bare rock, needing no lining. The inspector, when it was completed, walked the entire length with a carriage being propelled slowly behind him with its doors open to make sure no rocks projected too close. (But don't lean out in any tunnel, there may be more recent obstacles to take your head off.)

I have always been utterly amazed at the transformation from green sheep pastures at the north end to bleak slate heaps and industrial moonscape at the Blaenau Ffestiniog end. I first visited this spot 25 years ago when there wasn't a tree to be seen and it rained furiously; more recently in lovely sunshine I thought it might be softened by nature and clean-ups. It hasn't been.

We shoot out into a post-nuclear bleakness that is still dominated by the ruins of the slate trade. On our right is a massive mountain of slate waste that looks worryingly insecure, and everywhere there are signs of

THE NORTH OF ENGLAND: CHUFFING 'ECK THAT'S GRAND!

▲ D/DM

The Spectacular Lake District

▲ BV/VC

EDEN VALLEY   The Settle & Carlisle Railway passes through a pretty village

▼ BV/CW

RAVENGLASS STATION

The 'La'al Ratty' Line

▲ D/PG

CARLISLE Across the rooftops

▼ ME

SCARBOROUGH

FOR ILLUSTRATED BOOKLET POST FREE APPLY : The TOWN HALL SCARBOROUGH
OR ANY L.N.E.R ENQUIRY OFFICE

Greetings from
Scarborough

CUMBRIA Old cobbled street, Dent

▲ BV

▼ PCL/AD

Dracula

WHITBY Spooks and vampires

▼ D/A

Ribblehead
Viaduct

GREAT WESTERN: GOD'S WONDERFUL RAILWAY

Brunel's ghost looks on as his broad-gauge tracks are taken out.

▼ ME

PLYMOUTH Tamar Bridge

▲ D/PE

Clifton Suspension Bridge

ST MICHAEL'S MOUNT

▼ SXC

▲ PCL/DN

Newport

▼ D/FS

▲ PCL /CW

TORQUAY

▲ D/DG

TEIGNMOUTH Beach, boats and Brunel!

WALES RAILS

The breathtaking Snowdonia National Park

▼ D/Dj

ABERDOVEY

▲ BV

The fabulous Ffestiniog Railway near Blaenau

▲ BV

Elegant Llandudno

BRECON BEACONS NATIONAL PARK

▲ PCL/GL

▲ SXC

CONWY CASTLE *Spectacular!*

▲ D/BJ

▲ RJ

KNUCKLAS VIADUCT *On the Heart of Wales Line*

The Glorious Days of Steam

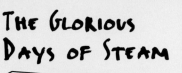

▲ F/E

Alresford Station
on The Watercress Line

▲ PCL/GL

GOATHLAND TRAIN

▲ BV

North
Yorkshire
Moors
Railway

▲ BS

Tending the fire at Weybourne, Norfolk

NORTH WALES AND THE MARCHES: a fantastic circular route FIVE

chopped-off high viaducts, inclined plane wagon routes and routes of narrow-gauge tramways in gullies. There is a shocking beauty in all this too.

The mine to the right was the largest in the world, with 26 levels, 50 miles of underground railways (that's about twice what we've done down this branch) and 1,400ft in depth.

On the right we see a siding of the 1ft 11^1/$_2$in gauge Ffestiniog Railway, and pass the old station terminus of our own route. In fact there were at least four stations here at different times, but ironically Ffestiniog, the first railway to arrive, which came here horse-drawn as early as 1836 but was cut off by a reservoir in the 1960s, was the last to arrive too. It returned in 1982 when a useful connection with the Conwy Valley Line was established at our terminus, **Blaenau Ffestiniog**, built where the Great Western had its station on a route coming from the south. The Ffestiniog is highly recommended as a way to continue to the Cardigan Bay coast, but check times before leaving Llandudno to avoid a long layover here.

The Ffestiniog Railway: Blaenau Ffestiniog to Porthmadog
(1hr 10mins, 13^1/$_2$ miles)

This book cannot include full descriptions of Britain's 100-plus steam railways and centres, but this one is briefly mentioned because it forms part of a north Wales circuit, linking the Conwy Valley with the Cambrian Coast Line, and is recognised as part of the national system by timetabling websites and ticketing.

It's a glorious ride and soon after **Blaenau Ffestiniog** you can see down to the left the reservoir that submerged the route – bits of trackbed poke up according to water levels – making the deviation we are travelling on necessary to rejoin it in the 1980s. There is also Britain's only rail spiral (where a line loops under itself to lose height) at **Ddault**, one of several ways in which this recalls the Darjeeling Line in India (monsoon rain sometimes being another!).

The station to alight to connect with the coast line is at **Minffordd**, although if you have an hour before the connection, carry on across the cob (causeway) to picturesque **Porthmadog**, and walk up the main street to the main-line station.

Cambrian Coast Line***, magnificent main of Harlech

(Pwllheli to Shrewsbury including Aberystwyth, 3¹/2hrs, 118 miles)

This line isn't just one of the great railway journeys of Britain. It is one of the great railway journeys of the world. You simply mustn't miss it. It is Wales's answer to England's Settle & Carlisle, or Scotland's West Highland.

As I'm describing it unusually in the Up direction – that is, towards London – I'll dispense with the left/right suggestions and use seawards and inland, so it's easier to follow in either direction. And to save space I'll describe only the best bit in detail – from Porthmadog down to Machynlleth. Sit on the seaward side for the best views.

Pwllheli, at the very north end of the Cambrian Coast Line, is on the Lleyn Peninsula, pronounced (badly) 'Clean'. 'That's because no-one ever had a dirty weekend here,' a friend of mine once quipped. But the area it sits in is that deeply beautiful top arm of the great bowl of Cardigan Bay which totally defines Wales's west side. A holiday camp up here has given the railway much traffic from the English Midlands since the 1930s.

In 20 minutes and through **Abererch**, **Penychain** and **Criccieth** we reach the fascinating seaside town of **Porthmadog✱**, where those coming from the Ffestiniog Railway from the north can join. And it is a mecca for rail fans, because across the road from Porthmadog station is the terminus of another narrow-gauge steam outfit, the Welsh Highland Railway (WHR), the massive rebuilding effort of which should have linked up with Caernarfon by the time this book comes out.

By the way, rail experts will tell you that the flat crossing at Newark on the East Coast Main Line is the only one left in Britain. It isn't.

As we leave Porthmadog, the WHR station is on the inland side. Just after that we cross a flat crossing with the WHR's link to the Ffestiniog at the other end of this small town. And that definitely *is* unique, being a crossing of two gauges, protected by signals on both systems.

We are passing round the head of the bay and crossing the River Glaslyn, with great views inland of the Glaslyn Estuary with its mountain surrounds, Snowdon the highest looming beyond. We reach **Minffordd✱**, where the FFESTINIOG RAILWAY coming from the mountains inland passes over our heads. That railway crosses the bay to reach a cob or causeway, built by the enterprising William Madocks who created this whole place – Port Madock.

Talking of creating places, Minffordd is where you get off to visit by bus (or a long walk) the amazing fantasy village of Portmeirion.

It became internationally known because it starred in the 1960s' cult TV series *The Prisoner* and offers a range of rescued Italianate buildings, domes, pillars, arches and statuary which would have been not so odd in Tuscany but which stood out like an orange in a coal heap against the relatively grim slate-and-chapel teetotal no-nonsense heritage of Welsh Wales.

We carry on with glimpses of the next estuary, then to seaward, through **Penrhyndeudraeth**, with views of Portmeirion, looking back across the water, while we cross the estuary on a bridge shared with a minor toll road on which the railway used to charge a toll, to reach **Llandecwyn**. Next the tiny stations of **Talsarnau** and across a smaller river to Tygwyn. Looking back on the seaward side, as we approach **Harlech**✝✝ you can see the mountains of the Snowdonia massif.

Harlech Castle is one of the most romantic ruins you can imagine, and part of an immense chain created by English kings to subdue this land. But as it's high on the cliff above, you have to get off to see it properly (and this makes this station a good ending for a day out in itself). Thousands of labourers, masons, carpenters and others were conscripted from all the English shires to undertake this massive task, assembling at Chester in an effort not unlike building the pyramids.

Oddly, the flat land seawards wasn't here when the castle was built; the station would have been on the beach. As we roll southwards there are fantastic views of Cardigan Bay, of the whole Lleyn Peninsula to the tip and the fab beach. Area of sandy beach per person on a sunny September day as I rolled past: a guesstimated $2^1/2$ square miles. Area of sandy beach per person at Bournemouth the previous weekend: an estimated $2^1/2\text{ft}^2$.

These beaches follow us down past **Llandanwg**, **Pensarn**✝ (crossing yet another estuary head), **Llanbedr**✝, **Dyffryn Ardudwy**✝, **Talybont**✝ and **Llanaber**, with the odd outbreak of spotted mobile-home disease. Rock armour defends the line here and there.

The setting of the small seaside town of **Barmouth**✝✝ is a total beauty to look out for.

South of the station we cross the estuary on a spectacular wooden viaduct, with a splendid outlook on sea and mountains, which was famously closed when attacked by a shipworm in the early 1980s, threatening the whole route's survival in the same way that the Ribblehead Viaduct crisis did for the Settle & Carlisle.

Barmouth Bridge

It also gave the unlikely headline: 'Shipworms stop trains.' But to be fair to the Toredo worm, really a mollusc, there weren't many wooden ships left for it to molest, so the bridge timbers must have seemed fair game. The railway should have copper-bottomed them, as ship owners once did to deter the critters.

Anyway, it was eventually fixed, much to the relief of parents who had to drive their children to school round an immense diversion up to the top of the estuary rather than letting them catch the train. In fact an 1886 book told of the alternative to the long way round by road, shortly before the railway viaduct was finished. On the south side of the estuary before the bridge was opened there was a station called Barmouth Ferry. From there, it complained:

...there are two miles to drive in an open car [carriage], followed by a walk from 50 to 300 or 400 yards, according to the state of the tide, over the rough pebbly beach, to reach the small boat which has only one man to manage it. The sail is often very rough, and nearly half-a-mile in length. If it is low water, there is a bar of rough gravel (perhaps 300 yards long) in the centre of the estuary, over which it is necessary to walk, and then another boat has to be taken to reach Barmouth — a mode of proceeding not very convenient for ladies and children.

Black's Picturesque Guide to North Wales, 1866

The first section of this long timber viaduct as you head south is in fact metal, because it used to roll open to let vessels pass upriver. Not any more, at least not while we're crossing.

On the south side is a halt, **Morfa Mawddach**, then the strange station at **Fairbourne**. Odd not just that no Welsh version of the name is offered at the station or on maps, and that a large miniature (if that makes sense) railway system is based here, which can be seen to seaward. This runs all the way to the tip of the arm of land sticking across the bay towards Barmouth, and in an odd recreation of the situation described in 1886 above, meets a boat to take you to Barmouth. Nice afternoon out from Barmouth in a circular route.

Along this stretch to seaward you will, several time's see tank traps (those concrete blocks that were supposed to stop Panzers) and pill boxes, dating from World War II. Why anyone expected the Germans to come all this way round to attack Britain, when they couldn't even command the narrow Straits of Dover, is a puzzle. Anyway, Dai's *Dad's Army* was ready.

The railway builders then had a problem here – the flat coastal plains had run out and the shoulder foothills of Cader Idris Mountain fall fairly sharply into the sea. The railway had to be cut into a ledge in the cliffs about 100ft up, with the road clinging to its own ledge a little higher up. This gives us superb views as we screech around the corners out across Cardigan Bay. There's even a concrete rock shelter with a sloping roof to shed any landslides as we carefully pick our way along at 15mph.

Nor is this Friog avalanche shelter an extravagance. At least twice trains have been hurled onto the rocks below, killing the crew. Once on New Year's Day 1883, and once in 1933. Now the loose cliff above has been so substantially fixed with concrete and steel that the danger is less, you'll be glad to know.

Llwyngwril follows and soon we're on the flat again, really speeding along a straight, right beside the beach for a couple of miles through **Tonfanau*** into **Tywyn***. Tonfanau, by the way, escaped closure when little-used halts were axed in the 1980s because of 'educational journeys' – which turned out to be just one schoolboy. Well done, lad, or sir by now, for keeping it open.

After the station, look on the inland side for the terminus station of the TALYLLYN RAILWAY, which comes down from the slopes of Cader Idris – the fourth narrow-gauge railway we've seen today.

The Welsh seem to have these railways like Edinburgh has architectural wonders – you can't believe how many they feel they need, but you're glad they do. They are all very different in character, it must be said, and this one was the first preserved line in the country: in fact it never actually stopped, just was taken over by enthusiasts (many English, of course). Like the Ffestiniog, this was originally for getting slate down from the hills. The unhurried nature of this railway is perhaps demonstrated by the fact that they stage man-against-train races, and it's not a foregone conclusion.

Next is another very pretty stretch as we squeeze around a headland and into **Aberdovey****. From here looking south you can see the other end of Cardigan Bay.

There's a tunnel – the first of a series along this hilly north shore of the Dovey Estuary, but after the first one there's pretty **Penhelig**, a charming seaside village cove. We follow the estuary northeast, dipping in and out of tunnels until we race across the flat flood plain, cross the River Dovey, and curve into **Dovey Junction***. This is a very unusual station, having no village or even road to it. Its only purpose was to allow people to change to the Aberystwyth branch, which joins us from the right. Being beside the river it was a bit prone to flooding, so recently the track was raised a little to avoid the hazard. There was a signal box keeping lonely vigil here last time I ran through. What a setting to work in! Many years ago, I left a camera in this remote place and wrote to them in a forlorn hope. Two days later it arrived in Hitchin, Hertfordshire, free of charge and packed in a box with ancient railway timetables and details of special trains.

Few people get off here because changing can usually be done at the next station, **Machynlleth***, a far more elaborate job with original building, café, town, alternative energy centre (in fact they were doing wind power, solar heating, recycling and recycled toilets here 30 years before anyone else woke up to it, and were probably derided as sandal-wearing bearded ex-hippies. Now the government tells people to do the same.).

We then run quickly east across the small womanly waist of Wales towards England, through **Caersws**, **Newtown**, **Welshpool** (the last station in Wales, so they squeeze in another steam narrow gauge, this one being rather rural, the WELSHPOOL AND LLANFAIR RAILWAY) and then we follow the infant River Severn and enter England to join the WELSH MARCHES LINE coming up from Cardiff.

We turn north a little way into **Shrewsbury**, a splendid station with connections in all directions. Our approach is guarded by the largest manual signal box in Europe on our right.

The ABERYSTWYTH BRANCH* is short and runs down the other, south side of the Dovey Estuary from Dovey Junction, before crossing a headland to **Borth** on the Cardigan Bay coast, again with wonderful views. And guess what joins us from the left (south) as we follow the pretty Ystwyth River valley into the seaside resort and university town of **Aberystwyth**? Yes, another narrow-gauge steam railway (number six today!).

This one, the VALE OF RHEIDOL RAILWAY**, is again different in character, taking a really scenic mountain route up to **Devil's Bridge**. Recommended.

Aberystwyth is typical of the great Edwardian seaside resorts in having a station too big for today's trains (like Llandudno above). In fact this was the grandest on the Cambrian Railways system, and the little Rheidol steam trains have sensibly been diverted in from their previous terminus to share some of it, which makes changing trains easy.

The platforms were once used by the Manchester and Milford Haven Railway heading to south Wales, a connection the Welsh Assembly would do well to restore. Mind you, how many people ever wanted to go from Manchester to Milford Haven on a wintry afternoon? Surprisingly, perhaps, there is such a service, by another, faster route.

For the last link in a Chester to Chester circular route round North Wales, see page 184.

The Marches Line*: lawless borderlands and half-timbered charm

Newport to Shrewsbury (1hr 50mins, 95 miles)

Newport's amazing clock sculpture

The trouble with a London-centric view of Britain is that it stops you thinking of some terrific cross country railways. One of these is the MARCHES LINE*, which stitches North Wales to South Wales running up the borderlands – and mostly through England.

Starting at Newport on the Great Western route from Paddington to South Wales, the line runs, after some industrial hinterland, through a beautiful land of big rivers, rolling hills, long views, great country walks, historic towns and castles and a wonderful quality of life that has something to do with not being near anywhere big.

The term 'marches' is used across Europe to denote borderlands; the 'marcher barons' ruled their own patches of this rather lawless region.

We start in industrial, or post-industrial, south Wales. **Newport** has a rare transporter bridge and an amazing clock sculpture; **Cwmbran** is a new town, **Pontypool and New Inn** were in the heart of the coal and tinplate industries, but the countryside improves around **Abergavenny**. We enter England to reach **Hereford**, with its historic centre and cathedral. Birthplace of Charles II's favourite mistress (and that Charles had plenty to choose from), Nell Gwyn. And junction for the COTSWOLD LINE.

She was perhaps fortunate to avoid the ducking stool preserved at the church at the next stop **Leominster** (pronounced 'Lemster'). **Ludlow** has many gorgeous buildings and a castle spectacularly set by the River Teme. **Craven Arms** is the junction for the HEART OF WALES LINE* (see page 186) and has the fortified manor Stokesay Castle nearby. **Church Stretton** is on the slopes of the Long Mynd and **Shrewsbury** offers a fabulous medieval town set in a loop of the Severn, plus a major railway station with a five-way junction, with routes to the Cambrian Coast Line, south Wales, Birmingham, Crewe and Chester. The town has a Welsh Bridge across one loop of the river and an English Bridge across the other – a little like Carlisle, another border town.

This brings us to the end of the Marches Line officially, but most trains continue north.

Shrewsbury to Chester*, in the company of Telford, bad jokes and lethal crossbows (55mins, 42 miles)

This superb section offers some real treats, is a useful link, and forms part of the north Wales circuit of train routes.

Keep an eye out on the right (east) going north from **Shrewsbury** after **Gobowen** for the glorious aqueduct slightly below us, where colourful

barges drift along high in the air. After **Chirk** (which has a castle you can visit just over a mile from the station, rail ticket holders get two-for-one) comes another spectacular aqueduct on the other, west side, with wonderful views of the Ceiriog Valley. Telford-built, these were marvels of their age and still seem extraordinary; yet again the railway chose the same route as the canal and made it quickly nearly redundant – but not quickly enough that they could convert the aqueducts into viaducts, thankfully. Telford, by the way, got a whole new town named after him and if you came to Shrewsbury from Birmingham by road or rail, you will have passed Telford the town; we see his great coaching road from here to Holyhead, now the A5, again at the Menai Strait with his superb suspension bridge.

Chirk (just in Wales) also has a chipboard factory that receives freight

trains of logs from the Highlands of Scotland and elsewhere, and thus helps preserve lines in remote forested regions. Log branches, as it were.

Ruabon, although having a neat Tudor-style stone station, hasn't a lot to offer but is a short bus ride away from Llangollen, which picturesque place offers a standard-gauge steam railway beside a pretty chattering river (the Dee, which we will see bigger at Chester), more canals... and lesbians! By which I mean the famous Ladies of Llangollen, who scandalised early 19th-century society by preferring their own company to the men they were supposed to marry – or at least

Ladies of Llangollen

gave people something to gossip about. Today, probably, no-one would raise an eyebrow if Llangollen lesbians came in six packs, but then it was a matter of great curiosity. If you remember, Queen Victoria shortly afterwards deleted that part of anti-gay legislation because she didn't believe it was possible!

Wrexham General follows and the 1912 station building is in the GWR's handsome French pavilion style – look at the roof detail. But Wrexham is more complex than it seems. You may have spotted another railway crossing under us just before the station, with a station just east of our line. This wings round to join us at Wrexham General and uses Platform 4 on our far left (west) and then continues in the rural **BORDERLANDS LINE** to Shotton on the North Wales coast (where it has a high-level station near the other one) and on over the River Dee into the Wirral, where it connects with Liverpool trains. You could also use it to go from Wrexham to North Wales without leaving the principality, if that matters, but in fact all Welsh north–south trains have to pass through at least Shrewsbury to Ludlow in England.

Another complexity at Wrexham is that there were, when I visited, two unused bay platforms on the east side (our right) facing south. They were disused because a rambling cross-country service once reached Barmouth on the Cambrian Coast Line. Must have been fun.

Now they are used for a direct service to London Marylebone via Shrewsbury and Telford by an independent operator, which has had rave reviews.
Local bad taste joke:

Driver: My express train doing 95mph hit some badgers near the station.
Guard: Wrexham?
Driver: Yes it does.

Moving swiftly on, a quick run into **Chester**, which we approach from the Holyhead direction, having joined the coastal line at **Saltney Junction**.

Chester trivia: It is apparently still legal to shoot a Welshman with a crossbow if he comes within the city walls after midnight. One of those laws that have never been repealed. Well, people say so but it's probably doubtful legally, and obviously morally. And there is/was a three-Welshman limit. But it does tell you something about the past relationships in the border badlands... and the present one, when the rugby's on.

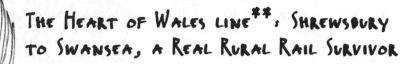

THE HEART OF WALES LINE**: SHREWSBURY TO SWANSEA, A REAL RURAL RAIL SURVIVOR

This is an absolutely delightful rural ramble across the real Wales, with broad valleys of towns and villages, plus some dramatic mountain scenery. There used to be rural railways all over the place, mostly gone, so this 121-mile line is a rare survivor and worth savouring.

But it ain't quick or posh, being more like a local bus at times. The guards I spoke to were surprised I was going all the way – they certainly weren't.

And although a quicker train was leaving Shrewsbury for Swansea at about the same time – it left 45 minutes later but got there a minute earlier by heading south on the main line to Cardiff and then west along the coast on high-speed tracks, I preferred the bumbling eccentric little one-car train (sometimes as many as three in the summer!). It's like catching the local train across India, instead of the air-conditioned express. You see a boy dancing with a snake, baskets of live chickens and a holy man. Well not the snake in Wales, but something *real* about these places. You see the lovely countryside in relaxing time, instead of a high-speed blur, not sure where you are. This is a rail cruise, no commuter crush, no Intercity rush.

One more note of caution. There probably aren't any refreshments for the four hours – that's because sane people use the train for short bits, stopping for a lunch, hike or cycle, not end-to-end. Sometimes it's worth being a little insane, and this is one of those times. Just bring something to eat and drink, or stop off after checking the timetable, or indeed overnight. The scenery and relaxation make it all worth it. It's a cliché but nevertheless true: it's a return to a pace of life we have sadly lost. Make the effort to stop rushing and it's worth it.

Llandrindod Wells

Builth Rd
Cilmeri
Garth
Llangammarch Wells
Cynghordy
Sugar Loaf
Llandovery
Llanwrda
Llangadog
Llandeilo
Ffairfach
Ammanford
Llandybie
Pantyffynnon
Pontarddulais
Llangennech
Llanelli
Bynea
Gowerton
Swansea

Fishguard

Cardiff,
London Paddington

The route described from Shrewsbury: Sugar Loaf and battlements (4hrs, 121 miles)

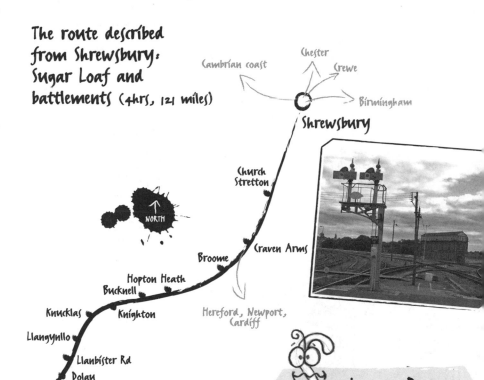

Cambrian coast

Chester

Crewe

Birmingham

Shrewsbury

Church Stretton

↑ NORTH

Craven Arms

Broome

Hopton Heath

Bucknell

Knucklas   Knighton

Llangynllo

Hereford, Newport, Cardiff

Llanbister Rd

Dolau

Pen-y-Bont

Your tiny train doesn't look in the slightest embarrassed to be in such an important station as **Shrewsbury**, with its bridge over the Severn along the platforms' south end, leading to a clattery set of diamond crossings and Europe's biggest manual signal box in the form of **Severn Bridge Junction Box**, set high up in the triangle of three routes. Hence the many semaphore signals waving about. The massive box has 170 levers to pull. As a railwayman said: 'It works, it's safe and it's easy to fix.' So let's hope the meddlers leave it there.

Having said that, our route today was advertised as 'London to Swansea by LMSR' in the 1930s, which was roundabout to put it mildly compared with the GWR line from Paddington. In those days the LMS wanted to get to Swansea

LOOPY PRICES

If you are starting on the main line anywhere between Swansea, Cardiff and Shrewsbury, you can get a bargain run-round ticket to do the whole loop including the Heart of Wales Line in a day. However, if you have plenty of time, see my note about the virtues of stopping off on the Heart of Wales (see opposite). Doing the whole loop has got to be seven hours on trains, which will appeal only to, well, loopy people like me! Mind you, you can always doze off with a beer on the Paddington train after Swansea. It'll be well worth it, whatever you decide.

for its freight, but later people discovered what a gem the line was and tourism developed.

I'd sit on the left in the mountain section; if it's crowded, do so from the start. Note: many stations are request stops – tell the guard where you intend to stop and, when waiting, wave at the driver before he speeds past.

Setting off, we take the right-hand fork and soon the CAMBRIAN COAST LINE (see page 178) diverges right from us. On the left is Shrewsbury Town Football Club, and on the far right (west) stand Welsh hills. We are soon doing a nice lick along the welded rails of the main line through the Welsh marches, the border country – a performance which one suspects might not be maintained in the interior of rural Wales. One suspects right.

The border often seems an economic one round here, drawn round rough bits of hillsides covered in sheep, letting the Welsh have them but leaving the salients of lush farmland to the English.

But that isn't the case with the long hills ahead. They are an island of hill country in Shropshire; perhaps the 'blue remembered hills' of *A Shropshire Lad*. So that nails that theory as we approach **Church Stretton**, the main line builders clearly aiming for the one gap in the hills. The Long Mynd is the hill to the right (west) and Caer Caradoc the biggest on the left (east).

We now descend in a thrilling series of sweeping curves and you can't help but think, blimey these little things can't half go. It's like Danny DeVito turning in an impressive 400 metres hurdles.

Soon we're slowing for the token allowing us on to the branch at Craven Arms signal box. We cross over to 'wrong line' at the station itself, for the Heart of Wales Line takes off right after it. Now we are climbing and curving away on old clickety-clack lines at branch-line speed. Only one track; we're alone now for hours.

But we're not in Wales yet. **Broome** (milepost $2^3/4$) (I'll provide the mileposts because they are easy to spot on this route and it's fun to find out how far along you are at any point) and **Hopton Heath** (milepost $5^1/2$) **Bucknell** (milepost 8) and then we coast downhill through charming woodland to the pretty town of **Knighton** (milepost $12^1/4$), which is in Wales. But the station isn't!

We cross the border – marked by the ancient Offa's Dyke on the right – and soon reach **Knucklas** ($14^3/4$ miles from the junction, the mileposts tell us).

Look ahead right for the spectacular **Knucklas Viaduct** with castellated entrance and battlemented parapets along the sides.

In 1925, a fox being pursued by hounds made the mistake of running along the viaduct.

He was met not by a train but by a gang of workmen carrying their tools. The panicking fox leapt over the parapet and fell 69ft to his death. The workmen were so astonished they carved 'fox' into the parapet where he leapt.

We climb from this to a long tunnel (most tunnels are climbed to, when you think about it, but this includes the 980ft summit of the line) and **Llangynllo** (milepost $18^3/4$), **Llanbister Road** (milepost $21^3/4$) and **Dolau** (milepost $25^1/2$), where you shouldn't miss the enchanting collection of signals in the garden to the left.

A mega meandering river on the right, steep rock cuttings and a tunnel bring us to **Pen-y-bont** (milepost $28^1/4$). The four concrete flower containers on the right here are embossed Safety, Speed, Comfort and Efficiency. Laudable attitudes to impress on the staff (where there were any), and I might buy my local station two more: Value and Punctuality, but here I have no reason to complain.

At 32 miles we come to the splendidly restored Victorian station of **Llandrindod Wells**, where there is a passing loop and even two platforms! There's also a plaque on the platform where a very young Queen Elizabeth II put her first foot in Wales from the Royal Train in 1952.

An annoying weak bridge slows us to a crawl at 37 miles (which I hope is fixed by the time you get there), followed by **Builth Road** (milepost $37^1/2$). 'Road' in an old station name means it's nowhere near the place it's supposed to serve, like 'Parkway' in many more modern ones. This was a major junction, however, with the Mid-Wales Line which crossed underneath, long gone.

There's a high bridge over a wide river, and two short tunnels, then **Cilmeri** (milepost $39^1/2$), which has a monument to where Llyweln the Last was killed by an English trooper in 1282, ending Welsh hopes of nationhood.

Next **Garth** (milepost 43) and **Llangammarch Wells** (milepost $44^1/2$) (one of a mere 13 places beginning with 'Llan' on this route). This is where another enemy of the Welsh popped up 630 years later. The Kaiser of Germany stayed here incognito in 1912.

But drama is coming, with high hills ahead and to the left. We climb to the tiny halt at **Sugar Loaf** and are now $50^3/4$ miles along the line.

Like the Sugar Loaf hills in various places, this might puzzle anyone younger than 150, for sugar came in enormous towering pinnacles (a bit like the shape of the London Gherkin building sometimes, at other times more like a pyramid or plum pudding). In those days the grocer cracked you a bit off with a hammer. It certainly gave a different meaning to 'one lump or two?'.

The guard told me that in 20 years he'd never picked up anyone at this little platform, although he'd dropped off quite a few, and that raises the question of whether they disappear into the hills like Welsh goblins. Well obviously they walk downhill to the next station, but dammit, doesn't it make you want to turn up there with ten people and freak out the driver by making him stop? Next holiday, I'll be there.

Meanwhile sit on the left if you can. Ahead is a massive rock wall, so we plunge into **Sugar Loaf Tunnel**, 1,001yds, through which we whiz on smooth welded rail (it's amazing that on other routes guys go miles inside the hills to check, grease and tighten the joints. Sometimes you can glimpse the outline of white painted recesses in the side where they shelter when a train enters, which is why drivers hoot as they do). The halt just passed was for the cottages of the track workers, so their children could go to school and their wives to market, just once a week. Unlikely though it may seem, there's another Sugar Loaf Tunnel in Britain, near Hull.

We come out in totally wilder scenery, with a high mountain to our right and long, beautiful views to our left down to the lush Bran Valley which leads to lowlands where we will be spending most of the next hour. There are long views south of the Brecon Beacons; the Sugar Loaf is the pyramid hill back left. We curve left round to get an angle to descend, and leap over a dramatic **Cynghordy Viaduct** (milepost $53^3/4$) over the River Bran. Soon we are approaching civilisation again – well, old railway vans used as chicken sheds on the right.

Cynghordy (milepost $54^1/2$) miles done by the mileposts, is our first stop on this side of the tunnel, then **Llandovery** offers a passing loop and one of those crossings that works by the driver pulling a string.

Now we race across a fertile wide valley floor created by the River Towy. This hidden shangri-la is not at all your grim Welsh hillsides and is as lovely as Shropshire. In fact more like Devon, if we must make comparisons.

After **Llanwrda** we cross the broad river at an angle, and we are 25^1/2 miles by the mileposts. 25^1/2? Yes, the mileposts are now counting down to the far junction for historical reasons. **Llangadog** (milepost 23^3/4) is followed by two more river bridges, including one massive girder number, **Glanrhyd Bridge** which is new and strong because in 1987 an exceptional flood on the Towy had undermined the old bridge, which collapsed under the train. The driver and three passengers were killed.

Llandeilo has a token exchange and a little-used double track (which the line clearly was once all the way beyond here). In the refreshment room here, ladies used to bring an urn of tea onto the train with footmuffs in winter. Sounds like a good idea to me!

Ffairfach (milepost 17^1/4), **Llandybie** (milepost 12^1/4), **Ammanford** (milepost 11^1/4) and **Pantyffynnon** (milepost 10^1/4) with 1892 GWR signal box, token exchange and proper signals, leads us to a more industrial south Wales, although there's a lovely valley to the right, such things being oddly mixed up in Wales, as they were in the north of England's Industrial Revolution too. This area was rich in anthracite coal, so branches ran all over the place.

The signal box, by the way, is what the driver has been communicating with every time he has got out at a passing loop, to get permission to enter the next section. He hasn't been phoning up the bookie for a bet on the 2.15 at Chepstow. Well, that too possibly.

At **Pontarddulais** (milepost 5^1/4) note the way the car park diverges left, which gave a more direct route to Swansea than the current very Welsh arrangement. Soon we get double track at last. At **Llangennech** (milepost 3), a bay is visible to the left, and at **Bynea** (milepost 1) note the ivy-covered ruin to the left. At **Llandeilo Junction** the milepost announces 0. The next one says 224^1/4 (from Paddington, whose main line we have joined) on the short run through freight yards to **Llanelli** (milepost 225^1/4), our furthest point west today. We reverse and speed down the main line through **Gowerton** (milepost 219^1/2) and a long tunnel to **Swansea** and welcome refreshments, plus express trains to Cardiff and London.

It's been a beautiful trip, and this is a handsome station, and a city that gave us Dylan Thomas and Catherine Zeta-Jones can't be all bad. But don't hang around. Get aboard your next train or in the pub before they announce the return train to Shrewsbury: all 35 place names in Welsh, then every request stop in Welsh (another 22) then every one in English, then the request stops – over 100 names in total – argh, I'm going to throw myself in the River Tawe!

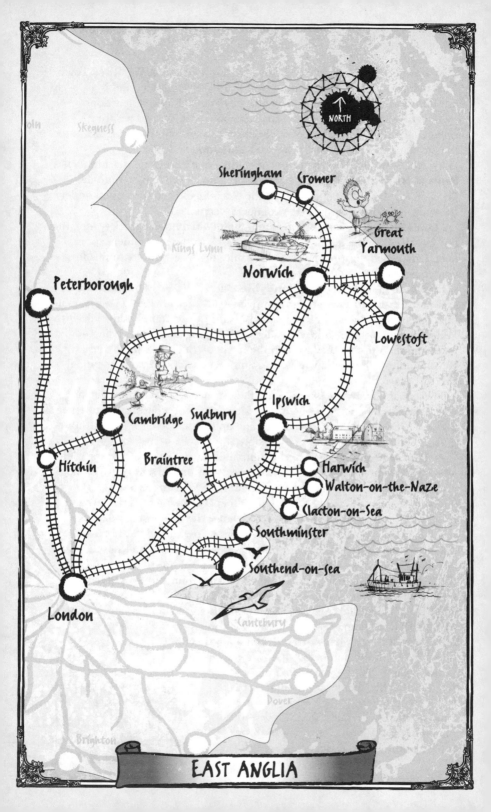

EAST ANGLIA

EAST ANGLIA: A CIRCULAR TOUR TO SEE THE BEST OF THIS UNIQUE REGION

If you want to get from London to Norwich and back in a hurry, you'd be a fool not to take the electric main line from Liverpool Street (and this is detailed towards the end of this chapter on page 209). If you're *not* in a hurry, however, you'd perhaps be a fool to take it. Much greater treats await by going a more roundabout route. There are some total gems, and the branch lines in East Anglia are just the best. Superb.

What I'm suggesting is a tour, over at least two days (with a stop in Norwich). Even better with a few days to stop at Cambridge, if you like that sort of thing, and a few in Norwich to sample its superb rural and seaside branch lines. That really will be a great trip, guaranteed.

So while the routes described are useful for anyone using any part, I'm writing about them in the order of a suggested six-stage tour (not including side trips down branch lines), starting with London King's Cross to Cambridge. The first part, to Hitchin, is described on page 2 as part of the East Coast Main Line. Then we continue below with Hitchin–Cambridge–Ely–Norwich, then Norwich–Lowestoft; then Lowestoft–Ipswich; then finally Ipswich–London Liverpool Street.

If, however, you do want to explore the excellent and varied branch lines in Essex and Suffolk, these are described on page 212. The best Norwich to seaside branch lines are described on page 200 and 203.

Bargain Anglia

Given that East Anglia has a fabulous set of cross-country and branch lines to explore, to historic towns and wonderful seaside, it's great that it has bargain go-anywhere tickets which allow you to stop off wherever you like.

EXPLORE
EAST ANGLIA
IT'S QUICKER BY RAIL
Full information from any LNER Office or Agency

▲ ME

These are priced at various levels, depending on how much of the system you want to roam and for how long. They also often include connecting buses. Be careful, however, to make sure you do not accidentally travel beyond the area they cover, or you could face penalties. Most are not valid before 08.30 on weekdays.

Here are some examples with 2009 prices as a guide, starting local and going further afield:

Bittern Line Rover

(Norwich/Cromer/Sheringham line) Includes Coasthopper buses from the end of the line along the north coast to Hunstanton, and the Broadshopper buses inland. Cost: £6 adult, child £3.

Anglia Plus Rover

(Recommended, a huge chunk of East Anglia away from London and the East Coast Main Line). Consider your day out a rail cruise.

It covers the three seaside branches from Norwich, the East Suffolk Line down to Ipswich, the cross-country Norwich–Cambridge Breckland Line, the connecting lines from Cambridge or Ely to Ipswich, plus the Felixstowe branch from Ipswich. The cost is currently £13 adult and accompanied children travel for only £2. This could offer fabulous days out from anywhere in the area, eg: Norwich–Lowestoft (best East Anglian line for scenery), the charming East Suffolk Line, maybe stopping at Woodbridge for two or four hours, then a fast train back from Ipswich to Norwich. Or Cambridge to Norwich via Ely, then a trip down a seaside branch and return, stopping for tea in Ely. Ipswich to Cambridge, or Ely for the cathedral, and back via Norwich. Includes buses in Norwich, Great Yarmouth, Bury St Edmunds and Ipswich.

NB: the three-day version of the Anglia Plus Rover costs £26 per adult, yet the accompanied children are still only £2 and bikes are free (normally £1). Even better, you choose which three days within a seven-day period. This could make a lot of sense if you take my advice and travel up from King's Cross to Norwich via Cambridge and back down the East Suffolk Line via Ipswich. You would need to buy singles from King's Cross to Cambridge and Ipswich to Liverpool Street, and make sure you have the correct tickets before straying over boundaries. Call ☏ 0845 600 7245 for details and to book. Valid after 08.45 Monday–Friday, all day other days, and until 02.00 the following day.

HITCHIN TO CAMBRIDGE: teetotal recall, dozy crossing keepers and snooty dons
(40mins, 26 miles) (East Anglia circular tour leg 2, leg 1 started on page 2)

Ely, Norwich, King's Lynn

Cambridge

Foxton

London Liverpool St

Shepreth

Meldreth

NORTH

Royston

ECML to York, Scotland

Baldock   Ashwell & Morden

Letchworth

Hitchin

London King's Cross

Hitchin#, a market town named after the River Hiz (except in droughts, when it's the Hizn't, locals say), is where the **CAMBRIDGE BRANCH** curves off east from the **EAST COAST MAIN LINE**. **Letchworth** is quickly reached and was the world's first Garden City, set up in 1903. Like all successful pioneering efforts, it's difficult to appreciate now as it looks like any other 1930s' or '50s' suburban sprawl. But it dates from far earlier, and was the first time someone thought homes for workers could be laid out with trees and gardens, and the industrial areas kept separate instead of smoke-filled slums next to factories. This place changed the world, planning wise.

The Garden City in the late 20th century still housed many idealists, Esperanto speakers, vegetarians, pacifists, bearded sandal wearers (of both sexes). It was also alcohol-free to start with – the only pub, The Black Squirrel (the creatures really are that colour locally), serving fruit juice, etc. This had unintended consequences. People went to nearby villages for alcohol and in order not to lose their driving licences used bikes and, in at least one case, a horse. The horse got a pint at each pub too, so one chap was arrested for being drunk in charge of his horse, and for the horse being drunk too. Another consequence was that the last train back from the next stop – the town of Baldock, an old coaching crossroads with more pubs than shops, it seemed – was full of giggling drinkers. And the bar of the *Cambridge Buffet Express*, coming back up this line from London in the evenings, would be doing a roaring trade with gents knowing they were heading to a 'dry' town. Even though their wives were waiting, it was not unknown for them to carry on to Cambridge, and come back on the next service. 'So sorry, dear, working late again…'

Baldock# is pub-filled and ancient, with a wide pleasant high street filled with pubs and cafés now bypassed by most traffic. The countryside begins to open up. **Ashwell and Morden** is one of those hopelessly optimistic stations that was nowhere near either place. Ashwell village is worth the mile or so hike up the lane, with two good pubs and a pretty spring that is a source of the Cam. It should have been called Ashwell Road, or in modern parlance, Ashwell Parkway.

Along this next stretch is a level crossing, now operated by those automatic half barriers. In the days when it had wooden gates, it was looked after by a chap who liked his beer. Occasionally in dark or fog, when he'd slept in, the early morning train would arrive at Cambridge with the crossing gates (having been left closed to trains) on its front buffers. By a quirk of fate, because of the angle of the road, when this happened the oil lamp from the top of the gate would fly right through the bedroom window of the crossing keeper, ending his lie-in rather dramatically.

After **Royston** – the last outpost of Hertfordshire, and the only place in the planet with a paper called the *Royston Crow* – the rolling hills end and we're definitely in East Anglia. We whiz through **Meldreth**, **Shepreth** and **Foxton**. After a sharp curve to the left we join the WEST ANGLIA MAIN LINE from London Liverpool Street coming in from the right, then reach **Cambridge✦✦** station. It is unusual in that it retains the original idea of most early British stations of having one long platform face, like a dock where ships may call (plus, in this case, bay platforms at either end). There is therefore a set of scissor points (an X-shaped crossing between two tracks) halfway down this platform so that trains may use either half of the very long platform. In fact most of Brunel's Great Western stations were like this, before it was found better to have separate Up and Down platforms and tracks.

The elegant arcaded frontage (Francis Thompson, 1845) features arms of the colleges and local bigwigs in the spandrels of the arches.

It was late on in the railway age, in 1842, that it was decided that Cambridge would, after all, be connected by railway with London, Peterborough and Suffolk. The powers-that-be at the university were horrified on three counts:

Foreigners and the uneducated would come to Cambridge;

Trains would run on the Sabbath, bringing ungodly noise and traffic to the town;

And students might be tempted to use the routes and gain access to evil, sinful places they should not go to such as racecourses, fairgrounds, theatres or brothels.

Right on all three counts, old chums, one is tempted to say. As with Oxford, the university's hostility to the railway caused the station to be far away from the city centre, in this case a bus ride away (the buses are directly outside the station).

THE BRECKLAND LINE*: Cambridge to Norwich — islands in the Fen to blasted heath
(1½ hrs, 68½ miles) (East Anglia circular tour leg 3)

This useful connecting BRECKLAND LINE* not only makes a lot of round East Anglia trips possible, but is well worth the trip in itself. Starting from **Cambridge**** the historic university city that needs little introduction, the line crosses at Ely from the once-waterlogged and still river-riddled fertile fens to the Breckland, the sandy heathland offering a totally different wildlife habitat, which straddles the Norfolk–Suffolk border. It's one of the driest places in Britain in terms of rainfall. Like many such bits of poor agricultural land, it has attracted wildlife, naturalists, hunters, forestry and the army. Beyond this, the line links to the superb city of Norwich, set on the complex lake and river system of the Norfolk Broads, and hub of a brilliant network of railway routes itself.

First stop beyond **Waterbeach*** is **Ely***, which, after being joined by the BURY ST EDMUND'S LINE we reach at the riverside rather than the town centre. Looking up at Ely from the railway you can see not only why it was once the Isle of Ely, before these marshes around were drained to make flat fields, but also how it can have then been a stronghold for Saxon resistance to the Norman invaders. Plus, it makes a superb site for the cathedral which, with its unique and magnificent lantern tower, looks out over the flat fens for miles. Directly east of the station is the river, with a marina, and open farmland.

Baedeker's 1906 guide, by the way, says about the route from Cambridge: 'The line traverses the unattractive *Fen District*.' I beg to differ. But he goes bonkers about the cathedral, and rightly too: it's unique.

It's an unusual place too in railway terms. Despite being a tiny town, it has five lines, approaching from the south (Cambridge); east (Ipswich); west (Peterborough); north (King's Lynn, the FEN LINE); and northwest (Norwich, the Breckland Line). These last three combine at Ely North Junction about two miles north of the station, with a rare avoiding loop enabling trains to go from, say, Norwich to Peterborough without going into Ely station and reversing.

After this, the Breckland Line proper starts. It is strangely reminiscent of mid 20th-century British Railways, with its jointed track (clickety clack, etc), semaphore signals, signal boxes, telegraph poles with their wires rising and dipping beside the train, and no electrification masts (unlike the modernised line from Cambridge to Ely and on to King's Lynn). With the occasional steam excursion, the illusion is complete and you'd think the new young things were Cliff Richard and Cilla Black – on black-and-white television, of course.

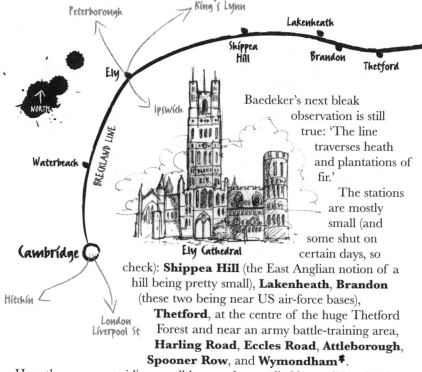

Peterborough

King's Lynn

Lakenheath

Shippea Hill

Brandon

Thetford

Ely

Ipswich

↑ NORTH

Waterbeach

BRECKLAND LINE

Cambridge

Hitchin

London Liverpool St

Ely Cathedral

Baedeker's next bleak observation is still true: 'The line traverses heath and plantations of fir.'

The stations are mostly small (and some shut on certain days, so check): **Shippea Hill** (the East Anglian notion of a hill being pretty small), **Lakenheath**, **Brandon** (these two being near US air-force bases), **Thetford**, at the centre of the huge Thetford Forest and near an army battle-training area, **Harling Road**, **Eccles Road**, **Attleborough**, **Spooner Row**, and **Wymondham✝**.

Here there are vast sidings, well kept and controlled by traditional point rodding (those bars on the ground which push the points open and closed) and semaphore signals, which may be something to do with the appearance of military trains carrying light armoured vehicles from time to time. They go up the branch to the north which is also the home of the MID-NORFOLK RAILWAY, a mainly diesel-preservation outfit which reaches Dereham, 11½ miles, and intends to go further north to Fakenham (which should be the spiritual home of Meg Ryan). At the time of writing there was a walk between the two railways, although a closer junction station is planned. Wymondham (pronounced 'windem') station also houses a fine restaurant and a railway museum. Old abbey nearby.

As we approach **Norwich✝✝** we pass a nature reserve and then go under the GREAT EASTERN MAIN LINE from London, which loops around (having lost its own terminus in the city) to join us and puts us back under electrification wires. Indeed we cross the River Yare on what I am told is the only

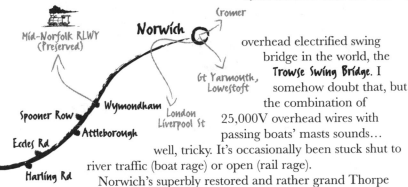

overhead electrified swing bridge in the world, the **Trowse Swing Bridge.** I somehow doubt that, but the combination of 25,000V overhead wires with passing boats' masts sounds... well, tricky. It's occasionally been stuck shut to river traffic (boat rage) or open (rail rage).

Norwich's superbly restored and rather grand Thorpe station is well located for the wonderful cathedral, castle, shopping centres, medieval city and pubs, riverside walks, etc. Plus it's the jumping-off point for three great branch lines to the seaside (see next page).

For the next stage in the East Anglia circular tour, skip to page 205.

REALLY RECOMMENDED FOR THE RIDE

Whilst not part of the East Anglia tour, the following lines are nevertheless worthwhile.

Ely–Peterborough–Leicester: cross-country connector (1½hrs, 82½ miles)

Before looking at Norwich's three lines to the coast, let's briefly remember that line from Ely to Peterborough. Through trains from Norwich or Cambridge usefully run via this route to reach the **EAST COAST MAIN LINE** at Peterborough (for York, Leeds, Newcastle, Scotland) and continue on a charming route via Melton Mowbray to Leicester (**MIDLAND MAIN LINE**, for Nottingham, Derby, Sheffield). And some even carry on to Liverpool, connecting at Nuneaton or elsewhere with the **WEST COAST MAIN LINE** (Birmingham, Manchester, Glasgow). Norwich to Birmingham is 176 miles by rail.

Not only is this line west from **Ely**✱ useful, it's also beautiful, peacefully passing over the flat fens (see for how many miles you can look back to Ely Cathedral) and its many waterways, through **March** and **Whittlesea** to **Peterborough**✱ (steam railway, river, cathedral) and then increasingly pretty countryside through **Stamford**✱ (charming market town, bookshops), past huge Rutland Water to **Oakham**✱ (castle, own tiny county – Rutland) and **Melton Mowbray**✱ (pork pies, cheese) through valleys filled with ideal villages, bountiful farms and gentle rivers to join the main line at **Syston Junction** and run south to **Leicester** (red cheese, ethnic diversity, cathedral).

Plus there's the **FEN LINE** – Ely to King's Lynn is an electrified line heading north from Ely to the coastal town (30mins, 26 miles). Some through trains from London go to Lynn.

Once Bittern... the Bittern Line**, Norwich–Cromer–Sheringham

(1hr, 30 miles)

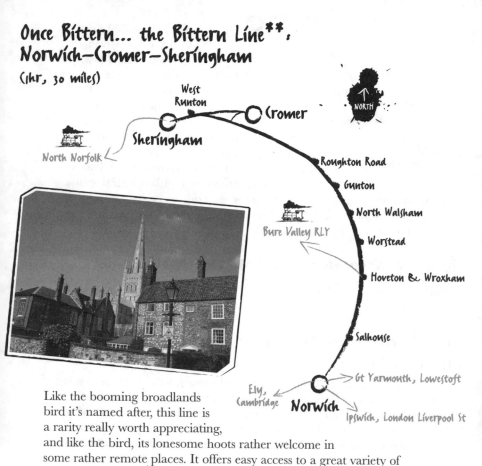

West Runton

Cromer

NORTH

Sheringham

North Norfolk

Roughton Road

Gunton

North Walsham

Bure Valley RLY

Worstead

Hoveton & Wroxham

Salhouse

Ely, Cambridge

Gt Yarmouth, Lowestoft

Norwich

Ipswich, London Liverpool St

Like the booming broadlands bird it's named after, this line is a rarity really worth appreciating, and like the bird, its lonesome hoots rather welcome in some rather remote places. It offers easy access to a great variety of countryside and sea shore, plus endless leisure activities, *plus* two steam railways start directly from its stations, *plus* two great seaside resorts. What more do you want?

From magnificent **Norwich's**** stately French Renaissance-style station, you pass along the top side of the triangle that takes the London and Cambridge lines south.

We come alongside the River Yare (as in Yarmouth) on our right, and the river switches to our left for a few hundred yards by the village of Thorpe St Andrew. Or does it? When the railway was built crossing the snaking river twice here, it was easier to make the New Cut for the river on the right so that ships could reach Norwich without having to build two expensive swing bridges.

Right after this, we take **Whitlingham Junction** left (north) while the Yarmouth and Lowestoft lines go straight on. First stop is **Salhouse**, from which you can walk to one of the quieter bits of broadland on the River Bure, with the village plus pub on the way.

When all heavy goods were moved about Norfolk on wherries – those lovely great sailing barges with massive sails – you could have reached Norwich by water from here, but only via Great Yarmouth. What took the train ten minutes took them perhaps three days, so you can see why the railways took over. **Hoveton and Wroxham** are a pair of villages either side of the Bure, which we cross before the station. The river is much busier here and you can hire boats or take pleasure trips on the river and hire bikes. Wroxham Broad, a couple of miles down river, is dubbed 'The Queen of the Broads' for its beauty. By the way, if you hail from afar, broads are lakes, so the US airmen taken during the war to see the 'beautiful broads of Norfolk' felt somewhat aggrieved.

You can also take the nine-mile **BURE VALLEY STEAM RAILWAY**, a narrow-gauge line from here that uses an old branch-line trackbed to reach Aylsham, a market town. You can buy discounted through tickets at your starting station. Look out for the tracks by the signal box on the left if you are continuing.

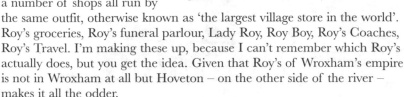

Wroxham is also home to a strange department store, Roy's of Wroxham, which consists of a number of shops all run by the same outfit, otherwise known as 'the largest village store in the world'. Roy's groceries, Roy's funeral parlour, Lady Roy, Roy Boy, Roy's Coaches, Roy's Travel. I'm making these up, because I can't remember which Roy's actually does, but you get the idea. Given that Roy's of Wroxham's empire is not in Wroxham at all but Hoveton – on the other side of the river – makes it all the odder.

Next stop is **Worstead**, which has given its name to worsted cloth. Sheep do eat up men, they once said, as they replaced farm workers because of their profitability. But sheep also build church towers – or rather the money from their wool did throughout Norfolk, which explains the tall towers and huge churches that were often excessive even when built. The enormous and splendid church, visible on the right after the station, is known as the 'Wool Church'.

The small market town of **North Walsham**✝ has the 'Weavers' Way' footpath and a motorcycle museum. Pretty **Gunton**✝ station, built for the convenience of a nearby aristocrat, now a private home, is in good walking country. **Roughton Road** soon brings us to **Cromer**✝ (famous for crabs, sandy beaches, a pier with a theatre, a massive church tower you can climb for superb views, a lifeboat museum and shops) and a railway oddity. The train reverses here and takes another track along the coast through **West Runton** (excellent station gardens, shire horse centre nearby) to reach **Sheringham**✝✝, a pretty little fishing village with miles of beaches (but thronged with tourists in summer). Here you can board the continuation of the track in the form of the steam **NORTH NORFOLK RAILWAY** or 'Poppy Line' which takes a very pretty cliff-top route further west to Weybourne and Holt. As you enjoy the full-sized express engines and carriages all lovingly preserved, you will learn that this and the line to Cromer are all that remains of the M&GNR (Midland & Great Northern, known locally as the Muddle & Go Nowhere) a system that has otherwise vanished but once reached Norwich and Yarmouth and even Lowestoft from the Midlands. Or just enjoy the splendid views from the cliff tops. Again, you can get a bargain-priced inclusive ticket from your starting station. (Bittern Line Rover ticket: see page 194).

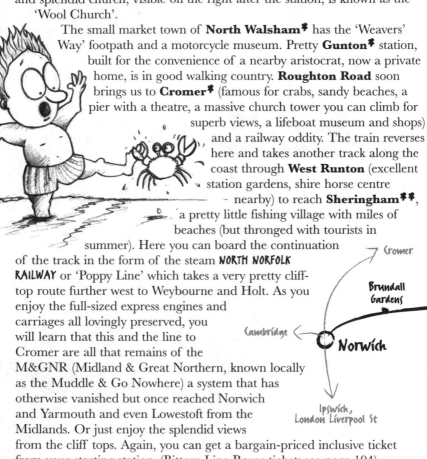

Cromer

Brundall Gardens

Cambridge

Norwich

Ipswich, London Liverpool St

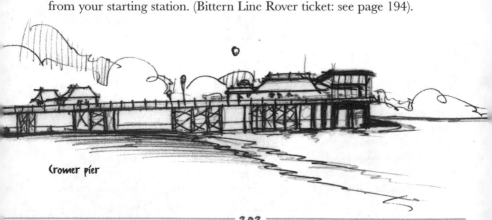

Cromer pier

The Wherry peculiar Wherry Lines**

The first of the Wherry lines isn't part of the East Anglia tour, but is recommended. For the second Wherry Line and continuation of our tour, see page 205.

Norwich–Great Yarmouth (37 or 31 mins, 27 or 18½ miles)

The route to Great Yarmouth is, frankly, completely crackers. In the nicest possible way. If it were Ireland, it would be called very Irish. But the Irish can't hold a candle to East Anglia when it comes to railway barminess.

Perhaps I should say the *routes*, plural, to Great Yarmouth *are* bonkers. You set off from **Norwich's**** grand station in a normal fashion on the same track as the Bittern Line until **Whitlingham Junction**. Then, still a little less logically, you reach **Brundall Gardens** and **Brundall** (so close together you wonder why they didn't bundle Brundall together) and then something odd happens. Trains either go left or right, yet they all go to Great Yarmouth. Except the Lowestoft ones, which go right.

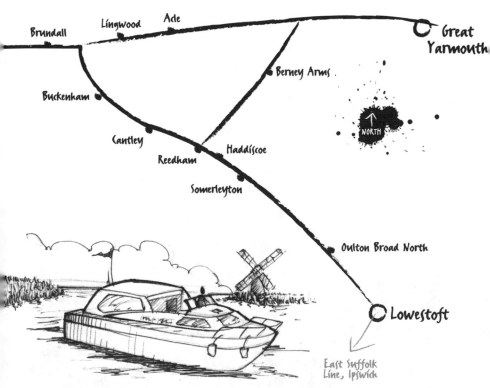

There is no sane way of explaining this. The ones going left at the junction carry on to **Lingwood** and **Acle** (which is on the River Bure, a base for river trips to the northern Broads, but not very near the village) and after much marsh, farmland, windpumps and distant church towers, are rejoined by the track taken by the errant cousins who mischievously took the other route further south, apparently heading directly for Vienna. But where have they been in the meantime? That route after Brundall also crosses flat, remote marshes to **Buckenham** and **Cantley** before reaching **Reedham**, where it gives up on dreams of Vienna (which route seems to carry on) and swerves left (north), suitably chastised and heading straight for Great Yarmouth, tail between its legs.

Here on this last stretch is the one possible yet unlikely explanation for the whole fiasco: a station called **Berney Arms** that has no road access. What a marvellous pub, with access only by water or train! It does meals, but book ahead if you don't want a long boozy wait. There's also some great walking and, in Breydon Water, enough mud to fill in the Suez Canal, plus glorious Norfolk light to start and end the day.

The theory is that someone important at the railway liked this boozer, and as it had no other access, the apparently unnecessary line was retained. Really useful lines all over the place in East Anglia were being axed by the dozen, and yet they saved this oddity. Well, if you travel it, you'll be rather glad they did, barmy Berney Arms or not. Strange, you may think as you arrive at **Great Yarmouth** (cheap-and-cheerful seaside resort, lots of accommodation, Nelson memorabilia).

Oddly, when you look at the strange layout of the Wherry Lines, you may notice that sideways they mirror exactly the layout of a wherry boat's rigging. Wherry peculiar.

NORWICH—LOWESTOFT**: Queen of the Lot
(40mins, 23¹/₂ miles) (East Anglia circular tour leg 4)

This is the queen of East Anglia branch lines, my favourite, the fairest of them all (and that's a tall order, given the last two). As explained in the last section, we set off sharing the route of the Bittern Line trains, but quickly diverge from them after twice crossing the Yare, then diverge from some Great Yarmouth trains after **Brundall Gardens** and **Brundall**, then after marshes and woodland at **Buckenham** and **Cantley**, with the Yare tracking us to our right all the way, diverge from the rest of the Yarmouth trains at **Reedham**✼✼. Vienna or bust! Well, let's settle for Lowestoft.

Now it gets really picturesque. We go through a cutting to emerge, with a bit of luck, onto the high **Reedham Swing Bridge** over the Yare. Note how the signal box controls the river and trains. The boats are controlled by a red flag which looks like a prop from *Dr Zhivago* (and in winter it can feel like that Russian epic here). The track curves down to reach the level of the marshes. There are excellent pubs in Reedham, and not that it bothers us, a tiny car ferry down a lane somewhere.

If you think the layout of the railways round here is eccentric, you should look at the map – or chart, rather – of the waterways. We follow the artificial New Cut between the Yare and the Waveney, both of which rivers are heading for Great Yarmouth. The Waveney runs further south along the Suffolk border. God knows what the tides make of this odd arrangement, but when the rivers were the main route for cargo around Norfolk, this Cut cut (!) several miles for boats travelling between the two rivers, and avoided troublesome Breydon Water and some low bridges.

The Waveney, by the way, reached the sea twice: once at Lowestoft and once at Yarmouth.

The rivers round here are often above the land level – honestly – because the marshes shrank when drained. That's what all those 'windmills'

are for (or were for), to pull water from the ditches up into the rivers. And yes, pedantically, they are windpumps. So the enormous white or tan sails of boats – the really big ones being the wherries – sail past higher than the fields, and higher than the railway at this point. It's odd being on boats and looking down on fields. It's also odd being on a train looking up at a boat.

Next stop is **Haddiscoe⁎** which, typically for the railways, is not near the village of that name but close to St Olave's where the riverside Bell Inn is reputedly the oldest pub in Norfolk. We cross the Waveney on **Somerleyton Swing Bridge**, whose far end rests in Suffolk. A massive bolt secures the bridge in line with the land rails, you'll be glad to know, and the signals cannot allow trains over without the bridge being in the right position. **Somerleyton⁎** is a fascinating and pretty village with much history: thatched cottages, stately home, old church. The first hovercraft was tested here. The Duke's Head pub offers discounts on meals to Wherry Line ticket holders (T 01502 730281).

Oulton Broad is a bit of water that extravagantly has two stations. Ours is **Oulton Broad North**, serving this pleasant Lowestoft suburb and the water beloved by boaties. It is the only Norfolk Broad I can think of that is lined with homes and isn't in Norfolk! Pubs include The Wherry Hotel (discount for Wherry Line tickets holders: T 0845 230 5678; W www.elizabethhotels.co.uk, and the Lady in the Lake, known by local wits as the Bitch in the Ditch. There are also a lot of ghost stories attached to this place, including a ghost wherry which, presumably, doesn't need swing bridges opening.

Just after OBN station, the **EAST SUFFOLK LINE** runs in from the south (right).

Lowestoft⁎ is still a busy working port and seaside resort and, as it's the most easterly point in Britain, markets itself as the Sunrise Coast – which doesn't apply when North Sea fogs roll in! When I visited there was still one of the old enamel signs in the correct Eastern Region (and you can't get more eastern) colour high up on the outside wall proclaims: 'British Railways: Lowestoft Central'. Both British Railways and the rival Lowestoft stations have long, well, gone west, but this station, much larger than most modern trains require, has happily survived.

The lovely East Suffolk Line**: Lowestoft to Ipswich (for London): swinging stuff

(1½hrs, 49 miles) (East Anglia circular tour leg 5)

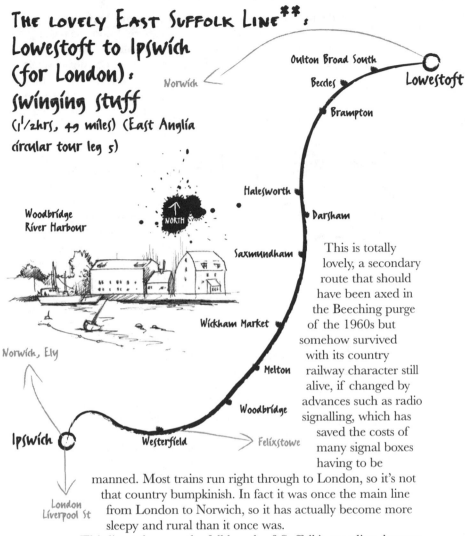

Oulton Broad South

Beccles

Brampton

Lowestoft

Norwich

Halesworth

Woodbridge River Harbour

Darsham

Saxmundham

Wickham Market

Norwich, Ely

Melton

Woodbridge

Ipswich

Westerfield

Felixstowe

London Liverpool St

This is totally lovely, a secondary route that should have been axed in the Beeching purge of the 1960s but somehow survived with its country railway character still alive, if changed by advances such as radio signalling, which has saved the costs of many signal boxes having to be manned. Most trains run right through to London, so it's not that country bumpkinish. In fact it was once the main line from London to Norwich, so it has actually become more sleepy and rural than it once was.

This line takes you the full length of Suffolk's coastline, but not along the coast. Instead it runs a few miles inland through market town and sleepy village, and charming it is too.

We start by running nearly back to Oulton Broad North on the Norwich route, but swerving south over **Oulton Broad Swing Bridge**, with good views up and down the waterway, to reach **Oulton Broad South**. If you have come up via Norwich that's the fourth railway swing bridge which is probably a world record in so few miles.

Next stop is **Beccles***, a lovely town on the Suffolk side of the River Waveney and you can see by the ludicrous curve we arrive on and the size of the station that there was once a main line heading north, now gone. There was yet another country line across to the Great Eastern Main Line, so Beccles once had four routes. By the time you get there, I hope its passing loop has been reinstated as planned, because that will allow a more flexible hourly service on this mostly single-track line. Beccles is the dwile-flonking (a strange sport involving hitting each other with beer-soaked floor mops) capital of the world, and is also known for its printing centre, and as the home of Nelson's parents.

Brampton (not near its village) is followed by **Halesworth**✴, a small, prettily set town (and jumping-off point for the seaside town of Southwold, which once had its own narrow-gauge railway from here, (spot the embankment diverging left). We have a bit of double track down to Saxmundham, and to **Darsham** (again away from the village, with a rather odd level crossing across the busy A12 road). There are lots of wartime pioneering radar bases and US air-force history round here. The freight branch from Sizewell nuclear power plant trails in left.

Saxmundham✴, a great name and not a bad old country railway station, comes complete with two platforms. It's a charming small town and note its thriving small shops, such as baker, butcher, grocer, etc, for it is famously 'the town that said no to Tesco', the supermarket giant that now dominates many British towns.

We then pass through **Wickham Market**, and on to **Melton** (once a home for the county's 'pauper lunatics', but not any more) and **Woodbridge**✴✴ (very pretty, worth a wander around with rare Tide Mill, and harbour on the River Deben). The track becomes double again, the busy FELIXSTOWE BRANCH trails in from the left and **Westerfield** whizzes past. We then make a great loop around Ipswich at high level, THE GREAT EASTERN MAIN LINE joins from our right and we finally reach **Ipswich**.

Oddly, because of the fast trains from Ipswich, you could go either way along the East Suffolk Line to reach Norwich. But Ipswich is the station to change for London Liverpool Street if your train isn't going straight through. Make sure you have a through ticket or they'll clobber you – even a few yards from the station.

For East Anglia circular tour leg six, overleaf, though the remaining fast run down to London isn't described in detail.

Enfield, Hertford, Stansted Airport, Cambridge

Romford

London Liverpool St

LONDON LIVERPOOL STREET TO NORWICH VIA THE GREAT EASTERN MAIN LINE (plus fabulous branches)

(2hrs, 115 miles) (And the last leg of the East Anglia circular tour — in which case it's Ipswich to London)

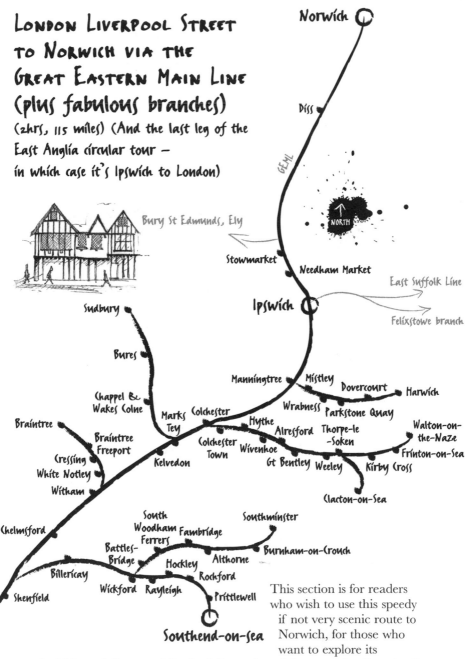

Norwich

Diss

GEML

NORTH

Bury St Edmunds, Ely

Stowmarket

Needham Market

East Suffolk Line

Ipswich

Felixstowe branch

Sudbury

Bures

Manningtree · Mistley · Dovercourt · Harwich

Chappel & Wakes Colne

Wrabness · Parkstone Quay

Marks Tey · Colchester

Hythe · Alresford · Thorpe-le-Soken

Walton-on-the-Naze

Braintree

Braintree Freeport

Colchester Town · Wivenhoe

Frinton-on-Sea

Cressing

Kelvedon

Gt Bentley · Weeley · Kirby Cross

White Notley

Witham

Clacton-on-Sea

Chelmsford

South Woodham Ferrers · Fambridge

Southminster

Battles-Bridge

Althorne · Burnham-on-Crouch

Billericay

Hockley

Rochford

Shenfield

Wickford · Rayleigh

Prittlewell

Southend-on-sea

This section is for readers who wish to use this speedy if not very scenic route to Norwich, for those who want to explore its wonderful branch lines, and for the information of those touring East Anglia as recommended at the beginning of this chapter and finishing off by joining this route at Ipswich and speeding down to London Liverpool Street.

It is not given the mile-by-mile description the rest of that tour has enjoyed. London Liverpool Street is a great and grand terminus, and still has boat trains for the continent (via Harwich) plus the newer Stansted Airport traffic and direct trains to most of East Anglia. For more about this station, see opposite.

The GREAT EASTERN MAIN LINE (named after its original company) has understandably always been more concerned with speed than rural beauty, so it races through parts which start off, to be frank, a little dull. Fine for head-in-the-paper commuters, not so great for sightseeing (see page 193 for a more picturesque route to Norwich). It's not just me, either.

You have to admire the honesty of the Baedeker guide of 1906 when it stated:

> **The run from Liverpool Street Station to (12½M.) Romford (White Hart), a small town (13,656 inhab,) noted for its ale, with good golf-links, is uninteresting.**

A century later, little change there you may feel.

Back to Baedeker: 'Kelvedon (Star and Fleece) the birthplace of Charles H Spurgeon (1834–92)'. Who? Well, they wrote after his death: 'It is not possible to make a true estimate of the work of Charles H Spurgeon. It is too near to us.' Now it is not quite so near, we find he was a preacher, who wrote a great many books. A modern guide says when discussing **Kelvedon** under the 'celebrity' heading: 'I'll get back to you on that one.' Or as a modern website puts it 'quite a safe place to be after dark'. Er... that's it.

Chelmsford, the first large town out from London, is not on most people's must-see-before-you-die list, although it is by no means ghastly.

Things get a bit better with **Colchester***, which has a fascinating history including Roman emperors, war elephants and Boadicea, painter John Constable and a celeb-studded present. The electrified main line rattles quickly on to **Ipswich**, then takes off directly north to Norwich (more in the earlier line section, page 199). On the other hand, all is not lost round here, thanks to the many great branch lines, see pages 212–13.

A Sea-Going Railway Hero

ME/TLN

Liverpool Street station contains a unique memorial to a railwayman who attacked an enemy submarine – while on duty. Captain Charles Fryatt was the master of the Great Eastern Railway ferry *Brussels* which had just left Harwich in 1915, bound for the neutral Netherlands, when a German U-boat surfaced nearby and demanded his surrender. The U-boat had a deck gun as well as torpedoes, and such craft had already shown no compunction about attacking unarmed civilian vessels. Captain Fryatt rang down to the engine room 'full speed ahead' and turned his bows towards the U-boat, which, unsure of stopping the ferry, did a crash dive to escape. The episode made the German navy a worldwide laughing stock and Fryatt a hero.

The following year Fryatt's ferry was surrounded by German destroyers and they captured him. They took him ashore to occupied Belgium, tried him on a trumped-up charge and shot him. Such was the national anger that many shells fired at German trenches had 'For the Murderers of Captain Fryatt' painted on them. After the war his remains were given a hero's funeral at St Paul's in London, and then taken by special train for burial at Dovercourt near Harwich, where he had lived with this family. His grave is still marked in that churchyard: 'Captain Charles Fryatt, Illegally Executed by the Germans.'

The station has also suffered from history in being bombed with great loss of life in both world wars, by terrorists (nearby) twice in recent years, and it played a very different role in the arrival of the Kindertransport trains of saved Jewish children fleeing the Nazis in the late 1930s. Those now elderly people, one told me, have never forgotten this place, or what Britain did for them.

It's a lot to think on as you wait for the 11.08 to Clacton.

Also not to be missed at the award-winning brightly modernised Liverpool Street, go up the stairs opposite the platforms to see the brick frieze. And, high above Captain Fryatt's memorial, the proud words 'Great Eastern Railway'.

Have you twigged to these great branches?

Having been just a little underwhelmed by the GREAT EASTERN MAIN LINE, it must be said that it offers more than half-a-dozen interesting branch lines up until Ipswich, plus more beyond, and they all offer different fascinating aspects and great countryside to explore. Leaving aside the London inner suburban branches, they are, going east:

On a Y-shaped route southeast from **Shenfield**, the SOUTHEND VICTORIA LINE (to **Southend** major seaside resort – think long pier, cockney days out, sticks of rock, mud) and branching off that at **Wickford**, the CROUCH VALLEY LINE to **Southminster** on an estuary and 45 miles from London (the former is an electrified double track, so no mere sleepy branch).

On the left (north) of the main line there's the six-mile single-track BRAINTREE BRANCH taking off at **Witham** and passing through **White Notley**, **Cressing** and **Braintree Freeport** (a sort of jumped-up shopping mall) to **Braintree** – perhaps you didn't know Essex could be so rural. If you suspect the strange mileposts are counting down to something more distant, you're right. It once went to Bishop's Stortford.

Also to the north, the GAINSBOROUGH LINE* to Sudbury takes off at **Marks Tey**, and was briefly known as the Lovejoy Line during the heyday of that TV programme (12 miles single track, not electrified; massive viaduct and railway museum at **Chappel & Wakes Colne**; scenery as immortalised by Constable past **Bures**; Gainsborough Museum at **Sudbury**).

Heading right (south) at **Colchester**, there are two more electrified double-track coastal branches, again in a 'Y' shape: THE SUNSHINE

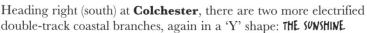

COAST LINE* to **Clacton-on-Sea** and **Walton-on-the-Naze** (the Y divides at **Thorpe-le-Soken**). Both termini have piers, and are about 18 miles from Colchester. The Clacton trains tend to run through from London. The Walton trains run from Colchester and often take the short branch-off-a-branch line to **Colchester Town** station (but not on Sundays) before reversing along the other side of a triangle to regain their route.

At **Manningtree**, another important line takes off to the coast, the 11-mile MAYFLOWER LINE✝ to **Harwich**, which takes boat trains for ferries to Holland, running down a pretty peninsula beside the Stour Estuary. The junction is a triangle with all sides electrified.

At **Ipswich** the main line shoots straight north to Norwich, with very few stations and not much interest; more below. But a marvellous secondary route takes off up the coast from Ipswich and reaches Lowestoft, where a connection for Norwich can be made: the EAST SUFFOLK LINE is hugely worthwhile scenically (see page 207). There is also another branch to the coast just after Ipswich, coming off the East Suffolk Line.

The 12-mile FELIXSTOWE BRANCH LINE has a regular passenger service from Ipswich but is also hugely busy with shipping container trains from that port. It may even be double tracked by the time you read this, because it's so busy.

There's also a useful connecting cross-country BURY ST EDMUNDS LINE from Ipswich to Ely or Cambridge, which starts by splitting off from the Great Eastern Main Line to Norwich before it reaches Diss and heading west, then dividing for either of those cities near Newmarket.

And of course if you go to the end of the GREAT EASTERN MAIN LINE at Norwich (in which case note how you cross over the Cambridge–Norwich line on the approach, swoop round right to join it, and cross Britain's only overhead overhead electrified swing bridge at Trowse, ending up in the splendid Norwich Thorpe terminus), or get there via the East Suffolk Line, (more on page 207), you have a choice of four fabulous branches. They are all detailed elsewhere in this chapter: the two WHERRY LINES (see page 203), THE BITTERN LINE (see page 200), and THE BRECKLAND LINE (see page 197).

The WEST ANGLIA MAIN LINE is the rather grand name for the other major route out of Liverpool Street, which goes north up to Cambridge, with four branches *en route* to **Enfield Town**, **Hertford East**, **Chingford**, and **Stansted Airport** (all electrified). There's nothing wrong with this route either, but as it isn't very scenic and I recommend going to Cambridge from King's Cross (which is as quick, if not quicker), I won't describe it in detail.

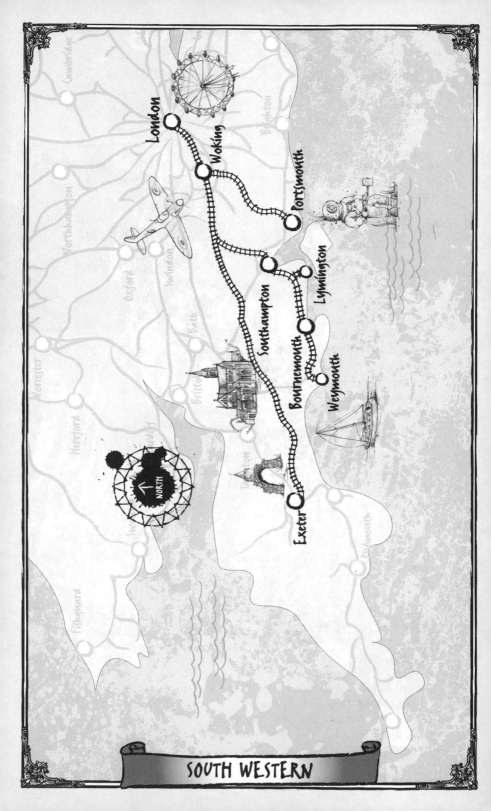

London
Woking
Portsmouth
Lymington
Southampton
Bournemouth
Weymouth
Exeter

Cambridge
Brighton
Northampton
Oxford
Swindon
Bath
Bristol
Worcester
Hereford
Taunton

NORTH

Fishguard

SOUTH WESTERN

South Western from Waterloo:
Take Me to the Sunshine

Waterloo: welcome to Britain's biggest and busiest station

Waterloo, where our journey starts (or ends), is Britain's biggest and busiest station. It covers 24.5 acres and also has the greatest number of platforms. It's arguable how many there actually are, however, depending on which you include: some put it at 32, which seems rather a lot until you start counting them. I can count 19 main line, five in what was until 2007 the International terminal, four in Waterloo East, an annex on the Charing Cross route (and once connected by a line right across the concourse!); two each for the Underground's Bakerloo, Jubilee, Northern and Waterloo and City lines, which gives a total of 36. I'm probably cheating by including Waterloo East, but hey, if you're boasting, don't leave stuff out.

The main part of the station alone is by far Britain's busiest in passenger numbers, with 61 million people ticketed through here in the last year recorded.

It's a fabulous and romantic station, whatever grumbly commuters may say. You can still meet beneath the old-fashioned clock, as did film stars and spies, intrepid explorers, illicit lovers, departing war heroes and those heading for the boat trains connecting with the great liners for New York.

The Kinks rock group made the station more famous with the song *Waterloo Sunset* in 1967 (trivia: although it was intended to be *Liverpool Sunset* until too many records came out about Liverpool, many Londoners consider it their anthem. Abba's song *Waterloo*, in as much it was about anything, was about the battle).

At the end of the lines in the main station are Britain's best buffers (sounds like a Frankie Howerd joke but go and have a look, they're like

battleship guns), some massive hydraulic Ransome & Rapier jobs. They are supposed to absorb the impact of a train at speed but have never been put to the test, as far as I know. They have gas flames under them in winter to stop them freezing and splitting (as did the four sets taken out of the platforms when

Benefits of an Early Start: the 1840 to Southampton

One odd benefit of the South-Western route out of London being so very early in railway history – the company started in 1831 – was that engines were at that time feeble. So the gradients of the main line from London to Southampton are extremely gentle, which has paid a dividend ever since in high speeds, comfort and fuel savings, whereas later railways could be built more cheaply, with more severe gradients and curves to conquer.

Indeed other routes operated from Waterloo – such as the Portsmouth Direct route through Haslemere built about 20 years later – are so twisting in places that you have to cling to your coffee with the lid on between stations, and trains even today on the steep bits sometimes slip to a halt on ground-up leaves in the autumn. Another loop through Alton to Winchester was called 'over the Alps' by steam-train drivers who had to struggle up it, which is one reason it closed beyond Alton (only for steam nuts to reopen it *because* it was so steep).

By contrast, the original main line is more level and straight. The first section to open was from the original London terminus at Nine Elms to Woking Common, which was in the middle of nowhere, more than a mile from the small village of Woking, population 600.

The ensuing century would see that town boom around the station and a whole new breed of people depend on it: we now call them commuters (interestingly because the railway company would *commute*, that is reduce and transform, the normal fare – so commuters have

Eurostar moved in. They had been stored at Woking and some total twit forgot they were full of water.)

The name 'Waterloo' came from the bridge built across the Thames not long before the station, and that was of course named after the battle not long before that – in 1815, changing history by defeating Napoleon's French army. In turn the battle is named after the little town in Belgium where it happened.

You could travel from Waterloo London to the small station of Waterloo Belgium via nearby Brussels in about four hours, which I have done. Waterloo, Merseyside might take a little longer. To travel to Waterloo, New Zealand (a three-plank halt last time I looked) or Waterloo, Ontario, or the three Waterloos in Australia would not be a day-return job.

▲ ME/ILN

Extending the South Western Railway

something in common with prisoners whose death sentences have been, to use the legal term, *commuted* to 40 years' penal servitude!). The leafy hills of Surrey would become the 'gin-and-Jag belt' by the 1950s, and it still is.

The railway soon realised the horse-race goers would form another regular clientele, with thousands flocking to trains for the Derby, and even for Ascot races (which then entailed a seven-mile walk each way to the races from Woking!). They still do, with at least four racecourses reachable from Waterloo, and the stations now a lot closer to the finishing post.

On 11 May 1840, the first train ran right through from London to Southampton. It was sent off by a brass band, took three hours and was greeted by a 21-gun salute. Nothing would ever be quite the same again.

The London one is certainly worth looking around. There's the award-winning sinewy, curving and undulating modernistic International station on the north side, completed to budget and timetable in 1993, with a very modern glass roof. The design by Nicholas Grimshaw could be irregularly curving because of computer-aided design. Apparently no two of the sheets of glass in the irregular roof are quite identical, which must be a pane (groan!) for glass repairs.

There's the magnificent Victory Arch on the outside of Waterloo. It's at the left of the concourse as you stand with your back to the platforms and faces outward, so you only encounter it coming from Waterloo Bridge on foot and commuters go through here for years and never see it. It commemorates a different war: 1914–18, and the many railwaymen who died fighting it. Have a look at the outside.

Notice the lanterns with a bundle of rods, or fasces, the Roman symbol of imperial power. Fascism, based on that power, had yet to be discredited.

This, and the rest of the imperial Baroque-style station buildings rebuilt in 1900–22, are by James Robb Scott. He was also the architect for the astonishingly modern Art-Deco station at Surbiton some ten minutes down our route (that station is now also listed for preservation). It seems impossible they are by the same man, or his team. Like saying Handel's *Messiah* and *Rock Around the Clock* were written by the same composer. Amazing. If you get a chance to look at both of them, they do have one thing in common: quality.

Waterloo also, bizarrely, had more platforms for the dead in the Necropolis station, at a site on the left as you leave by train. The tickets were one-way, naturally (see page 234). We, on the other hand, hope to return.

WATERLOO TO WOKING: another Britain's Busiest

(25mins, 24miles)

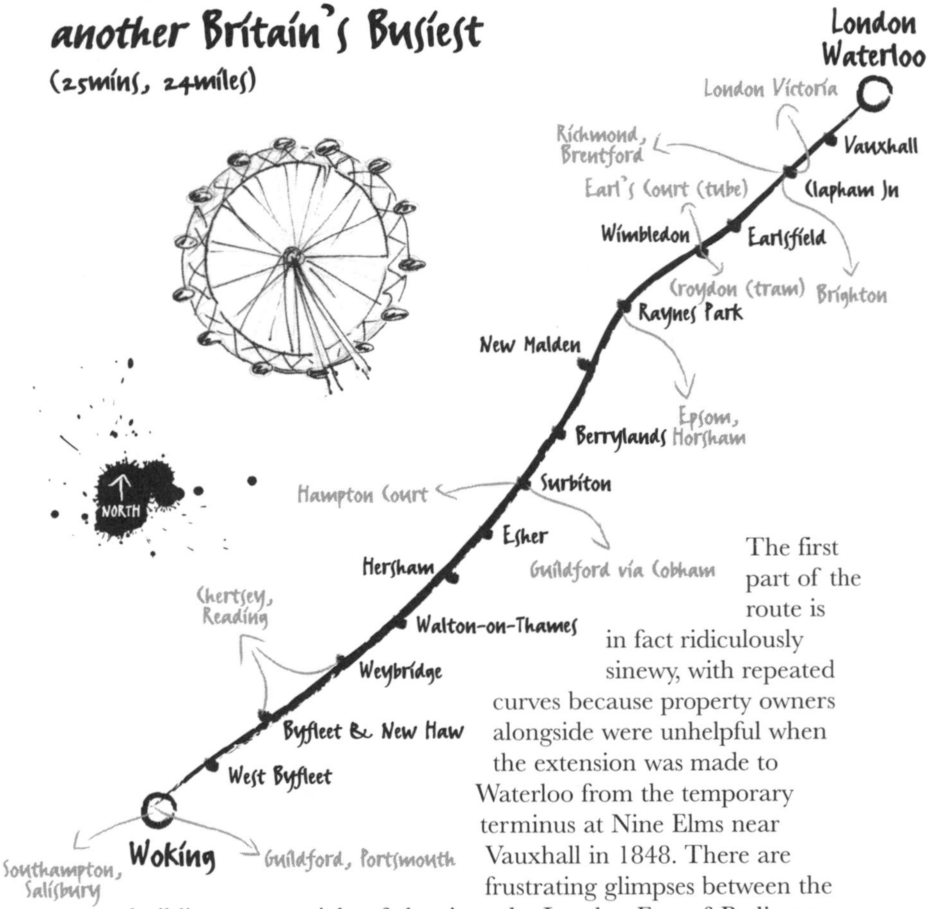

London Waterloo

London Victoria

Vauxhall

Richmond, Brentford

Earl's Court (tube)

Clapham Jn

Wimbledon

Earlsfield

Croydon (tram) Brighton

Raynes Park

New Malden

Epsom, Horsham

Berrylands Horsham

Surbiton

Hampton Court

Esher

Hersham

Guildford via Cobham

Chertsey, Reading

Walton-on-Thames

Weybridge

Byfleet & New Haw

West Byfleet

Woking   Guildford, Portsmouth

Southampton, Salisbury

NORTH

The first part of the route is in fact ridiculously sinewy, with repeated curves because property owners alongside were unhelpful when the extension was made to Waterloo from the temporary terminus at Nine Elms near Vauxhall in 1848. There are frustrating glimpses between the buildings to our right of the river, the London Eye, of Parliament, and of the Millbank tower block across the river near the Tate Britain art gallery, but they are unfortunately just glimpses.

At **Vauxhall**, as we lean into another curve, the surreal image of elephants and castles whiz past on our right amid chimney pots. This is because we are at the roof level of a neighbouring pub.

Oddly, all Russian railway stations are called Vauxhall because the main line from the southwest ended here before Waterloo was built and the Tsar, being shown round, said they should get a 'Vauxhall' for themselves. That may be apocryphal, but if so, the Russians probably named stations after the Vauxhall pleasure gardens nearby, because a pleasure park was called a *Vauxhall* in Russia at the time, and the first railway there went to one. A huge concrete flyover arises on our right and crosses over our heads to reach lines heading at right angles across us from Victoria to the Kent coast. This 6,000-ton monstrosity was built only just over a decade ago to bring Eurostar trains from France into Waterloo, a calculated insult to the French some claimed. Would we do such a thing? Really it was because the room for the long trains was here, not at Victoria. The French now go to St Pancras by a faster route. Anyway, they name their stations after military victories too. They just haven't got so many to choose from.

We whiz under several sets of lines from Victoria, which is across the river to our right, and one of these routes, which has crossed the river near the giant four-chimneyed former Battersea Power Station, crosses over us on a girder bridge at an angle then swoops around to our left to join us for

Britain's widest set of running lines for the last mile or two into Clapham Junction. So this stretch we are sharing with the Brighton Line and all its offshoots.

Here in the rush-hour you can have eight or so trains within sight at the same time, running in different directions on a bewildering expanse of railway.

Yet another line from west London arrives on our right just before **Clapham Junction**, said to be Europe's busiest station in terms of number of trains and certainly Britain's by that measure.

The first station here, called Falcon Bridge, was opened in 1863. Even then it was a junction between this line, the London & South Western Railway, and other lines. The population of the sleepy rural neighbourhood, known for market gardens, rocketed from 6,000 to 168,000 from 1840 to 1910, a dramatic transformation caused largely by the railway.

After the station the Brighton Line diverges left and we pick up speed through **Earlsfield**. A flyover which separates the fast from slow trains crosses over our heads as we approach **Wimbledon**. A huge train depot is on our right; from behind that an Underground line joins us and the famous All England tennis courts are on the far side of that, a stiff walk over the hill from Wimbledon station.

The junctions come thick and fast. One for Croydon trams to our left, then a burrowing junction (the diverging route burrows under the other track) which diverges at the platforms at **Raynes Park** for Epsom, another burrowing junction below us takes off

right over a level crossing to Kingston, and after **Surbiton** comes
a complex flyover using the brick viaduct which starts
climbing on our left and then crosses over our heads to
the right to reach Hampton Court and *then* a
burrowing junction which goes off left *en
route* to Effingham Junction.

Shah
Jehan
Mosque

You may not be able to see much if
trees are in full leaf, but down on the
right just before the flyover is an
equally complex miniature railway
system in someone's garden. I
suppose you'd have to be a train fan
to live in the shadow of this lot!

Surbiton's listed Art-Deco station can't really be appreciated by through
passengers, but soon we are speeding southwest through a string of small
stations. The racecourse on our left at **Esher** is Sandown Park.

After **Hersham**, **Walton-on-Thames** and **Weybridge** there's a huge
triangular junction on our right which takes a line to Virginia Water,
looping back to London a different way.

As we start slowing for **Woking**, the next major station, notice the elegant
Shah Jehan Mosque set amidst trees to our left. Mosques may be two-a-
penny in Britain today, but this was the first.

Woking is also central to H G Wells's 1898 sci-fi classic *The War of the
Worlds*. The Martians land near here and an early casualty of their heat-ray
is the dome of the Oriental College (now the mosque) and a train at this
very station which gets set on fire:

The light upon the railway puzzled me at first; there were a black
heap and a vivid glare, and to the right of that a row of yellow
oblongs. Then I perceived this was a wrecked train, the fore
part smashed and on fire, the hinder carriages still upon
the rails.

Well, I was going to say don't worry, you won't
encounter a Martian tripod fighting machine around
here, but actually there is one. Woking people seem to
have forgiven H G Wells, as they have recently
erected a sculpture of one of them outside a shopping
centre in the town. Not within heat-ray range of the
station, luckily.

After Woking, trains can stay on the main line
southwest for, ultimately, Southampton, Weymouth or
Exeter (in which case, read on), or head south on the
Portsmouth Direct route through Guildford (in which
case skip to page 236).

WOKING TO SOUTHAMPTON: Martians to maritime
(50mins, 55 miles)

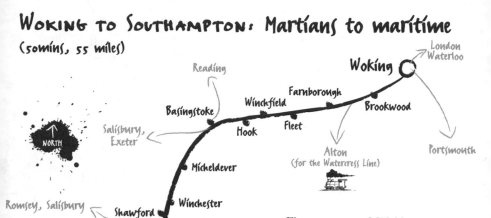

First stop out of Woking on the main line is **Brookwood**[*], which was once a junction for the dead, as the funeral trains from Waterloo Necropolis would reverse up into the massive cemetery on our left. There's a faded sign saying *Brookwood Cemetery* on the left before the station. The just-mentioned H G Wells's mistress, novelist Rebecca West, is buried here, as is Freddie Mercury of rock band Queen. For more on the fascinating death trains that ran to here, see page 234. There was also a branch on the other side on the main line to Bisley, still the top place for rifle champions to shoot. The train was nicknamed, of course, the *Bisley Bullet*.

The area starting here and continuing down through Hampshire through Aldershot and Bordon is thick with military bases, and you could pretty well place them by a geological map. They are wherever the barren, sandy land is; you didn't use top farmland for that kind of thing – or for firing ranges. In one case regiments were marched off trains from Southampton troop ships after a war, set up camp and simply never moved away.

Shortly after Brookwood, the Basingstoke Canal runs alongside on the right, down in the trees. We run right alongside, and as elsewhere the canal

had been heading for greater things – the south coast – but never got there thanks to competition from the railway, which followed a few years behind the canal builders. Indeed, the canal boomed in 1838–39, carrying supplies to build the railway, which then killed its trade. Happily it was saved by pleasure boating and fishing types, and more recently preservationists who have restored nearly all of it (apart from a tunnel near Basingstoke because that has been occupied by protected bats – now that *is* batty).

Meanwhile we see the rightmost track lift up and over, and one go left too, for the flying junction of the ALTON BRANCH.

THE ALTON BRANCH

The ALTON BRANCH* soon meets junctions from the north and south, **Ash Vale**, then 'home of the British Army' **Aldershot** and the pretty but busy town of **Farnham**. It becomes increasingly rural beside the meadow meanders of another branch of the River Wey through little **Bentley** until **Alton** is reached, giving a direct connection for the steam-powered WATERCRESS LINE** which continues another ten very attractive and hilly miles towards Winchester but stops short at the charming Georgian small town of Alresford. Recommended. Really worth a day out in itself. Back at Farnham in 2001, a train was delayed for 25 minutes while the driver waited for a snoozing badger on the track to wake up. The passengers all heartily approved. Only in England!

We zoom under **Pirbright Junction** for the ALTON LINE – Pirbright is a name well known to soldiers, as is Bisley Camp to our right, Aldershot to our left, and ahead – appropriately in a deep cutting – Deepcut Camp. In fact the village is named after the earlier deep cutting, parallel to us now, which carries the canal and suddenly swerves south and over our heads on an aqueduct (it comes after a high brick road bridge and leaked ominously onto the tracks until 1980, when it was relined). It seems a gloomy spot – Deepcut Camp was the scene of a series of suspicious suicides/deaths in recent years and has closed.

Cheer up. Next is **Farnborough**, which is known to aviation buffs – aeronaks if you like – for world-class air shows. The Royal Aeronautical Establishment, to give the base its proper name, was south of the station and used to have its own branch line trailing in from the left after the station. It was here only around a century ago – on 16 October 1908 – that Britain's first powered flight took place, the pilot being American 'Colonel' Sam Cody and the aircraft *British Army No 1*. He failed to convince the brasshats that the contraption had any use in warfare – unlike good old

▼ ME

horses, dear chap – and he died in a plane crash here in 1913. Today all the latest planes in the world come to Farnborough to show off, proving he was right all along. If you see nothing at all in the sky, it's probably a very stealthy stealth bomber.

Next stop is **Fleet**, named after Fleet Pond that the railway was built across. In medieval times it belonged to the monks – for fish to keep the abbeys going in winter.

The M3 motorway, racing us towards Southampton, appears on our right before **Winchfield** then lifts over our heads while we are in a cutting and reappears on our left before **Hook**. After some good straight flat four-track speeding, we slow for the junction at **Basingstoke**.

Here the Great Western Railway comes down from Reading in the north, trailing in from the right. Initially, the GWR had its own daft broad-gauge tracks, so every item of goods had to be transhipped between trains, as had passengers. After World War II, Basingstoke, which had lost its best property in the 17th-century Civil War siege, was built up into a huge London overspill town. Although the area may be uninspiring it does produce some amazing women: Jane Austen, Liz Hurley and the Duchess of York for example. The Anvil, which you may see to the left, is not a place to get hammered but a theatre.

Next at **Worting Junction** the Exeter and Salisbury route, the **WEST OF ENGLAND MAIN LINE**, makes a dramatic departure, diving off right, with a high-speed flyover for trains coming up from Southampton, towards which we swerve off left. (If you are on the Salisbury route, switch to page 243).

There is just one station in this 18½-mile section, which involves a climb to a summit at **Litchfield Tunnel**, eight miles from Basingstoke. But it's a gentle climb, of around 1 in 250, so feeble were the engines when this line was built. We are rising onto a chalk plateau which was once a seabed but is now an eastward extension of Salisbury Plain. That one station, **Micheldever**, comes after the two short **Popham tunnels** and is in a vast quarry, carved out by the railway to provide the chalk base for Southampton Docks.

We run gently downhill for ten miles to **Winchester***, highly recommended for its medieval town, great shopping and cathedral – which, like Waterloo, gave its name to a pop song. But because the station's in a cutting and the city's in a bowl of hills you don't see much from the train. Actually you can glimpse the cathedral about half a mile later, at about 7 o'clock if you consider the train's heading towards 12 o'clock. Or over your left shoulder if you prefer.

Did you know?

Winchester Cathedral was the title of the US number-one pop song in 1966 for the New Vaudeville Band and Crosby, Stills and Nash wrote the song Cathedral about the building.

The collapsing cathedral, which houses the remains of St Swithun, a number of kings and Jane Austen, was saved in 1906 by diver William Walker going under the waterlogged foundations and shoring them up. It took him six years underwater in total darkness. Unpaid. And he cycled from London!

As we run down through **Shawford** to **Eastleigh**, the River Itchen (one of the world's premier trout streams) becomes more and more evident in its meanders on our left.

Eastleigh, not the prettiest of places, is one of those railway towns such as Crewe, Swindon and Doncaster entirely created by the company. In fact the first station here was called Bishopstoke because that was the nearest village. Huge carriage works employing thousands grew up here, and it's still a four-way junction, with a line heading across country to Fareham.

Eastleigh's vital role in the last war is detailed overleaf, and indeed next stop is **Southampton Airport Parkway**, home of the Spitfire, and boasting the shortest stroll between train door and check-in desk in Europe. On the left after the station, a replica Spitfire is mounted near the tracks.

Next is **Swaythling**, then **St Denys**, spelt like the Paris football team. It was once called Portswood, but people took trains there thinking they were going to Portsmouth, so it was changed. One hopes no-one goes there now thinking it's part of Paris.

Tracks join here on the left from another, picturesque coastal route to Fareham. This curves right around the harbour to our left, so you can sometimes see the trains heading the same way as us, across the water.

On the left is **Northam train depot**, a modern privately owned outfit that is part of the reason why Eastleigh isn't needed so much now – the manufacturers maintain the trains.

We swerve off right – the original terminus was where the old lines still run straight on – and through a once-troublesome tunnel to **Southampton Central**, the main station having been moved here after the through route was provided. Here you will hear announced trains for Bristol and Salisbury, Leeds and Brighton. If you're going to Bournemouth and Weymouth, read on; if you're heading to Salisbury and Bath go to page 155.

Southampton's Railway in War and Peace: Blood, Sweat, Tears… and Seaborne Glamour

No British railway had a greater role in the two terrible world wars of the 20th century than the lines out of Waterloo run by the London & South Western, or Southern Railway as it became between the conflicts, because of its vital Channel ports.

On 5 August 1914, the War Office gave the railways 60 hours to organise the transport of the British Expeditionary Force to France. By the end of that month 711 trains had moved 130,000 soldiers, 39,000 horses, 344 heavy guns, 277 lorries and all the other equipment the army needed through Southampton to rush to the aid of France and Belgium. That it famously wasn't over by Christmas was evidenced by the grim reverse traffic: 7,822 ambulance trains left Southampton carrying 1,234,248 wounded by the end of the war four long years later.

The run-up to World War II saw Eastleigh performing a decisive role. A young designer at the Supermarine factory called R J Mitchell drew plans for a very elegant, fast fighter aircraft with elliptical wings. RJ, as he was known, was secretly dying of cancer while the prototype was built. After the first test flight, he eagerly rushed to see what the pilot wanted changing – they always needed certain things altering. 'Don't touch a thing' came the answer. It was a natural winner. They needed a name, and that of a querulous small animal, such as *Shrew*, was suggested. Then someone remembered its formidable eight machine guns and suggested *Spitfire*.

The Air Ministry ordered its first 300 of the planes, ready just in time for the Battle of Britain in these same southern skies. RJ didn't live to see his design turn the tide of history against barbarism. Today the airport alongside the railway is named after him. Had he lived, the honours would have been endless. And his aircraft carried on in more and faster versions – not until the jet fighter arrived was it outclassed.

Meanwhile the enemy knew Southampton's strategic importance for the docks, the railways and the aircraft works. It was hammered by bombing relentlessly in late 1940, to the point where normal life broke down and the city resembled 'a blazing furnace' night after night. The population fled to the hills and slept in the open, returning to clear up and restart war production every morning. The mayor was noted rather ignobly fleeing on the 3pm train every afternoon, well before the chaos the raids that night would bring.

In fact the Waterloo end of this line was the most heavily bombed railway of all: 92 hits in just eight months at the height of the Blitz. Navvies swarmed into the still-smoking craters and had trains running again within hours.

The railwaymen hit back by making Southampton, Poole and Weymouth down this line the centre of the build-up for the biggest seaborne invasion in world history. Even all the rather unnecessary and unprofitable duplications of route caused by company rivalry – the Great Western Railway had its own route down from Didcot to its own station at Winchester, for example, part of whose viaduct can still be seen forlornly standing

by the M3 – were for those few years running at full capacity, although they would quickly close after the war.

From D-Day to the end of 1944, a million US soldiers marched off trains at Southampton and onto ships for God knows what fate in France. The harbours of the south coast were thronged with every type of ship imaginable – the oddest things. An (obviously elderly) American friend of mine as a young tug captain had to tow a massive empty concrete box the size of an office block across to Normandy.

It had anti-aircraft guns on the corners. When they got there, they were ordered to sink it. It was part of the Mulberry Harbour, a way of invading a country without having to seize heavily defended and mined existing docks. No need to repeat the disaster at Dieppe.

Of course the railway saw the other side too. The bewildered child evacuees from France and the Channel Islands at the start. At the end, again the ambulance trains were waiting.

Yet another side of Southampton's railway history involved glamour and hope. The great liners from the doomed *Titanic* to the great *Queens* carried increasing numbers of the rich and famous as well as millions of emigrants whose last ride in Britain was down these tracks.

Huge flying boats seemed to promise new custom for the

railway from the rich. For those who never knew them (and to be truthful that included me, except on film), these were airliners with boat hulls instead of wheels which could therefore use waterways instead of runways. The wealthy passengers had the most luxurious trains run from London, fast motor launches to take them out on to Southampton Water, and then the roaring massive aircraft would create huge white bow waves as they raced across the sea, lifting off and turning towards America, South Africa and exotic destinations worldwide.

But travel changed rapidly after the war. The peak number of

sea passengers was in 1955, when 690,000 passed through here. After that, jet airliners took over, flying boats were scrapped, and it seemed the era of great liners was over. The railways turned their attention to serving airports instead.

Wrong, as it turned out. Today more and bigger liners than ever are docking at Southampton, this time for the burgeoning cruise market rather than getting anywhere fast. Some of the wealthier passengers are even taken there from London by special luxury trains. History repeating itself.

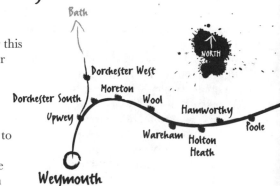

SOUTHAMPTON TO WEYMOUTH: the New Forest and two Hardys' Wessex
(1½hrs, 63miles)

You should sit on the left for this route (going west). Soon after Southampton comes **Millbrook** and on our left Southampton's *raison d'être* – the miles of docks with containers piled high, many to be lugged away by train.

Huge ships are visible here at the head of Southampton

Bath

Dorchester West
Moreton
Dorchester South
Wool
Hamworthy
Upwey
Poole
Wareham
Holton
Heath

NORTH

Weymouth

Water, the deep channel formed by the confluence of the Itchen and the Test (and dredged a lot deeper). Stonking great trains of containers head to and from the Midlands, the North and Scotland via Basingstoke and so lucrative is this traffic that the railway recently dug out all the tunnels and raised the bridges to get the bigger type of shipping boxes through.

Redbridge (junction right, for Salisbury and Bath route) and **Totton** (junction left, for Marchwood military port and Fawley refinery but not passengers) follow. Then at **Ashurst**✱ a transformation from grotty industry and unappealing suburbia miraculously happens – we are entering the New Forest and one of the most beautiful parts of this run.

The New Forest is (like the Holy Roman Empire or Lord Privy Seal) not what it says on the tin, being neither new nor a forest. It's a royal hunting ground dating back to Norman times and is largely gently rolling open heath. It has its own laws – enforced by the Verderers' Court – and is famous for the wild ponies which you can see from the train here and there. Here at last horses can behave as natural herd animals (which seems to be the females hanging out together being sociable while the bossy stallion runs round herding them up!). It's also fabulous for butterflies, lizards and snakes, etc.

Beaulieu Road✱ is one of those places cheekily named by railways that are nowhere near the place they purport to serve.

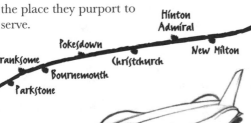

Beaulieu, meaning 'beautiful place' in French (though a Frenchman would be appalled to hear it pronounced as it is here – 'byoolee') is at least five miles away, with its National Motor Museum. This station and the others in the New Forest are a perfect start for wonderful walks.

Or indeed bike rides. At the next station, **Brockenhurst✦**, there are bike-hire outfits where you can find mountain bikes, cycle helmets and information about trails. Try Cycle Experience **T** 01590 624204 and Country Lanes **T** 01590 622627.

The Lymington Branch (10mins, smiles)

Brockenhurst✦ is also the junction for the recommended **LYMINGTON BRANCH✦**, a pretty, short run across typical New Forest heathland to Lymington River, the handsome small Georgian seaside town of Lymington (station **Lymington Town**) and across the river to the pier (called, er, **Lymington Pier**). Here ferries to Yarmouth on the Isle of Wight await, with fabulous views of Hurst Castle, the western Solent seaway to the Channel and the Needles (very tall, very thin – hence the name – chalk monolith rocks off the most westerly point of the isle).

This branch is the only place on the network where you can still ride in the 1950s'-built slam-door trains, which for the last half of the 20th century inhabited southern England in their thousands. It was found at the Clapham crash that these don't do too well (to put it mildly) when two crash end-on, so they were slowly phased out from the network. Here they operate under the old 'one engine in steam' branch-line rules – ie: you can't crash into other trains if there aren't any.

It's a pity these trains had to go because they were astonishingly reliable (more so than their replacements, which in at least one case recycled the 40-year-old motors in a 'new' train!) and would have happily soldiered on for another 40 years.

The extremely rare crash danger was a problem, but they were still around 40,000-times safer than driving in a car. And as for slam-door trains, you can bet there will be some teenagers growing up soon who just stand there with the door closed and have no idea why the train has moved off without letting them out...

Sway is next, and was home to an eccentric judge who retired from British India and decided that concrete was the coming thing in building materials. To prove his point, he built slender towers, such as the one you can see if you look left after the station, in Mogul style. The Sway towers didn't sway. He wanted to put a powerful light at the top, but the Admiralty objected, saying ships heading for the docks would plough into the New Forest.

After **New Milton** and **Hinton Admiral**, look left to see a large abbey-like church and a distant headland at **Christchurch**✦. The church has a story of a medieval miracle in its construction. The headland, Hengistbury Head, affords fantastic views across to the Isle of Wight and hosts kite festivals. Stroll down through the town (south, to our left) and take the foot ferry across the river (about two miles in total). The rivers before and after the station are the Avon and the Stour, which proves yet again that the English can be amazingly unoriginal about river names.

After the second river, you can catch a glimpse of the white cliffs of the Isle of Wight at about 8 o'clock direction, then **Pokesdown** and a short tunnel lead us into **Bournemouth**.

Bournemouth is a suitably grand station with massive overall roof and spacious interior. The seaside's rather discreet charms – this isn't raffish Brighton – are about a mile to the south. If you were interested in the early aviators back at Farnborough, it was here on 13 July 1910 that The Honourable Charles Stewart Rolls, aged 32, co-founder of Rolls-Royce, was the first Briton to be killed flying a plane. The crash was in front of a horrified crowd at a competition for the 'alighting prize' by which early aviators attempted to follow a course and land within a 100ft bullseye. From that day on, the red lettering on the radiator of a Rolls-Royce car became black.

▼ ME

Bournemouth Aviation Meeting. The Hon. C.S. Rolls in the air.

Still no salt water visible from the train, but don't worry, a treat is coming up. We whiz past a viaducted (if that's a word – well it is now) old triangular junction on our left which led to the old station of Bournemouth West (part of the legacy of competing companies before 1948) and through **Branksome** and **Parkstone** in increasingly leafy, not to say well-heeled suburban sprawl. By the time we reach **Poole**✦ (alight for Channel Island fast ferries), which we reach – oddly – by crossing a pedestrian shopping precinct, we are at the seaside at last! There are superb views to the left as we seem to cross the waves (well we do, on a causeway, not a hovertrain) of the expanse of Poole Harbour and the distant hills of the Isle of Purbeck – not really an island, but hills near Swanage.

The suburb to the far left is Sandbanks, variously and breathtakingly described as the priciest real estate of its type in Britain/Europe/the world, the sort of place where a tatty old beach hut will go for £4 million because of the ground it's on. No wonder you see (on the right) gleaming Sunseeker motor yachts built here, the Ferraris or stretch limos of the sea.

Brownsea Island (National Trust) is one of the few refuges of the native red squirrel (not driven out by its bigger, brasher, more sexually active American grey cousins as elsewhere) and has a castle *and* the birthplace of Boy Scouts and Girl Guides to show you. It can be visited by launch from Poole Quay (half a mile from the station). Just don't bring any grey bushy-tailed American chums.

In World War II the Germans were invited to bomb it, I'm told. A decoy Poole docks, with lights, was fabricated there while the real one escaped unscathed under the blackout. Or that was the idea. We cross Holes Bay on this causeway and then after **Hamworthy**✣ – note the signal box on the left of the train with its toilet on stilts! – and then cross Lychett Bay for more great views.

After **Holton Heath**, we have the Wareham Channel of Poole Harbour on our left. **Wareham**✣ is as lovely a small town as you can imagine, perched between two rivers, the Piddle (near the tracks here) and the Frome. Piddle, by the way, was changed to puddle by embarrassed 18th- or 19th-century gentry in nearby place names such as famous Tolpuddle and Affpuddle. Puddle it ain't.

There are tiny unspoilt medieval streets, a gas-lit cinema, no big hyperstores and some very eccentric ceremonies. This pretty place is what many British towns were like before town planners were invented: local butchers, bakers, quality produce and a sense of community.

SWANAGE STEAM

South of Wareham on the Isle of Purbeck is the totally lovely
SWANAGE STEAM RAILWAY which goes from that seaside town up to
Corfe Castle, the impossibly picturesque ruin perched on a hill above
the little town and station. The tracks actually continue up this way
to the junction on the left after Wareham (trains carrying oil
extracted from under Poole Harbour have used them), and an
unused bay platform awaits at the station. For some dunderheaded
reason, at the time of writing it has still not been reconnected to the
main line, despite about 20 years of trying. It may have been fixed
by the time you arrive, but if not, try not to say 'brainless
bureaucratic blundering busybody blockheads.' And any other
words beginning with 'B'.

We have now crossed to run beside the other river in its lovely meanders
(or swan-filled floods in winter), the Frome, which like us is heading for (or
from, in the Frome's case) Dorchester. The next station is **Wool** (which like
Tweed, Worsted, Axminster and Wilton is a place that's part of the
nation's fabric) and has a totally fascinating
Tank Museum up the road at Bovington, about
a mile away. Tank trivia: they were originally
called landships and were operated largely by
sailors. 'Tank' was a name dreamed up to fool
enemy spies into thinking they were some kind of
water tank. Well, nearly a century later, we're still using the decoy name…

As we approach Dorchester after **Moreton**, local hero Thomas Hardy is
buried on the right – well, actually only his heart, and even then it might
have been the wrong bit of meat – and local hero Thomas Hardy (the
other one, captain of the *Victory*), is commemorated ahead on our left.
Dorchester✦, Casterbridge in Hardy's novels, is a classic county town of
great charm with several museums (and Hardy stuff) and great pubs. Plus
Prince Charles's strange dream suburb, Poundbury, which is a bit like the
1960s' TV series, *The Prisoner* in its odd almost-authenticity. An attempt to
make an instant Wareham.

It has two stations: Dorchester West on the Great Western route (see
page 160) which still goes north inland and eventually reaches Bath or
Paddington, and Dorchester South, which we arrive at from rival Waterloo
and, being on a screeching curve, unlike the other straight line, is clearly
an afterthought, but is now the main line.

In fact, as in Bristol Temple Meads, the Waterloo line did go straight
into a terminus at right angles to the other line but after they were later

connected by a curve, reversing into the station became too much of a fag. It was supposed to go straight on to Exeter at one time, but never did.

I mention this because in 2007, *60 years* after the Great Western Railway (GWR) finally lost the battle for supremacy at Dorchester, so the Waterloo line became the main route, and both companies were nationalised as the same outfit, I met a GWR staff diehard who said: 'We always signalled them Waterloo trains at the junction as though they were the branch line and we were the main.' It was that kind of company, the GWR.

Now we run south to run over 'proper GWR metals' as my anachronistic acquaintance insisted on calling them to Weymouth. Note on our right – to the west – the enormous prehistoric hill fort of Maiden Castle, the only one with triple rings of earthworks. Like Stonehenge, the amazing thing about these hillforts (and there are several close to here) is how amazingly little we know about them. Like why are they there, for a start. They are far too big to be defended by the population of the times – there'd be one man every hundred yards as

Waterloo's Strange Death Railway: No Return Tickets

The macabrely fascinating London Necropolis Railway started running to Brookwood on the Southampton line in 1854. It was exclusive in that you travelled only once, and then only in one direction. The service was run for just one type of passenger: the dead. 'Coffin Tickets', issued right up to the 1950s, were not available as returns. It was a radical solution to the capital's literally bulging graveyards.

Funeral trains to Brookwood ran from the discreet London Necropolis station adjoining Waterloo (in fact jammed next to a turntable for locomotives) where steam-power hoists would raise coffins to the level of the hearse vans. In the spirit of the age, those were segregated between Anglicans and the rest, as were the mourners' waiting rooms and carriages. There was, in later years of the operation, a discreet stone-built entrance on Westminster Bridge Road marked London Necropolis.

Everything was done to maintain dignity and avoid the view, expressed by the Bishop of London when the scheme was first floated, that it was improper to convey corpses by anything as fast as a steam train.

At **Brookwood**, Surrey, a part of Woking, a vast city of the dead was laid out with every possible nationality and creed catered for, (and indeed judging by the number of graves marked 'resting' or 'fell the Roman legions marched over the ramparts. Weird.

And down through **Upwey** (near a former station originally called Upwey Wishing Well Halte) into **Weymouth**✱, which offers a curve of resorty sandy beach on one side, Georgian terraces, a charming little harbour and a huge naval one, and,

on the west side is the strange Chesil Beach (many miles long, and all the pebbles graded from one end to the other, separate from the shore mostly and linking to the even weirder Isle of Portland beyond). The railway, until about 20 years ago, ran though the town's streets in a tramway to connect with Channel steamers – the lines are still there – and even reached the Isle of Portland, but for us, this is the end of the line.

asleep', waking Woking might still be a possibility). If today you take the pleasant and fascinating walk along the route of the long siding which these mournful trains took, reversing back from Brookwood station, to two truly terminal stations (one Anglican, one for the rest), many interesting things will come to light.

Such as why the further station is home to Orthodox monks, incongruously set with their chickens on a former platform for the dead in deepest Surrey? (They are venerating the relics of the English King Edward the Martyr, an important saint for them, in the nearby special chapel.) There is a fascinating collection of people who finally met their Waterloo, as it were, to discover at Brookwood, so a stroll round makes a happy day out, if you like that sort of thing. There are also sections for every kind of religion and every sort of dead: Freddie Mercury, star of Queen, born in exotic Zanzibar but ended his days at Brookwood; the deeply eccentric explorer Gottlieb Leitner, responsible for there being a mosque the other side of Woking station; Turkish aviators killed in World War I; American sailors; the feminist author Rebecca West who was so critical of H G Wells's books that she angrily went to see the writer – and ended up having a son by him. Great people – and they're not going anywhere. There is also a totally fascinating book on the subject of this forgotten death railway (see booklist, in *Appendix 2*), and a good novel based on it.

THE PORTSMOUTH DIRECT LINE:
Woking to Pompey, ups and Downs

The Battle of Havant and Frog Wars

The extraordinary railway Battle of Havant had its roots in one question: with both Southampton and Brighton reached by rail from London by 1840, the rival companies eyed up the sizeable city of Portsmouth in between – who would seize that valuable prize first?

First the London & South Western Railway (LSWR) tried to grab the traffic by building a line from Eastleigh to Gosport in 1841, but this was the wrong side of the harbour: Portsmouth folk had to take a ferry to reach their town. Then the Brighton company built a line along the coast in 1847 to run right into Portsmouth. The LSWR retaliated by building a line round the top of the harbour to Cosham and running down into Portsmouth too. All the routes to London were very indirect and Portsmouth people complained.

The solution came in the form of swashbuckling railway builder Thomas Brassey, who had already built a line from Woking down to Guildford and then to Godalming by 1849. He next started to build a route through the South Downs to Portsmouth, which would cut the distance from London by 20 miles. The people of Portsmouth were delighted, but the LSWR and the Brighton company were appalled that the interloper would steal their lucrative trade.

Brassey in fact never intended to run a railway on his new route. He was a speculator and knew one of the other two would be forced to buy it. In fact they were in no hurry to disrupt their cosy share-out of traffic, but when a cheeky third company, the South Eastern, built a line as far as Guildford from Redhill, there was clearly a danger of that lot getting to Portsmouth and spoiling their set-up. So the LSWR moved swiftly to take the new line over – but a battle royal ensued.

Where the new direct route joined the Brighton company's tracks at Havant – as it still does – the LSWR thought it had obtained the right to run trains over the Brighton company's tracks into Portsmouth.

The Brighton boys begged to differ, and the connections of the new route rusted for a year while the wrangling continued.

On 28 December 1858, the LSWR lost patience and sent a goods train down towards Havant from Petersfield very early in the morning to surprise their rivals. It was not in fact carrying goods, but a task force of LSWR officials, engineers, burly navvies and all their equipment, plus heavy-handed railway police. As one modern rail historian put it: 'It was a Victorian rent-a-mob!'

The Brighton boys had, however, got wind of this and had also turned out an intimidating crew of their toughest labourers and their tools, overseen by managers who had vowed not to give way. They had removed the connecting points and placed a large engine on the tracks blocking the way, chaining it down. They saw the LSWR train stuck helpless and went smirking to eat a celebratory breakfast ignoring the shouts of abuse and protests from the other side.

On their return the Brighton boys were aghast to find the LSWR crew had moved the Brighton engine and reconnected the points, moving their own engine towards Havant. They were appalled and uprooted some rail behind the LSWR engine, marooning it. The insults and swearing of the two gangs of workmen – sleeves rolled up, and squaring up to each other (it seemed a bare-knuckle brawl was imminent) – was now drawing a crowd of onlookers, and of course normal trains along the south coast were blocked all the while.

Eventually the LSWR men, the more sober side, reconnected their line and made a strategic withdrawal, greeted by whoops of triumph from the Brighton boys, who decorated their engine with victory flags, and went off to celebrate again. The Battle of Havant seemed over.

But the LSWR legal eagles were busy, and the Brighton company was forced to allow trains through the very next month. The real winners of the Battle of Havant were the people of Portsmouth, who saw journey times and fares to London plummet as the now three routes and two companies fought for their custom (as they still do).

Such border battles were known as Frog Wars, named after the bit of metal that allows two tracks to cross. They include such tactics as removing junctions or running a slow goods train in front of your rival's express to hold it up. There were at least two other Frog Wars in Britain, and around a dozen in the United States – and all involved people getting hopping mad…

The route described: Woking to Pompey
(1hr 10mins/1½-2hrs from London, 50 miles)

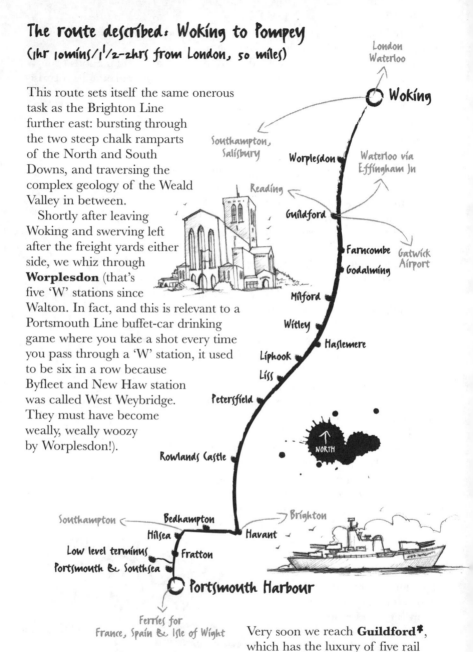

This route sets itself the same onerous task as the Brighton Line further east: bursting through the two steep chalk ramparts of the North and South Downs, and traversing the complex geology of the Weald Valley in between.

Shortly after leaving Woking and swerving left after the freight yards either side, we whiz through **Worplesdon** (that's five 'W' stations since Walton. In fact, and this is relevant to a Portsmouth Line buffet-car drinking game where you take a shot every time you pass through a 'W' station, it used to be six in a row because Byfleet and New Haw station was called West Weybridge. They must have become weally, weally woozy by Worplesdon!).

London
Waterloo

Woking

Southampton, Salisbury

Worplesdon

Waterloo via Effingham Jn

Reading

Guildford

Farncombe   Gatwick Airport

Godalming

Milford

Witley

Haslemere

Liphook

Liss

Petersfield

NORTH

Rowlands Castle

Southampton   Bedhampton   Brighton

Hilsea   Havant

Low level terminus   Fratton

Portsmouth & Southsea

Portsmouth Harbour

Ferries for France, Spain & Isle of Wight

Very soon we reach **Guildford***, which has the luxury of five rail routes out. After we cross over the A3 Portsmouth road on the approach (for the third time since Waterloo), two rail routes join us from either side, the one on the right from Reading and the one on the left from Effingham Junction, bringing trains a more roundabout way from Waterloo.

Guildford's historic town centre with cobbled streets and ancient pubs is on the hill to our left, the more modern university and cathedral on our right. I'd be surprised if you liked the cathedral, but then it did feature in the horror film *The Omen*. The devil boy screams when he gets out of a car and sees the gold figure on the tower. Talking of gold, the place name means 'gold (sand) ford' of the River Wey, which here cuts through the North Downs in a narrow cut, heading towards London to the left of the railway.

Guildford should be the county town of Surrey, but since London sprawled across the river and baggsied bits of Surrey, the county council has been nonsensically left in foreign territory at Kingston. I suspect they want London to think this is through inertia, but secretly plot to seize back the South Bank one day.

We tunnel through the chalk Downs, here very narrow, in two short bores and then burst out onto green river meadows. The Wey and its canal are on our left. Soon the **NORTH DOWNS LINE** curves off left across the river towards Redhill and Gatwick Airport, once a long tentacle of the distant Kent-based South Eastern Railway desperate to reach Reading (which they did, on the route that still exists). As recounted above, it was fear of this rival interloper reaching Portsmouth that pushed the London & South Western Railway to take over this line we are travelling on.

We rattle through **Farncombe**, which has level crossings at both ends of the platforms, and across the River Wey again into **Godalming**, whose insanely sharp curve is only partly explained by the fact that the end of the line was once nearby. There are lakes on the left which reminds me that nearby a mad millionaire built a ballroom – well, a kind of large conservatory – under one such lake. It's still there.

Then the increasingly rural **Milford** and **Witley**, the engine (or rather electric motors) now working hard to pull us up a steep and winding climb through forested woodland. The hills to our right include Hindhead, the summit of the A3 to Portsmouth, and a handy knoll beside the ancient route where they used to hang highwaymen who preyed on travellers from London. It overlooks a strange deep valley called the Devil's Punchbowl. The road is getting a tunnel to level it out a bit; we don't tunnel, however, climbing up to the rail summit at **Haslemere**, 43 miles from London. Here an extra platform and points allow trains to overtake each other. The signal box, unusually, is right on the platform on our left, and is still used.

Now it's an easy run down through **Liphook** (we're now in Hampshire, although we wander over the Sussex border twice by a few yards) then over a slight hump which is the watershed between the north-flowing infant River Wey – which joins the Thames all the way back at Weybridge – and the Rother which comes close to the tracks on our right at, and after, the next station, **Liss**, then heads south for the English Channel.

True, the Rother first heads east down the beautiful Weald Valley between the Downs for a while and finds a gap at Arundel to reach the sea. We will not take the easy way out and head for the imposing cliff of chalk that is the South Downs blocking our way, now visible in the distance. The name 'Rother' means 'red', as the river bed (and the other Rother in East Sussex) is, because of the ironstone which once made this a vital cannon-making area.

Liss, by the way, had a very strange military railway leading off north. It was odd because soldiers would often blow it up and rebuild it just for practice. It had a huge six-mile loop in the middle of nowhere with no point whatsoever except for soldiers to learn to play trains, and deliberately wreck them. Needless to say, with the build-up to the D-Day invasion of France in 1944, its many sidings were crammed and its routes busy round the clock. By 1969, it was closed and although steam fans gathered half-a-dozen engines here to start a preserved line, local residents stopped them. Today they'd probably beg them to stay. It's all gone now – its old route runs past my house – and can only be seen in the classic film comedy, *The Great St Trinian's Train Robbery.*

At **Petersfield**⁑, a pretty market town, the station is at least near the town centre, unlike at the last three stops where the towns or villages had to grow towards the stations set a mile or so from the original settlements.

As you near the imposing Downs (with the A3 on our right) you wonder how on earth the train is going to get over them. The road, also climbing, sensibly heads for the cleft between Butser – the hill on the right with aerials on top, and the highest of all South Downs at 886ft – and its neighbour Wardown to the left. In fact the road's cleft was cut considerably deeper, but on a curve so it didn't spoil the profile of the Downs.

Nearer and nearer we climb through wooded country beside the charming village of Buriton but we seem intent on suicide, heading for the hillside ahead like a torpedo heading for a battleship. Do we tie on the headscarf of the suicide pilot? No, with a hoot we disappear into the 485yd **Buriton Tunnel**. A Down train indeed.

Beyond the tunnel we travel down the dip slope – the gentle side, that is – towards the sea in a most pretty dry valley (so called because the chalk is porous, so the expected rivers aren't there) which is virtually uninhabited because the main roads never reached here and the railway has no halt. Look out for the isolated shepherd's church in a field on the left, reachable only by foot. There are several like this up on the South Downs.

Next station is **Rowlands Castle**⁑, on a sharp curve. The curves were made because of aristocratic interference – not unusual around Britain – so the line wouldn't be seen from Stansted Park. The Earl of Bessborough also required a needlessly complex double bridge to be built where we cross the road and these two to be smartly finished with flint panels to match local buildings. Still looks good.

HIGH SPEED... HIGH TECH...

▲ F/AS

PADDINGTON STATION

▲ SXC

Statue at
ST PANCRAS

▲ SXC

London Liverpool Street Station

Arrivals from:	Time	Plat.	Comments
Bruxelles Midi	12:57	5	On time
Paris Nord	14:29		On time
Paris Nord	15:29		On time
Bruxelles Midi	15:57		On time
Paris Nord	16:00		On time
Paris Nord	16:35		On time

Arrivals board,
St Pancras International

High speed along the Devon Coast

▲ SXC

East Anglia

COTTAGE EXHIBITION EDITION.

WHERE SHALL I LIVE

| GUIDE to Letchworth (GARDEN CITY) and CATALOGUE of Urban Cottages and Rural Homesteads EXHIBITION | PRICE 6D NET | Complete Plans and Specification and detailed cost of over 50 designs of MODEL COTTAGES, with special articles by noted Housing Experts |

FUTURE LIVING?

▲ ME

▲ PCL /RD

The beautiful Broads

▲ PCL/MD

South Beach at Lowestoft

COLCHESTER

▲ PCL/TM

Saxmundham Market

▼ PCL/MD

▼ PCL/TM

▼ BS

NORWICH Cathedral in the snow

A flotilla of wherries sailing serenely through the Norfolk Broads

South Western from Waterloo:
Take Me to the Sunshine

▲ PCL/TM

Oil seed rape, Hampshire

WEYMOUTH The harbour at night

▲ PCL/BL

▲ SXC

HMS Victory, Portsmouth

RUGGED DARTMOOR

▲ SXC

▼ PCL/CB

▼ SXC

SHANKLIN Isle of Wight

PORTSMOUTH Spinnaker Tower

Swanage Steam railway

80078

302

▲ D/M

South and Southeast: From Dirty Weekends to Bo Peep

BRIGHTON ROCK

OUSE VALLEY VIADUCT

Now, which path shall we take?

CANTERBURY

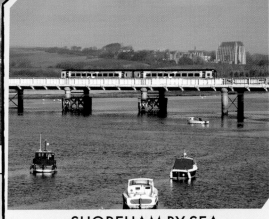

SHOREHAM-BY-SEA
A train crossing the River Adur

The famous White Cliffs

HASTINGS The Old Town

Rail Things...

▼ BV/DP

Signals at the ready

Crossing of gauges at Porthmadog

▼ A

▲ BV/DB

SEVERN VALLEY A traditional lever frame at Highley Station

Dorchester West bridge plate

WEY
209
161M 61CH

▲ BLV

PERTH Station clock

▲ BLV

Wanting to further have his cake and eat it, the earl (family name Brabazon Ponsonby) had a legal right to have all trains stop at Rowlands Castle for his convenience (again not unique). His more sensible descendants drove to Havant to catch the fast train.

The sharply curving junction with the coast line shows that the other line was here first. In fact this was the scene of the Battle of Havant between the two companies (see page 236). **Havant**, much built up in the last century, isn't the prettiest town on earth, but you can change here for the **WEST COASTWAY LINE** route left (east) to many attractions including Brighton. If you see a trend-setting railwayman here, he could be described as Havant guard.

Curving back and left as we enter Havant, near the signal box, you can see the direction of the route to Hayling Island, south of here. It's long closed, but worth mentioning because its swing bridge across the tidal channel was so rickety that the 'Hayling Billy' steam engines had to be tiny things dwarfed by their carriages. And also to mention the strange geography – the Solent coastline here has three narrow entrances giving access to three massive six-mile-long harbours, divided by three huge islands (the eastmost harbour, Chichester, being a double one), all oddly with a channel along their north sides, as we will find approaching Portsmouth, which is on the westmost island. All of this makes it heaven for boaties, not so great for railway and road builders.

We whiz through **Bedhampton** and under the A3M motorway as it swoops round to join the coastal A27 on our left (the road equivalent of Havant Junction). On the far side of this on our left is Langstone Harbour, the middle of the three, and although you can't see it, it's a seaweed-covered stone's throw away.

Soon we swoop left at a triangular junction and rattle over the tidal creek that runs across the top of Portsea Island, making Portsmouth an eminently defensible place. Indeed, the authorities were rather reluctant to let the railway pierce the defensive wall, which we do at the end of the bridge; when a rival company later reached here from Southampton, they would not allow another opening in case the French swarmed through. Hence the junction, because the two railways were forced to share one access to the island.

Even so, the military weren't happy to let the railway enter the inner ring of defences and so to start with the route stopped short of the town and harbour.

We pass **Hilsea**, opened in 1941 as a wartime halt to get workers to nearby munitions factories, and then **Fratton**, which has extensive sidings and the look of a junction for a line curving off southeast (which it was). If you went for a drink with the aforesaid French here, would you be Frattonising with the enemy?

Next is **Portsmouth & Southsea**, where we have a choice. Either the train goes into the rather elegant 1866 station on ground level (a terminus), or it climbs to high-level platforms in order to reach the line to the harbour station. If (as is likely when travelling from London) you take that route, the imposing Guildhall and war memorial, etc, are on your left, then the modern Gunwharf shopping centre and the spectacular Spinnaker Tower (Portsmouth's millennium project and a great landmark which you can go up). Soon we boom and rattle on to **Portsmouth Harbour*** station, for if you look down between the platforms you will see we are on a metal pier above the muddy shore.

This station was utterly destroyed in the relentless bombing this city endured in World War II, so none of it is more than 60 years old. By one of history's little ironies it wasn't, as it turned out, the French, whom Portsmouth had spent the previous five centuries worrying about, doing the bombing.

At the end of the pier waits the fast ferry to **Ryde*** on the Isle of Wight – cue the song *She's got a ticket to Ryde* – and another pier, on which another train waits. An exiled 1938 Tube train, unless they've modernised things, for the much-recommended **ISLAND LINE*** down to **Shanklin***. You can book your return tickets right through from London and walk only a few yards at each connection. Council busybodies witter on about integrated transport nowadays. This is how the Victorians did it. Brilliant. Still works. I can be on the beach on the Isle of Wight, from my home ten miles north

of the South Downs, in not much more than an hour. No car needed.

Meanwhile I can't list all the attractions of Portsmouth, but the Historic Dockyards (with massively important and very different ships *Warrior*, *Victory* and *Mary Rose*) along the shore to the train's right by a few hundred yards, are a superb start and worth a day out. In fact, as you're unlikely to appreciate all three in one day, you can get a passport-type ticket which lets you return. Alternatively there's a great walk past the new landmark Spinnaker Tower (near the harbour station, back beside the tracks a little, through the new Gunwharf shopping centre. Lifts to the top for a spanking view) round the little fishing harbour to pubs on Spice Island and the fort at the harbour mouth. You'll love it. You might reasonably suppose that the two unlikely Tube trains exiled to the Isle of Wight are as far south as they can get on British territory. But no! Two Tube cars are towed up and down the tiny Alderney Railway in the Channel Islands.

WATERLOO TO EXETER:
the West of England Main Line

History of a frontier line: a race to the death, the ACE and the 'Withered Arm'

It might seem bizarre that the charming, partly single-track cross-country route to Exeter from Waterloo through sleepy country stations, far slower than the high-speed Paddington to Exeter route, is called the **WEST OF ENGLAND MAIN LINE**. But the reason is mired in an unlikely Wild-West frontier history. This fascinating survival – most such duplicated routes on nationalisation were destroyed to leave just one route to each provincial city – has literally been a borderline case.

It marked the northern and western frontier between the Waterloo-based London & South Western Railway's empire and the hated arch-rival Great Western Railway, which came out of Paddington. Nearly everything these companies did in this border area in the second half of the 19th and first half of the 20th centuries was to do down and block the enemy as much as to serve the travelling public.

The LSWR had ambitions to grab some of the lucrative West Country traffic by building a line to Exeter (with secret desires to reach Plymouth and the north coast of Cornwall, and cream off some of the transatlantic liner traffic that then landed from America. Rich passengers and urgent mails would be put ashore onto fast expresses to London rather than continue up the Channel by ship).

Meanwhile the GWR was desperate to reach Weymouth, Southampton Docks and Bournemouth, despite the LSWR blocking its way.

Surprisingly, all those aims of both companies were achieved despite deliberate obstruction by the other outfit. Indeed, the unhelpful approach carried on well after nationalisation made them nominally all the same outfit in 1948 and has had dire consequences ever since.

Going back to the very early days, the LSWR had dreamed of extending its Waterloo–Dorchester line (see page 233) on to Exeter but looking at the massive cliffs and valleys around Bridport and Lyme Regis, this would have been horrendously expensive and so was never carried through.

Meanwhile it reached Salisbury, first from Southampton in 1847 and then more directly from London via Woking in 1857. It became clear that a far easier route to Exeter was possible by staying inland on flatter valleys, and this is indeed today's line which steers away from the coast in the lush green hinterland of farms, orchards and country towns.

Not only did the LSWR reach Exeter, but by going north a little on the Great Western and then striking west across the top of Dartmoor (and a now largely closed route) it eventually reached Plymouth, bizarrely coming into the city from the northwest. The stub ends of this Dartmoor route are still there as picturesque branch lines, but if only it had been kept...

The two companies raced their expresses at breakneck speed to get their wealthy passengers and mails from Plymouth and Exeter to London first. It is no coincidence that the GWR's *City of Truro* in 1904 became the first loco in the world to reach 100mph on their route from Exeter to London.

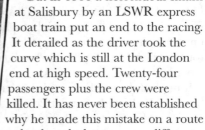

But in 1906 a horrendous smash at Salisbury by an LSWR express boat train put an end to the racing. It derailed as the driver took the curve which is still at the London end at high speed. Twenty-four passengers plus the crew were killed. It has never been established why he made this mistake on a route he knew well, but recent opinion suggests he thought he was on a different, less-curved track at the station which he could have just about rounded, not the one where he came to grief. It was the end of the GWR and LSWR racing each other, but not the end of doing each other down. Since then all trains passing through must stop at Salisbury.

Meanwhile the Waterloo HQ pressed on with branches to north Devon and north Cornwall seaside towns such as Padstow. In the 1920s' rivalry the Waterloo marketing boys thought of selling the premier train on this line to the public as the *Atlantic Coast Express*, soon nicknamed the *ACE*. I say the marketing team thought of it: actually a guard from Great Torrington scooped the three guineas first prize for the idea.

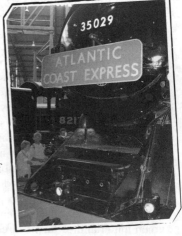

The train was a legend, with endless carriages detached for various branch lines at Waterloo – so you had to be very careful to get in the right bit – and racing hell for leather down through Woking and Salisbury behind great Pacific steam engines such as, appropriately, the West Country class. I recall as a small boy waiting at some remote West Country level crossing in a car and reading off the roof-level name boards of the different portions as it passed: Barnstaple, Camelford, Bude, Launceston, Tavistock, Padstow, Wadebridge, etc.

By the 1960s, the line to the north coast of Cornwall had become known as 'the Withered Arm' because it was being run down (and on the map it was arm-shaped). One reason was obvious: we were in a car that day watching it, after all.

But the other was more insidious. Some utter numbskull had decided that the Western Region of British Railways (as the GWR became after 1948) should have charge of the various previously Waterloo-run routes in the West Country, and eventually even the West of England main line west of Salisbury.

It was like letting the Gestapo run the escape route for Allied prisoners of war in the war that had just ended. Or letting a pack of starving Rottweilers look after kittens. Not wise. The Withered Arm, which had once been the proud *ACE*, was run badly, the timetables made deliberately so that fewer people would use trains and closure could then be justified. That Withered Arm dropped off and many north Cornish towns lost their trains for ever.

Then the remaining line between Exeter and Waterloo was singled in places so trains have to wait for oncoming traffic. True, other lines were getting the same treatment – hugely mistaken in view of the boom in rail traffic coming just ten years later – but old LSWR men felt that here the 'broad-gauge bastards' were getting their revenge. Branches and stations were closed, and it looked like Brunel's ghost was going to wreak havoc on those southerners who challenged the supremacy of the GWR so cheekily (and won the argument over track gauge).

At last, in the 1990s, a miracle happened. It was finally realised what an asset the beautiful **WEST OF ENGLAND MAIN LINE** was, and how useful it would be if the Great Western were blocked at, say, Taunton. It was realised that people from Southampton, Portsmouth and Salisbury *did* want to go to Exeter and beyond without going far to the north first or via London, so why shouldn't they? And it was realised what a loss the line would be to the small towns and villages between Exeter and Salisbury.

New trains arrived and the timetable speeded up again. It was made user-friendly with really useful connections at places like Woking and Salisbury. Catering arrived in the form of trolleys. Stations such as Templecombe reopened after determined fights by local people. Better signals, upgraded track and more passing loops helped.

I don't think those local people should rest until it is restored to double track all the way to Exeter. How about reopening the branches to Lyme Regis, Okehampton and Tavistock, for example? What would a line to Padstow do for local businesses and in combating greenhouse gases caused by road traffic? You'd get it if you were in Scotland or Wales. Fight and it can be done!

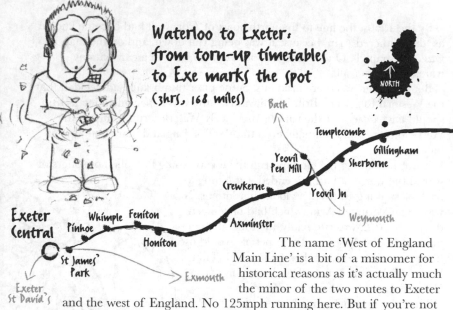

Waterloo to Exeter: from torn-up timetables to Exe marks the spot
(3hrs, 168 miles)

NORTH

Bath

Templecombe

Gillingham

Yeovil Pen Mill

Sherborne

Crewkerne

Yeovil Jn

Weymouth

Exeter Central

Whimple   Feniton

Pinhoe

Axminster

Honiton

St James' Park

Exmouth

Exeter St David's

The name 'West of England Main Line' is a bit of a misnomer for historical reasons as it's actually much the minor of the two routes to Exeter and the west of England. No 125mph running here. But if you're not in a screaming hurry what a beautiful ride through the best of the South, the loveliest countryside, past the greatest cathedrals, the most charming small towns and villages. It's certainly not the poor relation in terms of scenery.

London Waterloo to Basingstoke is described on page 219, but at **Worting Junction** we dive off right under the flyover and race westwards.

You may have noticed that the train is diesel; a noisy thrum while idling but a surprisingly good turn of acceleration and not at all noisy at speed. The reason is clear looking down right at the other track: the electric third rail has disappeared.

The landscape changes too, to a more open rolling chalk upland as we approach Salisbury Plain's vastness.

Overton comes at $55^{1}/_{2}$ miles (from Waterloo, the mileposts are those blue diamonds on the left), and at milepost 59 comes **Whitchurch**[*], followed by watercress beds in valleys on both sides of the line – it's a traditional Hampshire crop that loves the chalk streams that trout, and therefore anglers, also love. Indeed the Watercress Line, south of here on the end of the Alton branch, is so called because whole trains of this most perishable and peppery

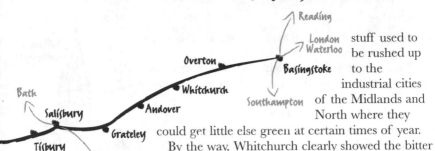

↗ Reading

↗ London Waterloo

Overton

Basingstoke

Whitchurch

Bath

Andover

Southampton

Salisbury

Grateley

Tisbury

Southampton

stuff used to be rushed up to the industrial cities of the Midlands and North where they could get little else green at certain times of year.

By the way, Whitchurch clearly showed the bitter rivalry between this Waterloo route and the enemy GWR, who also had a station here. Their north–south line from Didcot to Winchester crossed under this one close to our route's station, so passengers could have had a very useful interchange. The bloody-minded GWR put their station miles away at the far end of Whitchurch, a walk so far that it was out of the question.

Andover is basically the steam-age station, with a fine old wooden clock and cast-iron brackets holding up the canopies. Whether or not you find anything of interest in the light industrial sprawl of the town is up to you, but one comic said: 'It's called Andover because people who arrive go like this' (and he put his 'and over his eyes).

More watercress and a well-maintained military branch line to the right follow. Talking of military, we are now approaching the vast openness of Salisbury Plain which makes such good practice ground for tanks, guns and infantry.

Next comes **Grateley**. Good walking country but not Grateley exciting. Unless you get buzzed by military helicopters from the base a little south of here in a set of villages called the Wallops (the air base being neither Nether Wallop nor Upper Wallop but Middle Wallop, if you must know). Talking of odd names, the hamlet on the left after Grateley is Palestine.

The military aspect becomes perhaps a little more sinister as we cross into Wiltshire with the miles of high fencing and CCTV cameras on the left: the former chemical warfare base at Porton Down comes into view. It used to have its own station at which naïve volunteers would arrive for their experiments into 'common-cold research', not always successful (or rather, too successful).

If the carriage is flooded with yellow light around here, don't panic, it's not those military spooks. At least, not if it's April or May when rape plants flower in massive fields with extraordinary intensity. They make cooking oil, which Americans with a better yen for marketing call canola oil instead of rape oil.

Fine on the port bow – well, ahead sharp left – we can soon see the distant spire of Salisbury Cathedral, the finest such spire in England (although you have to get out of the train and cross the town centre to get a decent view).

Salisbury Cathedral

Then a single line curves left to offer a connection to the **WESSEX MAIN LINE** to Southampton, which itself curves in shortly from the left. As is traditional all over Britain, the land in the middle is given over to allotments, which must be alternately peaceful and then thunderously noisy.

Anyway, **Salisbury Tunnel Junction** at the west end of this triangle not surprisingly leads us into a short tunnel. Then we see a steam-age water tower on the left and the sharp curve which caused the 1906 accident (see page 244) brings us into **Salisbury**✳✳ station.

Leaving Salisbury the two tracks pass between sidings, then divide into an impressive four for a short while (the right-most pair is the **WESSEX MAIN LINE** for Westbury and Bath) and then our two diverge left, becoming a measly one beside the remains on the right of Wilton South station.

After about ten miles of lovely chalk stream and pasture, we arrive at a passing loop then **Tisbury** station (milepost $96^1/2$), followed by **Gillingham** (milepost $105^1/2$), which more sensibly has the loop in the station and **Gillingham Tunnel** (745yds). There's a station and tunnel with the same name in Kent, so be careful if booking there to add the word 'Dorset', which we are now in. This one is pronounced with a hard 'G', as in guilty.

Next comes **Templecombe**, which like most places with 'temple' in their name around Britain – I can think of at least a dozen – had links with that powerful and secretive Europe-wide organisation the Knights Templars. In 1185, they built a commandery at Templecombe where new Templars were trained before departing on Crusades to the Holy Land or to guard pilgrims. But they became so rich, so secret and so powerful – the *Da Vinci Code* in real life – that they were eventually destroyed by the kings of Europe whose power they threatened.

Many centuries later it seemed another story was coming to an end when Templecombe station was closed in the 1960s, after its complex connection with the crossing Somerset and Dorset route, also closed, had gone.

But locals had other ideas. After a prolonged campaign, they got this station open again and very pretty it is too. The strange way the singling of this remaining route was done meant that some stations had one platform so, at the time of writing, you have to wait outside the station in a loop for the oncoming train to pass you, which is frankly daft – why not have two platforms and wait at the station? Anyway, if you've got plenty of time it doesn't matter and the carefully timed operation is usually surprisingly slick.

The restored station is pretty and the garden well maintained (and has won awards), featuring a strange bronze statue of a man with his back to the railway tearing up the timetable. No jokes about this is how they run the trains round here – they are pretty punctual, I found – but I am mystified as to whether it was a protest against the station closing, or a celebration of its reopening. I did manage to find out that it's called *Tempus Pugit* (time fights, a joke on the usual sundial motto *Tempus Fugit*, time flies). And it is indeed a sundial, with the pages torn from the timetable forming the hour markers.

As a matter of fact we do get some double track now to **Sherborne**✻, where the old ruined castle – the price of being royalist in the Civil War is to be ruined – lies to the left as we approach the station. The 12th-century castle belonged to Queen Elizabeth I's favourite (and then favourite enemy) Sir Walter Raleigh, and was replaced by a new great house, still called Sherborne Castle though it's not one. The small town features lovely stone houses and a famous public school.

Back on the railway, it's worth keeping an eye open as we slow for Yeovil Junction four miles further on. We quickly cross over the delightful **HEART OF WESSEX LINE** (from Bath to Weymouth) in a cutting beneath us, then the connecting line trails in from the right behind the signal box (and note the triple semaphore signal for traffic coming off that line. If it seems odd to have three signals for one track, the point is they show which of three possible routes at the junction the train will take. That job is done on modern signals by the white 'feather' lights above the one signal).

Yeovil Junction, now the most important station in the area, was in fact the last of four to arrive. Two broad-gauge branches had arrived first – the second being the still-existing Yeovil Pen Mill, the station on the **HEART OF WESSEX LINE**, which opened in 1856.

The Waterloo standard-gauge line didn't arrive until 1860, and its original Yeovil Town station was replaced by today's Yeovil Junction when the Great Western brought a broad-gauge branch down to meet it.

Of course trains couldn't run through, but passengers could connect and goods were swapped in the transfer shed. Both the shed and the connection are still there, although as all the lines are now 4ft 8^1/$_2$in apart, through trains are possible.

The Down side (that is, going away from London) of the station and a few of the original buildings have all been saved by the Yeovil Railway Centre, which leases the site and uses it for railway heritage purposes. The old transfer shed contains a visitor centre, exhibition and café, and there are many events, train rides, steam tours calling, etc (**T** 01935 410420; **W** www.yeovilrailway.freeservers.com).

When leaving Yeovil, keep a sharp eye on the right, perhaps half a mile away, for a strange arch topped with a statue of a boy. This is *Jack the Treacle Eater*, which probably leaves most people none the wiser. It is one of a set of follies – architectural whimsies which must be by definition useless – set up around Barwick Park. Jack the Treacle Eater was a useful messenger boy who ran like the wind, fuelled by treacle, and is thus immortalised. If you like this sort of thing keep an eye out to the right for the Needle, a very sharp obelisk closer to the track after going under a road bridge (look back a little). I suspect they were both eyecatchers, that is things to look at in the distance.

We are climbing hard out of the valley now, and pass a reservoir and sailing club. Many of these stations have old goods sheds, such as the one at **Crewkerne**✦, next stop, and although these have new uses, their train-sized openings, usually bricked up, tell of days when nearly everything came and left by rail. Crewkerne, which has a fine Minster, is followed by **Crewkerne Tunnel** (207yds).

We pass some tall silos of some sort and sidings at **Chard Junction** (where you may have to wait on your return, if it's still single-track around here) but it's a junction for Chard no longer. All along this route now there are lovely lush meadows and crystal-clear meandering rivers. This peacefulness contrasts oddly with the pillboxes, low concrete or brick buildings with gun slits you may spot here and there in groups covering each other. The railway line and rivers were thought a good stop line to prevent invading Panzers racing for that Salisbury Plain tank territory we passed earlier, and thence to London. Hence the 'tank traps' – pointed concrete pillars the size of a fridge – still beside the track that would have blocked these lines. As stated elsewhere, thank God they were never used. They still stand more than 60 years later as testament to desperate days simply because they are too much bother to move, not because of preservationists.

Jack the
Treacle Eater

Cheer up, next stop is **Axminster** (which, like Wilton back down the tracks, gave its name to carpets) where a long-overdue £20 million track redoubling started in 2009, means an hourly service can be provided again. The old island platform on the right served the former Lyme Regis branch. After that there's a beautiful River Axe (not to be confused with the Somerset Axe, or indeed the Exe) Valley with great big meanders, content cattle and water fowl. That river hits the English Channel at a little place called Axmouth, by the way. Here TV chef Hugh Fearnley-Whittingstall is a local celebrity. We climb up to Honiton Tunnel (1,351yds).

At **Honiton** station there's a loop and by the next stop, **Feniton**, the characteristic red soil of Devon is evident. Downhill to **Whimple**, under the M5 motorway and through **Pinhoe**. Soon Exmouth Junction sees the AVOCET LINE from that seaside town on the east of the estuary trail in from the left. After the short Black Boys Tunnel, we whiz through **St James' Park** (just for local trains) and reach **Exeter Central**, a spacious station that was obviously built for more traffic than it handles today, with its 950ft platforms needed because the Up *Atlantic Coast Express* had to be assembled from perhaps five portions for its onward journey to Waterloo. When you consider that, unlike today's trains, the locos had to be detached from the front of each part, it was complex indeed. Down trains did the opposite, of course. Even so, Exeter Central still has bay platforms for the branch.

It is indeed more central than the other stations and ideal for walking (left) to the town centre, shops, pubs and cathedral. Note how sharply downhill are the tracks to link to **Exeter St David's** on the Great Western Main Line. In the days of steam, banking engines were needed to shove at the rear buffers to get trains up in the opposite direction, and when a gleaming steam special used these tracks not long ago, someone had forgotten that.

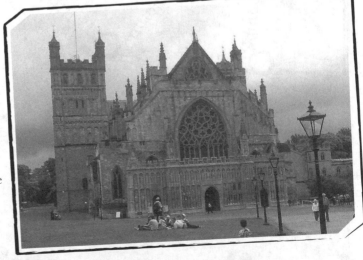

Result: it slipped to a halt and had to be humiliatingly rescued by an oily devious diesel. The *shame*!

For the branches from Exeter, see page 146. For the Great Western onwards to Plymouth see page 129.

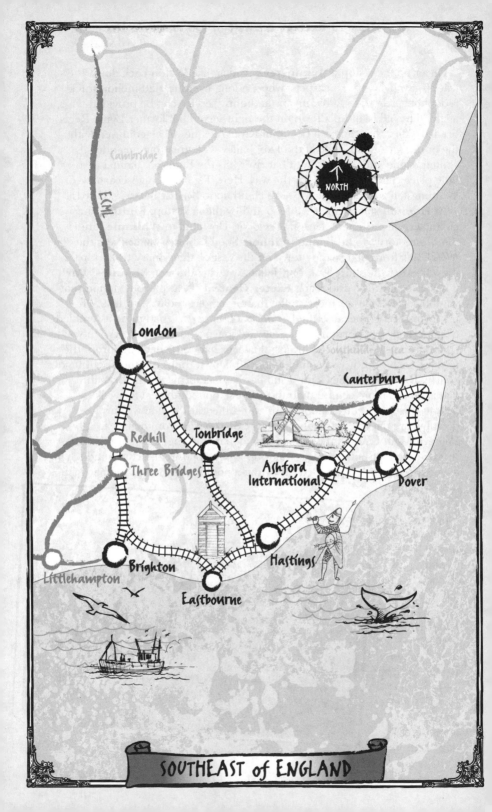

NORTH

Cambridge

E.C.M.L.

London

Canterbury

Redhill

Tonbridge

Three Bridges

Ashford
International

Dover

Brighton

Hastings

Littlehampton

Eastbourne

SOUTHEAST of ENGLAND

EIGHT

South and Southeast:
From Dirty Weekends to Bo Peep

The Brighton Line:
premier holiday route

The world-famous Brighton Line is not any old railway: it is Britain's oldest, best, most loved and most famous holiday line.

It created entire communities of commuters, whom it enables to live in lovely Sussex yet work in London.

It populated Brighton, 'London-by-Sea', with thousands of cockneys escaping the Big Smoke, and has given millions of others the chance of seaside air and fun, or a day at the races, crossing the perfect English countryside *en route*.

It even created the concept of the 'dirty weekend', with countless Mr and Mrs Smiths following a certain adulterous Prince of Wales, checking into countless seedy or, indeed, posh hotels, spied on by countless investigators for divorce-seeking spouses, featuring in dozens of B-movies and paperback novels. A prostitute being paid off by a rich author who later lied about it – wasn't that at Victoria?

It also spawned the harmless fun of 'Kiss Me Quick' hats, the sticks of rock, the garish piers with their naughty 'What-The-Butler-Saw' slot machines, the smell of fish and chips, candyfloss and cheap beer.

It hid the raffish gangsters of the great Graham Greene book, and film, *Brighton Rock*, giving the place a not-at-all respectable but rather fun feeling that endures today. Legions of 'luvvies' of theatre and screen have caught the late theatre train down from London's West End, and countless writers, intellectuals, politicians, gays, rebels, artists and jobbing journalists have inhabited Brighton, a town, now a city, with attitude. It has carried the political great and the good, and the fawning and fake, to the great party conferences there each autumn. The Brighton Line has created all this, and several towns and suburbs *en route*, virtually single-handedly.

Speeding dead queens, amorous princes and smelly princesses: Brighton's steamy royal history

The Brighton Line was one of the earliest in the south, work on it starting in July 1838. The great Robert Stephenson, the son of the father-and-son duo who had built the world's first passenger railway just 13 years before, had advised parliament against the direct route to Brighton, which would have cut through hills and thrown viaducts across valleys, and instead suggested going round the obstacles on a much longer route. Luckily for generations of commuters and holidaymakers ever since, his advice was ignored.

The tunnels on the route were so long, and so totally novel at the time, that some were whitewashed and lit by gas throughout to reduce passengers' nervousness at the new experience of hurtling into the underworld. The company selected a friend of Stephenson, John Rastrick, as chief engineer, and he rose to the challenge with bold, beautiful structures such as the beautiful Balcombe Viaduct.

The first train reached Brighton in September 1841. The *Brighton Gazette* pronounced proudly:

> The Brighton Terminus is a beautiful structure, and with the iron sheds in the rear, will not suffer from comparison with any railway terminus in existence. The offices and waiting rooms are most commodious, and are furnished with every convenience for passengers. Gas fittings for the whole terminus have been put up by Brighton and Hove General Gas Company.

As a direct result of the railway, Brighton's population doubled in the 30 years after opening and the saucy seaside town has never looked back.

The royals gave the place notoriety – in the form of an adulterous Prince of Wales and an ugly Mrs someone or other but then abandoned the place in Victorian times. Brighton being Brighton couldn't care less and hitched its skirts up and got on with having fun.

The Brighton Line, meanwhile, provided a few firsts. The first South of England railway to throw itself across the River Thames and reach London proper on the north bank. The first all-electrified main line in the 1930s. The first electric Pullman (luxury all-seat dining cars, that is) trains in the world, the much-missed *Brighton Belle*, finally pensioned off car by car to preserved railways and restaurants in 1972.

▼ ME

Brighton Belle

RECORD RUN

The fastest-yet London to south coast run was in 2005, when it was completed in a normal service train, a Southern Electrostar, in just 36 minutes 56.28 seconds. Some 103 years earlier a record had been set by a steam train at 48 minutes 41 seconds for the same route. The modern record run was from London Bridge and had the benefit of green lights all the way, and even permission to exceed the speed limits by 10mph, plus chaps standing at the footpath crossings to keep people out of harm's way – so don't expect to get there quite that quickly every day. The fastest run ever seen on screen, however, was the 'London to Brighton in four minutes' frequently shown on British television in the 1950s and '60s, when 'intermissions' were required between programmes; it can still be seen on DVD and video. The run starts normally enough, with a view of the clock at Victoria, and then after four minutes of speeded-up film hurtling at seemingly hundreds of miles per hour, with trains of the era flashing past on the opposite tracks, slows to a normal stop at Brighton, where the clocks shows just four minutes later. A fake, but fun.

The geographical obstacles and total treasures

The builders of the route from Victoria (the second terminus – originally it was London Bridge) faced huge obstacles for the day and age. There's the job of leaping across the Thames with heavy steam trains. After traversing the southern half of the wide London basin, a clay bowl stretching from Hampstead in north London to Sydenham Hill in the South, the route runs into the **North Downs**, a formidable ridge of chalks hills that leads east–west from Hampshire across Surrey to the north Kent coast.

The burrowing railway bursts out of these steep hills into the **Weald**, a great wide valley of the prettiest English countryside you can imagine. Dozens of charming historic small market towns with tile-hung cottages, hundreds of villages with black-beamed old pubs, modest sandstone churches next to greens where cricket is played, copses of woodland where pheasants roost, gently rolling farmland, hop gardens and oast houses, apple orchards, sandy heath covered with flowering broom and gorse – all these alternate in an ever-changing patchwork of small hills and streams in valleys and, from time to time, modest rivers.

Did you know?

If London Victoria has the feeling of a station in two halves, it's not surprising. The two stations were built separately by two different companies and it was not until they were merged in 1923 that a hole was knocked through to let you walk from one to the other. Even today, almost a century later, railwaymen still talk of the Chatham Side (east) and the Central Side (west). The frontages made clear the companies' rivalry – they blend well, but each was trying to outdo the other, or at least make its independence known.

The secret of the Weald, this demi-paradise, this other Eden (as someone else put it) which stretches east–west between the two barriers of the North and South Downs, shutting the wide valley off the outside world, is revealed by what happens at that western edge of the great valley. Here the broken, steep, wooded 'hangers' lead up to a higher chalk plain and on to Salisbury Plain and Stonehenge. Once, the North and South Downs were joined in a massive chalk dome, raised from the bed of a warm tropical sea where the chalk had been made by billions of creatures' shells. That chalk dome has been worn away, by ice ages, weather, and conservatory salesmen, to reveal the intricate patchwork of soils below, be they sands, clays, and marls, sandstone and ironstone. That's the reason why one bit of the Weald is barren heath, growing acid-loving conifers, perhaps quarried for a brick works and iron-making long ago, and yet yards away there is a fruitful apple orchard, or a high-yielding grain field, or a chestnut coppice. It is entirely dictated by the suddenly changing patterns of soil underfoot. Hence the pleasingly chaotic patchwork.

The 'scarp' – steep, cliff-like faces – of both sets of Downs face inwards, towards the Weald, the 'dip' – gently sloping – faces on the outside edges. This is the barrier confronting rail travellers speeding south. How to get through, or over, the wall of chalk.

The **South Downs** themselves have long been grazed by sheep, their pleasing close-cropped outlines likened by poets to female forms, or perhaps a line of moored battleships or massive whales lined up fore-and-aft as far as the eye can see. They too lead east–west and gave the ancient British a dry route, avoiding the dense oak forest in the Weald, to their sacred sites around Stonehenge. Going east, they form fabulous white cliffs, the Seven Sisters around Eastbourne.

There are few gaps in this 700ft-high wall through to the English Channel coast beyond, and these needed guarding with castles against the Viking invaders, and French raiders, seeking to attack wealthy Weald beyond. Later railway builders would put routes through these gaps too, but they would have been a long way round for the Brighton Line which decided to boldly go straight through both sets of Downs in unprecedentedly long tunnels.

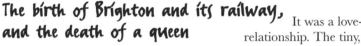

The birth of Brighton and its railway, and the death of a queen

It was a love-hate relationship. The tiny, impoverished and semi-ruined fishing village of what was then called Brighthelmstone began its path to fame, glamour and riches when in 1753 a Dr Russell of the nearby town of Lewes published a study of the health benefits of bathing in seawater, which until then had been regarded as something that you did reluctantly, as in drowning.

It was a follow-on to the great spa boom of the 18th century. Now the rich and sick made their way to Brighton, as it became known, and built elegant terraces there just as they had at Bath and Tunbridge Wells. But it was a certain Prince of Wales's adulterous love affair (more below) that made the place really fashionable as a sea-bathing resort in the 1780s and '90s, well before the railway arrived.

By the time of Queen Victoria, however, things had changed, because the railway had brought a very different class of clientele.

The young Queen Victoria, visiting Brighton in 1845, long before the disliked monarchy regained its popularity and public respect towards the end of her reign, found the democratic railway age had brought a lower class of person, a less respectful type – the 'cor blimey' cockney day tripper. She was not amused, abandoned the Royal Pavilion at Brighton and built a seaside home at Osborne House on the Isle of Wight, away from the prying eyes of common people. Nevertheless the London, Brighton & South Coast Railway felt it wanted to build a Royal Train with five luxurious carriages in 1897, as at least the next Prince of Wales (the future Edward VII) visited Brighton.

▼ ME/ILN

Luxury travel to Brighton

Queen Victoria's Funeral

Queen Victoria never used it; that's what histories will tell you anyway, but in fact she *did* once: when she was dead. In 1901, the late queen was conveyed in this train from Gosport (she died at her beloved Osborne) and was handed over by the rival London & South Western Railway to the London, Brighton & South Coast Railway's engine at Fareham, running nine minutes late. Driver Walter Cooper, told that the new king wanted above all punctuality, drove like a bat out of hell to get the old queen to Victoria as timetabled, and in fact got there early. Victoria, so nervous about train travel that she ordered no train on adjoining tracks to be in steam, and another locomotive to run ahead of her train to check the track, had demanded that no train carrying her during her life go over 40mph. She was conveyed in her coffin at more than twice that speed as the funeral train hurtled down straights, careered round corners and clattered screeching over junctions. If the queen had thought she wouldn't have been seen dead speeding on the Brighton Line, she was wrong.

It was a good thing there wasn't an accident, as much of Europe's royalty was aboard. Would they have Driver Cooper taken to the Tower? Not a bit of it: Kaiser Wilhelm of Germany and the rest sent a minion to congratulate the driver on a thrilling run. The racier Edwardian age had arrived.

Did you know?

Oddities at Victoria include: across the road on a traffic island, Little Ben – a miniature of the tower known as Big Ben at the other end of the same street; the London, Brighton and South Coast Railway war memorial; the fact that one of London's seven lost rivers, the Tyburn, passes near here which means that millions of gallons of water are pumped out of the Underground station each day; and that a World War II German Dornier aircraft lining up for an attack on nearby Buckingham Palace, from where the Royal Family had refused to be evacuated, fell in the forecourt after a Hurricane pilot who'd run out of ammunition deliberately rammed the enemy. Both pilots survived.

The double-crossing Prince of Wales

Brighton's royal connection concerns a spurned Princess of Wales whose husband preferred the company of a previously married woman and whose eventual funeral through Kensington, which the authorities tried to downplay, moved the entire population of London to unprecedented mass emotions and near-revolution.

She was exposed to constant lies about her private life by courtiers and the media, yet was in part the authoress of her own downfall, becoming an adulterer, as her husband certainly was. She appeared towards the end, scantily clad and with a most unsuitable playboy lover.

But this led to Britain's most eccentric building, the oriental fantasy that is the Royal Pavilion at Brighton; it should have now become clear that we are talking not about the late 20th-century Princess of Wales, Diana, but the early 19th-century one, Caroline.

Caroline of Brunswick married the unpleasantly priggish 'Prinny' in 1795, the deeply unpopular Prince Regent who was to become George IV, in a union that was more about diplomacy and settling his debts than it was about love. They soon became estranged as the prince spent more and more time with a previously married (scandal!) Catholic (more scandal!) commoner (yet more scandal!), a rather frumpy woman (well, no scandal about that bit) called Mrs Maria Fitzherbert at a farmhouse in Brighton.

In fact, Prinny had secretly married Mrs Fitzherbert in 1785, ten years before his therefore bigamous marriage to Caroline.

After the prince's official marriage in 1795, the court put it about that the new Princess of Wales was unfaithful and unhygienic, never changing her undergarments and eating mainly raw onions and garlic. She had consequently the most monstrous breath and bad teeth, one courtier complained.

Little was accurate: the unfaithfulness was true but only after she had been shabbily treated by the prince's flaunting of his mistress (is this at all familiar?). The prince, meanwhile, was indulging in the ultimate barn conversion with his Brighton bit on the side. The change from tatty old farmhouse to fantasy palace went through a few stages, but the key decision was calling in architect John Nash, who created the fabulously lavish Royal Pavilion.

Nash's onion-domed confection of a building in Brighton is utterly unforgettable, even if it's a bit vague in its precise style. As cleric Sydney Smith said at the time: 'The Pavilion looks as if St Paul's had slipped down to Brighton and pupped.'

LONDON VICTORIA TO BRIGHTON:
what to look out for from Thames
to Channel (1hr, 50³/4 miles)

Arrive in time to find a
window seat facing
forwards, preferably
on the left (east).
If possible go against
the rush-hour (ie: leave
London in the morning and
return in the evening)
because of overcrowding and higher
fares. Stopping trains are better
for seeing the countryside. To
state the obvious, if returning,
or starting, from Brighton,
reverse the rights and lefts.

As you leave **Victoria Station**
you cross what was once a canal
basin, bought from the Duke of
Westminster when the railway
terminus needed expanding. The old
pump house on the right, with
a stub end of the canal as you
reach the river,
are all that's left.

The **Grosvenor Bridge**, which
the train soon rumbles over, was
the first railway bridge to stretch across
the Thames. Only one pair of tracks was carried
when it was built in 1859, but more and more
tracks were added, on new bridges
built tight alongside, until there were
ten tracks. Some of this was
done by a
rival company,
which is why
Victoria even today
seems to be two stations side by side. In the 1960s, the bridges were
replaced track by track so there are ten narrow bridges abutting each other.

Looking right (west) along the river is Chelsea Bridge, Battersea Park on
the left and the much more elegant Albert Bridge beyond that, looking like

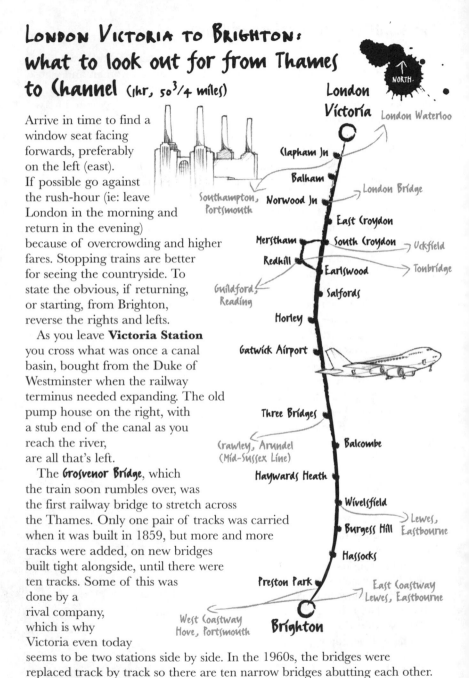

London
Victoria   London Waterloo

Clapham Jn

Balham   London Bridge

Southampton,   Norwood Jn
Portsmouth

East Croydon

Merstham   South Croydon   Uckfield

Redhill   Tonbridge

Earlswood

Guildford,   Salfords
Reading

Horley

Gatwick Airport

Three Bridges

Crawley, Arundel   Balcombe
(Mid-Sussex Line)

Haywards Heath

Wivelsfield

Burgess Hill   Lewes,
                Eastbourne

Hassocks

Preston Park   East Coastway
                     Lewes, Eastbourne

West Coastway   Brighton
Hove, Portsmouth

something that should adorn a wedding cake. In the park, by the water's edge, you can see the extraordinary Peace Pagoda, constructed in response to the bombing of Hiroshima in 1945.

On our left are the four massive chimneys of Battersea Power Station. London used to have several of these riverside giants, where the Thames could be used for cooling water and bringing in coal by barge, but they are all redundant now, one having become the Tate Modern art gallery.

If you peep behind the power station you get the first sight in the far distance of two towers the shape of the Eiffel Tower. They are key landmarks and sit on Crystal Palace Hill at Sydenham; the first major obstacles for our train to get round on its way to Brighton.

We curve to the right past a massive gasholder and, obliquely crossing above the main lines coming out of Waterloo (to our left), swoop round to join them. While you are doing this you may catch sight of the *Orient Express* or a vintage steam locomotive waiting in the depot below to our left.

Joining the Waterloo lines in an unbelievably broad mass of tracks, we soon come to **Clapham Junction**, Europe's busiest station in terms of trains. Its platforms are jammed in, some on ridiculous Southern Region curves (which meant trains south of the Thames have never had very long carriages, unlike those on main lines to the West and North).

A series of disconnected architectural incidents loosely linked by either bridge or subway.
David Atwell describing Clapham Junction station

Next we turn south, leaving the Waterloo lines to carry on southwest to Portsmouth, Southampton and Salisbury.

We rattle through unprepossessing south London and many junctions such as that at **Balham**, five miles out from Victoria (these distances are given on yellow mileposts on the east, that is left, side of the track, even to every quarter mile – one dot for each quarter).

This area was heavily bombed during World War II, and when the deadly V1 'doodlebug' rockets were introduced by the Germans – a sort of early cruise missile – they were fooled by British misinformation into thinking they were overshooting central London. So they put a little less fuel in them, which was good for central London. Bad for south London, which was clobbered instead, until they could be reliably shot down over Kent. Earlier, in October 1940 at the height of the Blitz, the worst disaster was here in Balham when a high-explosive bomb penetrated a shelter, killing or injuring 600 people.

From the train, the area seems pleasantly green and open. Having crossed Wandsworth Common before Balham, we now cross Streatham Common. After another junction you can now see the Crystal Palace television transmitter towers on the hill to your left. The Crystal Palace itself has long gone: it was the massive greenhouse-like structure put up in Hyde Park for the 1851 Great Exhibition, and then re-erected here as a hugely successful leisure attraction – until it burnt down in the 1930s. This hill was chosen for London's early television transmitters. The opposite hill in north London across the Thames Basin also

GRAND ENTRANCE TO THE GREAT EXHIBITION OF ALL NATIONS.

The 1851 Great Exhibition

had its own leisure palace, its own television transmitter, and its own branch line to its own station and Alexandra Palace, which hasn't burnt down yet.

Other rail routes plunge through Crystal Palace Hill (or Sydenham Hill as it was called before) in tunnels but we neatly avoid it. On its southern flank the football ground we can see on the left is Selhurst Park, home to Crystal Palace Football Club.

Selhurst railway depot on the left is followed by a fantastically intricate **Norwood Junction**, with lines dipping and diving all over the place. There are several on this scale in south London, so dense are the routes. This density, together with the once-massive tramway system, is why the Underground never really penetrated this sprawling area, which is in many ways – culturally as well as geographically – a separate city from the rest of London.

Here the route from **London Bridge**, now used by Thameslink trains (which usefully come from King's Cross, Luton and Bedford), joins the Brighton Line from the left. In fact, that route was the original for the Brighton Line, before the bridge across the Thames made the Victoria terminus the main one. Then just as we pass the 10^1/4 milepost, we reach **East Croydon**, where many Brighton trains stop. Croydon, seen from street level at any rate, has a high-rise city centre that looks vaguely American. Nowadays it's known for being the birthplace of model Kate Moss and for having expensively brought back the tram routes it once ripped up.

> 'Isn't this invigorating?'
> 'No, Sir, it's Croydon.'
> Platform exchange recorded by Richard Pike 1888

As we leave East Croydon the things that look like small tunnels on the massive retaining walls to the left (and also the right) are, if you are curious, refuges for track workers because the tracks are too close for safety.

Now the train starts getting into its stride, the landscape is a little more open, and the suburban streets less shabby, although like those earlier they owe their existence to the railway making it possible for people to live here.

Another line, for East Grinstead and Uckfield, diverges slowly to the left after **South Croydon**, and then a strange thing happens to our four-track Brighton Line. At a place called Stoat's Nest, two of the tracks – the slow lines – seem to disappear to our left. Soon we soar over them on a bridge. This is because our lines – the fast tracks – were built later, to relieve a two-track bottleneck and avoid the complex junction at Redhill, a town just ahead. It was easier not to follow the old route through the North Downs.

Note the steep chalk walls of the deep, deep cutting we are in, some parts retained with steel nets to stop the white stuff crumbling onto the tracks.

We now plunge into the **Quarry Tunnel** (2,113yds). At a lower level, the old slow lines are also burrowing through the chalk hills in **Merstham Old Tunnel**. One of these tunnels, a railwayman said, was the scene of a Christmas suicide of a woman from the old Cane Hill Lunatic Asylum, through whose former grounds we have just passed, and, he said, when the track was closed for repairs one Christmas, demented laughter could be heard in the darkness.

Cheered up by that thought, we whiz over the M25 London orbital motorway, the world's busiest. A glimpse to our right sees the bridge carrying the old slow lines also leaping across the chasm. Look back left to see the line of the North Downs under which we have just passed – not as impressive as the South Downs to come, but a major obstacle for early railway builders all the same.

BLOOD ON THE TRACKS

What appeared to be the victim of a terrible assault staggered from the 14.00 London Bridge train at Preston Park station, just before Brighton, on 27 June 1881. The ticket collector waiting there saw a man covered in blood, dishevelled, his collar and tie ripped from him, hatless (a rarity then) getting off the train. He said he was Percy Lefroy and had been assaulted and robbed in Merstham Tunnel (back on the North Downs) and, having been hit on the head, had lost consciousness. The alert ticket inspector noticed part of a gold watch chain hanging from his boot. Lefroy was taken to the police station, buying a collar and tie *en route*, where he was searched and found to have two counterfeit coins, which he denied all knowledge of. He offered a reward to catch his 'assailants'. It wasn't that straightforward, however.

The carriage in which he had been travelling was shunted into the sidings for examination. The compartment was covered in blood and there were three bullet marks and more dodgy coins. Lefroy was allowed to return to London but was followed by a bumbling detective called Holmes (no, really).

Meanwhile, track workers in Balcombe Tunnel found the body of a Mr Gold, a retired Brighton corn merchant, who had been stabbed

Redhill, the junction with two other lines which we are avoiding, was one of the classic sites of Victorian company rivalry, where one or the other company – the London, Brighton and South Coast or the South Eastern Railway – would employ obstructive tactics, stopping a long coal train across the junction, being slow with the signals to obstruct a rival service, or sending a slow stopper in front of the express, reducing it to a crawl. Typically for the era, there were three stations all inconveniently placed for changing from one train to another.

Now we have returned to several different railway companies using the same tracks (although this time round they don't own them) a more grown-up attitude prevails…

No wonder this new route was expensively cut to avoid the chaos at Redhill (or Reigate as it was then known). If, by the way, you are on the slow lines, they're not so bad, and in fact I recommend getting a stopping train on the way back, so you've more time to see the things we whizzed past too fast on the way down.

We rejoin the other lines at **Earlswood** after the short **Sand Tunnel** – we are now on the east side of the slow tracks, of course. The large hill in the far distance to the right (west) is Leith Hill, in Surrey, a spectacular viewpoint if you ever go there for a picnic, with a tower you can climb and robbed of a large sum of money, a watch and chain. The news was telegraphed to Holmes at Three Bridges station with orders not to lose sight of Lefroy. But the suspect entered a boarding house further up the line 'to change his clothes' and slipped out of a back door.

National outrage at the detective's incompetence followed when the story came out, and newspapers printed – for the first time – a likeness of a wanted man. He was tracked down living in London's East End under a false name. Lefroy, a journalist (in fact called Mapleton) was incredibly vain and at his trial asked to be allowed to wear full evening dress with a silk hat 'to impress the jury'. It didn't. He was hanged at Lewes on 29 November of that year.

In fact, Merstham Tunnel *was* the site of a grisly murder, but not until 1905. The mutilated body of one Mary Money was found there. She had been thrown from a train, but her killer was never found. Nor Miss Money's money.

amidst the trees at the top. A peaceful spot, but has not always been so: here an invading army of Danes was slaughtered in their hundreds by the Saxon king from Winchester.

Talking about wars, after you speed through **Salfords**, if you look at a field on the left you'll see a solitary World War II pillbox standing guard over the main line. I say solitary, but they were usually in groups of three, covering each other, in chains across the south of England. As small boys growing up in the Weald in the last 50 years would have noticed, they often covered a bridge over a river, or a main railway line that could be used by tanks to drive up towards London.

Those small boys clambered over them playing at war; but thankfully these rather crummy-looking pillboxes and their Dad's Army back-up were never tested against German Panzers. The reason for that was, of course, the 'Few' of the RAF who wheeled and soared and often died over this very ground in the long, hot summer of 1940. As you look over this landscape you realise that here and there a brave young man – of either side – still lies beneath some woodland where his aircraft buried itself after a death dive. They are occasionally dug up, even today.

Of all the aircraft involved, it is the Spitfire that above all carries the aura of that era. Once in a while a Spitfire returns to a Wealden town or village for an air show – I saw one from right here on the Brighton Line once – and thousands turn out for a glimpse of those beautiful lines, the confident purr of that Rolls-Royce Merlin engine and all that death and glory, packed into a tiny 31ft fuselage and 37ft elliptical wing-span. (More on the Spitfire's birthplace on page 226.)

The old people, who were children back then looking up at the planes fighting in a blue sky, look up again with watery eyes and remember a moment, right here, when the whole history of mankind and civilisation rested in just a few youthful, courageous, frightened hands…

After speeding through **Horley**, thoughts of 1940s' aviation are soon replaced by the more modern **Gatwick Airport** on our right. You'll probably see lumbering jumbo jets coming in from the left looking as if they intend to pancake on the train's roof. In fact the runway starts just beyond the station, on the right, and there's always something to see, perhaps aircraft going hell for leather down the runway, huge radar dishes sweeping round looking for the 17.50 from Hong Kong, not the 10.06 from Victoria.

And returning to war, the iron workings in the Weald were critical in another conflict – the 17th-century Civil War. The fact that parliament controlled Sussex meant that it controlled the making of cannon and shot and beat the Royalists. If it doesn't look very industrial today, consider that many places have 'Hammer' as part of their names.

Next station is the substantial **Three Bridges**, which serves the sprawling new town of Crawley and is also the junction for the picturesque MID-SUSSEX

LINE going southwest to Littlehampton. Read ahead now, as we climb a little from here and the route becomes two tracks before entering **Balcombe Tunnel**, because soon we enter the most scenic stretch, so you'll want to be looking out of the window after **Balcombe** station (the first one after the tunnel) and not so much at this book.

Here we speed too fast over the beautiful **Ouse Valley Viaduct**, a bridge whose great beauty and a certain secret is best appreciated by those not on the train, but walking below. You can, however, glimpse eight Italianate pavilions at either end.

To the left (east) you can glimpse the stately towers and flag of Ardingly College, a minor public school, pronounced – judging from cries of 'play the game, Ardingly!' at rugby matches many years ago – 'Arding-lye', to rhyme with 'tie'.

Looking down into the valley, you may search for the major river that eroded it and made this huge viaduct necessary. In fact, all you can spot is a stream about 6ft wide hardly worth the name river (or indeed any name at all). Yet once, with the aid of weirs, this River Ouse was broad enough a navigation route for canal boats to come up from Lewes down near the coast with the millions of bricks to make this viaduct, ironically for the railway that would destroy the waterway as a freight route.

After the viaduct, a freight line – remains of one of the less-than-sane routes built in the 19th century frenzy of inter-company railway rivalry – trails in from the left at the quaintly named **Copyhold Junction** (copyhold being a form of tenure, like leasehold, if you must know). We rapidly reach the town of **Haywards Heath**, which indeed was a blasted heath in the middle of nowhere until the railway came. The nearby town of Cuckfield, which was doing very well out of the stagecoaches to Brighton, and the stables and inns they required, vowed to resist the railway. The burghers bought up the land round the town to obstruct it. The result was that the railway swept away from that town and made a deep cutting in the empty heath, built a station here, and then a tunnel under the hill. Silly Cuckfield was ruined as Haywards Heath grew like topsy. It's now quite a town but frankly, a boring one. If you're the sort of person who finds brash and bawdy Brighton stimulating, Haywards Heath certainly isn't. Cuckfield, however, is a charming backwater with historic buildings, so maybe they weren't so stupid after all. But you can't get there by train.

Leaving the tunnel, you can begin to see the line of the South Downs, still a few miles off, an impenetrable but somehow noble wall of rather female shapes, striking fear into the thousands of annual London–Brighton cyclists as they approach (knowing the route goes right over the top at Ditchling Beacon) and no doubt seriously worrying the railway builders as they surveyed their route. They boldly carried straight on regardless, as do the cyclists.

Now 40 miles from London, we rapidly reach little **Wivelsfield** and **Keymer Junction**, where the **LEWES BRANCH** line for that ancient county town leaves to the left (you see a level crossing from this line). From Lewes, you can carry on to the coast at Newhaven on the **SEAFORD BRANCH** and Eastbourne on the **EAST COASTWAY** (see page 276), but you can access those directly from Brighton too. The branch to the left here is heading for the same gap in the Downs where those river barges once came up to build the last viaduct. Near the next station down that branch, Plumpton, by the way, the embankment contains thousands of bones from a mass grave from the Battle of Lewes in 1264. Is that what the railway means by a skeleton service?

Meanwhile we rattle our own bones through **Burgess Hill** and **Hassocks**, now closing fast with the looming Downs. Hassocks belongs with Ottoman, Pouffes, Sofas and Davenports as a kind of furniture, but in turn derived from a hassock or tussock of grass. People in the Middle Ages would pull up a grass hassock to kneel on the stone floor in church, and later made cloth footrests still called hassocks. Here there was a field full of such hassocks.

If you are seated on the left by the window, look high up as we approach the tunnel. Not only will you see the Jack-and-Jill windmills atop their hill, but also a glimpse of the extraordinary castellated tunnel mouth, and the little house oddly perched above it (more on page 270).

Then it's into **Clayton Tunnel** with its dark secrets – you may not wish to read what happened here once but rest assured such accidents are now impossible (see box on page 270) – and then we are really nearing Brighton.

After a bit of countryside we enter the much shorter **Patcham Tunnel**; and then a Brighton suburb, **Preston Park** station (start of an early railway murder story, see page 264). Preston Park, the green space with a clock tower in the middle of it on the left, was paid for, appropriately enough for raffish Brighton, by the profits of a bookmaker. It's amazing what a few bets on a horse can achieve, and the area has had many racecourses including Brighton's own at Kemp Town.

Soon the direct lines for Hove and the **WEST COASTWAY** dive off to the right into a tunnel of their own, and we pass the railway depot on the right known as **Lovers Walk**. It's possibly hard to see the romance in such places – unless you're an out-and-out train nut – and let's leave them to carry on with their coupling. On the other hand, Brighton just about invented the 'dirty weekend'.

From the left a stunningly high viaduct (another Rastrick job, 1846), way above the rooftops, brings the **EAST COASTWAY** line from Lewes, curving in to join us as we enter the grand, light and airy trainshed of the **Brighton** terminus. Note the superb ornamental frontage (no, not the royal mistresses, the station!) and the beautiful LBSCR clock inside, plus on the west side a plaque to signalling pioneer John Saxby.

THE CHILDREN'S FRIEND'S BRIGHTON

▼ ME

There isn't room here to describe everything that Brighton has to offer – perhaps such a place should be judged by its piers – but you can't go far wrong if you march straight out of the station and down to the glittering sea you can glimpse in the distance. On the other hand, turning left (east) at the first crossroads will take you down to the Lanes area for fascinating pubs and shops, and beyond that, the extraordinary Royal Pavilion (more on page 259). To the right (west) is more genteel Hove, which has traditionally considered itself snootily above Brighton and far more respectable. As Keith Waterhouse wrote, the sticks of rock there should have 'HOVE, ACTUALLY' written all the way through them. Best stick to Brighton.

THE SUSSEX DOWNS CASTLE THAT'S REALLY A RAILWAY TUNNEL — WITH A DARK SECRET

Britain's most eccentric, not to say exclusive, country cottage could well be Clayton Tunnel House, a rather unlikely bungalow perched above the unlikely castellated north entrance to Clayton Tunnel.

On one side it looks like a castle; above soar the glorious South Downs topped by the Jack-and-Jill windmills; before it lies the verdant sweep of the rolling Sussex Weald (so far, so good); and right in front a suicidal drop into a gaping hole below through which hurtle dozens of trains a day carrying holidaymakers and commuters.

Until recently, the bungalow housed railway workers, and is now a private family home. But its past contains a dark secret.

The house's origin and purpose are somewhat clouded, as indeed would have been its residents every few minutes in the age of steam. It hardly fits the extravagant Norman castle style of the tunnel portal created by John Rastrick, the genius responsible for Britain's most elegant railway viaduct across the Ouse Valley.

Nor would being showered in smuts, having a near-cliff for a front lawn and a suicidal drop for a back garden be most people's idea of a nice country cottage.

It is ironic that the medieval doom paintings uncovered in Clayton Church lie just a few steps to the east, depicting fearful scenes of death and the descent to the underworld. Fear of the underworld could account for the peculiar cottage's presence, and doom certainly lay in store for some early railway passengers.

When the railway was built in 1841, the question arose: would the inexperienced passengers' fears (they were carried in open carriages behind engines belching fire, steam and smoke) prevent their going underground in the line's longest tunnel?

The directors attempted to diminish these fears by whitewashing the tunnel's brick lining and lighting it throughout with gas jets. The cottage's resident probably helped maintain these lights, in an attempt to convince naïve people that heading into the tunnel wasn't to say farewell to daylight for ever.

But it was exactly that for the victims of the Clayton Tunnel Disaster of 25 August 1861, Britain's worst rail crash to date. By then the Brighton Line was booming, but signalling technology was still based on dispatching trains at five-minute intervals. Rear-end collisions were thus greatly feared, particularly in tunnels.

Ironically, Clayton Tunnel was the only part of the line given more sophisticated protection in the form of a single telegraph needle in each box at the ends of the tunnel which dipped one way or the other to indicate 'train in tunnel' or 'line clear'.

Disaster struck on a Sunday, which meant heavy excursion trains. It also meant that signalman Henry Killick at the south end was working a 24-hour shift so he could have his one day off later in the week. There was also a simple signal, the arm of which was supposed to be returned to 'danger' by the passing train wheels pressing a lever. This did not always work, and the Portsmouth excursion heading for London that morning failed to change it.

Killick telegraphed 'train in tunnel' to his colleague at the north end, but failed to put the signal to 'danger' before the Brighton excursion passed some three minutes later. He waved his red flag just as the heavy train steamed into the tunnel.

Worried, he frantically telegraphed the north box and soon received the reassuring answer 'line clear'. He assumed this meant the second excursion had left the tunnel – it hadn't, it was the *first* train the north box signalman meant. The second train's crew, having seen the red flag, had screwed down the feeble brakes and the train's 17 packed carriages slowly came to a halt deep in the tunnel, then started to reverse to see what was wrong.

At that moment, about four minutes after the Brighton excursion, came a third train – a regular timetabled train from Brighton to London. Killick, reassured by the telegraph's ambiguous message, waved his white flag. Had the earlier whitewash been kept clean and the gas lights been still lit, the driver might have seen his doom approaching. But as it was, the tunnel was sooty black and filled with smoke.

The resulting crash caused appalling carnage with 21 people dead and 176 injured.

More than 140 years later, the listed tunnel portal and cottage have been fully restored, and the railway, unable to sell off the home as it sits on operational railway land, rents it out.

BRIGHTON LINE BRANCHES

Historically, the London, Brighton and South Coast Railway was a triangle of railways with London at their apex and a broad base along the coast. Many of these routes, and those built by rivals, still exist, giving marvellous opportunities for great days out.

Redhill–Guildford*
(NORTH DOWNS LINE)
(30mins, 20 miles)

This is a particularly beautiful route along the valley at the foot of the North Downs, going west from **Redhill**, which is halfway down the BRIGHTON LINE. Very scenic, so often used for luxury steam excursions from London with dining cars, such as the British version of the *Orient Express* which, ironically, contains some of the lovingly refurbished cars from the old *Brighton Belle*. This non-electrified route leads to **Guildford***, a pretty Surrey town astride a gap in the North Downs, good for pubs and shopping, where it crosses the PORTSMOUTH DIRECT from London line (so triangular days out from London are easy), and goes on through wooded Surrey and Berkshire to **Reading** for the GREAT WESTERN MAIN LINE. Note some Brighton expresses avoid Redhill, so make sure you get the right train if you wish to change to this line.

Redhill–Tonbridge
(joining SOUTH EASTERN MAIN LINE)
(30mins, 20 miles)

This line, which goes pretty much due east, is Britain's longest straight, and was used by Channel Tunnel trains until they built their own route; the main line of this route use once started at Redhill but a direct route from London now curves into **Tonbridge** from the north, making the first bit now a minor route. A useful link from the Brighton line to **Ashford**, **Canterbury*** (pictured opposite) and the Kent ports of **Folkestone** and **Dover** though not wonderfully scenic or littered with places you must see. Much prettier and more interesting than Tonbridge is **Tunbridge Wells***, which would mean changing trains at the former for a short run south down the HASTINGS LINE.

Three Bridges–Littlehampton
(ARUN VALLEY LINE*)
(1hr 10mins, 32½miles)

This route, sometimes known as the MID-SUSSEX LINE, is beyond **Horsham** (junction for MOLE VALLEY LINE north), a gem, and boasts a station named after a public school, **Christ's Hospital** (which once had seven platforms and further branches north and south) and then heads south through great countryside to pretty **Billingshurst***, **Pulborough***, and **Amberley*** heading for a gap in the South Downs at

Arundel✱✱ (comments below). Connects, directly or via Littlehampton, with the WEST COASTWAY LINE at **Barnham**, so triangular days out are possible from the Brighton or Portsmouth lines. It continues to the seaside towns of **Littlehampton** or **Bognor Regis**.

East Coastway Line✱ (1³/4 hrs, 66 miles)   See page 276.

West Coastway Line
(1hr 20mins, 43 miles)
This line goes the other way from **Brighton** to Portsmouth. It goes to great places but is only at times scenic (with slightly boring bits at **Hove**, near **Shoreham** and **Worthing**) because you very rarely see the coast. It is briefly beautiful around Shoreham with views of the gap in the South Downs, Shoreham airport's 1930s'-style terminus, and the beautiful chapel on the hill. Ditto wonderful Arundel, with a castle and chapel guarding another gap in the Downs, although this line doesn't go as close as the ARUN VALLEY LINE, above (onto which you can easily change at **Barnham**). It's otherwise flat and dull. There are branches to the seaside at **Bognor Regis** (beach, pier, but not otherwise pretty or interesting) and **Littlehampton** (port, bit more interesting), **Chichester**✱, for cathedral, pubs and shops, **Fishbourne**✱ for Roman Palace, **Bosham**✱ for a walk round a beautiful tidal village (head south from station across main road), **Emsworth**✱ for great harbourside walk and pubs, possibly connecting to station at **Havant**, and **Portsmouth**✱ for historic dockyards and famous ships, Spinnaker Tower, pubs, shopping and Isle of Wight trips. You can also get trains from Brighton this way to Salisbury, Bath, Bristol and Cardiff, which may not be much quicker than going via London but is more scenic *en route* (see page 155). Book a seat if you can for those.

RECOMMENDED EXCURSIONS

Take the scenic OXTED BRANCH southeast from London (it branches off the Brighton Line at Croydon), then either the branch to **East Grinstead** for the BLUEBELL RAILWAY✱✱ or the longer UCKFIELD LINE✱ (the whole of which is recommended for the scenery although it serves nowhere very important) for **Eridge** and the SPA VALLEY RAILWAY✱✱. Both steam railways are in glorious countryside and were due to make their direct connections with the main-line stations mentioned in the near future, but at the time of writing were still a short bus ride away. Check before travelling, details page 310.

10 BRIGHTON LINE TRIVIA: FASCINATING THINGS YOU DIDN'T KNOW

1. There's a Brighton Line on the New York City Transit subway, and another on the Melbourne, Australia train network, both leading to stations called Brighton Beach, plus a line to New Brighton, again a seaside station, on Merseyrail in Northwest England.

2. The 19th-century company, the LBSCR, was nicknamed by its customers, sarcastically or not, as the Lay Back So Comfortable Railway.

3. The first London to Brighton Run, now run with vintage cars, started in 1896 to celebrate the Locomotives on Highways Act, which made it legal to use motor cars on British roads without a man carrying a red flag walking ahead. Not such good news, you may think. On the very first run, a girl was knocked down and many cars broke down so their occupants finished by train!

4. The beauty of the line at Balcombe clearly didn't work for everyone. In 1846, a heroic PC Shaw was killed while trying to remove a deranged women from the tracks there.

5. British bingo calls (bingo is a game involving numbered balls being randomly chosen and called out, players crossing out numbers on their card until the winner has no numbers left) include '5 and 9, the Brighton line, number 59'. It was a headcode (number on the front) on trains on that route. Aptly, perhaps, in those days, the number before was 'Make them wait, number 58'. The game is often played by two fat ladies, who are, of course, the call for 88.

6. Electrification of the rails is by a third rail (the thick one set slightly higher than the others), so illegally walking across the tracks is extra dangerous, and yes it is on when trains aren't coming (as one man who thought otherwise proved to his friends, fatally). Gaps in the third rail for badgers have been left at various spots on the network, even though this means electric locos, if not long electric trains, could become stranded.

7. It's all the Kaiser's fault. Oddly, the Brighton Line had started electrification before World War I with the more efficient overhead system, but there was just one snag... the equipment suppliers were in Berlin, suddenly enemy territory. So when the rapid expansion of the electric network started, the rival third-rail system won out. Although birds can hop happily along the live rail (as long as they don't touch anything else), it does lead to problems from time to time. A steam-engine fireman dropped his steel shovel once and there were brilliant arcs of sparks as his shovel was welded solid to the track.

8. Luvvies and kippers: the theatrical and arty types – 'luvvies', as they are known today – who have always used the Brighton Line, kicked up a stink (appropriately enough) when British Rail tried to remove kippers from the dining-car breakfast menu. The charge was led by the formidable Laurence Olivier – 'Larry, darling' in the dining car – and thundered through the letters page of *The Times*. It was only after the railway caved in and put them back on the menu that it was discovered that only one-sixteenth of a kipper a week was served per dining car. Today you can't even get a sixteenth.

9. At the time of writing, you can still see on the trains of the Brighton Line great stars of that era – such as Dora Bryan and Dame Vera Lynn – modern media types such as Julie Burchill and Annie Nightingale, and a surprising number of actors of the perennial British TV soap *Coronation Street*, who play gritty northerners but prefer to live down south. Eee oop, chook!

10. A student employed at a Brighton rock factory in the 1960s was once fired for making a quarter of a mile of the sticky souvenir candy with a very rude word written through it. The pink stuff was destroyed. Now it would probably sell for hundreds of pounds a stick on eBay to collectors.

BRIGHTON—HASTINGS—ASHFORD: towns, gowns and Downs
(1³/₄hrs, 66 miles)

This EAST COASTWAY* route east from Brighton, unlike the West Coastway Line west from there, is fun, fascinating and rewarding, and leads into the great MARSHLINK LINE. It is a total treat. And for some reason the lovely route, particularly west of Hastings, is sadly overlooked by visitors, even those who emerged from the Channel Tunnel only a few minutes away by Eurostar from one end of it. Their loss, your gain.

The route described: from Narnia to Bo Peep

The first part to Hastings from Brighton (both with direct lines from London) is called the EAST COASTWAY LINE. You immediately curve away right (east) from the London Victoria main line, on the impressive high 28-arch London Road Viaduct with views down onto people's roofs and back yards. It was designed by John Rastrick, the genius behind the splendid engineering on the Brighton Line from London. There's a great 1848 James Wilson Carmichael oil painting of this viaduct seen from the north and it's all open countryside: two women lean on a fence while cattle are driven along the dusty London Road far beneath the soaring arches.

Well the arches and road are still there but the countryside isn't. And when I say the arches are still there, in the case of the central arch not exactly. That arch over the road was destroyed in May 1943 when 24 German fighter bombers raided the town, leaving the tracks suspended over a chasm. It was rapidly restored although the raid killed 24 people. The south-coast towns were especially vulnerable to these kind of daytime hit-and-run raids.

London Road station is followed immediately by the Ditchling Road Tunnel (63yds), a lost junction for the closed Kemptown branch, **Moulsecoomb** and **Falmer**, which is adjacent to Sussex University. Two tunnels, Falmer (107yds) and **Kingston** (490yds), bring us into the pretty county town of **Lewes**, hemmed in by the South Downs and once a junction for six rail routes, with four still running.

The handsome station is a kind of Y-shape with us joining one arm of the 'Y'. To the left, the other arm brings the direct link to the London line. Note the disused platform filled in with gravel in between.

There are views of castles and ruins and the famous Harvey's brewery before we head east and see the white cliffs and river cutting through this gap – from the great Weald Valley inland to reach the sea. In that respect Lewes is like Arundel and Shoreham gaps further west along the line of Downs, and has had similar strategic importance since Roman times.

At **Southerham Junction** we diverge left across the river (while the seven-mile **SEAFORD BRANCH** races across the flat marshlands through **Southease** to **Newhaven**, a Channel ferry port, **Bishopstone**, and **Seaford**).

You may see hang-gliders leaping off the Downs to the left and as we pass **Glynde** (as in nearby Glyndebourne opera house in the hills a couple of miles north), and whiz through **Berwick** and **Polegate**. When we approach Eastbourne we turn sharply south off a lost route which went straight ahead but which we rejoin in ten minutes, if that makes sense – we're going to go into a terminus and then reverse out. We are doing two sides of a triangle with the top side missing.

As we head south we rattle over **Willingdon Junction** for that route to Hastings which joins us from the left and on the right there's a high 'splitting' semaphore signal – with one arm for each route to show trains coming out of Eastbourne which way they are going. We rattle through **Hampden Park** to **Eastbourne** (a ten-minute walk to beach and pier, station frontage in elegant not to say bonkers French style, which survived the platforms being bombed in the last war) and then reverse back again and over the junction, taking the eastern fork this time. As we near a well-preserved windmill ahead at Stone

Cross you can make out the old embankment direct from the Brighton Line which would have got us here at least ten minutes ago!

After **Pevensey & Westham** is a ruined castle on the left and **Pevensey Bay**. This place was important to the Romans, who built the fort here to ward off the Jutes and Saxons. The Saxons overcame heroic British resistance in AD491 and the Britons were massacred – those who escaped to France helping create what is now called Brittany.

As mentioned earlier, the '-sey' ending means island, as in Battersea and Chelsea, so a Saxon called Peve gave this place its name. They were in turn attacked by Vikings from the sea, which you may feel served them jolly well right. Then in 1066 William the Conqueror invaded here before the Battle of Hastings, the last successful invasion of these islands. It was besieged twice in the Middle Ages, and then this coast was heavily defended in both the Napoleonic Wars and World War II.

Perhaps it was in recognition of this little place's huge importance to our island history that C S Lewis chose the surname 'Pevensie' for the children in his book *The Lion, the Witch and the Wardrobe*. Certainly it was important to J M W Turner who painted the castle (well, a picture of it, not the castle, that was too big) and Kipling who lived nearby mentioned the village in his books as 'England's gate' – as history shows it was.

On to some charming little halts called **Normans Bay** and **Cooden Beach**, the shingle shore being only feet from our train, then **Collington**, **Bexhill** (semaphore signals in use) more beach views with rocks to protect the line from the sea, and fishing boats and beach huts adding to the seaside view.

As we enter the suburbs of Hastings, there are carriage sheds on the left then a junction comes trailing in from the left with the HASTINGS LINE from London Charing Cross through Tunbridge Wells, a recommended and very pretty run in the last 30 miles. This is Bo Peep Junction, named after a nearby pub. The Brighton company got here first in 1846 on our route: then the rival South Eastern Railway got here from the east (Ashford direction) in 1851, their direct London route through Tunbridge Wells coming last. The two companies were bitter rivals and obstructed each other for the first year, the 'new battle of Hastings' ending in a court case after which they decided to share access to Hastings station.

Bo Peep Tunnel (1,318yds) and then **St Leonards Warrior Square** until Hastings Tunnel (788yds) bring us into the substantial station at **Hastings**.

A massive old-style signal box to our left still operates the whole thing manually at the time of writing – look at the point rodding on the ground in front of it – and to the right (south) are great views of the castle ruins on the cliff top, looking over the roofs of the Old Town. (Beach, cliff railway, pier and picturesque fishermen's huts are all a short walk away. As featured in the television series *Foyle's War*.)

Hastings to Ashford: the Marshlink Line – where oast meets wets
(42mins, 26¼ miles)

Oast house

We soon enter **Mount Pleasant Tunnel** (143yds) and then reach **Ore** station where the electrification ends (so if your train isn't a diesel, it will fizzle to a halt). This odd extra bit of third rail was simply so that trains could be taken out of the way from Hastings and put in store at Ore, which little-known place comes as an odd final destination in announcements. 'Or what?' people wonder.

Now we reach the most charming and scenic part of the whole route. We wind on a curving single track through woods carpeted with flowers in spring past ridiculously small halts such as **Three Oaks** and **Doleham**, which do a good impression of being in the middle of nowhere. In winter, you half expect to meet the White Witch.

We join the River Brede Valley which is full of primroses and lambs in March, with oast houses (the white conical roofs used for hop-drying) up on the hills.

Winchelsea (the old station is for some reason across the level crossing from the present uninspiring structure) was nowhere near the town, and there are views across the marshes to Camber Castle. Again, the '-sea' or '-sey' ending means it was once an island. It is characterised as the smallest town in England, but has other claims to fame. It was the first planned town in England, being laid out in a grid pattern in 1277 to help fortify it against the French after the original had been lost to the sea. The other claim is that it is the head of the ancient confederation the Cinque Ports, a defensive and trading alliance that was typical of medieval Europe where nation states were hardly formed. Port, did you say? Winchelsea today sits on its little hill looking across the marshes at the distant sea which has retreated in the intervening centuries. As local lad Kipling put it of this place and others: 'ports of stranded pride.' A town that's really a village nowhere near its sea. Or, incidentally, its railway station.

Soon we enter the rightly famous little town of **Rye** on its own little hill ahead on the right. It has staggered platforms like many of the stations on this line – and the prettiest arrangement of the handsome little station buildings and signal box a model railway maker could devise.

Here's a passing loop too, with trap points directing us

Rye

harmlessly into sand-filled sidings rather than to face an oncoming train on the single-line section. It's all interlocked – the point and signal can't be changed until the oncoming train has cleared the section. Simple, safe and cheap – so when 'more modern' methods were adopted from the 1980s, a whole bunch of fatal accidents such as those at Cowden, Wilmslow and Paddington were directly caused by forgetting these techniques our ancestors had learned through painful trial and error.

More happily, Rye is famous not just for the pretty little harbour formed by the confluence of rivers, its narrow cobbled streets and ancient pubs, but also for fantastic literary associations it has had with writers such as Henry James, E F Benson and Rumer Godden (actually these three all lived in Lamb House in West Street, which you can visit, but there were plenty more). We plug onwards across river and onto the marshes which have been the haunt of invaders, defenders and above all sheep and smugglers for millennia (the breed of sheep known worldwide as Romney – 'excellent for show, wool and meat' – comes from here). The strange stories of smugglers led by parson/smuggler Dr Syn are recounted in Rye's Museum. On the hills stand churches, once on islands, and more oast houses, better known as an emblem of Kent, which we enter after the second level crossing.

Ham Sandwich on Rye, please

> The world according to the best geographers is divided into Europe, Asia, Africa, America, and Romney Marsh.
>
> From Ingoldsby Legends by Richard Barham

At **Appledore** the Dungeness branch line trails in from the right. It was once for passengers but now serves the nuclear power station of that strange pebble peninsula which points south into the English Channel. The tip of the peninsula is also reached along the coast by the miniature ROMNEY, HYTHE & DYMCHURCH RAILWAY, which is odd in that the towns aren't in that order, and which had a tiny armoured train during World War II. Very *Dad's Army* as it could probably have been derailed by a German army bratwurst. One of their favourite engines is *Dr Syn* (see *Rye* above).

Talking about defences, the train soon crosses the Royal Military Canal which is making the same route as us across the marshes. It was built to deal with the Napoleonic threat and then provided with pillboxes to cope with Hitler's ambitions. When you consider Roman, Saxon and Viking warriors came this way too, it's been a busy old spot, this quiet marsh.

After **Ham Street** (good name for a place showing rare pig breeds, which it is, although that's a long walk from the station; one day I will book a ticket from here to Sandwich, also in Kent, just to collect a Ham–Sandwich ticket) we get onto proper double-track railway and quickly reach **Ashford International**, a thoroughly modern junction for Eurostar trains to France (note the sweeping Ashford avoiding line viaduct behind the station. Architectural style: mid-Venusian space port; would suit upwardly mobile Treens led by the evil arch-fiend Mekon (well even if you've never read *Dan Dare*, you get the idea).

Even the stopping electric trains to London seem fast and modern after our branch line, not to mention the Javelin-Class ones which zoom up to St Pancras at 140mph.

There is nothing here to suggest you are in the same century as the sleepy halts and semaphore signals back the way you came. But you can be in Paris or Brussels in less than two hours from here. Or in the pub back in Rye in about 15 minutes, which is exactly what I did. Back a few miles and a couple of centuries…

HASTINGS DIRECT AND THE KENT COAST – catch the 1066

One more route strongly recommended in the south of England is the **HASTINGS LINE*** , sometimes known as the 1066 Line, from London. While this book isn't going to fully describe yet another route to the south coast, this has stretches as interesting and beautiful as the others.

Like them, it has to pierce the ridge of the North Downs to reach the broad and jumbled valley of the Weald, which it does with long tunnels. Unlike them, it doesn't have to pierce the South Downs, as they have already hit the sea west of here, at Beachy Head and the Seven Sisters cliffs. There are hills, but not the main chalk downs.

The route shares the **SOUTH EASTERN MAIN LINE** (SEML) out of London, through **Orpington**, **Sevenoaks** (long tunnel) to **Tonbridge**, where the **SEML** takes off east dead straight to Ashford and the Kent ports, while another line goes west for Redhill on the Brighton Line and thence to Guildford.

The Hastings Line, however, plunges south through **High Brooms** to **Tunbridge Wells** (tunnels, with the station at a low level to make a minimal impact on the elegant spa town), then increasingly pretty Wealden countryside through **Frant**, **Wadhurst**, several small stations including the Gothic-style **Battle**, to Bo-Peep Junction near the coast where it meets the line from Brighton (see page 278) and runs through **St Leonards Warrior Square** to **Hastings** (for comments see page 278).

Another top line in the southeast of England must be the KENT COAST LINE, reached by the CHATHAM MAIN LINE from London Victoria, speeding through Bromley South to the Medway towns of Rochester, Chatham and Gillingham and reaching historic **Faversham**. Here the train often splits with one bit going direct to Dover and another – this is the one you want – going round the coast through the seaside resorts of **Whitstable**, **Herne Bay**, **Margate**, **Broadstairs** and **Ramsgate**. You can go on from there to **Dover** and complete a loop back to Faversham if you wish. At Faversham there is the usual clanking and bonging and station announcements of joining and separating trains, but the chap who then lived in the old water tower to one side said the only time he couldn't sleep was on Christmas Day, when the strange silence was too much to endure!

Dover's stations – Dover Priory and Dover Western Docks – are surrounded by tunnels because of the famous white cliffs. Western Docks has a dramatic war memorial but then this is where millions of servicemen left and the wounded were shipped home. Only Priory is in regular use. Shakespeare Tunnel between Dover and Folkestone is named after Shakespeare Cliff. This in turn gets its name after failed King Lear who threw himself off it. He wouldn't have seen the fine, tall lancet-shaped tunnel mouths on the way down because: a) they weren't built yet, b) he was blind, and c) he was fictional.

NINE

FARE DOS AND FARE DON'TS

Basic stuff that could save you a packet

The **good news** about rail fares in Britain is that the turn-up-and-go principle has been saved. If you can get on the platform one minute before departure, with a valid ticket for that route, not even that one particular train or one particular seat, you can get aboard. A few minutes before and you can buy a ticket and get on, no reservations. You might not get a seat, but you should get there.

The **bad news** is that you'd be totally *stark raving bonkers* to travel long-distance like this if you don't have to. Fine for suburban or local trips, but buying the tickets on the day can mean you not only have to stand for half the distance but also pay through the nose (more like having your sinuses extracted with a rusty corkscrew, financially speaking) too. By which I mean the people in the comfy seats, while you stand, are paying a quarter of what you paid. So take a moment to read our guide to make your journey enjoyable and relatively cheap.

The **even better news** is that although British railways are expensive for those not in the know, with a bit of poking around and planning ahead, you can find tickets that are startlingly cheap. Fabulous deals! Just follow 1, 2, 3 below.

First a word. If it all seems too complex, you don't have to know what train company you are going with, what route you are going on or what the ticket is called. You could skip all this and go to the station, or the call centres, or the website (number 3 below) and just tell them when and where you want to go. It's not hard. But you won't always get the best deal, and you might get a very bad one. Knowledge is power…

1. BASICS

These apply to all the ticket types below. Natives should know most of this…

Class of ticket All the following tickets are First and Standard Class. For Standard, think Second; it's just politically incorrect to say 'Second Class' any more, although that's what it is. (Third Class fell out of favour a long time ago, some time after some passengers in open trucks arrived at London Paddington from the West Country frozen to death!) Nowadays, for First you get free tea and biscuits, freedom from misbehaving chavs, if there are any (but not boring business types braying into mobiles), comfy armchairs only three seats across rather than four or five, all facing a table, no airline-style cramming in. Not available on some local trains, or Scottish branches. Expensive, but can be discounted and can be got at a bargain rate at weekends or by advance booking (see below), so worth considering then. Even on weekdays, sometimes on company websites *First Class* is about as cheap as Standard, so don't rule it out. And if your employer is paying, stuff it, have the full English breakfast too. It's wonderful…

Single or Return

Fairly obvious choice, but the days when Returns were always cheaper are gone. Always check both options. Some long-distance journeys can be much cheaper buying two Singles and yet a commuter-distance journey, if you travel Off Peak Day, can be almost as cheap for a Return as a Single. Check the options rather than accepting the first price that comes up either online, on the phone, or at a booking office. Always say 'is it cheaper if I travel at a different time?'

Note: 'Return' simply means 'both ways', as opposed to a 'one-way' meaning 'Single'.

Train companies

There are about 20 train operating companies running trains on the national network. Information, connections, tickets and timetables work well as one national system, National Rail, although cheap tickets will be limited to one train company. Sometimes there's a real choice of route and/or companies – eg: London to Reading, Gatwick, Birmingham, Glasgow, Exeter (routes and companies), Hull, Shrewsbury, Wrexham, Sunderland (same routes, different operators) and on very long journeys you could be using trains of more than one company on one through ticket. You don't have to know about this but it is useful to find out the operating company for most longish journeys because if you can go on their website, special deals are offered to online customers. When you get down to individual company websites, they won't list the rival companies' trains, so always start off on the National Rail one (see below). The ticket offices in stations, however, are supposed to tell you about all companies on the route and their best deals, even if they work for a rival outfit. Yeah, right…

There is sometimes more choice than you would think. For instance, London to Birmingham offers four companies on three viable routes, and major differences in both price and time. In 2009, the obvious intercity-type operator was Virgin from Euston (Anytime Standard Return £132, Off Peak £40.40, Advance £28; 1hr 20mins). But then there's Chiltern Railways from Marylebone (£82, £32, £15–34; 2hrs 20mins) on a completely different route. Those two are listed by National Rail on the website and by the call centre and, of course, can be bought at all stations. What they *don't* tell you, unless you ask, is that you could start from Paddington (£132 Anytime, £40.40 Off Peak; 2hrs 12mins). And did you know there are yet *another* company's suburban local-type trains doing the trip on the main Euston route, run by London Midland (£64, £23, £15; 2hrs 20mins)? A very different travelling experience, but then up to £117 cheaper than the most expensive option. This degree of choice is unusual, but many cities have two companies or routes to choose from and all have different fare deals.

Children
Under fives go free, ages five to 15 are half price.

Discount railcards
No use to tourists, great for residents who use trains a lot. These are discounts of usually 34% on almost any fare (including the cheaper ones) obtained by certain types of residents by buying a card for a whole year, usually involving an application form and photos, and an address in the UK. Categories include: *16–25, Senior* (over 60), *Family and Friends* (you have to go in a group with a child), *Forces, Disabled, Annual Season Holder* (in the Southeast), and *Network Railcard* (misleadingly, that again means just the Southeast, after 10.00). It might seem simpler to have a *Stupid 26–59 Billy-no-mates Able-bodied Civilian Taxpayer* card for those who are not in these categories and charge them more for everything! Seriously, these cards are only worth having if you use trains regularly, as you have to pay an annual fee, but that should be recouped with one long return journey.

And no, you don't get paid for travelling if you are four of the above! Note, just to avoid any confusion, you don't get the discount for simply being one of these things, but for being one *and* having bought the card, at about £24 a year.

Rail passes
No use for residents, great for tourists. These passes such as BritRail and InterRail are not available to British residents but can be a good deal if you are coming from overseas. Because you don't have to buy a ticket, they make the following *Section 2* irrelevant. Details in *Other Deals* below.

Rover tickets
Paying a lot of money to have the freedom to rove around a certain area or region, possibly for a 'five days out of 14' type of deal. Also makes the next *Section 2* irrelevant, so go to *Other Deals*.

Oyster cards
Great for Londoners, useless for everybody else: you buy a smart card, with a certain amount of form filling online or at a station, prepay a set amount, say £20, and then get your London journeys such as Underground, suburban rail in some cases, and

bus, at a massive discount (about a third of what tourists pay). You never have to queue for a ticket again, and just swipe your card to get on and off the network. You just top up the cards online, at a station ticket machine or at a booking office, or even set it automatically. No Londoner should be without one. If you are visiting the capital regularly, or staying for a month or more, definitely get one (go to **W** www.tfl.gov.uk/tickets/, or to Tube stations or phone **T** 0845 330 9876). It does not operate on main-line trains, except a few short journeys into London. It may spread.

2. TYPES OF TICKET

Ticket types were simplified in 2008 from dozens of confusing sorts and names around the country to just three main types, easily understood from the name:

Anytime Very expensive, very flexible. You can catch any train on the day it's issued, or dated for first use, and if you get an Anytime Return, any train back within a month. You must have the return portion of a Return to use the outward portion of a Return (so dishonest people can't use it again or claim a refund for an uncancelled – that is, not clipped or stamped by an inspector and electronically marked by gates – outward ticket). It's refundable if not used and a break of journey is allowed. Any company on the route can be used. Get a seat reservation for medium to long journeys; it costs nothing and your ticket is still valid if you miss that train. By the way, I noticed that away from large cities, Off Peak sometimes starts very early (such as 05.00!) – so, if you know roughly when you are leaving, ask when Off Peak starts.

Examples (2009 prices) Glasgow–London one-way today or up to a month ahead, £135.50. First Class £199.50.

Off Peak Less expensive, less flexible. Cheaper travel on less busy trains, so not during rush-hour and certain other peaks. You are not committed to any particular train, but there are whole periods of the day where you are not allowed to use these tickets. You can buy them in advance or on the day, and must depart on the day specified on the ticket. You can break the outward journey for a stop of up to one night. There are **Off Peak Single** tickets, which means one-way in the cheap periods, and on the day specified on the ticket. **Off Peak Return** means you can come back any day within a calendar month, but only in the off-peak hours specified.

There are also **Off Peak Day Single**, and **Off Peak Day Returns**, with which you specify the one day you will use them (both ways, if return), which is printed on the tickets and again work in the cheap periods only. So if you need a cheap ticket to somewhere and back for a day trip, and don't want to specify your return train in advance (for example if you don't know how long exactly you will spend there) or have only decided to travel today, this is the one for you. Provided you are avoiding peak hours, of course.

On some routes there is an even shorter period of the day when you can get a ticket called **Super Off Peak**, which is even cheaper. Or rather, to be more cynical, they can get away with charging more to the people travelling close to the peak hours because the trains right after the peak hours' high fares were getting overcrowded.

You can get refunds for unused tickets (minus admin charges).

Examples (2009 prices) Glasgow–London one-way a month ahead or same day £107.80. Amount saved over Anytime ticket: £27.70.

Advance   Not at all expensive, not at all flexible. You buy them as Single tickets, so you can get different deals in each direction if you want a return, or come back a different way. You have to specify which particular train you are going on. You can alter the time of departure beforehand, but will be charged a £10 admin fee and any extra the other ticket would have cost.

These tickets operate a bit like airline tickets, in that there are some very good deals early on, but the price rises as those discounted seats get filled. So the early bird catches the worm, as it were. So by the time you decide to change, the other tickets will be more expensive, and there's no chance of using another company's trains. Advantage: good value. Unlike a few years ago, when it was ruinously expensive to make circular trips by coming back a different way, it's now cheap as chips to go on one route and come back on another, as I often recommend in this book. Disadvantage: no refunds. Yes, you lose it all if you decide not to travel, or get a lift in a car. Given the enormous cost of Anytime tickets, that's a risk worth taking. You will automatically get a seat reservation with the booking.

Examples (2009 prices) Glasgow–London a month ahead £12, £19.50, £32, £59.50 or £84.50 depending on which train you take.
The National Rail website offers both companies on this route (one goes to Euston, one to King's Cross). Interestingly, First Class is available on Advance a month ahead for just £52 upwards.
Amount saved: £123.50.
Booking just two days ahead: £19.50–£51. Amount saved: £116.

Lesson learned   On a long run, you'd be crackers to use Anytime tickets if you didn't have to. With two adults in the example, you could save £247 by buying the Advance tickets early enough. You could probably fly for as much as the Anytime ticket, or take a taxi. With a group of people you could almost buy the taxi! Or, amazingly, you could travel in the comfort of First Class with some Advance deals and still save £167 off the Anytime Standard-Class ticket. As said before, the downside is that you would lose at least £24 and maybe a lot more if those two people decided not to travel at all, and at least £20 if you changed your train time. Note how the saving falls as you get nearer the date.

Rail company website bookings   Can be cheaper, in our examples based on 2009 prices: Glasgow–London a month in advance (compare with above) was, with National Express's website, £12 (for some pretty unsociable hours, suitable for poverty-stricken insomniacs with infra-red scenery-viewing equipment who can get home at the other end perhaps after midnight), and upwards; there's also a £5 special offer.

Virgin Trains (slightly faster route): £17.50 (again for very unsociable hours), then £23 upwards.

First Class: £52 (unsociable hours), £86. Amount saved: £110.50.

Lesson learned   You can get even better deals online. First Class can become almost as cheap as Standard. And if you don't mind setting off before 06.00 or arriving after 22.00, there are some absolute bargains. Great for students, etc.

3. How to Get Times and Book Tickets

Not necessarily the same thing! It's two-stage. First, find out the times and fares for your journey. Then book your tickets.

Phone   Call T 08457 48 49 50 at cheap local rate from within the UK; from overseas, use your international access code then T +44 (0) 20 7278 5240. This is National Rail Inquiries and is an impartial 24-hour information service, not in itself a booking line. It will offer all companies on the route, and if there are long waits for a human advisor, you will be offered the Traintracker automated voice-activated service, which is pretty good. Either way, you will be forwarded to a company call centre to make the actual booking.

Web Go to **W** www.nationalrail.co.uk. When you come to buy tickets you may be redirected to a relevant train company. Check out the alternatives, make a note and then use the train company's own website. There might be special deals on these.

Independent train booking websites
W www.thetrainline.co.uk and **W** www.raileasy.co.uk are good for researching times, etc and quote similar fares, but they add booking fees, posting fees (depending on how quickly you want the tickets) or even fees for picking the tickets up at stations from automatic machines. I suppose the advantage is that you can get all the options and book on the one website.

In person Go to a booking office at a manned railway station, or use ticket machines on stations. Convenient for turn-up-and-go short journeys, but for goodness sake if you can avoid it *not on the day of travel for long distance*, otherwise you may pay five times, (yes five times!) too much. A tiny station with one chap isn't usually as good as a larger centre. To get good service, avoid the rush-hours at that office. Note: the Advance and Off-Peak savings are just as good from here as online (except company website deals) or by phone. It isn't two-stage in this case. Please take a couple of minutes to check out alternatives instead of paying the full whack. Ticket machines are often limited in scope – for instance, machines at some suburban stations will assume you want to travel from there on that day, not a month ahead from somewhere else.

Seat reservation If you are travelling more than 50 miles, *get one!* They come with most long-distance tickets and don't cost anything, and British trains can be horribly overcrowded (most of the routes this book recommends are less so, except the parts on the great main lines). Insist on your rights if someone is sitting in your seat and the train is full – if it is labelled as reserved they are just trying it on – or call the guard (conductor). Remember: British railways are now carrying more people than ever before (except maybe during wartime) and yet the network is a third smaller than in its heyday. You *will* encounter crowded trains unless you are very lucky. Book that seat, except for local journeys.

OTHER DEALS

Regional Rovers, Day Rovers or Rangers and Passes
These are very good value if you are exploring a whole region with several journeys. Thoughtfully, many of them offer a five-days-in-eight, three-in-five or a similar facility, because no-one (except those writing a guide to railways) wants to travel every single day. They simply mark off the days you are moving around.

There are also Day Rovers for the area, or Rangers for particular lines (usually post-morning rush-hour, and on scenic routes), and Evening Returns at bargain deals within some areas at even cheaper rates. Do ask if you are touring an area. These allow you to get on and off as it suits you.

There are also passes aimed at particular routes, such as the one in North Wales which allows you to circle this fabulous region on a set of great lines (including the steam narrow-gauge connecting Ffestiniog), or the Anglia Plus pass ('plus' often means travel on buses in the towns you arrive at is included in the ticket). Both these great tours are detailed in this guide. Do ask and look for leaflets. These terrific deals are sometimes mentioned in the text of this guide where it might help, but as they change and are called different things in different regions, it is a good idea to ask locally.

A very good combination if travelling on holiday would be booking well ahead for the long-distance part (saving heaps of money) then using Rover tickets to get around Devon and Cornwall, Wales, Scotland, East Anglia, North of England or whatever. For a couple or a family, this approach could save you hundreds of pounds – really! – compared with turning up and paying for each trip. It does tie you down at the start and finish (not too much of a problem if you are travelling on set dates, for example) but offers complete freedom once you are in your region. Wonderful.

There are about 200 of these ranging from Atlantic Coast Line Ranger to Wherry Lines Rover. Find out at the National Rail website (put 'Rover' in the search field), or ask at the call centre or station: 'I'm thinking of exploring [name of area], are there any Rover or Ranger tickets?' Again, better when clerks are not swamped with rush-hour traffic.

BritRail passes

These aren't cheap but are really a good deal for overseas visitors travelling a lot around the system. They *must be booked by overseas citizens from abroad*. It's too late once you get here. If you'd like to see a show in London, see Uncle Cameron in Edinburgh, tour the Highlands, visit Aunt Gwynneth in Wales and take in the best of Devon and Cornwall plus maybe Stratford-upon-Avon to see a Shakespeare play then go back to London, they are just great, and you don't have to specify when and where you travel. But if you just want to visit Gwynneth and maybe pop down to the seaside once, it isn't worth it.

Things have got better for BritRail pass buyers with two types of ticket: the Consecutive pass which covers, say, seven consecutive days, and the Flexipass which will give you, say, any eight days in two months. There are also discounts for Senior, Youth, Family, Party (that is group) and for sticking to certain 'regions', eg: England only, or Scotland only. Either could offer a fabulous tour, as this book shows.

And there is another discount for travelling off peak, which in this context means winter, when many scenic-area trains are pretty empty. Yes it'll be dark early, and cold, but could be useful as this covers Christmas and New Year (but don't forget to book seats around these holidays when trains are crammed and remember to check when the system shuts down for the holidays).

Also beware travel agents in your own country ripping you off with the high-level fares – they get a percentage, so £150 for a ticket that could cost £15 seems to them a better idea. Have a look on the web as above to see what fares are available for yourself. It's not hard, and although the computer may require a UK postcode to complete the booking, this can be any valid postcode (of which there are many visible on the net, or friends, relations, etc).

InterRail

This is an all-Europe pass, or can be limited to one or more countries, giving a three-days-in-ten, or ten-days-in-a-month type of deal. You can travel from Narvik way up in the Arctic Circle to the Straits of Gibraltar, or from the Iranian border to the west of Ireland. Fantastic. (But not in Britain if you're British – they apply to all of Europe except your own country.) Well worth checking out: see **W** www.interrailnet.com or enquire via travel agents. Having tried this, I'd say fine if you want to rush from one end of Europe to another, but to enjoy a country in depth by rail, not so suitable. This book is encouraging the latter approach – while not knocking the former!

First-Class upgrade, or Weekend First

Most train companies have an awful lot of expensive First-Class accommodation rolling around empty at weekends, so it is often possible to upgrade to First Class cheaply (£3–10). Do make sure it's OK with a train crew member to move *before* the ticket inspector comes along; don't just move to First Class and hope for the best, or you may get stung with a Penalty Fare. And *don't* try it on weekdays where you will have to pay the full, eye-watering, First-Class fare.

Megatrain

Sounds great – low-cost intercity travel from £1 – but it isn't that good or that simple. It's on the principle of cheap airlines where tickets start very cheap but in fact most people pay considerably more. You can only travel between certain stations (usually end to end) and on certain routes (at the time of writing largely those owned or co-owned by the Stagecoach group – that is South West Trains, East Midlands Trains and few others).

It turns out that it is part of the Megabus operation which offers similar point-to-point £1 bargain tickets, mostly on buses, and I mean not-very-new buses, not luxury coaches, judging by the one I once saw. But then what do you expect for £1? Great for students, or people on benefits, etc. Otherwise you'd be insane to choose a bus from Swindon to London, as the site suggested in 2008. Swindon exists only because it's on the railway.

Of course you're free to choose the bus... if you're a total traitor to Brunel's magnificent memory!

With a lot of forward planning, to be fair, you can get the £1 deal (plus booking fee) on a real train on a few routes. A friend of mine used it to get from London to Southampton for a sailing trip for just £1.50. One happy bunny. Not that bunnies go sailing much, but you know what I mean. **W** www.Megatrain.com.

Group travel

Many train companies offer discounts for groups, and surprisingly small groups (eg: four for the price of two), in recognition of the fact that people have cars, and by the time you have four or five people, the train fares become extremely uncompetitive.

AND LASTLY...

Check out up-to-date deals and advice on the very useful website: **W** www.seat61.com and don't forget **W** britainfromtherails.bradtguides.com!

Disclaimer

We have tried really hard to make this advice up to date and useful. We cannot, however, be responsible for any loss, damage, delay, tedium, etc which arises, whether it's foreseeable, error, or act of a whimsical malevolent fate. If the ticket people suddenly say you cannot claim refunds unless you are wearing purple pyjamas and are accompanied by all eight great-grandparents or that Latvian pogo-stick practitioners with blue hair must pay double... don't ask me for the cash. But I'll see you on the 10.00 train out of King's Cross.

THE INSIDE TRACK:
LOOK, LEARN AND ENJOY
THE RAILWAY WORLD

A WINDOW-GAZER'S GUIDE TO 'RAIL THINGS':
stuff to look out for on your journey

Mileposts Mileposts are measured from the London terminus, or another major junction. Within Scotland it could be to the terminus at say Edinburgh, or often where a later branch line diverges from a previous route (which may not exist anymore, to confuse things!). There are various formats; some have half and quarter miles marked on too, either with a fraction or with dots or dashes (one for each quarter), sometimes under the whole number of miles, often not.

Perversely, they are often wrong. For example, the mileposts in Cornwall exaggerate the distance from London Paddington by a mile or two because of a diversion at Saltash 100 years ago and a short-cut in Plymouth around World War II bomb damage. It doesn't really matter, because they are there to establish a location on the line: eg: a fault at 220 miles *by the mileposts*.

Black numbers on yellow posts are common but not universal and some ancient Victorian company cast-iron ones can still be spotted. Some lines from Waterloo have large blue diamond-shaped ones with bars for the quarters, facing the oncoming trains. This is useful for checking your train speed – a mile a minute is 60mph, so a quarter mile is 15 seconds at that speed, etc. It would be half that for 120mph.

Signals

Traditional signals Semaphore signals (the ones with waggling arms) still exist on the remoter parts of the system despite being 19th-century pre-electric technology – they operate by long cables being pulled by levers in signal boxes and were perhaps derived from railway policemen who held their arms out to say stop, slanted to say go, as the signals still do. Or possibly from the Navy's semaphore towers that used to carry messages from London to Portsmouth by towers fitted with waggling arms (if this seems far-fetched, consider that these towers were still being built just ten years before the first very similar signal box).

On the railways, an arm sloping at 45° – *up* in some regions such as the North Eastern and Southern, *down* in others such as the Western – means go. A yellow arm with a fish tail means a distant signal, which warns if the next home signal (red arm, square end) round the corner is going to be at stop, or 'at danger' as railwaymen call it. The beauty of these signals, also seen on preserved lines, is that with oil lamps showing through the glasses on the other end of the arm, they predate electricity entirely, never mind electronics. The disadvantage was that the lights were pretty dim in poor visibility conditions such as fog, and the lampman had to – and still does in one or two places – climb up to refill the things with paraffin and trim the wick. An arm at an angle, saying 'go' – or 'off' in railway parlance – tends to mean a train is expected, whereas with modern power colour-light signals, a green is often automatic and simply means the track ahead is clear.

Signal wires and point rods If you see cables strung alongside the track with small pulleys at about ankle height, these are signal wires. Not electric wires – no, no, before all that! – but for pulling with the great levers in signal boxes. You can follow them along to their signals. If they disappear, the signal is probably on the other side of the train, with a pulley going under the track.

The signals are returned to danger by a counterweight, so if the cable snaps, it's fail safe. Square rods resting on rollers are for points (the movable bits of rail that make you switch tracks). As these need to be pushed as well as pulled, they can't be cables. It was all very reliable and very safe, but you need many manned signal boxes down a line – some busy junction stations need two or three – which works out very expensive in this day and age. One power box at Carlisle, for example, replaced 44 boxes (which each needed manning all round the clock in shifts). A retiring signalman, by the way, was told by the management that his 40 years spent in the same box was a long time. To which he replied: 'It's not as long as I'll be in the next one!'

Modern Signals Electric-light signals resemble traffic lights but are far more complex, and are fitted with lenses to shine a mile into a driver's view. Unlike with cars and traffic lights, a train doing 125mph cannot hope to stop when it sees a red light, so advance warning is necessary. On such a route there will be four lights in each signal. Green is go. The first warning is double yellow (as it is brightest) then there will be single yellow (so it's safer if one yellow bulb failed, although they very rarely do), then red, which must not be passed. As the signals are largely automatic, it is common for signals at caution to clear as the driver slows because a train ahead has moved ahead one section. This is happening if you feel a train repeatedly slowing and then the brakes easing off – the system is very busy but still moving. The red signal is the bottom one, not to help colour-blind drivers – they aren't allowed, applicants are weeded out by tests – but to ensure that any heavy build-up of snow on the hoods of the lights will not block the most important signal. And it is nearest to the driver's eye-level.

On slower routes, there are three-aspect lights – red, yellow and green – and in remote areas a blend of semaphores and colour lights could have two-aspect lights replacing distant signals with green or yellow. In Scotland, for example, this can be seen to avoid signalmen pulling a cable $1^{1}/2$ miles long.

Don't freak out if you seem to pass a red signal next to your carriage. As the signal is reset by the front of the train passing onto the next section, this may happen before the back of the train reaches it. It is protecting your backside, that's all. The signal behind will at the same time switch from red to yellow, the one behind that from yellow to double yellow, and the one behind that from double yellow to green. That's how trains are kept safely apart.

Future signals may have no signals on the track, just in the cab. The 'block' section of track which keeps trains apart could thus move with the train, not be fixed on the track. This is the European Union's idea for keeping trains moving.

'Feathers' These direction indicators are a series of five white lights leaning out from the signal head. When lit, they show the route the train will take the points in that direction at a junction. At a complex junction you could have three or four sets at different angles, and they are important to show the driver that his route is correctly selected. Obviously, the speed limit for a sharp turn is completely different from going straight ahead (no white lights), so it's vitally important that these signals are heeded. If the turning has a severe speed limit on an otherwise fast line, signalmen may use a 'controlled approach' where the train is slowed by the usual series of signals as if to stop at a red at the junction, which clears to green plus the 'feathers' as the train slowly approaches. With the old semaphore signals each route has its own signal, which gave the initially puzzling sight of two or more signals – called splitting signals – over the same track.

Banner or repeater signals Where a signal round a bend can't be seen, such as at a left-curved platform, there is often a white disc halfway along the platform with a black arm on it, either sloping to indicate the hidden signal is green or yellow, or straight if it will be red. When at slope, they look like the 'end of speed limit' signs on roads, which, of course, they are not!

Shunting or ground signals Small signals on the ground are only for local shunting (or 'switching', in North America). Two reds means stop, the angled white means proceed at slow speed to the next signal. The old mechanical ones are white discs which rotate.

Pair of blue lights facing the oncoming drivers Accompanied by a painted fixed red signal and a sign saying 'STOP Obtain token and permission to proceed'. This is radio signalling for remote single-track lines, much used in Wales and the Scottish Highlands. Because grids between the rails can stop a train passing through without a radio token for the next section this makes it safe for trains to pass each other at loops without head-on crashes being possible. The whole line is controlled from one centre instead of a signal box at each station, so while this may not be as picturesque as the old semaphore signals the cost saving is enormous and may have saved some remote lines from closure.

Gradient posts Although smooth steel wheels-on smooth steel rails makes railways far more efficient than roads in energy, they can't, however, do steep hills, hence the need for all those cuttings, embankments, viaducts and tunnels to level things out. A gradient of 1 in 17 would be very steep for a railway: 1 in 60 is bad enough. These gradient posts, with arms both ways sloping, not accurately, but enough to simply suggest up, down or level, were more important in steam days. A fireman had to shovel like crazy to keep a head of steam up a long drag like the one up to Shap on the West Coast Main Line. Nearing the top he would have to be careful not to waste more coal, only for the driver to then have to fight to keep a heavy train within speed limits on the way down. Every train is a potential runaway on a long downhill without control, even today, so these gradient posts are still useful to tell drivers when to pour on the power and when to shut it off and put a hand on the brake.

Speed limits Speed-limit signs on the railways are black numbers on white circles with red rings round them, just like those on the roads. Drivers learn where these are initially from an old hand. It's no good taking a 100mph train right up to a 30mph curve; you couldn't stop. So when the Press mock a train not running because the driver 'didn't know the route' (their scorn being you just follow the rails), in fact they are wrong. The driver needs to know where the signals and speed limits are sited. Like pilots of aircraft on automatic pilot, drivers keep a regular lookout, but then you don't have to steer the thing. They are keenly looking out for those critical signals and speed limits, however. The speed limits may have arrows on them in which case it means it applies only to a diverging route. There can be temporary speed limits too, for repairs, etc, the end of such sections being marked by 'T', for 'terminates'. There are a few speed limits in the old style: metal cut-out yellow numbers.

Whistle boards On similar white circles to speed-limit signs, the letter 'W' stands for 'whistle', which is pretty anachronistic as steam engines had whistles and modern trains have horns. If you see a 'W', probably to your left, or hear a hoot, keep an eye out a quarter-mile further for what it might be protecting – possibly a crossing or footpath. Or if just a hoot, men working on the line. They raise an arm not just in greeting but to tell the driver they've seen him and all is safe. On curved track, a chequered flag is sometimes waved, and a horn blown, by a lookout man to alert a crew further away who cannot see the approaching train.

Loops Freight wagons seeming to whiz past backward on your left will probably be a stationary freight train which has been 'looped' to let your express train zoom past unhindered. A 'loop' is a third track (on a double-track route) of at least half a mile in length joined by points at both ends and controlled by signals. Freight wagons are often limited to 60mph or so, so they need to be cleared out of the way on busy routes. Not a problem when there are four tracks, but a real headache for signalmen on twin-track routes, which most are. They have to calculate how long a lumbering slow train will take to get to the loop, and then the slow speed that may be required for the points leaving the main line to get the last wagon clear in time, ideally, for the double-yellow warning lights, three signals to the rear, to be changed to green so the express doesn't slow at all. On single-track routes, such as those snaking across Wales and the Scottish Highlands, loops allow trains to pass in opposite directions, so they are used by passenger trains too. You can spot empty loops and the signals controlling them as you pass round the system. A siding is not a loop because it's not joined at both ends.

Junctions See page 304.

Clocks

We often associate clocks with stations nowadays – railways are nothing without time – but have you considered there was no need for standard time in Britain until railways arrived? Bristol time, by the sun (noon is defined by the sun at its highest), should be 12 minutes behind London time. No problem until you had timetables to keep to. And take time – as it were – to appreciate the beauty of certain station original clocks, be it a small-town station where the wooden case clock has miraculously survived (such as Aldershot), or the magnificent ones at Waterloo, Paddington, Brighton, Glasgow Central and Perth. They are all unique, often embellished with forgotten railways' names, and have you considered how many sweethearts, adulterers, spies, departing soldiers or desperate refugees have met right under them? It's a wonder the tears haven't worn the pavement away…

Bridge plates

These oval plates on bridges give you the distance, usually from London or Edinburgh, in miles and 'chains'. A chain will be a mystery to metric people: it's the length of a cricket pitch, 22yds, and was literally a chain at one time – surveyors used them for measuring. Under the figures will be an acronym describing the route, eg: 'ECML' for the East Coast Main Line or 'BHL' for the Berks & Hants Line, or an abbreviation such as 'WEY' for Westbury to Weymouth.

Electrification

There are two main systems: south of the Thames, most routes use a **third rail** beside the other two, raised slightly on insulating pots and on the far side at platforms in case passengers slip onto the track. It's an older system at 750V DC which means it has to have cables as thick as your arm (look at the connectors where there is a break in the third rail) and supply substations every three or four miles. There have to be gaps for crossing tracks and level crossings, and some are left for wildlife such as badgers to take their customary routes. While the voltage sounds not huge, the amperage available is, so the danger is considerable. I spoke to one railwayman who once saw a soldier step on one whilst running across the tracks to catch a train. 'There was a bang and he flew up and landed dead.' And a steam driver dropping a metal-handled shovel: 'With a series of blinding blue arcs it welded itself between the conductor rail and the running rail'. And I've seen the oddest thing: a swan, caught between the two rails amid flashes and sparks. This was on a bridge over a south-coast marshy river. The driver got down and somehow scooped up the swan, climbed down the riverside and set it down. And all this in thick fog – I wouldn't have believed it if I hadn't seen it with my own eyes, along with all the other passengers leaning out of the windows and applauding the driver as he came back up. I don't know if he had the power turned off, but it seems not. In most countries he would have run the thing over and kept to time.

The second system is the more powerful **25KV overhead** line. Because of the higher voltage, and being alternating current, this needs only a wire as thick as your thumb and substations about every 40 miles, so it is much cheaper. It does, however, need all that clobber of overhead catenary and masts, and if this is installed at too lightweight a level for the speeds of the trains, it will all come tumbling down from time to time (as with the East Coast Main Line, which is being expensively rectified). Sometimes bridges have to be raised to accommodate this system, used on both main lines to Scotland and also from London to Norwich and some connecting routes. Some English trains change from one system to the other *en route* – eg: the Thameslink trains from Gatwick to Bedford. The Eurostar trains from the Channel Tunnel used to use third rail to Waterloo, reaching a maximum of 100mph with difficulty, but now they use 25KV to St Pancras and easily reach 180mph (the difference being in the standard of the track as well as the power supply). Less dangerous to pedestrians, apart from drunks who urinate from metal bridges. Don't even think about that.

Types of rail

If you are on a modern, heavily used or high-speed line, the chances are your rails and those of the opposite track (which, after all, are the only ones you can see once you're in the train) will be **flat bottomed**, held down with clips such as **Pandrol** clips, those figure-of-eight springy things. The rails will be very long or possibly **welded** into miles. The **sleepers** will be concrete or steel, the sheer weight of the things making it impossible for rails to expand or contract with temperature changes. In the old days, this expansion was a danger in really hot weather because the track could become buckled and wavy, leading to derailments. So old-fashioned track, still used on some secondary routes and rural branch lines, had to be in shorter lengths with gaps to allow for expansion.

These were joined by **fish-plates**, with two or four bolts, so called because originally they were fish-shaped, and the joints give that old clickety-clack, clickety-clack, sound. The sleepers in this case are often tarred wood, and the rails bull-headed (that is, not flat bottomed but look like they could be used upside down). In that case they are held upright by cast-steel **chairs** screwed to the sleepers, and kept tight by wooden or steel wedges. This 19th-century form of track is still often found around the system – in fact, the London Underground uses a version of it so they can change broken rails quickly.

Patterns repeating: canals and roads

Railways often follow canals that follow roads into the same gaps in the hills. Indeed, this demonstrates wonderfully the four-stage transport revolution from narrow medieval-style mud tracks to modern transport.

The first stage was the building of proper surfaced **coach roads** with gradients that stage coaches could handle. On your train trips you will glimpse many of these, and from time to time you may also see the octagonal toll houses on the road edge that the turnpike trusts used to pay for. A spectacular case of a coach road being joined later by a railway is at the Menai Strait in Wales. Here, the all-important Irish Mail Coach Road was dramatically taken across to Anglesey with the world's largest suspension bridge, created by the brilliant Thomas Telford (the 'colossus of roads') and opened in 1826. The railway arrived just a few years later with George Stephenson's Britannia Bridge, a pioneering iron tubular box bridge, the trains it carried including, of course, the *Irish Mail*.

In a monumental misjudgement, the **canal** system was finished just in time for the railway to follow and make them obsolete, or at least little-used. Just like the railway, the canals needed to find the easiest routes through the hills and often ended up alongside (eg: Taunton, Hemel Hempstead to Tring, Standedge, Bathhampton to Bath, Newbury to Pewsey, Banbury to Oxford, Swindon to Stroud, Chester to Shrewsbury). In fact these canals actually enjoyed a boom transporting railway-construction materials, building their own gallows as it were, and then two centuries of genteel decline or closure. In a few cases the **railway** was built along a canal bed (the West London Line from Clapham to Olympia, or Aberdeen to Inverness, see page 53). In Strood, Kent, the railway was laid through a canal tunnel which, being cut through bare chalk, was perhaps not the best idea. It recently had to be shut down for proper lining, although it had lasted for more than a century without too many rockfalls.

Of course one canal system that didn't get replaced was the Caledonian Canal. A half-hearted attempt to follow it with a railway fizzled out halfway. But as this book relates, you can ride the great routes that thump over the swing bridges at both the North Sea and Atlantic ends of this great canal. Often the great canal aqueducts, many created by the same Thomas Telford, were soon flanked by railway viaducts (eg: Chirk, Rochdale), for both

systems had to leap across valleys and cut through hills, both
having to be far more level than roads, though the railway
needing much gentler curves.

Yet later, we see **motorway** engineers looking at the same hill
and river crossings and often coming up with the same conclusions
(eg: Taunton, Lancaster to Shap, Watford Gap). Echoes of the past
were heard, as the railway was (and often is) the best way of
bringing in road-building materials for the rival system that might
destroy it. Perhaps a fifth stage in the revolution will be new **high-
speed rail** links, like the French TGV, finding routes alongside
motorways – it's already started with the Channel Tunnel rail link.

It gives each kind of traveller something to look at and think
about, and often the railway alongside a motorway leaves even
speeding cars satisfactorily falling far behind; 186mph on a
Eurostar, 70mph in a Mondeo or 4mph on a narrow boat – you
pays your money and takes your choice; at least on a train you can
always safely wave to the people doing the other things without
worrying about steering.

Barmy curves
There are some screeching curves on what are
now main lines because they were in fact built second: Dorchester
South, Havant and Romney spring to mind. This becomes even
more absurd when the original line has since been removed – as
with approaching Farnham from London, or indeed Fareham
from Portsmouth, or on the way to Skegness – creating a terribly
slow curve in the middle of nowhere, for no obvious reason. North
of Arbroath there's another one – it's something to look out for,
and as the mileposts are often numbered according to the
vanished routes, it explains the odd changes in distances.

Seaside termini
Because their custom was massive before the
British discovered cars and costas, these stations were immense,
and today often handle tiny two-car trains when they used to
handle endless long expresses in their heyday. Architecturally,
those that haven't been knocked down or sold off are just
fascinating; although some are shabby, others have been
beautifully restored. Wemyss Bay, Llandudno, Aberystwyth,
Penzance, Brighton and Scarborough are among those worth
seeing. You do rather get the feeling, where the original station
stands, of the tiny trains as minnows swimming where proud pike
and stately salmon used to prowl.

Basics: a few technical rail terms explained

Burrowing junction	Where a joining line dives under the main line
Flat junction	Where a joining line meets the main line on the level
Flying junction	Where lines join, with one on a bridge over the other
Flat crossing	Where two lines cross, not join, on the level
Halt	Small station
Pilot engine	Attached at the front for extra power or up a hill
Banking engine	Pushing at the rear for the same purpose
Point rodding	Metal bars running at ground level to work points
Point	Movable rails making trains switch from one track to another
'Up'/'Down'	As in 'Up Line' means towards London (or Edinburgh or another main centre) and 'Down' (as in 'Down Line') means away, whatever the compass direction or slope of the track

A note for North American readers

'Two nations divided by a common language', someone joked about Britain and America. Nowhere but in railways are the two branches of English more sharply divided. British English takes its railway terminology from the stagecoaches that the first railway carriages so closely resembled. Thus the guard is the man in charge, not the American conductor, and passengers ride in a coach or a carriage (although sometimes the American word car is used too). Here's a few examples. British usage first, North American second.

Coach or carriage	car
Driver	engineer
Engine	locomotive
Goods train	freight train
Guard	conductor
Guard's van	caboose
Level crossing	grade crossing
Open wagon	gondola
Permanent way	roadbed
Permanent way gang/platelayers	surfacemen/tracklayers
Points	switch
Porter	redcap
Shunting yard	switchyard
Signal box	tower
Signalman	dispatcher
Sleeper	tie (although in different context, sleeping car)

Train Trivia

Railway initials: satire by acronyms

Railway companies in the system's heyday were known by initials, as some
are again today. Unfortunately for the companies, the disrespectful
travelling public didn't always attach the right meaning to them, but their
satirical names often contained much truth (NB: Rlwy = Railway):

Initials	Official meaning	Satirical meaning
GWR	Great Western Rlwy	Great Way Round (pre Severn Tunnel) Goes When Ready God's Wonderful Rlwy (by fans) Gresley was Right (by enemies)
GC	Great Central	Gone Completely
GNER	Great North Eastern Rlwy	Got No Engine Ready
LBSCR	London, Brighton & South Coast Rlwy	Lay Back So Comfortable Rlwy
LNER	London & North Eastern Rlwy	Late & Never Early Rlwy
LM&SR	London Midland & Scottish Rlwy	Lazy, Mucky & Slow Rlwy
L&Y	Lancashire & Yorkshire	Languish & Yawn
M&GNR	Midland & Great Northern Rlwy	Muddle & Go Nowhere Rlwy
MS&L	Manchester, Sheffield & Lincolnshire	Money Sunk & Lost
SECR	South Eastern and Chatam	Slow, Easy and Comfortable
S&D	Somerset & Dorset	Swift & Delightful
WIMR	Woolmer Instructional Military Rlwy	Will It Move Rlwy

How to read the rails you see and the nuclear question

Broad shiny steel top	Regularly and heavily used, and used within the last week.
Narrow shiny-steel track centred on top	Used within the last week but also maintained in top-top condition.
Wiggly, broad, shiny top (looking lengthways), with dips at rail ends (looking sideways)	Heavily used suburban or freight line where speed is low; badly maintained. If they're very bad, they're probably near a power station. Or South London.
Perfectly aligned thin, shiny top as if drawn with computer, looking lengthways or sideways	Someone's spent a lot of money – *Neeee-NAAAAW!!! Vroom!! schwoar-schwoar schwoar-schwoar schwoar-schwoar schwoar-schwoar schwoar-schwoar schwoar-schwoar Vroom!!* Silence – oh yes, that's why.
Bright autumn leaf yellow top	Occasionally used, and used recently, but not since it last rained.
Rust-red top	Rarely used, every few months.
Deep-brown top	Out of use, possibly not used for years.
Black top	Brunel may have been the last person to ride a train here.
Glowing orange in the middle of the night	Used by a nuclear-waste train that was leaking.

The latter is, of course, a joke. They don't leak. In 1985 the authorities staged a crash (always fun) with a 100-ton diesel loco plus four passenger carriages speeding into a nuclear flask parked sideways on its wagon across the Old Dalby test track in Nottinghamshire. The loco, a driverless class 46 doing around 90mph, was spectacularly stuffed; the flask, however, was chipped, but did not leak.

By a cosmic bit of timing, a visiting delegation of American locomotive manufacturers was making a sales pitch at a British Railways office where the crash was screened on television. A BR manager turned to the Americans deadpan in the silence after the horrendous smash and said: 'And that, gentlemen, is our standard acceptance test for freight locomotives.'

USEFUL INFORMATION

BOOKS ON RAILWAYS: read between the lines

On Scottish railways
Anything by John Thomas is brilliant.
Eg: *The West Highland Railway* first published 1965 but updated.
House of Lochar.

On West Country branch lines
Pearson, Michael *Great Scenic Railways of Devon and Cornwall* Wayzgoose.
Excellent on detail, atmosphere and history.

On railway history
Wolmar, Christian *Fire & Steam: A new history of the railways in Britain*
Atlantic Books. Thorough, readable, well told.

On railway accidents and safety
Rolt, L T C *Red for Danger* Sutton Publishing or The History Press. Brilliant,
painstaking, yet oddly enthralling analysis of what caused railway smashes.

For children
Awdry, Rev Wilbert *Thomas the Tank Engine* Started off when the priest had
to entertain a child suffering from measles and made a pretend engine out
of a matchbox and gave it a voice. In fact the title is just one of a series.
The later ones, written by that child (Christopher Awdry) grown up, are not
nearly so good and harder to read aloud, so make sure of the author when
buying. Suited to children four–nine.
Nesbit, Edith *The Railway Children* Penguin Classics. If you can read this to
your children (aged five to 95) with dry eyes, well… Filmed several times,
the two best versions featuring Jenny Agutter, once as the child and once
the mother, both times brilliant. Perhaps in 30 years the Old Gentleman
can become the Old Lady for her third visit.

Thrillers
Martin, Andrew *The Necropolis Railway* Faber and Faber, £7.99. A pacey,
atmospheric mystery novel set on the railway described in *Chapter 7* of this
book – and the first of several on railways by this author.

Bradt Eccentrics also from Benedict le Vay

Eccentric Britain, 2005   *Eccentric London*, 2007
Eccentric Cambridge, 2006   *Eccentric Oxford*, 2004
Eccentric Edinburgh, 2004

For a full list of Bradt titles, go to **W** www.bradtguides.com.

Great poems

Auden, W H *Night Mail* 'This is the Night Mail crossing the border,
Bringing the cheque and the postal order…' – hear the rhythm of the train.
Betjeman, John *Dilton Marsh Halt* (see page 158), perfect, and *Pershore
Station, or a Liverish Journey First Class*. He makes you nostalgic for the past.
Eliot, T S *Skimbleshanks – The Railway Cat* Part of his humorous *Old Possum's
Book of Practical Cats* collection. Certainly gave people a different view of
oh-so-serious Eliot, who was Betjeman's school teacher by the way.
Heaney, Seamus *The Railway Children* Just beautiful evocation of Ulster
childhood.
Thomas, Edward *Adlestrop* Classic scene setting by World War I hero and
Edwardian poet par excellence.

Steamy affairs: historic and preserved railways

There's nothing so nostalgic as a steam train drawn through beautiful
countryside with that chuff-chuff, chuff-chuff, the evocative smell of coal
fires, the great big windows you can open, the old-style stations with
wooden signal boxes and a guard with a proper peaked cap coming round
to clip your traditional card ticket. A serious chap on the platform in
uniform, including a waistcoat with the railway's initials on the burnished
buttons, waving a cloth green flag and blowing his Acme Thunderer for all
it's worth as the couplings take up the slack and ease you forwards…

Luckily, Britain has the best collection of steam branch lines, museums
and excursions in the whole world. There are four ways of enjoying this
great heritage:

 working steam lines;

 steam centres (where exhibits may be working, and many fascinating
relics on show, but no cross-country route);

 steam excursions; and

 museums (these can include all types of train, not just steam).

A recommended selection of steam railways

Here's a recommended selection organised by the chapters in the book; all are working steam lines unless stated otherwise. They are rated with '**❀**' for scenic beauty, '**✔**' for good exhibits and '**NG**' for narrow-gauge track.

East Coast Main Line

National Railway Museum ✔✔✔ York; **T** 0844 815 3139; **W** www. nrm.org.uk. Simply the best in the world, and free, *and* within easy walking distance from York station. Allow plenty of time at this near-nirvana for rail fans. Not a working railway, however. See page 8.

Nene Valley Railway ✔ Change at Peterborough (and bus, taxi or walk); **T** 01780 784444; **W** www.nvr.org.uk. See page 4.

Scotland

Strathspey Railway❀✔ Change at Aviemore; **T** 01479 810725; **W** www.strathspeyrailway.com. See page 45.

The *Jacobite*❀❀❀✔ Fort William to Mallaig timetabled regular service on the main line; **T** 01524 732100; **W** www.steamtrain.info. See page 36.

North and Midlands

Keighley & Worth Valley Railway❀✔ Change at Keighley; **T** 01535 645214; **W** www.kwvr.co.uk. See page 80.

North York Moors Railway❀❀✔✔ Change at Grosmont; **T** 01751 472508; **W** www.nymr.co.uk. See page 74.

Peak Rail❀ Change at Matlock; **T** 01629 580381; **W** www.peakrail.co.uk. Part of the lost Derby–Manchester route. See page 73.

Ravenglass & Eskdale Railway❀❀✔ **NG** Change at Ravenglass; **T** 01229 717171; **W** www.ravenglass-railway.co.uk. See page 98.

Settle & Carlisle❀❀❀ and **York to Scarborough**❀ See excursions, below.

Great Western

Bodmin & Wenford❀✔ Takes off at Bodmin Parkway; **T** 0845 125 9678; **W** www.bodminandwenfordrailway.co.uk. See page 136.

Dartmoor Railway❀❀ **W** www.dartmoorrailway.co.uk. At the time of writing, the railway's long-term future and ability to connect with the main line was unclear. There are summer Sunday services in normal trains from Exeter to its base at Okehampton, however. See page 147.

Didcot Railway Centre ✔✔✔ **T** 01235 817200; **W** www.didcotrailwaycentre.org.uk. A unique collection, but confined within Didcot Parkway station limits. See page 119.

Paignton & Dartmouth Steam Railway❀❀✔ Change at Paignton; **T** 01803 555872; **W** www.paignton-steamrailway.co.uk. See page 150.

South Devon Railway❀❀✔✔ **T** 0845 345 1420; **W** www.southdevonrailway.org. Mentioned at Totnes on the main line where it connects. See page 130.

Wales

Fairbourne Railway ~~NG~~ Change at Fairbourne; T 01341 250362;
W www.fairbournerailway.com. See page 180.

Ffestiniog Railway*‡‡✓✓ NG Change at Blaenau Ffestiniog (from
north) or Minffordd (from south); T 01766 516000; W www.festrail.co.uk.
See page 177.

Talyllyn Railway*‡✓ NG Change at Tywyn; T 01654 710472;
W www.talyllyn.co.uk. The first preserved line – in fact it never really
closed. See page 181.

Vale of Rheidol Railway*‡✓ NG Change at Aberystwyth;
T 01970 625819; W www.rheidolrailway.co.uk. From seaside resort to
mountain waterfall. See page 182.

Welsh Highland Railway*‡‡✓ NG Change at Porthmadog;
T 01766 516000; W www.festrail.co.uk. This newly rebuilt, long
narrow-gauge line through the mountains will be an absolute cracker. See
page 177.

Welshpool & Llanfair Light Railway*✓ NG Change at Welshpool;
T 01938 810441; W www.wllr.org.uk. Delightful rural ramble. See page 182.

East Anglia

Bure Valley Railway ~~NG~~ Change at Wroxham; T 01263 733858;
W www.bvrw.co.uk. See page 201.

East Anglian Railway Museum ✓ Change at Chappel and Wakes
Colne, discount if you come by rail; T 01206 242524; W www.earm.co.uk.
See page 212.

North Norfolk Railway*✓ Change at Sheringham; T 01263 820800;
W www.nnrailway.co.uk. Coastal views and great stations. See page 202.

South Western

Mid Hants Railway (The Watercress Line)*‡✓✓ Change at Alton;
T 01962 733810; W www.watercressline.co.uk. Fabulous stations and superb
scenery – take your time. See page 223.

Swanage Railway*‡‡✓ Change at Wareham; T 01929 425800;
W www.swanagerailway.co.uk. Top-notch Enid Blyton-style scenery,
seaside to ruined castle, see page 233.

South and southeast

Bluebell Railway*✓✓✓ Change at East Grinstead, the grand-daddy of
standard-gauge preserved lines, in countless films; T 01825 720800;
W www.bluebell-railway.co.uk. See page 273.

Spa Valley Railway* Change at Eridge; T 01892 537715;
W www.spavalleyrailway.co.uk. Don't miss High Rocks halfway,
see page 273.

Steam excursion operators

These change from time to time, so buy *Railway Magazine* from station bookstalls if you want an up-to-date list of trips (and diesel or electric excursions if that's your thing). They generally offer a whole day out on the main line, at proper speeds (unlike the more relaxed preserved branch lines). With catering, trips on these fabulous trains and lovingly restored locomotives are understandably not cheap, particularly at the luxury end of the market:

Vintage Trains T 0121 708 4960; W www.vintagetrains.co.uk
Railway Touring Company T 01533 661500;
W www.railwaytouring.co.uk
Venice Simplon Orient-Express T 0845 077 2222;
W www.orient-express.com
Pathfinders T 01453 835414; W www.pathfindertours.co.uk
Steam Dreams T 01483 209888; W www.steamdreams.com
West Coast Railway Company T 01524 732100; W www.wcrc.co.uk

TOURIST INFORMATION CENTRES

Here follows a quick-reference list of tourist information centres that might be a useful starting point for local information:

Aberdeen T 01224 288828; E aberdeen@visitscotland.com;
   W www.aberdeen-grampian.com
Aberystwyth T 01970 612125; E aberystwythtic@ceredigion.gov.uk;
   W www.tourism.ceredigion.gov.uk
Appleby T 017683 51177; E tic@applebytown.org.uk; W www.visiteden.co.uk
Arbroath T 01241 872609; E arbroath@visitscotland.com;
   W www.angusanddundee.co.uk
Arundel T 01903 882268; E arundel.vic@arun.gov.uk;
   W www.sussexbythesea.com
Aviemore T 01479 810930; E aviemore@visitscotland.com;
   W www.visithighlands.com
Bangor T 0870 121 1251; E bangor.tic@gwynedd.gov.uk;
   W www.gwynedd.gov.uk
Barnstaple T 01271 375000; E info@staynorthdevon.co.uk;
   W www.staynorthdevon.co.uk
Bath T 0906 711 2000 (premium rate); E tourism@bathtourism.co.uk;
   W www.visitbath.co.uk
Beccles T 01502 713196; E becclesinfo@broads-authority.gov.uk;
   W www.broads-authority.gov.uk

Berwick-upon-Tweed T 01289 330733; E tourism@berwick-upon- tweed.gov.uk;
  W www.berwick-upon-tweed.gov.uk
Betws-y-Coed T 01690 710426; E tic.byc@eryri-npa.gov.uk;
  W www.eryri-npa.gov.uk
Blaenau Ffestiniog T 01766 830360; E tic.blaenau@eryri-npa.gov.uk;
  W www.eyri-npa.gov.uk
Bodmin T 01208 76616; E bodmintic@visit.org.uk; W www.bodminlive.com
Bournemouth T 0845 051 1700; E info@bournemouth.gov.uk;
  W www.bournemouth.co.uk
Boston T 01205 356656; E ticboston@boston.gov.uk; W www.boston.gov.uk
Bradford-on-Avon T 01225 865797; E tic@bradfordonavon.co.uk;
  W www.bradfordonavon.co.uk
Brighton T 0906 711 2255 (premium rate); E brighton-tourism@brighton-
hove.gov.uk; W www.visitbrighton.com
Bristol T 0906 711 2191 (premium rate); E ticharbourside@destinationbristol.co.uk;
  W www.visitbristol.co.uk
Cambridge T 0871 226 8006; E tourism@cambridge.gov.uk;
  W www.visitcambridge.org
Carlisle T 01228 625600; E tourism@carlisle.gov.uk; W www.historic-carlisle.org.uk
Carnforth T 01524 241049; E ingletontic@hotmail.com; W www.ingleton.co.uk
Chester T 01244 402111; E tis@chester.gov.uk; W www.chestertoursim.com
Clacton T 01255 686633; E clactontic@tendringdc.gov.uk;
  W www.essex-sunshine-coast.org.uk
Cromer T 0871 200 3071; E cromerinfo@north-norfolk.gov.uk;
  W www.north-norfolk.gov.uk
Dawlish T 01626 215665; E dawtic@Teignbridge.gov.uk;
  W www.visitsouthdevon.co.uk
Dorchester T 01305 267992; E Dorchester.tic@westdorset-dc.gov.uk;
  W www.westdorset.com
Durham T 0191 384 3720; E touristinfo@durhamcity.gov.uk;
  W www.durhamtourism.co.uk
Eastbourne T 0871 663 0031; E tic@eastbourne.gov.uk;
  W www.visiteastbourne.com
Edinburgh T 0131 473 3600; E info@visitscotland.com; W www.edinburgh.org
Ely T 01353 662062; E tic@eastcambs.gov.uk; www.ely.org.uk
Exeter T 01392 665700/665255; E tic@exeter.gov.uk; W www.exter.gov.uk/visiting
Exmouth T 01395 222299; E info@exmouthtourism.co.uk;
  W www.exmouth-guide.co.uk
Falmouth T 01326 312300; E info@falmouthtic.co.uk; W www.acornishriver.co.uk
Fishguard T 01437 776636; E fishguard.tic@pembrokeshire.gov.uk;
  W www.pembrokeshire.gov.uk
Fort William T 0845 225 5121; E Fortwilliam@visitscotland.com;
  W www.visitscotland.com
Frome T 01373 467271; E enquiries@frometouristinfo.co.uk;
  W www.frometouristinfo.co.uk

Glasgow T 0141 204 4400; E glasgow@visitscotland.com; W www.visitscotland.com
Grange-over-Sands T 015395 34026; E grangetic@southlakeland.gov.uk;
   W www.grangeoversands.net
Great Yarmouth T 01493 846345; E tourism@great-yarmouth.gov.uk;
   W www.great-yarmouth.co.uk
Guildford T 01483 444333; E tic@guildford.gov.uk; W www.guildford.gov.uk
Harlech T 01766 780658; E tic.harlech@eryri-npa.gov.uk; W www.eryri-npa.gov.uk
Harrogate T 01423 500600; E CustomerServices@harrogate.gov.uk;
   W www.harrogate.gov.uk
Hastings T 0845 274 1001; E tic@hastings.gov.uk; W www.visit1066country.com
Henley-on-Thames T 01491 578034; E henleyvic@frenchjones.co.uk;
   W www.visithenley-on-thames.co.uk
Hereford T 01432 268430; E tic-hereford@herefordshire.gov.uk;
   W www.visitherefordshire.co.uk
Holyhead T 01407 762622; E Holyhead@nwtic.com; W www.eryi-npa.gov.uk
Inverness T 01463 252401; E inverness@visitscotland.com;
   W www.visithighlands.com
Ipswich T 01473 258070; E tourist@ipswich.gov.uk; W www.visit-ipswich.com
Kyle of Lochalsh T 01599 534276; W www.visitlochalsh.com
Lancaster T 01524 841656; E lancastertic@lancaster.gov.uk;
   W www.citycoastcountryside.co.uk
Leeds T 0113 242 5242; E tourinfor@leeds.gov.uk; W www.leeds.gov.uk
Lewes T 01273 483448; E lewes.tic@lewes.gov.uk; W www.lewes.gov.uk
Liskeard T 01579 349148; E tourism@liskeard.gov.uk; W www.liskeard.gov.uk
Littlehampton T 01903 721866; E littlehampton.vic@arun.gov.uk;
   W www.sussexbythesea.com
Llandrindod Wells T 01597 822600; E tourism@powys.gov.uk;
   W www.tourism.powys.gov.uk

Llandudno T 01492 876413; E llandudnotic@conwy.gov.uk ; W www.conwy.gov.uk
Looe T 01503 262072; E looetic@btconnect.com;
   W www.visit-southeastcornwall.co.uk
Lowestoft T 01502 533600; E touristinfo@waveney.gov.uk;
   W www.visit-sunrisecoast.co.uk
Machynlleth T 01654 761244; E mactic@powys.gov.uk;
   W www.tourism.powys.gov.uk
Marlow T 01628 483597; E tourism-enquiries@wycombe.gov.uk
Morecambe T 01524 582808; E morecambetic@lancaster.gov.uk;
   W www.citycoastcountryside.co.uk
Newbury T 01635 30267; E tourism@westberks.gov.uk;
   W www.visitwestberkshire.org.uk
Newcastle T 0191 478 4222; E tourism@gateshead.gov.uk;
   W www.visitnewcastlegateshead.com
Newquay T 01637 854020; E info@newquay.co.uk; W www.newquay.co.uk
Newton Abbot T 01626 215667; E natic@Teignbridge.gov.uk;
   W www.visitsouthdevon.co.uk
Norwich T 01603 727927; E tourism@norwich.gov.uk; W www.visitnorwich.co.uk
Nottingham T 0844 477 5678; E tourist.information@nottinghamcity.gov.uk;
   W www.visitnottingham.com
Oban T 01631 563122; E info@oban.org.uk; W www.oban.org.uk
Paignton T 01803 558383; E paignton.tic@torbay.gov.uk; W www.torbay.gov.uk
Pembroke T 01646 622388; E pembroke.tic@pembrokeshire.gov.uk;
   W www.pembrokeshire.gov.uk
Penzance T 01736 362207; E pztic@penwith.gov.uk; W www.visit-westcornwall.com
Pitlochry T 01796 472215; E pitlochry@visitscotland.com; W www.perthshire.co.uk
Plymouth T 01752 306330; E plymouthbarbicantic@visit.org.uk;
   W www.plymouth.gov.uk
Poole T 01202 253253; W www.pooletourism.com
Porthmadog T 01766 512981; E porthmadog.tic@gwynedd.gov.uk;
   W www.gwynedd.gov.uk
Portsmouth T 023 9282 6722; E vis@portsmouth.gov.uk;
   W www.visitportsmouth.co.uk
Pwllheli T 01758 613000; E pwllheli.tic@gwynedd.gov.uk; W www.gwynedd.gov.uk
Rhyl T 01745 355068; E rhyl.tic@denbighshire.gov.uk; W www.denbighshire.gov.uk
Rye T 01797 226696; E ryetic@rother.gov.uk; W www.visitrye.co.uk
Salisbury T 01722 334956; E thecouncil@salisbury.gov.uk; W www.salisbury.gov.uk
Scarborough T 01723 383636; E TourismBureau@scarborough.gov.uk;
   W www.scarborough.gov.uk
Settle T 01729 825192; E settle@ytbtic.co.uk; W www.settle.org.uk
Sheringham T 0870 225 4838; E sheringhaminfo@north-norfolk.gov.uk;
   W www.north-norfolk.gov.uk
Shrewsbury T 01743 281200; E visitorinfo@ahrewsbury.gov.uk;
   W www.visitshrewsbury.com

Skegness T 01754 899887; E skegnessinfo@e-lindsey.gov.uk; W www.funcoast.co.uk
Skye T 01478 612137; E portree@visitscotland.com; W www.visithighlands.com
Southend T 01702 215620; E vic@southend.gov.uk; W www.southend.gov.uk
Stirling T 01786 475019; E pirnhall@visitscotland.com;
   W www.visitscottishheartlands.com
St Andrews T 01334 472021; E standrews@visitscotland.com; W www.visitfife.com
St Ives T 01736 796297; E ivtic@penwith.gov.uk; W www.visit-westcornwall.com
Sudbury T 01787 881320; E sudburytic@babergh.gov.uk;
   W www.babergh-south-suffolk.gov.uk
Swansea T 01792 468321; E tourism@swansea.gov.uk; W www.swansea.gov.uk
Taunton T 01823 336344; E tauntontic@tauntondeane.gov.uk;
   W www.tauntondeane.gov.uk
Teignmouth T 01626 215666; E teigntic@Teignbridge.gov.uk;
   W www.visitsouthdevon.co.uk
Tenby T 01834 842402; E tenby.tic@pembrokeshire.gov.uk;
   W www.pembrokeshire.gov.uk
Thurso T 01847 893155; E thurso@visitscotland.com; W www.visithighlands.com
Torquay T 0870 707 0010; E tourist.board@torbay.gov.uk; W www.torbay.gov.uk
Truro T 01326 270440; E tic@truro.gov.uk; W www.truro.gov.uk
Tunbridge Wells T 01892 515675; E touristinformationcentre@tunbridgewells.gov.uk;
   W www.visittunbridgewells.com
Tyndrum T 01838 400246; tyndrum@visitscotland; W www.visitscotland.com
Tywyn T 01654 710070; E tywyn.tic@gwynedd.gov.uk; W www.gwynedd.gov.uk
Weymouth T 01305 785747; W www.weymouth.gov.uk
Whitby T 01723 383636; E tourismbureau@scarborough.gov.uk;
   W www.discoveryorkshirecoast.com
Wick T 01955 611373; W www.visitjohnogroats.com
Winchester T 01962 840500; E tourism@winchester.gov.uk;
   W www.visitwinchester.co.uk
Windermere T 015394 46499; E windermeretic@southlakeland.gov.uk;
   W www.golakes.co.uk
Windsor T 01753 743900; E windsor.tic@rbwm.gov.uk; W www.windsor.gov.uk
Woodbridge T 01394 382240; E wtic@suffolkcoastal.gov.uk;
   W www.suffolkcoastal.gov.uk
Workington T 01900 606699; E workingtontic@allerdale.gov.uk
Wroxham T 01603 782281; E hoveton.info@broads-authority.gov.uk;
   W www.broads-authority.gov.uk
Wymondham T 0870 225 4844; E wymondhamtic@btconnect.com;
   W www.south-norfolk.gov.uk
York T 01904 550099; E info@visityork.org; W www.visityork.org

INDEX